T0311859

Globalisation, New and Emerging Technologies, and Sustainable Development

This book explores the capacity of the Danish innovation system to respond to key societal challenges including the green imperative of achieving growth with environmental sustainability and the need to adapt to new and possibly disruptive changes in technology, often referred to as the Fourth Industrial Revolution.

The book is divided into four main parts. The first describes the evolving characteristics of the Danish system of research and innovation with special attention to the role of policy at the national and regional levels. The second part focuses on interorganisational relations, including the position of Danish firms in national and global value chains. The third part examines changes in labour markets and in the educational and training system, and it considers the impact of new technologies including robotics and artificial intelligence on employment and skills. The fourth part turns to issues of climate change and environmental sustainability including an assessment of the Danish economy's success in meeting the challenges of the UN Sustainable Development Goals.

The book will be of particular interest to small countries, of which the Danish innovation system is representative, but it also appeals more broadly to an audience interested in innovation systems and policies to support economic development.

Jesper Lindgaard Christensen is Associate Professor of Industrial Dynamics at Aalborg University Business School, Denmark. His research focuses on SME development and entrepreneurial finance, economic geography, innovation systems, the dynamics of specific industries, entrepreneurship and innovation policy.

Birgitte Gregersen is Associate Professor of Economics at Aalborg University Business School, Denmark. Her research focuses on studies of national systems of innovation, university–industry linkages, role of public sector for innovation, innovation policy and sustainable development.

Jacob Rubæk Holm is Associate Professor of Industrial Dynamics and Quantitative Methods at Aalborg University Business School, Denmark. His research focuses on regional, industrial and structural change over time, ranging from studies of specific industries or specific regions, to theoretical and methodological contributions with an evolutionary angle.

Edward Lorenz is Emeritus Professor of Economics at the University of Cote d'Azur, France and part-time Professor at Aalborg University, Denmark. He is Visiting Professor at the University of Johannesburg, South Africa. His research focuses on the internationally comparative analysis of business organisation, employment relations and innovation systems.

Routledge Studies in Innovation, Organizations and Technology

Digital Business Models
Perspectives on Monetisation
Adam Jabłoński and Marek Jabłoński

Developing Capacity for Innovation in Complex Systems
Strategy, Organisation and Leadership
Christer Vindeløv-Lidzélius

How is Digitalization Affecting Agri-food?
New Business Models, Strategies and Organizational Forms
Edited by Maria Carmela Annosi and Federica Brunetta

Social Innovation of New Ventures
Achieving Social Inclusion and Sustainability in Emerging Economies and
Developing Countries
Marcela Ramírez-Pasillas, Vanessa Ratten and Hans Lundberg

Sustainable Innovation
Strategy, Process and Impact
Edited by Cosmina L. Voinea, Nadine Roijakkers and Ward Ooms

**Globalisation, New and Emerging Technologies, and Sustainable
Development**
The Danish Innovation System in Transition
*Edited by Jesper Lindgaard Christensen, Birgitte Gregersen, Jacob Rubæk Holm and
Edward Lorenz*

For more information about this series, please visit: www.routledge.
com/Routledge-Studies-in-Innovation-Organizations-and-Technology/
book-series/RIOT

Globalisation, New and Emerging Technologies, and Sustainable Development

The Danish Innovation System in Transition

Edited by Jesper Lindgaard Christensen, Birgitte Gregersen, Jacob Rubæk Holm and Edward Lorenz

Routledge
Taylor & Francis Group

LONDON AND NEW YORK

First published 2021
by Routledge
2 Park Square, Milton Park, Abingdon, Oxon OX14 4RN

and by Routledge
52 Vanderbilt Avenue, New York, NY 10017

Routledge is an imprint of the Taylor & Francis Group, an informa business

© 2021 selection and editorial matter, Jesper Lindgaard Christensen, Birgitte Gregersen, Jacob Rubæk Holm, Edward Lorenz, individual chapters, the contributors

The right of Jesper Lindgaard Christensen, Birgitte Gregersen, Jacob Rubæk Holm and Edward Lorenz to be identified as the authors of the editorial material, and of the authors for their individual chapters, has been asserted in accordance with sections 77 and 78 of the Copyright, Designs and Patents Act 1988.

All rights reserved. No part of this book may be reprinted or reproduced or utilised in any form or by any electronic, mechanical, or other means, now known or hereafter invented, including photocopying and recording, or in any information storage or retrieval system, without permission in writing from the publishers.

Trademark notice: Product or corporate names may be trademarks or registered trademarks and are used only for identification and explanation without intent to infringe.

British Library Cataloguing-in-Publication Data
A catalogue record for this book is available from the British Library

Library of Congress Cataloging-in-Publication Data
Names: Christensen, Jesper Lindgaard, editor.
Title: Globalization, new and emerging technologies, and sustainable development: the Danish innovation system in transition/edited by Jesper L. Christensen, Birgitte Gregersen, Jacob R. Holm, Edward Lorenz.
Description: Abingdon, Oxon; New York, NY: Routledge, 2021. | Series: Routledge studies in innovation, organization and technology | Includes bibliographical references and index.
Subjects: LCSH: Technological innovations–Economic aspects–Denmark. | Technology and state–Denmark. | Sustainable development–Denmark. | Denmark–Foreign economic relations.
Classification: LCC HC360.T4 G56 2021 (print) | LCC HC360.T4 (ebook) | DDC 338.489/07–dc23
LC record available at https://lccn.loc.gov/2020048927
LC ebook record available at https://lccn.loc.gov/2020048928

ISBN: 978-0-367-48047-9 (hbk)
ISBN: 978-0-367-74739-8 (pbk)
ISBN: 978-1-003-03775-0 (ebk)

Typeset in Bembo
by Deanta Global Publishing Services, Chennai, India

Contents

List of figures   x
List of tables   xii
List of contributors   xiv
Preface   xvi
Acknowledgements   xviii

**Introduction: Globalisation, new and emerging
technologies and sustainable development – the Danish
innovation system in transition**   1
JESPER LINDGAARD CHRISTENSEN, BIRGITTE GREGERSEN,
JACOB RUBÆK HOLM AND EDWARD LORENZ

PART I
The systems approach and policy agenda   11

1   **The emergence of innovation policy as a field: The
    international context and the Danish experience**   13
    JESPER LINDGAARD CHRISTENSEN AND JAN FAGERBERG

2   **The performance, challenges and related policies of the
    Danish research and innovation system**   33
    JESPER LINDGAARD CHRISTENSEN AND METTE PRÆST KNUDSEN

3   **Entrepreneurship, experimentation and innovation: Future
    policy for innovative and growth-oriented entrepreneurs in
    Denmark**   53
    KRISTIAN NIELSEN, MICHAEL S. DAHL, BRAM TIMMERMANS AND
    JESPER LINDGAARD CHRISTENSEN

4   **The Danish regional innovation system in transition**   70
    INA DREJER AND JESPER LINDGAARD CHRISTENSEN

PART II
Value chains, innovation and inter-organisational relations   89

5 Supplier firms in transition – the case of Denmark   91
POUL HOUMAN ANDERSEN, INA DREJER AND CHRISTIAN RICHTER ØSTERGAARD

6 Collaborative business models in innovation systems – the
   case of physical infrastructure   111
LOUISE B. KRINGELUM, ALLAN NÆS GJERDING AND YARIV TARAN

7 Collaboration as a cornerstone in public sector innovation –
   the case of Denmark   130
JØRGEN STAMHUS AND RENÉ NESGAARD NIELSEN

PART III
Technology, employee learning and the labour market   147

8 The impact of robots and AI/ML on skills and
   work organisation   149
JACOB RUBÆK HOLM, EDWARD LORENZ AND JØRGEN STAMHUS

9 Work organisation, innovation and the quality of working
   life in Denmark   169
EDWARD LORENZ AND JACOB RUBÆK HOLM

10 Work policy and automation in the fourth
    industrial revolution   189
PETER NIELSEN, JACOB RUBÆK HOLM AND EDWARD LORENZ

11 Firm innovation and tertiary continuing education   208
JESPER ERIKSEN AND JACOB RUBÆK HOLM

PART IV
Green transition and sustainability   229

12 Firms' contribution to the green transition of the Danish
    national system of innovation – changes in technological
    specialisation, skills and innovation   231
CHRISTIAN RICHTER ØSTERGAARD, JACOB RUBÆK HOLM AND
EUNKYUNG PARK

13 **The measurement and performance of the Danish innovation system in relation to sustainable development** 252

BIRGITTE GREGERSEN AND BJÖRN JOHNSON

Index 267

Figures

1.1 The frequency of industrial, science and technology policy
terms according to Google. Source: https://books.google.com
/ngrams, accessed on November 23, 2019   15

1.2 The frequency of the innovation-policy and innovation-
system terms according to Google. Source: https://books
.google.com/ngrams, accessed on November 23, 2019   18

2.1 R&D intensity in Denmark compared to the OECD and EU28   36

4.1 Regional and local share of government funds allocated for
R&D 2008–2020. Source: Statistics Denmark. FOUBUD:
Government Budget for Appropriations or Outlays for R&D
by grant-awarding organisations and price unit   74

4.2 An overview of levels and actors in the 2019 version of the
Danish Business Promotion System. Source: Ministry of
Industry, Business and Financial Affairs (2019)   76

5.1 Development in industry employment across regions
(% of total employment). Source: Calculations based on
own survey data   92

5.2 Development in value added across regions (current US$,
index 1997 = 100). Source: Calculations based on own
survey data   92

5.3 Visual overview of value creation activities pursued by the
three types of supplier. Source: Calculations based on own
survey data   100

8.1 Robot use in Denmark. Source: Calculations based on own
survey data   154

8.2 AI/ML use in Denmark. Source: Calculations based on own
survey data   156

8.3 Learning mechanisms. Source: Calculations based on own
survey data   157

9.1 The relationship between learning organisations and discretionary learning. Source: 3rd ECS, 2013 and EWCS, 2015   184

10.1 FTE AMU/employment. Source: Statistics Denmark. www .statistikbanken.dk; VEUAMU1, VEUAMU10, RAS93, RAS07 and RAS309   194

10.2 Benefits/income. Source: Statistics Denmark. www .statistikbanken.dk; INDKF112   196

10.3 Composition of benefits. Source: Statistics Denmark. www .statistikbanken.dk; INDKF112   197

11.1 Number of students who have started CE by year and type of programme. Source: Calculations based Danish administrative data   213

12.1 Evolution in the share of green patents of total patenting. Source: Patent applications in green patents defined as 'selected environment-related technologies' (ENV-TECH) filed under the PCT inventor country of residence. OECD statistics   236

12.2 Evolution in the number of green patents in Denmark 1999–2016. Source: Patent applications filed under the PCT inventor country of residence. OECD statistics   237

12.3 Evolution in the share of green patents in Denmark 1999–2016. Source: Patent applications filed under the PCT inventor country of residence. OECD statistics   237

12.4 Changes in distribution of green patents across subgroups in Denmark 1990–2016. Source: Patent applications based on patent families filed under the PCT inventor country of residence. OECD statistics. Note: climate change mitigation (CMM). The shares sum to more than 100%   238

13.1 Overall and average performance by SDG, Denmark 2020. Source: Sachs et al. 2020; data from online database for Sustainable Development Report 2020   256

Tables

5.1	Industries included	96
5.2	Comparing findings from two surveys on Danish suppliers' collaboration with their most important customers	97
5.3	Principal factor analysis – rotated factor pattern	99
5.4	K-means clustering – cluster means	100
5.5	Industry and size distribution of the different supplier types, as well as location of the most important customer	102
5.6	Characteristics of the different supplier types	103
5.7	Multiple logistic regression model of supplier types	104
6.1	Data collection	118
6.2	Parameters affecting the development of collaborative business models (CBMs)	119
7.1	Percentage of workplaces which have implemented at least one type of innovation in 2015–2016 (unweighted)	134
7.2	Types of innovation by sector, 2015–2016 (%)	134
7.3	Public sector workplaces: did your workplace collaborate with one or more of the following during the development of your latest innovation?	135
7.4	To what degree do you agree or disagree with the following statements concerning your workplace? (%)	138
7.5	Employee involvement in the initiation of the latest innovation	140
7.6	Ranking of most frequent collaborative partnerships between employees and other actors	141
8.1	Work organisation clusters	152
8.2	Models for using technologies	160
8.3	Models for skill gaps	163
9.1	Establishment organisational forms in 2013: EU27	172
9.2	Establishment organisational forms across the EU27 in 2013	174
9.3	Logit regressions predicting product or service innovation	176

9.4 Frequencies of forms of work organisation for the EU27: 2005, 2010 and 2015   178

9.5 Frequencies of the four forms of work organisation across the member states of the EU27   180

9.6 Inequality in access to learning opportunities in work in Denmark: 2005, 2010, 2015   182

9.7 Logit regressions predicting the likelihood of employee outcomes in Denmark, 2015   183

10.1 Labour market flexibility   194

10.2 Source of competencies in 2019   195

10.3 Skills among the unemployed: 2019   196

11.1 OLS regression of innovation outcomes on having former tertiary CE participants among employees   218

11.2 IV regression of innovation outcomes on having former tertiary CE participants among employees   220

11.3 OLS and IV regressions of indicators for collaboration with a university on having an employee with tertiary CE degree   222

11.4 IV regressions of innovation outcomes on having former participants in CE among employees and controlling for collaboration with universities for innovation purposes   223

12.1 The top 20 largest holders of green patents in Denmark 2000–2017   239

12.2 Share of green jobs and green education in 2014   241

12.3 Model on characteristics of green innovative firms compared to non-green innovative firms   244

12.4 Job creation by innovative firms 2014–2016   246

Contributors

Poul Houman Andersen is B2B Marketing Professor at Aalborg University Business School, and Professor II of Supply Chain Management at the Norwegian University of Science and Technology.

Jesper Lindgaard Christensen is Associate Professor of Industrial Dynamics at Aalborg University Business School.

Michael S. Dahl is Professor of Entrepreneurship and Organisational Behaviour at Aalborg University Business School.

Ina Drejer is Professor of Impact Studies and Innovation at Aalborg University Business School.

Jesper Eriksen is PhD student at Aalborg University Business School.

Jan Fagerberg is Professor Emeritus at TIK-Research Centre, Oslo University

Allan Næs Gjerding is Associate Professor of Business Administration at Aalborg University Business School.

Birgitte Gregersen is Associate Professor of Economics at Aalborg University Business School.

Jacob Rubæk Holm is Associate Professor of Industrial Dynamics and Quantitative Methods at Aalborg University Business School.

Björn Johnson is Associate Professor Emeritus at Aalborg University Business School.

Mette Præst Knudsen is Professor and Head of Research at the Department of Marketing and Management, Southern Danish University.

Louise B. Kringelum is Assistant Professor of Strategy and Business Models at Aalborg University Business School.

Edward Lorenz is Professor at Aalborg University and Emeritus Professor of Economics at the University of Côte d'Azur, France. He is Visiting Professor at the University of Johannesburg, South Africa.

Kristian Nielsen is Associate Professor of Economics and Entrepreneurship at Aalborg University Business School.

Peter Nielsen is Associate Professor Emeritus at the Centre of Labour Market Research (CARMA), Department of Politics and Society, Aalborg University.

René Nesgaard Nielsen is Associate Professor of Strategy and Innovation Management at Aalborg University Business School.

Christian Richter Østergaard is Professor of Innovation and Regional Industrial Development at Aalborg University Business School.

Eunkyung Park is Associate Professor of Innovation Studies and Globalization at Aalborg University Business School.

Jørgen Stamhus is Associate Professor of Economics at Aalborg University Business School.

Yariv Taran is Associate Professor of Innovation and Organisation at Aalborg University Business School.

Bram Timmermans is Professor of Innovation and Entrepreneurship at the Department of Strategy and Management, NHH Norwegian School of Economics in Bergen, Norway.

Preface

In the past couple of decades the world has seen the emergence of a number of societal crises and challenges. They include the financial crisis, climate change, the global COVID-19 crisis, effects from increased migration, and several others. In coping with these challenges, changes in technologies, behaviour and policies have occurred and these in turn have created increased flux and change. A key characteristic of many of these challenges is the broad effects they entail, spanning the economic, environmental and political spheres, which in turn urge a holistic view on the challenges. This has spurred a debate on how innovation plays a role, and the term 'innovation' has been broadened beyond new products and processes to encompass social and institutional innovation. In particular, in dealing with a holistic, broad view on the challenges, a systems approach to innovation is appropriate.

Consequently, this book explores the capacity of the Danish innovation system to respond to key societal challenges. Even if the focus is on Denmark, the challenges dealt with in the book are shared with a number of other economies, especially small, open economies.

In an increasingly globalised world, one can ask if national innovation systems are still relevant. We argue this is still the case, and especially the COVID-19 global pandemic crisis in 2020 accentuated a discussion of the role of the nation state in providing critical infrastructure, regulating mobility within and between countries, and stimulating research and innovation for developing vaccines and treatment.

Several of the main contributions to the previous literature on innovation systems are from members of the Innovation, Knowledge, Economic Dynamics (IKE) research group at Aalborg University, Denmark. The IKE research group has, over recent decades, continuously contributed to large research projects on innovation systems and projects with a systemic perspective. The research has evolved over time to focus on the problems and challenges facing Denmark and other countries. This makes IKE researchers particularly well positioned to analyse the Danish innovation system and its challenges, and the contributors to this book are mainly researchers affiliated to IKE.

We believe the messages in the book are important, but they are, of course, not finite answers, rather a contribution to, and hopefully stimulation of, a continuing debate.

Aalborg, Denmark
January, 2021
Jesper Lindgaard Christensen, Birgitte
Gregersen, Jacob Rubæk Holm, Edward Lorenz

Acknowledgements

We wish to thank the authors who contributed both with their own chapters and with comments to other chapters. We also wish to express our gratitude to external reviewers and to IKE group members for their support and constructive participation at IKE research seminars where earlier drafts of chapters were presented and discussed. This added to the quality of the chapters.

Shagufta Haneef provided great assistance in the process of editing the various chapters. We also thank the staff at Routledge Publishers for their patience, understanding and receptiveness regarding the process and the idea for the book in the first place.

Introduction

Globalisation, new and emerging technologies and sustainable development – the Danish innovation system in transition

Jesper Lindgaard Christensen, Birgitte Gregersen,
Jacob Rubæk Holm and Edward Lorenz

Introduction

This book explores the capacity of the Danish innovation system to respond to key societal challenges, including those linked to processes of globalisation and increasing competition from lower-cost emerging market economies, the impact of emerging and possibly disruptive technologies on productivity, skills and employment, and pressures for environmental sustainability and the transition to green energy systems. In this way, the book seeks to provide a broad, but at the same time, focussed understanding of the Danish national innovation system in transition. This is of interest beyond the Danish case as most countries face similar challenges (Fagerberg et al. (eds.) 2015).

What makes the Danish case interesting?

In many respects, the Danish case stands out as successful and a good point of departure for tackling these challenges. For several years, the Danish economy has been able to maintain low rates of unemployment and inflation, a balance of trade surplus, healthy public finances and a large foreign exchange reserve. Living standards are amongst the highest in the world, and Denmark also shows high performance in aspects not captured by GDP measurements, illustrated by its ranking fifth in the world in the Inclusive Development Index in 2018 and its Gini coefficient of 0.26, indicating a relatively egalitarian economic structure (OECD 2020). The public sector is relatively large, reflecting a welfare state model where education, social care for children and the elderly (including pensions), healthcare and infrastructure are mainly provided by the public sector and financed via the tax system. Many of the Danish production and innovation strongholds have their point of departure in public sector demand and regulation. For several years, the World Bank Doing Business Index has ranked Denmark consistently in the global top five. In other benchmarking exercises such as the EU Innovation Scoreboard, the Danish innovation system consistently belongs among the so-called 'innovation leaders' together with other small countries (Sweden, Finland, the Netherlands and Luxemburg). Moreover, the research system is demonstrating high performance.

A key question in this book is to what extent the Danish innovation system in its current stage is able to respond to key challenges on the horizon and maintain its high living standard. To discuss this, the book takes a closer look at key features of the Danish innovation system and considers how it is being put under pressure from globalisation, disruptive technologies and the transition to more sustainable production and consumption. While the empirical point of departure is Denmark, the challenges are not isolated to the Danish case or to small, open economies of which Denmark is an example. For this reason, the book is of general interest for the analysis of national innovation systems and policies to support their development.

Why is the national innovation system a relevant analytical focus?

Thinking about economic development in terms of innovation systems has evolved from a marginal position in the 1980s to a widespread approach adopted by researchers and policymakers alike today. This development was spurred partly by academics. The first studies of national innovation systems are from the late 1980s and early 1990s (see Freeman 1987; Lundvall (ed.) 1992 (reprinted 2010); Nelson (ed.) 1993; Edquist (ed.) 1997). Sharif (2006) and more recently Chaminade et al. (2018) provide an update on the national innovation system perspective and how it has evolved since the 1980s. Another driver of the upsurge of an innovation systems approach was policy needs at the time (cf. Chapter 1 in this volume). In particular, academics working in the Organisation for Economic Co-operation and Development (OECD), and the general efforts of the OECD to promote national innovation systems (NIS) thinking as a basis for policy formulation (and their collaboration with Eurostat to provide solid innovation statistics) were instrumental in the widespread adoption of the NIS concept (Chaminade et al. 2018; Lundvall (ed.) 2010; Rakas and Hain 2019).

In innovation systems research, the notion of 'system' has generally referred to an understanding of innovation as a process, which takes place in an interaction between agents in a specific institutional and historical context. This is important for how analyses of innovation systems are pursued. A mechanistic presentation of the elements of a system often misses important aspects of how the system functions. Whereas the functioning of a watch or a computer can be understood through breaking up their components into pieces, innovation systems are governed by informal institutions and historical contexts and trajectories that make the system not only more than its individual parts, but often different from the sum of its parts (Anderson 1972).

This may be seen as one of the common cornerstones of innovation systems thinking both in the analysis of nations and in the extension of the approach to cover different types of systems such as regional innovation systems (Cooke 1996; Asheim and Isaksen 1997; Cooke et al. (eds.) 2004), sectoral innovation systems (Breschi and Malerba 1997; Malerba (ed.) 2004), technological innovation systems (Carlsson and Stankiewicz 1991; Bergek et al. 2008), and ecosystems, a term which recently has been put on the agenda to describe both innovation and entrepreneurship systems (e.g., Stam 2015).

A related literature focuses on systems transformation, introducing a multilevel perspective (e.g., Geels 2004) and incorporating analyses of the dynamics of specific technological evolutions. Over the years, innovation systems analysis has been taken up in developing countries as well (Arozena and Sutz 2000; Lundvall et al. 2009; Niosi (ed.) 2018) where the role of system-building and the impact of the informal economy become particularly visible. Trust, reciprocity, social capital, norms for collaboration and other behaviour are generally important aspects of getting innovation systems to function, particularly in developing countries. In developed countries challenges for the economy continue to point to the relevance of the innovation systems approach (Fagerberg et al. (eds.) 2015).

The different system levels are not mutually exclusive but often interact and may complement each other, pointing to the multilevel nature of the analysis. The book adopts an approach showing how innovation dynamics at the enterprise, regional and national levels are embedded in a set of interrelated supporting institutions including the research and development (R&D) system, the education and training system, the structure of labour markets and distinctive networking arrangement shaping patterns of interactive learning among firms and organisations.

Despite increasing globalisation and international institutional coordination, nation states still constitute relevant environments for interactive learning and innovation. One reason for this is diversity, meaning that there are still significant differences between countries in relation to their production structure and specialisation patterns, institutions, policies and knowledge infrastructures. Production structures and specialisation patterns are only slowly changing in cases where key production factors, including knowledge and learning, have a high degree of local, sectoral and technological foundation. A second reason is national policies that affect the regulation of institutions related to the process of innovation and structural change (including labour markets), the provision of infrastructure (both 'traditional' and knowledge infrastructure) and finally the nation as an expression of a 'common culture' supported by political power and the state (see for instance Lundvall (ed.) 2010; Weber and Truffer 2017; Chaminade et al. 2018 for further elaboration). Although on a tragic background, when COVID-19 developed into a global pandemic crisis at the beginning of 2020, the role of the nation state in providing critical infrastructure, social security and compensation to private businesses hit by lockdowns, and in regulating mobility within and between countries, became very clear.

The impact of the COVID-19 crisis

The chapters in this book were in most cases completed prior to the outbreak of the global COVID-19 crisis at the start of 2020, and hence generally do not incorporate effects from this change. However, this does not make insights from the chapters any less relevant. On the contrary, in many cases, the dynamics described are reinforced by the crisis. For example, the competitive performance of firms and nations is likely to depend even more on the quality of their digital capabilities and infrastructure as the COVID-19 pandemic has led to increased use of distance working. In itself, the business churning caused by the crisis will lead to innovations, but it is likely that it will also have effects on what has been termed the digital divide, especially in geographical space. The COVID-19 pandemic will affect global value chains (GVCs) both due to the disruption of transport and logistics provision and to the way plant closures in specific segments and locations can affect production all along the supply chain. Related to this, many of the policy initiatives discussed in the chapters are even further accentuated during the pandemic as state aid for businesses has boomed. Of course, it is an open question whether the effects of the COVID-19 pandemic are temporary or will have a long-lasting impact on patterns of outsourcing, production location, consumption patterns, CO_2 emissions and wider effects on the environment.

Content and structure of the book

Several previously edited volumes include single chapters on the Danish national innovation system (Freeman and Lundvall (eds.) 1988; Dosi et al. (eds.) 1988; Lundvall (ed.) 1992; Nelson (ed.) 1993; Edquist and Hommen (eds.) 2008). Lundvall (2002) provides a more comprehensive analysis of the Danish innovation system based on a large empirical study, which was organised around four themes and analytical levels: the firm level, inter-firm interaction, the institutional context and the innovation system as a whole.

In some respect this volume can be seen as an update on the key characteristics of the Danish innovation system. However, while this volume builds upon these earlier contributions, it is also novel in explicitly analysing the Danish system in the context of contemporary transformation pressures, particularly those pertinent to smaller open economies. Moreover, compared to earlier contributions, there is a greater emphasis on the impact of technological change, reflecting the widespread view that new and potentially disruptive technologies are having major impacts on economic and social life.

The book focuses on selected aspects of the innovation system which are grouped in four sections:

- the innovation systems approach and policy agenda
- value chains, innovation and inter-organisational relations

- technology, employee learning and the labour market
- green transition and sustainability.

These aspects are selected not only because they are important parts of any innovation system but also because they focus on areas that are currently undergoing substantial transition pressures and are of particular relevance to the Danish innovation system.

The innovation systems approach and policy agenda

Part I starts out by providing an overview of the history of innovation systems thinking and of the emergence of innovation policy in Denmark (Chapter 1 by Christensen and Fagerberg). When explaining the upsurge of innovation policy, the authors point to important inspirations from the theoretical and empirical understanding of innovations in the 1970s and 1980s and find that innovation system thinking was gradually incorporated into Danish innovation policies up to the turn of the century. At that time, innovation systems thinking became an established part of policies. The second chapter focuses on the performance of the Danish research and innovation system and on the emerging challenges it faces. As explained in Chapter 2 by Christensen and Knudsen, the Danish NIS has performed extremely well by any of the usual indicators and over the last decade has persistently ranked in the top three in the EU Innovation Scoreboard. Distinctive strengths of the Danish system include its high level of investment in human resources and public R&D, and the strengths of its research system as measured by several types of indicators, e.g., scientific publications. Despite the Danish system's overall exemplary performance, there are weaknesses that may hamper the future performance of the system. In particular, it is unclear if the system is able to leverage the well-performing research system to innovation in the small firm segment.

The chapters in Part I of this book also focus on several broader societal challenges that the Danish system currently faces, and on how policies play an important role in tackling these challenges. This includes designing entrepreneurship policies that balance creating opportunities for experimentation while avoiding unnecessary duplication and waste of resources (Chapter 3 by Nielsen, Dahl, Timmermans and Christensen). Similarly, using the case of a re-organisation of the Danish business promotion system, Chapter 4 by Drejer and Christensen analyses how Danish regional innovation policy has been shaped by different theoretically founded rationales since the turn of the millennium. The chapter discusses the proximity aspect of links between actors in the innovation system and whether links between actors are being adequately addressed in current policy changes, and whether a simplification of the system and a reduction in the number of actors risk leaving some firms lost. This problem area closely relates to a more general question on the appropriate level of policies and the number of actors involved in policies at different levels of aggregation.

Value chains, innovation and inter-organisational relations

Part II of the book explores the relation of interactive learning to innovation in both the private and public sectors. One area of considerable concern in developed countries linked to processes of globalisation and to technological catch-up in emerging market economies has been the impact of outsourcing on local suppliers. New technologies based on digitalisation and the Internet of Things (IoT) have dramatically increased the possibilities for global coordination of value chains and have improved conditions for doing business in a wide range of low-cost countries.

Chapter 5 by Andersen, Drejer and Østergaard in this part explores the diverse ways in which local Danish suppliers have responded to this challenge. It demonstrates that while a dominant focus has been developing the necessary capabilities for collaborating with customers in the development of new products and technologies, strategies that are more detached can be observed for sectors with a high degree of standardisation of products and services.

Chapter 6 by Kringelum, Gjerding and Taran focuses on the case of fourth-generation ports, an example of innovation in infrastructural projects, which despite often being neglected in economic analyses plays a central role in maintaining industrial competitiveness. Ports are considered hubs for transportation of physical goods, but also, and increasingly, as coordinators and disseminators of knowledge, hence creating a micro-system of high importance to the regional innovation system. This part of the book also focuses on public sector innovation and on the forms of collaboration between the public and private sector actors that support innovation (Chapter 7 by Stamhus and Nielsen). The evidence points to an important role for collaborative innovation and within this approach employee-driven innovation, where employees collaborate with external organisations and institutions in the generation of innovation, stands out as particularly important.

The impact of new and possibly disruptive technologies including smart robotics, 3D printing, artificial intelligence and smart sensors and the IoT have caught the attention of policy makers around the globe. Areas of impact include the global supply chain and infrastructural projects as discussed in Part II. More generally, these new technologies are seen as holding out promise for promoting more sustainable patterns of consumption and production in the economy as discussed in Part IV of the book.

At the same time, at the level of the labour market there is widespread concern that the adoption of these new technologies will result in large scale job losses as well as in growing inequality through the increasing ability of firms to automate routine mid-level jobs in both services and in manufacturing.

Technology, employee learning and the labour market

Part III of the book explores these challenges through an analysis of the evolution of work organisation, skills and labour market structure in Denmark.

Chapter 8 by Holm, Lorenz and Stamhus uses the results of a unique employee-level survey to develop what is a world-first survey-based investigation of the impact of the adoption of artificial intelligence on skills needs and mismatches and their relation to different forms of employee training. The chapter shows how robotics, artificial intelligence and machine learning have diffused in the Danish economy. While robots have been in use for decades, they have been largely confined to the manufacturing sector and this is only changing slowly despite novelties such as cobots and private service robots. Artificial intelligence and machine learning have rapidly diffused across all sectors of the economy so that large shares of the workforce across occupations and industries use such technologies regularly. Chapter 9 by Lorenz and Holm provides up-to-date insights into the relation between the skills and knowledge needed for successful innovation on the one hand, and the use of learning forms of work organisation that provide employees with opportunities for learning through their daily work activity on the other. The chapter shows that while the access of employees in Denmark to such learning opportunities is relatively high by European standards, there has been a downward trend since 2010 pointing to the need to develop policies, especially around vocational training that can support the adoption of learning organisations.

Chapter 10 by Nielsen, Holm and Lorenz in this part also contributes to the policy debate on the impact of new automation technologies on jobs and employment by arguing first for the prevalence of voluntarism in technology adoption. This voluntarism has implications for policy, which is summed up in the argument that labour market policy needs to be more than policy for the unemployed; it must be a work policy that also encompasses the employed. Such a policy is needed in order to meet the challenges posed to the national innovation system from technological change, and to 'future-proof' the labour market to assure labour market inclusiveness.

The final chapter in Part III, Chapter 11 by Eriksen and Holm, deals specifically with the education and training system in the Danish national innovation system. The chapter zooms in on continuous training programmes for lifelong learning and demonstrates a shift over time from short spell vocational programmes, where participants acquire specific vocational skills, to a focus – in monetary resources if not in participant numbers – towards tertiary level programmes developing managerial competencies. The chapter demonstrates that having employees participate in such tertiary level continuous education is indeed associated with increased innovation at the firm.

Green transition and sustainability

Part IV of the book turns to the challenges of climate change and sustainability more broadly, which are increasingly recognised as amongst the most important challenges confronting developed and developing countries alike.

Achieving more environmentally sustainable patterns of production depends on leaving smaller environmental footprints. This in turn implies a need for new knowledge in the production process both in terms of the skills of the workforce and in the use of codified technical and scientific knowledge. Chapter 12 (Østergaard, Holm and Park) of the book provides evidence on firms that undertake green innovation and how the requirements for the workforce of such firms are changing, either because new skills are necessary for undertaking green innovation, or because they are in demand as a consequence of green innovation. The analysis shows that the education and training system in particular must be adapted if Danish firms are to lead and not just follow in this transition.

Appropriately, the concluding Chapter 13 by Gregersen and Johnson in this part of the book turns to the UN Sustainable Development Goals (SDGs) and assesses the performance of the Danish economy in meeting the challenge. The chapter turns to a more general assessment of the implications of the SDGs for how we measure innovation performance and the degree to which standard measures of innovation performance successfully inform policy makers towards a sustainability transition. There is a need for transformative capacity, i.e., an ability to mobilise major innovation and investment activities to restructure the society to meet the challenges in a wider, long-term perspective.

References

Anderson, P. W. 1972. More is different. *Science*. 177(4047), 393–396.

Arozena, R. and Sutz, J. 2000. Looking at national systems of innovation from the South. *Industry and Innovation*. 7, 55–75.

Asheim, B. and Isaksen, A. 1997. Location, agglomeration and innovation: Towards regional innovation systems in Norway? *European Planning Studies*. 5, 299–330.

Bergek, A., Jacobsson, S., Carlsson, B., Lindmark, S. and Rickne, A. 2008. Analyzing the functional dynamics of technological innovation systems: A scheme of analysis. *Research Policy*. 37(3), 407–429.

Breschi, S. and Malerba, F. 1997. Sectorial innovation systems: Technological regimes, Schumpeterian dynamics and spatial boundaries. In Edquist, C. ed. *Systems of Innovation: Technologies, Institutions and Organizations*. London: Pinter Publishers, 130–156.

Carlsson, B. and Stankiewicz, R. 1991. On the nature and composition of technological systems. *Journal of Evolutionary Economics*. 1, 93–119.

Chaminade, C., Lundvall, B.-Å. and Haneef, S. 2018. *Advanced Introduction to National Innovation Systems*. Cheltenham: Edward Elgar.

Cooke, P. 1996. The new wave of regional innovation networks: Analysis, characteristics and strategy. *Small Business Economics*. 8, 159–171.

Cooke, P., Heidenreich, M. and Braczyk, J. eds. 2004. *Regional Innovation Systems. The Role of Governance in a Globalised World*. 2nd ed. London: Routledge.

Dosi, G., Freeman, C., Nelson, R., Silverberg, G. and Soete, L. eds. 1988. *Technical Change and Economic Theory*. London: Pinter Publishers.

Edquist, C. ed. 1997. *Systems of Innovation: Technologies, Institutions and Organizations*. London: Pinter Publishers.

Edquist, C. and Hommen, L. eds. 2008. *Small Country Innovation Systems. Globalization, Change and Policy in Asia and Europe*. Cheltenham: Edward Elgar.

Fagerberg, J., Laestadius, S. and Martin, B. R. eds. 2015. *The Triple Challenge for Europe – Economic Development, Climate Change and Governance*. Oxford: Oxford University Press.

Freeman, C. 1987. *Technology Policy and Economic Performance: Lessons from Japan*. London: Pinter Publishers.

Freeman, C. and Lundvall, B.-Å. eds. 1988. *Small Countries Facing the Technological Revolution*. London: Pinter Publishers.

Geels, F. W. 2004. From sectoral systems of innovation to socio-technical systems: Insights about dynamics and change from sociology and institutional theory. *Research Policy*. 33(6–7), 897–920.

Lundvall, B.-Å. ed. 1992. *National Systems of Innovation: Towards a Theory of Innovation and Interactive Learning*. London: Pinter Publishers.

Lundvall, B.-Å. 2002. *Innovation, Growth and Social Cohesion, The Danish Model*. Cheltenham: Edward Elgar.

Lundvall, B.-Å. ed. 2010. *National Systems of Innovation: Towards a Theory of Innovation and Interactive Learning*. London: Anthem Press.

Lundvall, B.-Å., Vang, J., Joseph, K. J. and Chaminade, C. 2009. Innovation system research and developing countries. In Lundvall, B.-Å., Joseph, K. J., Chaminade, C. and Vang, J. (eds) *Handbook of Innovation Systems and Developing Countries – Building Domestic Capabilities in a Global Setting*. Cheltenham: Edward Elgar. 1–30.

Malerba, F. ed. 2004. *Sectoral Systems of Innovation. Concepts, Issues and Analyses of Six Major Sectors in Europe*. Cambridge: Cambridge University Press.

Nelson, R. ed. 1993. *National Innovation Systems. A Comparative Analysis*. New York: Oxford University Press.

Niosi, J. (ed.) 2018. *Innovation Systems, Policies and Management*. Cambridge: Cambridge University Press.

OECD. 2020. *Income Inequality (Indicator)*. doi:10.1787/459aa7f1-en (Accessed on August 19, 2020).

Rakas, M. and Hain, D. S. 2019. The state of innovation system research: What happens beneath the surface? *Research Policy*. 48, 103787.

Sharif, N. 2006. Emergence and development of the national innovation systems concept. *Research Policy*. 35(5), 745–766.

Stam, E. 2015. Entrepreneurial eco-systems and regional policy – a sympathetic critique. *European Planning Studies*. 23(9), 1759–1769.

Weber, K. M. and Truffer, B. 2017. Moving innovation systems research to the next level: Towards an integrative agenda. *Oxford Review of Economic Policy*. 33(1), 101–121.

Part I

The systems approach and policy agenda

1 The emergence of innovation policy as a field

The international context and the Danish experience

Jesper Lindgaard Christensen and Jan Fagerberg

1.1 Introduction

This chapter traces the development of scholarly interest in innovation and innovation policy in the Western world in general and in Denmark in particular, ranging from the early post-war period to the early years of the new millennium (Christensen and Knudsen 2021 for an account of more recent innovation policy developments in Denmark). Whereas we take a broad view of innovation and innovation policy, we do give special attention to the development of systems views on policy.

Today, innovation policy has become a part of the standard political vocabulary, but this was not always the case. In the early post-war world, it was common to view innovation as applied science, and science policy received increased attention by both policymakers and scholars. In fact, there was more focus on inventions than on innovation, understood as the introduction to the market of technologically new products or the implementation of new production processes.[1] However, as explained in the second section of this chapter, it gradually became clear that there was more to innovation than science alone, and that the conditions under which firms were able to innovate and upgrade technologically also needed to be understood. As a result, a rich body of knowledge on innovation in firms, including its relationship with other societal factors, emerged,[2] and this, together with other developments, influenced policy. The increasing interest in innovation policy, particularly in Europe, was related to the spread of system approaches to the study of innovation and its effects (e.g., 'national systems of innovation'), which became common in several European countries around the turn of the 20th century.

In the third section, the focus of the chapter shifts to Denmark, and how innovation policy instruments gradually evolved as a result of policy needs, changes in the understanding of innovation, business cycles and innovation policy development elsewhere. The evolution of empirical knowledge about innovation, of the conceptual and theoretical understanding of the phenomenon, and innovation policy practice in Denmark are also investigated. The final section of the chapter considers the lessons from the study for policy processes.

1.2 The evolution of innovation policy in the post-war period

How far back in history interest in – and experimentation with – innovation policy can be traced is an open question. Innovation is clearly not something new, and policy instruments that affect innovation, in one way or another, have existed for a long time but may not have been explicitly termed as innovation policy. Hence, the use of the concept of innovation policy is fairly recent. In fact, it only started to be systematically used by academics and policymakers in the early 1980s. One of the early proponents of innovation policy, Professor Roy Rothwell at the Science Policy Research Unit (SPRU) at the University of Sussex in the UK, described it as follows: 'Innovation policy is essentially a fusion of science and technology policy (patents, technical education, infrastructural based pure and applied research) and industrial policy (investment grants, tariff policy, tax policy, industrial restructuring)' (Rothwell 1982, p. 3). He went on to distinguish between three different types of 'innovation policy tools': 'supply' (financial support, for example), 'demand' (purchases), and what he called 'environmental', which referred to the legal and regulatory framework, amongst other things.

Figure 1.1 gives an idea of the prevalence of the policies (or rather the associated terms) that, according to Rothwell, took part in the 'fusion'. As the figure shows, industrial policy was already a well-established term in the early part of last century. The term got a boost in the 1970s and early 1980s, a period when the growth of the capitalist world economy had slowed down considerably compared to the early post-war period, and many established industries in Western economies felt increasing competition from Japan, commonly regarded as a champion of industrial policy (Johnson 1982). However, from the mid-1990s onwards, the usage of the term declined steeply, as direct public interference with industry and individual firms in particular, which many associated with the term, gradually lost credibility. This can be seen as a result of the widely held view that industrial policy during the economic downturn in the late 1970s and early 1980s tended to support (and prolong the lives of) uncompetitive firms that would eventually go out of business anyway, rather than foster fertile ground for new growth. However, it was probably also a reflection of the political changes associated with political leaders such as Reagan and Thatcher (e.g., the turn to neoliberalism) that had taken place in leading capitalist economies in the preceding years.

Science policy, by contrast, was virtually unheard of before the early 1960s, and the term 'technology policy' is of even more recent origin (Lundvall and Borras 2004). During the early post-war period, governments and public opinion in Western countries became gradually more aware of the important role science and technology played in economic and military spheres.[3] This also led to the funding of research and data collection of relevance for the topic. The OECD's scheme for how to collect data on R&D, the so-called 'Frascati Manual', appeared in 1962 (OECD 1962), and the first research centres at

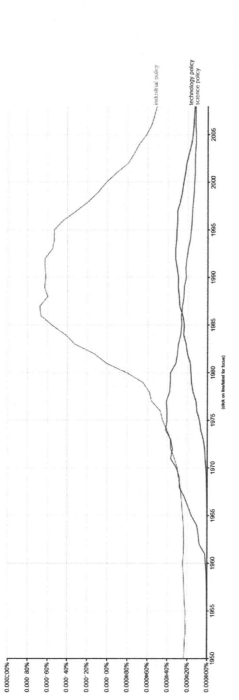

Figure 1.1 The frequency of industrial, science and technology policy terms according to Google. Source: https://books.google.com/ngrams, accessed on November 23, 2019.

universities focusing on the issue, such as the Science Policy Research Unit (SPRU) in the UK and the Research Policy Institute (RPI) in Lund (Sweden), emerged shortly afterwards.

The dominant perspective among observers during these early years was what later became known as 'the linear model' (Kline and Rosenberg 1986), which purports that economic growth stems from advances in science (Bush 1945). Based on this perspective, the challenge of policy is to ensure that scientific activity in universities, research institutes and firms is properly funded, and that scientific knowledge is disseminated. According to the arguments in favour of this model, policy is needed because the 'public good'[4] nature of scientific advance would result in a widening gap between private and social returns and lead rational actors (i.e., firms) to dramatically underinvest in R&D compared with what would be optimal for society as a whole (Nelson 1959; Arrow 1962).[5] In order to alleviate negative effects on a country's economy, various forms of public support for knowledge production and dissemination, such as universities, research institutes, technology transfer schemes, and intellectual property rights (IPR) systems may be justified.

While the 'linear model' has been, and continues to be, influential among academics and policymakers, it gradually became clear that the thinking underlying that model overlooked a number of important factors. In particular, it paid too little attention to the specific conditions under which firms search for, absorb, create and transform knowledge into goods and services, or in other words, innovate (Cohen 1995). This is perhaps understandable, as there was very little empirically supported knowledge on this subject available at the time. In fact, one of the first research projects initiated by the founding director of the SPRU, Christopher Freeman, aimed to fill this knowledge gap. The project, named SAPPHO, surveyed 'success and failure in innovation' in British firms (Rothwell et al. 1974). Another influential survey on innovation in firms, this time based on US data, was that of Levin et al (1987).[6] Since the early 1990s, the so-called 'Community Innovation Survey' (CIS) has mapped innovation activities in European firms, and similar surveys have been conducted in other parts of the world (see Fagerberg et al. 2010 for an overview). These surveys – and the research to which they led – gave a more nuanced picture of innovation (Fagerberg 2004). For example, it turned out that innovative firms did not, for the most part, attach high importance to using legal means, such as patents, to fight off imminent threats from imitators, but instead focused on being first in the market. Explanations of these research findings emphasised several mechanisms allowing firms to profit from knowledge investment: knowledge may be contextual in nature, difficult to copy and exploit, dependent on various forms of complementary assets, etc. Moreover, rather than jealously guarding their secrets, the surveys and research that followed showed that firms cooperated extensively with other actors, especially customers (users) and suppliers, while universities – the main actors in the linear model – were used much less frequently as a direct collaboration partner for innovation.

In the early years of innovation research only a small number of researchers in a few universities and countries were taking part. However, during the decades that followed, societal as well as scholarly interest in innovation increased, and today many thousands of scholars worldwide are active in this area, which often falls under the umbrella of 'innovation studies' (Fagerberg and Verspagen 2009). The accumulation of information and knowledge about this phenomenon has been accompanied by theoretical developments, three of which deserve particular mention here. First, a new theory of knowledge-based firms and economic evolution, drawing on behavioural theory as well as the older contributions by Schumpeter (1934, 1942), was developed by Richard Nelson and Sidney Winter. Their 1982 book, *An Evolutionary Theory of Economic Change*, is the most cited work in innovation studies (Fagerberg et al. 2012). Second, in the tradition of Schumpeter, Christopher Freeman, Carlota Perez and others focused on the role that specific (revolutionary) technologies, particularly ICTs, played in fostering economic growth (Freeman et al. 1982; Freeman and Perez 1988; Freeman and Louçã 2001), paving the way for greater attention – particularly in the 1980s and 1990s – being given to 'technology policy' (Figure 1.1). Third, and possibly most important from a policy point of view, the findings from empirical innovation research on the interactive nature of innovation led to the development of a systems approach to innovation (Freeman 1987; Lundvall 1992; Nelson 1993), which particularly emphasised the interactions between the various actors and institutions in the system for the (innovation) performance of the system as a whole. Although the approach can be (and has been) applied at different levels of aggregation, the earliest and arguably most influential contributions in this research tradition focused on the national level, hence the term 'national innovation system' (NIS). This quickly attracted the interest of policymakers, not least because the OECD did a lot to propagate the approach during the 1990s and 2000s (OECD 1997, 1999, 2002). In this conceptual development, narrow and broad perspectives surfaced. The former, narrower perspective primarily focused on the R&D system of a country and the public organisations supporting it, whereas the broader perspective both included a wider array of formal institutions into the analyses, such as the education and training system and regulation of labour markets, and emphasised to a larger extent the informal institutions that facilitate the interactions between core agents in the system (Edquist 2004). These two perspectives lead to some extent to different policy implications.

Figure 1.2 illustrates the spread of the term 'innovation policy' and 'innovation system' over time. As the figure shows, the term was rarely used before 1980, and then often with a different meaning than it holds today.[7] As mentioned, the term became more common in the early 1980s, when SPRU professor Roy Rothwell started to advocate its use as a 'fusion' of previous policy approaches of relevance for innovation. However, it did not take off then and, on the contrary, became less popular over the next 10–15 years. Indeed, as the figure shows, the take-off only occurred after the development and subsequent spread of the 'innovation system' approach. Although we cannot infer from

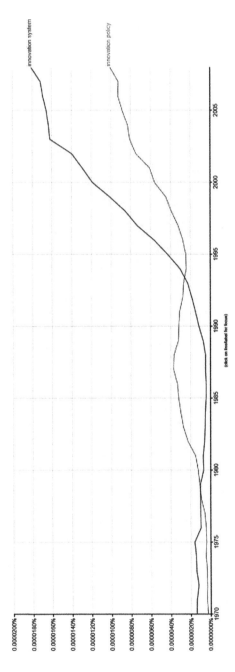

Figure 1.2 The frequency of the innovation-policy and innovation-system terms according to Google. Source: https://books.google.com/ngrams, accessed on November 23, 2019.

this that the use of the innovation system concept drives the use of 'innovation policy' it does indicate that the two phenomena may be closely related.

How can this upsurge in the interest in innovation policy be explained? One possible reason why the older policy forms gradually began to attract less interest was that they did not work as expected. First, investing in science was not the potent mechanism for increasing growth that the 'linear model' had envisaged. The effects, if any, often took a long time to materialise. Second, industrial policies, as implemented during the post-Second World War period, were criticised for lacking criteria for what merited support and for being susceptible to being hijacked by various vested interests. The innovation studies community, with its emphasis on innovation as the driving force of economic development (Schumpeter 1934, 1942), provided a way out of these dilemmas for policymakers by pointing to the development and diffusion of innovation as the central policy goal. This shift was also legitimised by economists with the development of the so-called 'new growth theories' (Romer 1990),[8] which also focused on innovation as the driving force of economic growth. To be operational, however, it is not sufficient to have a goal; it is also necessary to identify the factors, and eventually, the policy instruments, that influence the extent to which the goal can be achieved. The NIS approach helped identify several of these factors, which explains its rapidly increasing popularity throughout the 1990s and 2000s. In particular, its emphasis on the interactive nature of innovation led to the development of innovation policy instruments that aimed to bring different parts of the system, such as the financial system, the education and training system, the R&D system and – not least – the industrial system, together in the pursuit of innovation. The strong focus on the complementarities between the various processes (and policies) affecting innovation, to which the innovation systems approach gives rise, has also led to an increased emphasis on identifying factors that hamper the dynamics of the system (so-called 'blocking' factors, see Bergek et al. 2008). For instance, one such factor may simply be a lack of demand, which may be remedied through, say, increased use of public procurement as a policy instrument (Edler and Georghiou 2007; Edquist and Zabala-Iturriagagoitia 2012). Hence, the focus on complementarities between different factors influencing innovation processes highlights the importance of policy coordination, which over the years has received increasing attention (see e.g., Fagerberg 2017). Moreover, because of the generic and complex nature of innovation, a range of different policy fields needs to be taken into account, which requires a holistic perspective on policy (Borras and Edquist 2019).

1.3 The early development of Danish innovation policy

In this section we trace the evolution of Danish innovation policy in the post-Second World War period until the early years of the present century. We start by discussing the broader industrial and political context for policymaking, followed by an analysis of the evolution of the innovation policy stance in the chosen period (more recent policy developments are dealt with in Christensen and Knudsen 2021). Finally, we focus in more detail on two issues highlighted in Section 1.2, namely policy coordination and the evolution of a knowledge-base for policymaking.

1.3.1   Context: Danish industrial background

Post-war industrial development in Denmark was characterised by intense urbanisation, which created problems for rural areas. This led to policies supporting industrial development in these areas, such as 'The Development Plan for Regions' (Egnsudviklingsloven) in 1958. Policy formation in the subsequent period also featured this regional perspective, and emphasised the idea of growth poles, which was inspired by French theorists (Perroux 1955). In 1970, Danish municipalities were merged into larger entities,[9] while at the same time, some of the national policy areas relevant to framework conditions for firms were decentralised to regions, an intermediate tier between the national level and municipalities, which correspondingly became more important actors in the formulation and implementation of policy.[10]

Moreover, technological development and innovation in the broad sense were recognised as important for industrial development and competitiveness in the 1970s and 1980s (Industriministeriet 1990). The background for this point of view was that Danish unit labour costs were for a long time at the high end of the European spectrum and hence the competitive edge for Danish producers was based on quality, design and uniform standards. To keep productivity high, firms in Denmark across a variety of industries (including agriculture) effectively assimilated and implemented new technology in products and processes, including information technology and process optimisation technologies. Moreover, studies suggest that Danish firms generally focused more on process innovation and on incremental improvements than on radically new products (Christensen and Kristensen 1995; Lundvall 2002). However, this is not unusual for small, open economies (Christensen and Kristensen 1997). These background conditions are valid even today. The regional level remains important in policymaking (see, though, a debate on this in Drejer and Christensen 2021), and the application of knowledge into products and firms in traditional sectors continues to be a policy focus and competitive edge of Danish industry.

1.3.2   Policy development

Substantial discussions on policies for technological development and innovation started to emerge in the late 1960s and early 1970s. In particular, industry associations were not satisfied with the limited industrial application of research, and suggested a (partial) transformation of research policies towards policy initiatives supporting the development of new products and processes in firms (Christiansen and Sidenius 1988). Until then, the few discussions on this subject primarily concerned productivity and research; however, these policy discussions only yielded very few policy initiatives. These initiatives included tax deductions for R&D expenditures, firm-specific subsidies, and the Law on Technological Service in 1973. This law led to increased government involvement in the financing and management of technological assistance to businesses (Dalum et al. 1991).

The economic crisis following the steep increase in oil prices in October 1973 provided at least part of the background for the increased policy focus on technological and industrial change. Until then, both unemployment and balance of payment problems were almost non-existent, but this changed dramatically in the aftermath of the increase in oil prices. At that time, Denmark was 100% dependent upon imported energy. The oil crisis in 1973 (and later in 1979) spurred industrial and technological development of substitutes for oil energy, first towards a greater dependence on imported coal, but increasingly towards exploiting North Sea gas, improved insulation and other improvements in energy efficiency, as well as domestic, renewable energy sources like wind. This is an important part of why today Denmark is a net exporter of energy, has a large share of exports of energy technology, and has a high share of electricity production stemming from renewable energy sources, in particular wind energy.

Industrial policies in the 1970s were few, not very systematic and only partly focused on technological development in a broad sense. In fact, technology policies in Denmark generally supported the diffusion of technologies rather than the development of new technologies (Edquist and Lundvall 1993). One example is the development of the agricultural sector. In several branches of this sector, the R&D effort is organised on a branch level, coupled with a system for the diffusion and implementation of knowledge (Christensen et al. 2011). Another example is policies that support the development of a strong segment of intermediaries acting as links between R&D institutions and firms, thereby making scientific knowledge more easily accessible for industry (Erhvervsfremme Styrelsen 1999).

However, the beginning of the 1980s witnessed a change in the industrial policy stance (Christiansen and Sidenius 1988). Specifically, starting in 1983, a policy focused on 'programmes' was implemented, inspired by similar policies in Sweden and the UK. Its primary objective was to support the development of specific generic technologies,[11] primarily by supporting R&D and the diffusion of technology. These 'programme policies' were also the start of including a broader spectrum of actors in policy formulation and implementation. This goes not only for trade associations, but also for a number of different ministries involved in industrial policy, such as the Ministry of Environment. One of the actors in the development of policies was The Technology Council (Teknologirådet), established in 1986 with the purpose of assessing the consequences of technological development and spurring a broad debate in society around where technological development was going and how it might impact the lives of ordinary people. It was the first organisation of its kind in the world and has been a source of inspiration for several other countries.[12]

Policy changes in this area were also influenced by broader political changes. For example, a liberal government replaced the social democrats in 1982[13] and changed the country's macroeconomic policies, introducing a fixed exchange rate policy, liberalising capital flows, and hence diluting the power of monetary policy. Coupled with austerity in fiscal policies, the result was that room for manoeuvre – and availability of policy instruments – in macroeconomic policy was reduced. As a result, the need for alternative policy instruments, industrial (or technology) policy for example, increased. In fact, while the total expenditures for technology policy increased only slightly during the 1980s, the share of funds for 'programme policy' in total technology policy expenditures rocketed.

Simultaneously, the number of specific subsidies increased. There were more than 40 by the end of the 1980s, and they became increasingly difficult to assess for potential users.[14] Subsidies and programme policies gained a relatively larger share of technology policy at the expense of the technological services. However, this changed at the beginning of the 1990s when the funds for industrial policy were reduced and the number of specific subsidies was reduced dramatically (Dalum et al. 1991). The negotiations on the fiscal budget in 1990 were influenced by industry associations that requested a reduction in corporate taxes. The right-wing government followed their recommendations by reducing corporate taxes by ten percentage points, but it subsequently financed that loss of income from taxes by substantially reducing the allocation of funds for industry support. According to the fiscal budget for 1990 the allocated amount was reduced from DKK 1920 million to 1274 million, and the following years also witnessed cuts in funds allocated for industry support.

The reorientation of policies in the 1990s considered the improvement of framework conditions as the primary goal (Erhvervsudviklingsrådet 1994). The move towards a less interventionist policy stance during this time was inspired by discussions in other countries about the ineffectiveness of selective policies. Both 'picking the winner' and 'programme policies' became terms with a negative connotation. Relatedly, a number of 'resource area studies' had been conducted (Erhvervsudviklingsrådet 1994). These studies were initiated by the Council for Industrial Development (Erhvervsudviklingrådet) with the purpose of providing a new framework for advising the government on policies. In particular, the studies sought to get a better insight into which parts of the businesses share similar factor inputs and other framework conditions. The studies spanned not only traditional sectors but also firms, public and private knowledge institutions, suppliers, etc. that shared factor conditions and contributed to fulfilling a specific demand. There was a strong emphasis on innovation in the individual analyses and, additionally, a cross-sectoral analysis on innovation (Erhvervsudviklingsrådet 1994, p. 4). The subsequent policy development process involved a range of different actors, in total 29 groups, with representatives from firms, organisations and relevant ministries. They came up with a number of suggestions, many of which were also implemented (66 out of 152, according to Erhvervsfremme Styrelsen 1997c).

Another policy change was increased attention to the links in the innovation system; new policy instruments were introduced making firms eligible for a grant only if their projects involved collaboration with a partner with specialised knowledge (e.g., 'The Centre Contracts'). This was also the decade when the Danish network programmes were introduced (1989–92), and these were subsequently copied in numerous other countries.

In summary, Danish innovation policies moved from firm-specific subsidies to programme policy in the 1980s, and then towards a policy aiming at improving framework conditions for industry.[15] Nevertheless, there was at this time a quite strong emphasis in public policy on technology based innovation and R&D. Policy formulation in the latter part of the 1990s was inspired by innovation systems thinking, particularly that of the 'DISKO-project' (Hedin et al. 2008; Lundvall 1999), the 'LOK-project' (Erhvervsfremme Styrelsen 1997b) and also by policies abroad, especially as expressed in the reports by the OECD (1994, 1997, 1999). Hence, the turn of the 21st century marked the transition to a much more systematic approach to innovation policy. This policy change was consolidated after November 2001 when a new government initiated institutional and policy reforms. The Council for Technology and Innovation was established, and the Ministry of Knowledge, Technology and Development (MVTU) was formed as a merger between the Ministry of Research and parts of the Ministries of Education and Business Development. One of the key obligations of the new ministry was to conduct an integrated science, technology and innovation policy. The publication of reports and reforms of the institutional set-up of the knowledge and innovation system following the establishment of MVTU made a significant impact on consolidating innovation policy as a specific policy sphere, and the government expressed explicitly in their political programme that the reforms had the intention to create stronger links between education, research and innovation. More recent policy developments are dealt with in more detail in other chapters in this volume (see especially Christensen and Knudsen 2021; Nielsen et al. 2021; Drejer and Christensen 2021; all this volume).

1.3.3 Policy coordination

The adoption of a systems approach led to increased emphasis on cross-ministerial coordination, as the framework conditions were found to cross traditional sector boundaries, and also to encompass conditions that would traditionally have fallen under the purview of several ministries such as the Ministry of Education, the Ministry of Labour and the Ministry of Research. Policy coordination was, however, an issue even earlier on. For example, in 1993, the Ministry of Industrial Policy Coordination was established. The ministry had limited resources, and only existed one year as an independent ministry. It did, however, signal a broader and a more cross-ministerial approach to industrial policy, something that has been prominent in Danish innovation policies since that time. Nevertheless, at the time there was a relatively large degree of turbulence in policymaking, and this made it difficult to substantially change the existing policy stance. For example, in the 1990s and up until 2001, the average term of a Minister of Research was less than one year.

Policy development is related not only to the general understanding of innovation processes, but also to the fact that innovation has become more complex and interactive (Borras and Edquist 2019), and that it is affected by (and relevant for) several different areas of policy. For example, a firm's ability to innovate is increasingly dependent upon different types of institutions, such as labour market institutions and the educational system, etc. (see also —Part III in this volume). This in turn requires policymakers to cross several traditional boundaries; for example, policies that stimulate the share of highly educated people in (small) firms also increase the rate of innovation. In fact, in several cases, it is a prerequisite for success in innovation policy that the absorptive capacity (and hence the education level) is increased (OECD 2010). Collaborations between programmes in the Ministry of Industry and Ministry of Education are, however, not always easily achieved (Erhvervsfremme Styrelsen 1997a).

1.3.4 The knowledge base and other drivers of innovation policy – inspiration from theory and academia?

In the above explanation of how Danish innovation policies developed, we have already given indications of what triggered specific policy changes. Specifically, we indicated that policies are often (but not always) informed by several types of sources, such as e.g., empirical (statistical) knowledge on innovation and diffusion, inspiration from abroad, trade organisations, firms, academia, evaluations, single events and 'user' feedback. In this subsection, we particularly focus on one policy driver, namely how statistical knowledge on innovation evolved, why and what the consequences were for policy.

The first survey on innovation in Denmark was published in 1981 (Høgberg 1981). It was commissioned by the National Technology Board (Teknologistyrelsen) and, interestingly, was intended to form a basis for a decision on whether an 'innovator' education degree programme should be established in Denmark. It was shown, according to firms answering the survey, that innovation in Denmark was, and would increasingly be, dependent upon collaboration and assimilation with partners outside the firms.

From the so-called 'CIS 0' (covering innovation from 1984–1988), a Danish pilot study prior to the EU CIS surveys, more systematic empirical knowledge of innovation began to appear (Industri- og Handelsstyrelsen, Industriministeriet 1990). At the time Danish academic interest in innovation was scattered and limited to a few people, research groups and policy circles. In fact, innovation was not very high on the agenda before the early 1990s. The CIS 0 encompassed roughly the same questions and the same structure as the later innovation surveys coordinated by Eurostat. Although these later surveys were harmonised between (12) European countries, and theoretically informed (Smith 2004), they were initially carried out fairly infrequently, operating on a four-year cycle, and primarily focused on technological product and process innovations in the manufacturing sector.[16] Even R&D statistics were not highly prioritised. In fact, only one civil servant in the Ministry of Research had private sector R&D and R&D statistics as part of his or her responsibilities.

The results from the CIS surveys created awareness of innovation and were extensively referred to in both regional and national innovation policy deliberation (Christensen and Kristensen 1994, 1995, 1997). One of the results from innovation surveys that had a policy impact was that Danish firms demonstrated a high propensity to collaborate on innovation (Christensen and Kristensen 1997; Erhvervsfremme Styrelsen 1999; Lundvall 2002). This is especially true regarding interactions with customers and suppliers for developing innovation. Danish firms generally interact more frequently with these types of collaborators compared to firms in other countries. However, up until recent innovation surveys, the opposite was true for collaboration with universities (ibid.). The latter can be explained by the presence of a well-developed system of technological intermediaries which specialise in disseminating useful new technological knowledge to businesses, hence limiting the need for direct interaction with universities.

The high propensity for collaboration on innovation is not confined to inter-firm collaboration. Also, intra-organisational interaction across departments and between workers was considered important for stimulating idea generation and innovation (Erhvervsfremme Styrelsen 1997b). This led some unions to propose a policy effort to stimulate 'worker-led innovation'. This was seen as a way of democratising the innovation processes in firms and to stimulate workers' influence on their work and work organisation, cf. Lorenz and Holm 2021. Thus, in the mid-1990s, there was a growing recognition of the complementary benefits of organisational innovation and the upgrading of skills for technological innovations in products and processes (Lundvall 2002). As a result, stimulating knowledge transfer between collaboration partners has been a high priority, and it has a long history in Danish innovation policy (e.g., Erhvervsfremme Styrelsen 1997a, 1997b). Whereas in theory this could be about knowledge transfer between any actors in the innovation system, in practice the policy priority has primarily been to stimulate knowledge flows from knowledge institutions, in particular universities, to private firms.

The OECD was an early and active participant in mapping different aspects of innovation activities, and also paid special attention to interactions among actors, often referring explicitly to innovation systems in their mapping and evaluation of member states' systems (cf. Section 1.2 in this chapter).[17] Other countries' strategies and programmes also inspired Danish policymaking, although domestic influences were arguably of greater importance (*Mandag Morgen* 1994, 1995).

Generally, research in innovation studies rarely leads directly to policy initiatives. However, there are several cases where research – and researchers' participation in reference groups – have inspired innovation-focused policymaking in Denmark. It was mentioned earlier that advances in the systems approach to innovation (e.g., Lundvall 1992; Edquist 1997) had this effect, but more formal evolutionary theorising (Metcalfe 1995a, 1995b) also had a certain influence (e.g., in *Mandag Morgen* 1994, 1995; Christensen and Kristensen 1995; Lundvall 1999). It is also clear that some large-scale research programmes were instrumental in providing the background knowledge for a range of policy initiatives. This goes for projects such as the DISKO-project (Lundvall 1999), the LOK-project (management, organisation, competences) (Erhvervsfremme Styrelsen 1997b) and the so-called 'resource område studier' (resource area studies) (Erhvervsudviklingsrådet 1994). In particular, policy makers within the Ministry of Industry were actively engaged in a dialogue with academics regarding developments in the general understanding of innovation processes.

Within the ministries, it has been considered important to actively upgrade academic skills. In addition to the direct contact between academics and policymakers, the fact that the people currently being hired in the ministries are trained in modern innovation theory as a part of their university education has had an impact. A second channel of influence of innovation theory is the use of innovation scholars in various reference groups for evaluations. For example, the ministries often demanded in their calls for tender that consultancy firms should include academics in project steering committees, and sometimes the ministries themselves established such groups. This may be seen as a way to translate the academic understanding of theory to a more practical, policy-relevant setting.[18]

1.4 Concluding remarks

The purpose of this chapter has been to discuss how the knowledge base for innovation policy has evolved internationally and relate this to Danish experiences for the period leading up to the turn of the millennium.

As shown in Section 1.2, the turn to a more holistic and systemic approach to innovation policy in Europe during the 1990s was influenced by several factors, such as a changing economic context (presenting new challenges for policy), the emergence of new theoretical perspectives (innovation systems theory, evolutionary economics) and new types of empirical evidence on the working of innovation (e.g., from innovation surveys). Denmark, as demonstrated in Section 1.3, was no exception to this trend and, on the contrary, exactly the same trend and factors were present. Thus, Denmark was far from being a passive adopter of new, fashionable policy approaches originating elsewhere. In fact, Danish policy makers were early movers with respect to developing an empirical knowledge base for innovation policy making, and some of the research that influenced the development of the new approach was of Danish origin (Fagerberg and Sapprasert 2011).

During the past few decades there have been changes not only in our under-standing of the innovation process, but also in our understanding of how that process evolves. One such change is increased complexity and pace of change (Iammarino and McCann 2013). Innovative products now come about with a variety of inputs and often require knowledge from a range of different dis-ciplines. Firms, innovation scholars and policymakers alike now understand innovation not only as new products and processes, but also as new forms of organisations, new complementary services to manufacturing products, new forms of marketing, etc. Similarly, academics and policymakers now recognise the need to study and stimulate innovation in private as well as public ser-vices, as elaborated in other chapters in this volume. One implication of this increasing complexity and broader perception of innovation is that policymak-ing needs to take into account a number of different policy areas that are not usually coupled.

Although it was recognised early on that a more integrated policy approach would be appropriate (*Mandag Morgen* 1995; Erhvervsfremme Styrelsen 1997a, 1997b; Lundvall 1999), there have in the Danish case been continuing barriers to implementing this kind of policy coordination (Erhvervsfremme Styrelsen 1997a). Adding to the generic explanations discussed above, coordination problems in the Danish case relate to at least two factors. First, the Ministry of Finance had a strong say through budget control but does not really play a coordinating role in innovation policymaking. Therefore, innovation policies were pursued more or less independently in different ministries, e.g., Research, Education, Business Development, Environment and Agriculture (in fact there have been changes over time in which ministries cover which fields). Second, policies were (and still are) pursued with heavy 'user' involvement. Whereas this may be positive for legitimisation of policies it adds to the complexity of the political process. Nevertheless, despite these obstacles for policy coordina-tion, we found that there was a shift from very fragmented policies towards a more integrated, systemic and holistic approach to policymaking during the 1990s, particularly towards the end of the period (Regeringen 2000a, 2000b).

Moreover, post-war industrial evolution has been characterised not only by various business cycles, but also by fast, turbulent changes, which foreshadow challenges for innovation policy. Some of the means of dealing with this in Danish policy have been to develop and deploy flexible, temporary policy instruments, along with dialogue on trends with leading-edge firms, trade associations, branch organisations and knowledge institutions. The tradition of calling in opinions from these actors has persisted until today.

A recent attempt to map innovation and research policy studies (Ministry of Education 2015) pointed out that the link between the research commu-nity and the policy community in Denmark remains fragile. To find ways to strengthen this link without undermining the relative autonomy of the two communities is a challenge for both. Policy learning will always reflect a combination of experience-based insights and political influences. Having an ongoing dialogue with scholars engaged in scientific research aiming at understanding the innovation process may be helpful in avoiding that policy falls victim to fashion or under the dominant sway of vested interests.

Notes

1 Following Schumpeter (1934, 1942), the founding father of innovation theory, innovation studies distinguish sharply between invention (new ideas) and innovation (the introduction of such idea in the economic and social sphere). See Fagerberg (2004) for further elaboration. Hence, the central elements in innovation are 'novelty' and 'use/application'. The standard source for how to measure innovation with survey instruments, the so-called 'Oslo Manual', defines innovation as: 'An innovation is a new or improved product or process (or combination thereof) that differs significantly from the unit's previous products or processes and that has been made available to potential users (product) or brought into use by the unit (process)'. (OECD/Eurostat 2018, 20).

2 This is illustrated by the fact that later (2005) the definition of innovation as described in the Oslo Manual broadened as also new forms of organisation and marketing became part of the definition, and the word 'technological' was removed from the definition.

3 In the early years, this increase of interest was especially pronounced in the US, and the US military establishment played an important role in fostering it. See Fagerberg and Verspagen (2009) and references therein for more details.

4 In economic theory a 'public good' is something that cannot be appropriated, hence can be used by everybody free of charge.

5 This has led to large empirical literature on the measurement of social and private returns to research and development, see e.g., Griliches (1979, 1992).

6 Levin et al. (1987; also known as the Yale-survey) focused on the appropriability conditions in US industry based on a survey in which 650 R&D executives in more than one hundred industries took part. The results showed that conditions for appropriating returns from investments in innovation vary a lot across industries.

7 For example, there are examples of publications focusing on 'innovation policies' in specific companies or organisations (which today might have been labelled 'innovation strategies' or 'innovation management').

8 For an overview and discussion see Verspagen (2004).

9 As explained in Drejer and Christensen 2021 (this volume), in 2007 there was another major merger of the municipalities into fewer, larger ones.

10 Generally, regions have had an important role in Danish innovation policy. This was spurred particularly by the implementation of the Law on Industrial Policy in 1990, and the Law on Municipalities' and Regions' Participation in Industrial Policy in 1992 (Erhvervsministeriet 1995). This coincided with a change in national policies focusing less on intervention towards getting framework conditions in place, which left more room for regional actors to act in a direct, proactive manner.

11 For example, the Teknologisk Udviklingsprogram (Technological Development Programme), entailed a biotech programme, a programme for developing and using new materials, a programme for Food Technology and a programme on Strategic Research in Environmental Technologies (Industriministeriet 1991, 1992).

12 Consequently, an intense debate was sparked when it was abolished in 2011.

13 Generally, there is no direct link between the political orientation of the government and the emphasis they put on innovation policy.

14 This is illustrated by the fact that software was developed to guide users through support schemes, and the availability of consultants that specialised in helping firms apply. As illustrated in Drejer and Christensen, 2021, some of the same discussions and changes have occurred in 2019.

15 A nuanced analysis would show that changes were incremental in many cases, and several policies and instruments existed across more than one period.

16 The so-called Oslo Manual published jointly by the OECD and Eurostat in different editions in 1992, 2005, 2015, and 2018 contains the theoretical background, definitions and survey methodologies for the CIS innovation surveys.
17 The EU played a marginal role in inspiring innovation policies, and primarily had their influence through the establishment of innovation statistics in collaboration with the OECD.
18 Despite this influence of theory, data and academia, the causality may also go in the opposite direction. Policy initiatives are sometimes formulated, and only subsequently arguments for the policy are produced through new data and reports on innovation.

References

Arrow, K. 1962. Economic Welfare and the Allocation of Resources for Innovation. In *The Rate and Direction of Inventive Activity*, ed. Nelson R. R., 609–625. Princeton: Princeton University Press.

Bergek, A., Jacobsson, S., Carlsson, B., Lindmark, S. and Rickne, A. 2008. Analyzing the Functional Dynamics of Technological Innovation Systems: A Scheme of Analysis. *Research Policy* 37: 407–429.

Borras, S. and Edquist, C. 2019. *Holistic Innovation Policy: Theoretical Foundations, Policy Problems, and Instrument Choices*. Oxford: Oxford University Press.

Bush, V. 1945. *Science: The Endless Frontier*. Washington, DC: United States Government Printing Office.

Christensen, J. L., Dahl, M. S., Eliasen, S., Nielsen, R. N. and Østergaard, C. R. 2011. Patterns and Collaborators of Innovation in the Primary Sector: A Study of the Danish Agriculture, Forestry and Fishery Industries. *Industry and Innovation* 18(2): 203–225.

Drejer, I. and Christensen, J. L. 2021. Chapter 4: The Danish regional innovation system in transition. In *Globalisation, New and Emerging Technologies, and Sustainable Development – The Danish Innovation System in Transition*, ed. Christensen, J. L., Gregersen, B., Holm, J. R. and Lorenz, E. L. Abingdon, UK: Taylor & Francis.

Christensen, J. L. and Knudsen, M. P. 2021. Chapter 2: The performance, challenges and related policies of the Danish research and innovation system. In *Globalisation, New and Emerging Technologies, and Sustainable Development – The Danish Innovation System in Transition*, ed. Christensen, J. L., Gregersen, B., Holm, J. R. and Lorenz, E. L. Abingdon, UK: Taylor & Francis.

Christensen, J. L. and Kristensen, A. 1994. *Innovation i danske industrivirksomheder*. Copenhagen: Erhvervsfremme Styrelsen.

Christensen, J. L. and Kristensen, A. 1995. *Innovation og Erhvervsudvikling*. Copenhagen: Erhvervsfremme Styrelsen.

Christensen, J. L. and Kristensen, A. 1997. *Et historisk og internationalt perspektiv på innovation i dansk industri*. Copenhagen: Erhvervsfremme Styrelsen.

Christiansen, P. M. 1992. *Statslig erhvervsfremme – struktur, beslutninger, koordination*. Industri- og Handelsstyrelsen.

Christiansen, P. M. and Sidenius, N. C. 1988. Forsknings- og Teknologipolitik i Danmark. Politik og Institutioner. *Politica, Bind* 20: 3.

Cohen, W. 1995. Empirical Studies of Innovative Activity. In *Handbook of the Economics of Innovation and Technological Change*, ed. Stoneman, P., 182–264 Oxford: Blackwell.

Cohen, W. and Levinthal, D. 1990. Absorptive Capacity: A New Perspective on Learning and Innovation. *Administrative Science Quarterly* 35: 128–152.

Dalum, B. et al. 1991. *Internationalisering og erhvervsudvikling*. Industri- og Handelsstyrelsen.

Edler, J. and Georghiou, L. 2007. Public Procurement and Innovation-Resurrecting the Demand Side. *Research Policy* 36: 949–963.

Edquist, C. ed. 1997: *Systems of Innovation - Technologies, Institutions, and Organisations*. London: Pinter.

Edquist, C. 2004. Systems of Innovation: Perspectives and Challenges. In *Oxford Handbook of Innovation*, ed. Fagerberg, J., Mowery, D. and Nelson, R., 181–208. Oxford: Oxford University Press.

Edquist, C. and Lundvall, B.-Å. 1993. Comparing the Danish and Swedish Systems of Innovation. In *National Innovation Systems. A Comparative Analysis*, ed. Nelson, R. R., 265–298. Oxford: Oxford University Press.

Edquist, C. and Zabala-Iturriagagoitia, J. M. 2012. Public Procurement for Innovation as Mission-Oriented Innovation Policy. *Research Policy* 41: 1757–1769.

Erhvervsfremme Styrelsen. 1999. *Vidensinstitutioner og Innovation*. DISKO-projektet: Rapport nr. 8. Copenhagen.

Erhvervsfremme Styrelsen. 1997a. *Samspil Mellem Regional erhvervs- og arbejdsmarkedspolitik*. Copenhagen.

Erhvervsfremme Styrelsen. 1997b. *Forandring til fremtiden*. Copenhagen.

Erhvervsfremme Styrelsen. 1997c. *Dialogue with the Ressource Areas – Danish Experiences*.

Erhvervsministeriet. 1995. *Regionalpolitisk Redegørelse*. Copenhagen.

Erhvervsministeriet/Industri-og Samordningsministeriet. Various years since 1993. *Erhvervsredegørelse*.

Erhvervsudviklingsrådet. 1994. *Erhvervsudviklingsrådets redegørelse*. Copenhagen.

Fagerberg, J. 2004. Innovation: A Guide to the Literature. In *The Oxford Handbook of Innovation*, ed. Fagerberg, J., Mowery, D. and Nelson, R, 1–26. Oxford: Oxford University Press.

Fagerberg, J. 2017. Innovation Policy: Rationales, Lessons and Challenges. *Journal of Economic Surveys* 31: 497–512.

Fagerberg, J., Fosaas, M. and Sapprasert, K. 2012. Innovation: Exploring the Knowledge Base. *Research Policy* 41: 1132–1153.

Fagerberg, J. and Sapprasert, K. 2011. National Innovation Systems: The Emergence of a New Approach. *Science and Public Policy* 38(9): 669–679.

Fagerberg, J., Srholec, M., & Verspagen, B. 2010. Innovation and Economic Development. In *Handbook of the Economics of Innovation*, ed. B. Hall and N. Rosenberg, Vol. II, 833–872. Amsterdam and Oxford: North Holland.

Fagerberg, J. and Verspagen, B. 2009. Innovation Studies – The Emerging Structure of a New Scientific Field. *Research Policy* 38: 218–233.

Freeman, C. 1987. *Technology Policy and Economic Performance: Lessons from Japan*. London: Pinter.

Freeman, C., Clark, J. and Soete, L. 1982. *Unemployment and Technical Innovation: A Study of Long Waves and Economic Development*. London: Pinter.

Freeman, C., Louçã, F. 2001. *As Time Goes by: From the Industrial Revolutions to the Information Revolution*. Oxford: Oxford University Press.

Freeman, C. and Perez, C. 1988. Structural Crisis of Adjustment, Business Cycles and Investment Behaviour. In *Technical Change and Economic Theory*, ed. Dosi, G., 38–66. London: Pinter.

Griliches, Z. 1979. Issues in Assessing the Contribution of Research and Development to Productivity Growth. *Bell Journal of Economics* 10: 92–116.

Griliches, Z. 1992. The Search for R&D Spillovers. *Scandinavian Journal of Economics* 94: S29–47.

Hedin, S., Ikonen, R., Tynkkynen, V., Edvardsson, I. and Gunnarsdottir, R. 2008. *National Overviews of Regional Innovation Policies and Case Studies in the Nordic Countries.* Nordregio Working Paper, 2008:2, Stockholm.

Høgberg, L. 1981. *Industriel Innovation.* Århus: Jydsk Teknologisk Instituts Forlag.

Iammarino, S. and McCann, P. 2013. Introduction: Multinational Enterprises, Innovation and Geography in Today's Globalized World. In *Multinationals and Economic Geography: Location, Technology and Innovation*, pp. 1–29. Cheltenham: Edward Elgar Publishing.

Industri- og Handelsstyrelsen, Industriministeriet. 1990. *Innovationsaktivitet I Dansk Industri 1984–1988.*

Industriministeriet. 1990. *10 Erhvervspolitiske temaer.*

Industriministeriet. 1991. *Erhvervspolitisk redegørelse.*

Industriministeriet. 1992. *Pejlemærker for fremtidens erhvervspolitik.*

Johnson, C. 1982. *MITI and the Japanese Miracle: The Growth of Industrial Policy, 1925–1975.* Stanford: Stanford University Press.

Kline, S. J. and Rosenberg, N. 1986. An Overview of Innovation. In *The Positive Sum Strategy: Harnessing Technology for Economic Growth*, ed. Landau, R. and Rosenberg, N., 275–304. Washington, DC: National Academy Press.

Levin, R. C., et al. 1987. *Appropriating the Returns from Industrial Research and Development.* Brookings Pap. Econ. Act. Microeconomics, 783–820.

Lorenz, E. and Holm, J. R. 2021. Work organisation, innovation and the quality of working life in Denmark. In *Globalization, New and Emerging Technologies, and Sustainable Development – The Danish Innovation System in Transition*, eds. Christensen, J. L., Gregersen, B., Holm, J. R. and Lorenz, E. London: Routledge.

Lundvall, B.-Å. ed. 1992. *National Systems of Innovation: Towards a Theory of Innovation and Interactive Learning.* London: Pinter Publishers.

Lundvall, B.-Å. 1999. *Det danske Innovations System.* Disko-projektet, sammenfattende rapport nr.9. Copenhagen.

Lundvall, B.-Å. 2002. *Innovation, Growth and Social Cohesion. The Danish Model.* Cheltenham: Edward Elgar Publishing.

Lundvall, B.-Å. and Borras, S. 1997. *The Globalising Learning Economy: Implications for Innovation Policy.* Brussels: European Commission.

Lundvall, B.-Å. and Borrás, S. 2004. Science, Technology, and Innovation Policy. In *The Oxford Handbook of Innovation*, ed. Fagerberg, J., Mowery, D. C. and Nelson, Research Review, 599–631. Oxford: Oxford University Press.

Mandag Morgen. 1995. *Innovationskraft 2000.* Debatoplæg om en ny dansk innovationspolitik.

Mandag Morgen. 1994. *Det danske forsknings, teknologi- og innovationssystem.* Baggrundsrapport til OECD evaluering.

Metcalfe, J. S. 1995a. The Economic Foundations of Technology Policy: Equilibrium and Evolutionary Perspectives. In *Handbook of the Economics of Innovation and Technological Change*, ed. Stoneman, P., pp. 409–512. Oxford: Blackwell.

Metcalfe, J. S. 1995b. Technology Systems and Technology Policy in an Evolutionary Framework. *Cambridge Journal of Economics* 19: 25–46.

Ministry of Education. 2015. *Mapping the Research on Research and Innovation in Denmark.* Copenhagen: Ministry of Education.

Nelson, R. R. 1959. The Simple Economics of Basic Scientific Research. *Journal of Political Economy* 67: 297–306.

Nelson, R. R. ed. 1993. *National Innovation Systems: A Comparative Study.* Oxford: Oxford University Press.

Nelson, R. R. and Winter, S. G. 1982. *An Evolutionary Theory of Economic Change.* Cambridge, MA: Harvard University Press.

Nielsen, K., Dahl, M. S., Timmermans, B. and Christensen, J. L. 2021. Chapter 3: Entrepreneurship, experimentation and innovation: Future policy for innovative and growth-oriented entrepreneurs in Denmark. In *Globalisation, New and Emerging Technologies, and Sustainable Development – The Danish Innovation System in Transition*, ed. Christensen, J. L., Gregersen, B., Holm, J. R. and Lorenz, E. L. Abingdon, UK: Taylor & Francis.

OECD. 1962. *The Measurement of Scientific and Technical Activities: Proposed Standard Practice for Surveys of Research and Experimental Development.* Paris: OECD.

OECD. 1994. *Review of Denmark's Science, Technology and Innovation Policies. Examiners' Report.* Paris: OECD.

OECD. 1997. *National Innovation Systems.* Paris: OECD.

OECD. 1999. *Managing National Innovation Systems.* Paris: OECD.

OECD. 2001. *Innovative Networks. Co-Operation in National Innovation Systems.* Paris: OECD.

OECD. 2002. *Dynamising National Innovation Systems.* Paris: OECD.

OECD. 2010. *Innovation to Strengthen Growth and Address Global and Societal Challenges. Ministerial Report on the OECD Innovation Strategy.* Paris: OECD.

OECD/Eurostat. 2018. *Oslo Manual 2018: Guidelines for Collecting, Reporting and Using Data on Innovation.* 4th ed. The Measurement of Scientific, Technological and Innovation Activities.

Perroux, F. 1955. Note sur la Notion de Pole de Croissance. *Economie Appliquee*, January-June.

Regeringen. 2000a. *Regeringens erhvervsstrategi – kort fortalt.* Albertslund: Schultz Information.

Regeringen. 2000b. *Fra strategi til handling.* Auning: Datagraf.

Romer, P. M. 1990. Endogenous Technological Change. *Journal of Political Economy* 98: 71–102.

Rothwell, R. 1982. Government Innovation Policy: Some Past Problems and Recent Trends. *Technological Forecasting and Social Change* 22: 3–30.

Rothwell, R., Freeman, C., Horlsey, A., Jervis, V. T. P., Robertson, A. B. and Townsend, J. 1974. SAPPHO Updated – Project SAPPHO Phase II. *Research Policy* 3: 258–291.

Schumpeter, J. A. 1934. *Theory of Economic Development.* Cambridge, MA: Harvard University Press.

Schumpeter, J. A. 1942. *Capitalism, Socialism and Democracy.* New York: Harper.

Smith, K. 2004. Measuring Innovation In *The Oxford Handbook of Innovation*, eds. Fagerberg, J., Mowery, D., Nelson, R., 148–178. Oxford: Oxford University Press.

Verspagen, B. 2004. Innovation and Economic Growth. In *The Oxford Handbook of Innovation*, ed. Fagerberg, J., Mowery, D. C. and Nelson, R. R., 487–513. Oxford: Oxford University Press., E. and 2021.

2 The performance, challenges and related policies of the Danish research and innovation system

Jesper Lindgaard Christensen and
Mette Præst Knudsen

2.1 Introduction

For years the Danish research and innovation system has performed tremendously well by any of the standard indicators, and the research performance is among the best countries in Europe (European Commission 2020). Likewise, Denmark has consistently, since the early 2000s when systematic comparative measurements began, been at the top of the EU Innovation Scoreboard (European Commission 2001). Despite this position as an innovative leader in Europe, some warning signs are noticeable. The main (relative) weakness lies in the problems in transferring and transforming R&D-based knowledge into commercial use, particularly in the main segment of companies, small and medium sized companies (SMEs). Thus, even when aggregate system indicators remain high in international comparisons, some disaggregated areas and development trends point to potential challenges for the Danish system.

This is the story in this chapter, which we unfold by presenting the innovation system and identifying these challenges. An international evaluation panel recently (March 2019 – October 2019) looked into the Danish research and innovation system (European Commission 2019). The panel pointed to several challenges for the system and came up with a number of recommendations. Specifically, the panel recognised the strong research system and sectoral strongholds (e.g., life sciences and energy), but also pointed to weaknesses and challenges in (among others) a limited number of large, R&D-intensive firms, and a decreasing number of firms conducting R&D. Moreover, the links between large and small firms in innovation activities remain limited. The panel's primary concern is that Denmark is not making the most out of its superior research system in terms of business innovation (European Commission 2019). The latter complies with our main focus area in this chapter.

The conclusions from the panel are particularly interesting in the context of this volume. The panel points to specific adjustments that can be made to fine-tune the individual institutions in the system and the links between these to promote innovation. This is in accordance with innovation system thinking where core points are links between actors in the system. However, the overall conclusion of the panel is that Denmark has hitherto been relatively vague in specifying where the innovation should go. There have been attempts to provide innovation action plans (2012 and 2017), but a holistic strategy that explicates value propositions forming the basis for directionality and prioritisation is still to be developed, the panel argues.

Much in accordance with the points made by the evaluation panel, we particularly envisage the main challenges that are likely to hamper the future performance of the innovation system, and at the end of the chapter we discuss innovation policies that are better geared towards providing direction than the innovation policies pursued thus far. Hence, we give special attention to the research system and how it links with innovation, while recognising that innovation is dependent upon a much wider range of factors.

We consider the Danish case to be both interesting and relevant for other countries for at least two reasons. First, the high rankings on leading indicators, especially of research but also of several innovation indicators, have attracted international interest, and in this way the Danish research system could be considered a role model for other countries. Second, in the 1990s, a discussion evolved around what was termed the 'Swedish paradox', i.e., that Sweden led world rankings of R&D intensity but showed mediocre performance on innovation. This paradox was, though, soon broadened to a small country paradox and further to a European paradox as other countries showed similar patterns (Dosi et al. 2006). Thus, the observations in Denmark are paralleled in other countries and the possible solutions are transferable under the right circumstances. Whereas there are numerous studies of research and innovation in Denmark (see a detailed account of these studies in Christensen and Fagerberg 2021, this volume), there are fewer studies on the link between research and innovation, hence system performance and the associated implications for policy learning. This chapter contributes to filling this gap, as well as providing an overview of current policies and selected relevant innovation system features.

We pursue the analysis in the following steps. We first provide a short note on the fundamental issue of relating innovation input and output indicators and interpret this as system performance, the core problem area in this chapter. In Section 2.3, we list some of the key indicators for R&D and innovation in Denmark compared to Europe in order to provide an overall picture of the performance and problems for the Danish innovation system. Section 2.4 elaborates on the overall challenge of transforming research to innovation and the most recent policies pertaining to the challenge and improvement of innovation performance. In Section 2.5, we briefly pose hypotheses as to why there might be problems in transferring research to innovation. Before concluding, Section 2.6 points to four stepping stones that contribute to explaining why Denmark is still faring well in innovation despite the challenges described in this chapter. Section 2.7 rounds up the chapter by summarising and discussing the research and innovation system and policies in relation to broader societal objectives. Moreover, we point to the observation that innovation policies are now extensively discussed in relation to societal objectives and increased directionality of policies.

2.2 From research to innovation and R&D performance to innovation performance

Theoretically, the link between research and innovation was a central issue early in the upsurge in innovation studies (Mansfield 1984; Pakes and Griliches 1984), and different 'generations' of models for understanding this input to the innovation process was developed during the 1950s and the following decades. These models include linear models, coupling models, networked models, systemic models (see Christensen and Fagerberg 2021, this volume for an elaboration of these models). A large share of public funding for research goes to funding research at universities, and a recurrent issue for debate in connection with these funds is the balance between funding fundamental research and applied research, and related, to what extent the research leads to (immediate) applicable, useful knowledge and innovation. Generally, the road from research to innovation has been thoroughly discussed and described, whereas the paths from research system performances and how they transform into innovation system performances remain a key debate for policy development.

At first sight, it seems simple to relate known, established input indicators such as R&D expenditure to output indicators such as patenting. Indeed, a number of contemporary rankings pursue this endeavour. For example, the Global Innovation Index[1] calculates a so-called innovation efficiency ratio for 129 countries, defined as the ratio of the output sub-index score over the input sub-index score (Denmark ranking seventh in 2019, where input score is fifth and output twelfth). Similarly, the European Innovation Scoreboard (EIS) has a composite index ranking European countries according to their innovation performance. However, such measurements have been criticised. One criticism is around the measurement techniques; for example, the EIS mixes input and output indicators for its ranking, which in turn often is interpreted as a performance measure (Edquist et al. 2018). Another type of criticism is centred around the mere system performance measure. For example, Liu et al. (2014) argue that one should look at specific parts of the outputs in innovation systems and relate these to specific inputs as the true strengths of innovation systems are their abilities to efficiently induce a process to transform certain inputs to outputs. A third line of debate on system input-output relations is that systems exist in several realms, be they regions, sectors or technologies, and the efficiencies of innovation systems should be related to these specific realms (Weber and Truffer 2017). In this sense too, aggregated performance measures risk being flawed and will not capture that specific parts of the system entail so-called system resources, that is, important factors that in a balanced process facilitate the smooth operating of the system and the effective transition of input resources to output.[2]

Although the central story in this chapter also looks at relations between input and output factors for innovation, we do adopt a critical view on the simplistic measurements and include considerations on specific Danish innovation drivers.

2.3 Research and innovation performance in Denmark

R&D intensity (expenditure on R&D as a percentage of gross domestic product, GDP) in the OECD rose from 2.34% in 2017 to 2.38% in 2018, whereas for Denmark we observe a fairly stable R&D intensity above 3% (see Figure 2.1). Danish R&D intensity is therefore relatively high at 3% of GDP, exceeding both the OECD and the EU28 averages. The ratio increased during the financial crisis partly due to decreasing GDP. Public R&D is stable and around 1% of GDP and remains among the highest in the EU.

Business enterprise R&D expenditure (BERD) as a share of GDP has, in the 2008–2017 period, been stable at around 1.8%, which is relatively high in international comparison, whereas the OECD average is around 1.4% and the EU28 average is 1.14% (2017). Denmark is exceeded only by countries like Sweden, Switzerland and South Korea, and is substantially above the EU average. The number of researchers per thousand of the labour force speaks to the R&D intensity capacity. This figure for Denmark slightly increased from 14.5 to 15.2 from 2015 to 2018. This is significantly higher than both the EU28 and OECD averages of 8.06 and 8.1 (2017).

Whereas the aggregate figures indicate a smooth development, they hide substantial changes regarding firm and sectoral composition of R&D performers.

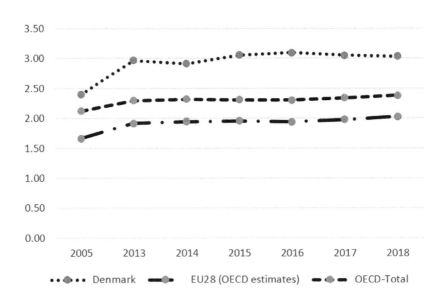

Figure 2.1 R&D intensity in Denmark compared to the OECD and EU28

The higher education sector (HES) is the main beneficiary of public R&D funds. The external share of funding of university research from non-profit private foundations and organisations is the highest among the OECD countries, and the overall external funding (including funding from business and international sources) in 2015 was the second highest among the OECD countries (OECD 2017a; Styrelsen for Forskning og Innovation 2018). Public funding of research and innovation (R&I) is also provided through international programmes. The Danish share of total EU funding from the EU framework programmes is high relative to the size of the population, as Denmark's success in obtaining €122/inhabitant is only exceeded by The Netherlands (Styrelsen for Forskning og Innovation 2018). Furthermore, a review of Danish doctoral education from 2017 (Styrelsen for Forskning og Innovation 2017c) found that the Danish system is functioning well, and Danish doctorate theses are of a high international standard. In 2016, 399 PhD titles per million inhabitants were awarded (fourth in the OECD) totalling 2279 PhDs awarded (OECD 2020).

A further indicator of R&D performance is the granting of patents, where Denmark's proportion of applications for world patents normalised by billion GDP was 6.24 in 2015, well above the EU average of 3.53. The patent applications per million population is also high and increasing, from 562 to 626 from 2007 to 2017 (WIPO 2018). This puts Denmark at seventh place in the OECD top performers. Much of the patent performance originates from energy-related technologies like wind energy in which Denmark is highly specialised (WIPO 2018).

Moreover, scientific publications are an indicator of R&D performance. Denmark has obtained an overall increase from 1166.12 in 2009 to 2228.92 in 2016 for the number of international scientific co-publications per million population. According to Styrelsen for Forskning og Innovation (2018), both the volume and citations of Danish publications are in the OECD top five in 2012–2016, and Denmark has the highest share of publications co-authored between HES and business; a similar top ranking applies to international co-authorship, as almost 60% of Danish publications are co-authored internationally. The 2012–2016 period produced 19,755 scientific publications per million Danish inhabitants (third in the OECD) and Denmark is top in the OECD with respect to its share of the top 10% most cited publications (19.8 in Denmark).

As this presentation of the Danish research system demonstrates, Denmark has a top-performing system that strongly engages and succeeds in research output. To engage with the link to the innovation performance, we present in an equal manner key indicators from the Danish innovation system.

Innovation performance is high and has been so for the past ten years, as evidenced by the EIS which has rated the country an innovation leader with consistent and significant performance. Overall, the latest EIS shows that in 2019, the composite indicator was 146 compared to the EU average of 134 (European Commission 2020). This composite index has been fairly stable since 2012 (ranging from 143 to 147).

Underlying the stability of the composite index, we see some disturbing developments. First of all, since 2013, Denmark's overall score on the EIS has declined by three percentage points, in a period when comparable European countries have improved. Supporting the analysis of these research systems, Denmark has fared well on input measures like the research system (knowledge creation) and an innovation-friendly environment (establishing supportive framework conditions). For instance, between 2013 and 2019, Denmark improved on attractiveness of research systems and firm investment. However, the drop across all indicators for *innovators* is disconcerting. Denmark dropped on all three indicators in the period from 2012 to 2019. A decline is also reported in the share of innovating SMEs collaborating with others (−31). Further performance drops are also reported on impacts on sales and employment. Again, a drop is noticeable in sales of new-to-market and new-to-firm innovations (−84, which is the largest drop by all EU countries).

Hence, the innovation indicators concerned with the innovation performance of SMEs stand out as significant. Here, Denmark is much closer to the EU average, compared to most other indicators. For example, 33% of Danish SMEs introduced product or process innovation and only 23% were innovating in-house. This is below the shares of other innovation leaders and is a cause for concern. Observing these declines calls for a more coherent analysis, where the answers expectedly require a research programme alone to solve. In Section 2.5, we nevertheless propose some plausible hypotheses regarding such explanations.

2.4 The main R&I challenge: ensure effective use of high-quality public research and business R&D for innovation

Section 2.3 presented an overarching challenge for the Danish innovation system, which is concerned with the links between research and innovation. In the vocabulary of the international evaluation panel, research and innovation stand out as 'silos' in Denmark and need to be integrated to a higher extent in order to leverage on the excellent Danish research system (European Commission 2019).

The Danish government launched a comprehensive and novel Strategy for Research and Innovation on December 6, 2017 (Regeringen 2017). One of the two main objectives of the R&I strategy was to increase the *quality* of Danish research from its current high level, which was an attempt at focusing the efforts even further to keep up with international research standards. The second objective was that research must benefit society (the *relevance* goal).

These goals were supported by 28 initiatives. For the research quality goal, the specific initiatives include creation of individual career paths, recruitment and incentives for talented researchers as well as a new performance-based funding model for the universities, new research system infrastructures and stimulating international research collaboration. The relevance goal was supported by activities related to strategic funds and capacity for technological research, focus on digitalisation as well as value creation in firms from research and focus on the connectivity and coordination between public and private funding of research. Moreover, technology transfer from higher education for societal use will be stimulated, and both higher education quality and more STEM graduates are policy objectives. Hence, the R&I strategy included initiatives to strengthen research in technology and technology transfers from universities to business.

Following the approval in parliament of the law on simplification and reorganisation of the business support system (see Chapter 4 in this volume, Christensen and Drejer 2021, for further details), the Innovation Fund Denmark (IFD) introduced three new programmes starting from January 1, 2019 that target commercialisation of research by providing incentives for researchers to engage in innovation and entrepreneurship: InnoFounder, InnoExplorer and Industrial Fellow. The InnoBooster programme (established in 2014) aims to support the innovative capabilities of SMEs. In addition to the IFD, support is provided by the Danish Growth Fund (DGF) for ongoing business development in sectors of high societal importance, and generally for innovation. The funding of such investments through the DGF is stimulated by an increased financial volume and new funding instruments.

According to the law on reorganising the business support system, the DGF should in the future have even more focus on early stage/seed funding of entrepreneurs and have clearer borderlines to the Innovation Fund. This has spurred the DGF to introduce four new initiatives that address this ambition: a matching facility for business angel investments, early engagement loans, increased co-investments with early-stage investors and adjustments of existing growth loans to target earlier stages. The strategy of the DGF is to co-invest with private actors. Currently, funding for innovative start-ups is also provided through the Innovation Fund (grants) and innovation incubators.

Denmark has four innovation incubators which offer a combination of traditional incubator services and early-stage gap funding for start-ups some of which stem from university spinoffs or university knowledge. The innovation incubators invest €10,000 (DKK 74,400) in pre-seed funding for proof of business and a subsequent seed capital accompanied by counselling for entrepreneurs. The funding of approximately €25m (DKK 185m) annually is provided by the Danish Agency for Higher Education and Science (Styrelsen for Forskning og Innovation), but with the reorganisation of the business support system, these organisations are being phased out over a three-year period from January 1, 2020 that allows the current 300 portfolio companies to still be guided by the innovation incubators.

To further incentivise private firms to carry out R&D, the government increased the tax credit for R&D expenditure progressively from 100% to 110% in 2026. Moreover, the Researchers Tax benefit scheme, where specialists from abroad can work for a period in Denmark and enjoy a tax benefit, was extended from five to seven years. It also improved coordination between the different funding instruments, between universities and simplified the administration of R&D programmes. The concentration of business R&D (see Section 2.5) is recognised in the Danish Agency for Higher Education and Science as a potential problem, which calls for research to understand the impact of it. The Danish Agency for Higher Education and Science has therefore initiated research to understand reasons for and implications of this phenomenon (Styrelsen for Forskning og Innovation & DASTI 2019).

The R&I strategy has been followed by separate strategies for digitalisation and growth in life sciences. Moreover, Denmark is a member of the European Spallation Source (ESS), which is part of a European investment in research facilities oriented towards research in new materials. Denmark is committed to invest DKK 2bn (€269m) from 2014–2022 on this initiative.

As this description also highlights, a particular challenge is related to the linkages for innovation as these are important gateways to access and transfer knowledge, but clearly also connected with the overall challenge of the 'unconnected silos', as the main driver in the research system is the university, whereas the main drivers in the innovation domain are businesses.

Compared to the EU average, the European Innovation Scoreboard 2020 (European Commission 2020) indicates that Denmark has experienced a significant decline in the indicator on linkages from 164.1 in 2010 (EU index 100 in 2010) to 149.7 (2019), while the index for the EU has only changed slightly in the period from 95.3 to 99. An important share of the drop can be attributed to *innovative SMEs collaborating with others* (from 215.5 to 120.7). A second observation is that, in 2016–2017, technology transfer offices (TTOs) at universities experienced small decreases in patenting, license agreements, partnership or funding agreements with businesses and spin-offs. However, from a longer-term perspective, the tech-transfer from HES to business is relatively stable and seems to have reached a consolidated level of output and a significantly increased experience base. These indicators speak to the overall connectivity of key actors in the innovation system, which has been a policy focus for many years, but improvements continue to be needed.

Public funds contribute around €300m for innovation infrastructures, primarily the 17 innovation networks, the seven Approved Technology Group (ATG) institutes (consultancy companies, which are certified for receiving a grant and contract for specific work (and a small share of operating costs) demanded by government). Further initiatives include four innovation incubators, and the schemes of the IFD, including the InnoBooster, Industrial PhD, Grand Solutions and Eurostars schemes. In 2018, the funding of the networks expired, and a new two-year funding worth DKK 190m (2019) was granted to the networks (2019–2020).

A strengthening of parts of the Research and Technology Organisations (RTO) system (including the 'GTS – Advanced Technology Group Institutes') has also previously been prioritised. A view to include private actors in the development of the ATG institutes and consolidation of the number of publicly supported innovation clusters are among the policies. In Denmark, business support is provided at national, regional and municipality levels. Mainly, efforts at the national level will be strengthened in the new organisation of the system at the expense of institutions at the regional level, which will be reduced.. At the same time as simplifying the system, the reorganisation of the business support system can challenge possibilities to maintain and strengthen the interactions between actors and knowledge flows in the system, something that has been emphasised as highly important.[3] An elaboration and further assessment of this policy reform can be found in (Drejer and Christensen 2021, this volume).

2.5 A set of explanations for the inefficiency of links between research and innovation

The main challenge points to the partially inefficient links between research results and innovation, but what are possible explanations for this missing link? Are policies inadequate or missing the target? Are there structural and/or behavioural explanations? Answering these questions begs a large research programme, and therefore we only provide some selected explanations and urge for more research into these specific problems, which are not only observed in and relevant for the Danish innovation system.

The first of these possible explanations relates to the fact that Danish R&D is highly and increasingly concentrated. Looking at specific industries, pharmaceuticals and biotechnology are by far the largest R&D-performing sectors in Denmark, and Denmark is on a global scale (relative to size) the leading investor in this industry. At a firm level, among the Danish firms conducting R&D, the global producer of insulin, Novo Nordisk, dwarfs the rest of the firms in terms of R&D volume. In fact, it invests more in R&D than the rest of the top ten firms combined, is 22nd among all R&D performers in Europe, and 80th globally.[4]

Moreover, the general trend over the past decade is that R&D is increasingly concentrated in fewer large firms. For instance, the number of firms investing in R&D decreased between 2009 and 2015 by 25%, and a small group of 64 firms increased its share of overall BERD from 35% to 56% in that period (Styrelsen for Forskning og Innovation 2017b). The top 20 firms increased their share from 2008–2016 to 54.7% of total BERD (Styrelsen for Forskning og Innovation 2018). There are 190 large firms (with more than 250 employees) conducting R&D in Denmark, and while they make up 8% of the population of firms conducting R&D they perform 72% of total BERD. Moreover, the R&D intensity of large firms is much higher than in SMEs and increased in the abovementioned period by 50% whereas it remained more or less constant in other firms (Styrelsen for Forskning og Innovation 2018).

In itself, a high concentration of R&D is not necessarily a problem for the innovation system as long as knowledge dissemination and widespread use of R&D are well established. However, the concentration potentially challenges a wider use and application of both public and private R&D, because effective dissemination and use of R&D often require both a strong system for dissemination of knowledge and absorptive capacity among firms to absorb and utilise knowledge from other sources for commercial purposes (Cohen and Levinthal 1990). With only a small share of firms doing substantial intramural R&D, the absorptive capacity at the system level is likely to be smaller compared to a situation with more equal distribution.

A second, related, explanation questions if the demand and capacity for using R&D is present in the SMEs. The Danish Council on Research and Innovation Policy (Danmarks Forsknings- og Innovationspolitiske Råd 2019) introduced the concept of 'innovation ready' firms to characterise companies that have the necessary preconditions and capacity for utilising R&D-based knowledge. These businesses demonstrate higher growth than other comparable firms, and they are more likely to get more out of business promotion efforts. Therefore, a recommendation following the analyses was that business promotion should be targeting these companies and should be aimed at increasing other firms' capacity to become 'innovation ready'.

Third, the policy changes we have described, such as closing the innovation incubators and several other related programmes, having fewer, more centralised cluster organisations and eliminating the regional tier in business promotion, indicate that over time, policies have been less focused on maintaining links in the innovation system. The diminishing systemic approach in policies encouraged the Danish Council on Research and Innovation Policy (Danmarks Forsknings-og Innovationspolitiske Råd 2016) to call for more systemic innovation policies. Likewise, the international evaluation panel points to bridging the silos in Danish innovation policies and to work towards a more holistic policy that targets the system's functioning (European Commission 2019). They claim in particular that R&I is more independent than in several other countries, and that increased performance may be obtained by seeking to integrate elements in a systems perspective. Chapter 4 in this volume (Christensen and Drejer 2021) is supportive of these arguments as it demonstrates a move towards fewer actors in the business promotion system and more distant links between these actors, and between the actors and their 'client' firms.

2.6 Stepping stones towards maintaining high innovation performance

Even as we point to weaknesses in the link between research and innovation, Denmark has kept its high rank on the European Innovation Scoreboard and similar rankings. Explaining some of these strongholds may not only provide some explanation as to the previous high performance but can also potentially be future innovation drivers. We therefore label these as stepping stones.

2.6.1 Innovation stepping stone 1: public sector innovation

Christensen and Fagerberg (2021, this volume) demonstrate that the definition and measurement of innovation has developed over time from a narrow focus on technological product and process innovations to encompass organisational innovation and marketing innovation. Simultaneously, studies of the carriers of innovation processes have widened beyond private sector firms by pointing to the role of innovation in the public sector and civic society. Particularly, these are important to the total innovation system (see also Stamhus and Nielsen (2021, this volume)). The Danish innovation system has been upgraded through deliberate policies on public sector innovation.

The specific Danish policy approach to public sector innovation has forged a close link between digital access and use of information and technology. The stated objectives are to promote good governance, strengthen democracy and use digital technology to improve society (www.digst.dk). Historically, Denmark has applied a shared digitalisation strategy across the public sector. From its beginning in 2001, when citizens could send emails to public offices, until 2020 when the fifth shared digitalisation strategy is now at its conclusion, a range of initiatives have supported the public sector in being efficient and increasingly digitalised. The strategies envisage that the use of new technology and media facilitates citizens and businesses in accessing public information and technology, which in turn should increase collaboration between the public sector and civil society, hence contributing to the public sector innovation culture.

An example of a Danish policy initiative is that Denmark appointed a Minister for Public Sector Innovation and Modernisation for the first time (2016), with the objective of improving public sector innovation, digitalisation and governance. In addition to innovating how the public sector operates, Denmark also used public procurement extensively to spur innovation. Denmark's strategy on intelligent procurement entails several initiatives aimed at stimulating innovation, such as the 'innovative public-sector purchases'[5] scheme, which aims to make it easier for public sector institutions to obtain innovative new solutions (Gallup 2010). The report shows that Denmark performs well on using public procurement to stimulate innovation, as Denmark is rated the best in the EU.

Another part of public sector innovation is how it interacts with and supports the private sector, including businesses. It is often debated whether administrative burdens and regulations are hindering small business development, which is why this is also subject to internationally harmonised measurement and ranking (e.g., as in the EU SBA Factsheet). Regarding the interaction between SMEs and public administration, Denmark performs generally better than the EU average on nearly all parameters. This good performance is reflected in the World Bank Global Indicators of Regulatory Governance[6] where Denmark scores the maximum of points on its measurements.

Together, the various efforts to increase public sector innovation has meant that the public sector not only functions well but is also constantly changing in response to demand. In turn, this is a stronghold in the innovation system, and potentially also a stepping stone for new innovative efforts, as it constitutes a part of the framework conditions for private sector innovation. In this way, the public sector innovation may be part of re-establishing strong links through e.g., public-private innovation partnerships.

2.6.2 Innovation stepping stone 2: national innovation strategy

The Danish government launched a comprehensive second strategy for R&I in 2017 (Regeringen 2017). This strategy was preceded by the first national innovation strategy, 'Denmark – a nation of solutions' in 2012. The first strategy was seen as facilitating a paradigm shift in innovation policies. The three main focus areas of this strategy were:

1. *Innovation driven by societal challenges:* demand for solutions to concrete societal challenges must be given higher priority in the public sector innovation effort.
2. *More knowledge translated to value:* focus on more effective innovation schemes and better mutual knowledge transfer between companies and knowledge institutions.
3. *Education as a means to increase innovation capacity:* a change of culture in the education system with more focus on innovation and value creation.

The second strategy had two main goals:

1. Danish research must be at the highest international quality *(the 'Nobel' goal).*
2. Research must benefit society *(the relevance goal).*

These goals were supported by 28 initiatives. It is part of the *Nobel* goal to set up a '*Nobel pact*' with the objective of reaching the highest level of research quality and rewarding excellence. For the *Nobel* goal, the specific initiatives include the creation of individual career paths, recruitment and incentives for talented researchers as well as a new performance-based funding model for the universities, new research system infrastructures and stimulating international research collaborations. The *relevance* goal is supported by activities related to strategic funds and capacity for technological research, focus on digitalisation as well as value creation in firms from research and focus on the connectivity and coordination between public and private funding of research. Moreover, technology transfer from higher education for societal use is stimulated, and both higher education quality and more graduates from STEM education are policy objectives.

The strategy is based on high public R&D investments for support. Nevertheless, public R&D investments dropped slightly below 1% in 2016 because of budget cuts and stayed below the 1% target in 2017 (OECD 2020). The government has confirmed its commitment to keeping public R&D investments at 1% of GDP.

The national innovation strategy formulated in 2012 was the first national strategy to be formulated in a comprehensive manner to grasp the multidimensionality of innovation. However, even if strategies, and the broad involvement of businesses and other stakeholders in the creation of innovation strategies, is a stepping stone for further collaboration, the need for more directionality in the policies and a systemic perspective on innovation policy remain clear as is the need to address the connectivity of the system and of the individual initiatives. Hence, despite these early attempts at framing innovation policy in an overarching strategy framework, the Peer Review of the Danish R&I System in 2019 forcefully argued for and recommended:

> The second set of recommendations addresses the opportunity to further elevate Denmark's innovation performance by outlining an overarching innovation strategy. Despite many individual strategies and action plans, Denmark currently lacks such a strategy, which is limiting the country's ability to create positive, system-wide effects from the alignment of individual innovation policy actions.
>
> (European Commission 2019: 2)

It is therefore positive to notice the policy intentions, but the realisation and the path towards a comprehensive and systemic innovation policy driven by an overarching strategy framework remains to be realised. The COVID-19 pandemic is further challenging such a development as the short-term drop in GDP may influence the absolute public investment levels in R&D following the pandemic. At the time of writing, it does seem that R&D investments will be maintained as the government intends to allocate substantial public grants to research, however, research funds are now primarily allocated to prioritised areas such as research in green transitions.

2.6.3 Innovation stepping stone 3: the quality and availability of human resources

It has been a standing phrase in the debate on Danish industrial competitiveness that Denmark has few natural resources and is therefore heavily dependent upon the human workforce resources. Education, training and lifelong learning have consequently been prioritised and an adequate supply of skilled and highly skilled labour is a prerequisite for raising Danish innovation performance. Recently, lack of highly qualified labour has spurred labour market reforms to increase the supply, and labour imports have alleviated problems with shortages of skilled labour. However, there are limits to how much labour supply responds to further labour market reforms, and demand for labour from neighbouring countries (especially Poland) is not fulfilled because demand for surplus labour is now at least as high within the countries that usually contribute immigrant workers as in Denmark.

Regarding highly skilled labour, Denmark has strengthened the industrial PhD and postdoctorate programmes and pushed students to complete studies in time. The development of innovation-related and entrepreneurial skills has been enhanced in courses and programmes throughout the education system. STEM-related studies have been upgraded as all projections (e.g., Økonomi- og Indenrigsministeriet 2018) show that there will be a shortage of skilled labour including people with STEM skills and skilled craftsmen, and that general problems of shortages of labour in all areas are increasingly observed. The shortage of skilled labour is primarily felt in the peripheral regions. For increasing innovation, it is not only a matter of deep technical skills like STEM, but also the future requirements of the skills profile of workers, which require more 'soft' competences like collaborative capabilities to function in increasingly networked environments (European Commission 2016; OECD 2017b; Vækstforum Nordjylland 2016). The chapters in Part III of this volume focus on this problem area and provide detailed information on the future, the skills profiles needed in light of increased digitalisation, AI, robots/cobots and automation.

In an innovation system perspective, the links between actors and alignment between research and innovation programmes, as discussed above (and by the evaluation panel) require competences among actors in the system to actually provide bridges between silos. This was also recognised by the evaluation panel, and points to a need for learning and competence development not only in businesses, also in the policy system.

2.6.4 Innovation stepping stone 4: innovation for sustainability and the environmental challenge

For decades Denmark has been strong in technological development, industrial use and sales of 'green' products and services. Much of this stronghold has been driven by policies and regulation, and this is still the case. As part of the 2014 Climate Act, Denmark established The Danish Council on Climate Change, which provides recommendations on climate initiatives in the transition to a low-carbon society.[7]

Its tasks are:

- to evaluate the status of Denmark's implementation of national climate objectives and international climate commitments
- to analyse potential means of transitioning to a low-carbon society by 2050 and identify possible measures to achieve greenhouse gas reductions
- to draw up recommendations to help shape climate policy, including a selection of potential mechanisms and transition scenarios
- to contribute to the public debate.

In this way, The Council on Climate Change provides recommendations to the Danish parliament on the EU goals for reduction of CO_2. This is partly accomplished through independent analyses presented in policy-oriented reports. The Danish government has over a longer period focused strongly on developing and utilising new technology for sustainability and climate change. It is widely agreed that technology constitutes the single most important solution to accomplish the goals for carbon emission reduction. In 2019, the Danish parliament took a strong step in signing a new climate act focusing on the continued green transformation of the Danish economy. This act was confirmed in a law in June 2020 and sets a framework for Danish climate policy based on binding intermediate targets every five years towards the target of climate neutrality by 2050. One of these targets is a 70% reduction in carbon dioxide emissions by 2030 (compared to 1990) (see Gregersen and Johnson (2021, this volume) for a discussion on the problems with measurement and evaluations in this area).

These targets are ambitious and require strong political focus but are at the same time deeply ingrained in the Danish political DNA through active policies developed and implemented over the last 30 years to pursue a green transformation through support for replacing traditional fuel sources with renewable sources. Attaining these goals is a complex and ambitious task. Not all sectors can contribute equally, therefore the government established 13 sectoral Climate Partnerships (Klimapartnerskaber) in November 2019. These are expected to define their contribution and routes to achieving goals for the reduction of emissions and are governed by a Green Business Forum involving a wide range of stakeholders.

As all relevant stakeholders in the national system of innovation agree that technology is the main driver for achieving the goals for green transformation and the climate challenge, the focus by the government has been a strong investment strategy. This investment strategy is implemented through the European Horizon 2020 programme and the Danish Innovation Foundation. This has been stimulated through the financing of research towards this agenda. In 2020, the Innovation Foundation dedicated DKK 700m to grand solution projects directly targeting the 70% reduction target. These funds were part of the dedicated funds by the Danish parliament of DKK 1,542m towards the 70% reduction target out of a total reserve of DKK 1,925m. In this way, 80% of the reserves are directly dedicated to the green transformation. Although political negotiations are still to be finalised. the proposal for the 2021 fiscal budget entails DKK 750m for research into green transition and carbon dioxide emission reductions.

With regards to the driver for sustainability and climate change, a strong historical focus on green transformation, as seen in the climate acts, and dedicated funds for research in technologies enabling the green transformation and reduction of carbon emissions are the core ingredients (seen from a policy perspective) constituting the stepping stone.

2.7 Concluding remarks

The Danish innovation system is performing very well. This is despite the observation that, with respect to some innovation output measures, the innovation potential of the system is not fully utilised, and that emphasis must increasingly be placed on the main challenges of leveraging the high-performing research system for innovation (cf. Section 2.4).

We follow the voices stating that the road from research to innovation is not linear; rather, it is long, complex and highly dependent on the functioning of the innovation system. Some examples include the distribution of the research activities, the links between core actors in the system and the importance of the 'soft' factors, illustrated for instance with public innovation. Somewhat relatedly, we point out that the variables behind the composite innovation index often used in the EIS only captures parts of the complexity.

An extensive debate unravels discussing whether the EIS is not only partial, but maybe also flawed (Edquist et al. 2018). Moreover, the link between the EIS position of a country and explicit and instructive normative policy implications is less than trivial. We propose that a broader view of innovation and relevant innovation system actors include public sector innovation, civic society innovation, generally a holistic, societal engagement and the incorporation of informal institutions governing the functioning of the system. This is argued to be decisive to societal coherence, which in turn is an important prerequisite for innovation.

With these more general remarks on the challenges of measuring and diagnosing the innovation system, we return to the recommendations. Where to take the next generation of Danish innovation policies? Different types of innovation policy have recently been extensively discussed (Kuhlmann and Rip 2018; Robinson and Mazzucato 2019), often taking an approach which is in stark contrast to the traditional market-based rationale in which the state has a very limited role. On the contrary, much of the discussion on 'mission-oriented' and 'challenge-oriented' policies[8] is centred around the argument that the state, and other public actors, should provide direction for industrial and technological development through policies. In its extreme consequence, the COVID-19 crisis spurred extensive and strong state interventions and directives to enhance research and innovation as the pandemic unfolded.

In their underlying theoretical understanding of innovation, mission-oriented policies are not fundamentally different from system-oriented policies. Proponents of these policies also adhere to the evolutionary, system-oriented view of innovation. But in the normative dimensions, there are clear differences as the policy advice in the mission-oriented approach is given a more proactive role and to a larger extent provides new direction rather than merely attempting to fix failures. A key feature of the understanding of innovation and evolution in this approach is the role of experimentation. It is likely, and acceptable, that firms and policies alike fail; in fact, it is by experimentation and learning from both successes and failures that policy developments occur. It might sound somewhat contradictory that experimentation and system are key features of this approach. This is not necessarily so, as experiments do in fact benefit from being embedded in a well-functioning system (Lindholm-Dahlstrand et al. 2019) where knowledge on policy learning is effectively diffused.[9]

The idea that policies should be guided by 'grand challenges' and that the state is able to give directions for the development is also found in Danish policies. For example, the RESEARCH2025 programme defines areas where future problem areas are addressed and the strategy from the former government explicitly point to societal challenges as an important guide for policy formulation (Styrelsen for Forskning og Innovation 2017a). The RESEARCH2025 catalogue provides sectoral priorities in line with the smart specialisation priorities and was created in a process involving a variety of stakeholders including businesses, organisations, ministries and Danish knowledge institutions. Moreover, through Innovation Fund Denmark, the Grand Solutions programme is part of RESEARCH2025, and the funds are allocated towards targets such as climate change and sustainable solutions to challenges.

The societal challenges in Denmark include alleviating the climate change crisis, but also rising costs of serving an ageing population combined with a demand to maintain the quality of the social welfare system, increased regional disparities and pressures on the labour market. Although policies are increasingly oriented towards meeting 'grand' societal challenges, these challenges are to a varying degree only partially or indirectly linked to the specific R&I challenges. Almost by definition, R&D can have direct effects on societal challenges, for example, 'welfare technologies' are promoted to alleviate the demand for human resources in health and elderly care, 'telecare' technologies are used to allow easy medical treatment in geographical areas without sufficient coverage of medical doctors, and 'energy-efficient' technologies are being integrated to support smart cities for the reduction of pollution. Thus far, these are however not directly linked and await further integration. Hence, we call with others for a comprehensive and holistic innovation policy for Denmark.

Notes

1 https://www.globalinnovationindex.org/gii-2019-report.
2 Weber and Truffer (2017) maintain that despite some disagreements in the literature on innovation systems, the majority of studies of innovation systems adhere to the view that six processes are at the core of systems: knowledge generation and diffusion, entrepreneurial experimentation, guidance of search, resource mobilisation, market formation, legitimisation (p.113).
3 In particular, The Danish Council for Research and Innovation Policy (Danmarks Forsknings-og Innovationspolitiske Råd 2016) points to inadequate links between key actors and a fragmented innovation infrastructure. The Council recommends a more holistic, systemic approach to innovation policy.
4 https://iri.jrc.ec.europa.eu/scoreboard/2019-eu-industrial-rd-investment-scoreboard.
5 http://markedsmodningsfonden.dk/innovative_purchases.
6 https://rulemaking.worldbank.org/.
7 https://klimaraadet.dk/en/frontpage.
8 There are differences between mission- and challenge-oriented policies. For example, there were well-defined paths for technological development associated with the clearly formulated mission to put a man on the moon. Regarding the societal challenges like maintaining welfare during changes in demography, global warning and climate change

etc., solutions are not pre-defined and may require several different missions (Boon and Edler 2018).

9 A prominent regional policy approach, smart specialisation, likewise has this emphasis on experimentation. In the way smart specialisation was originally formulated, the key feature was that it is a policy processes involving experimentation, recognising and utilising locally embedded resources and existing strongholds, and involvement of key stakeholders in an entrepreneurial discovery process (Foray et al. 2009).

References

Boon, W. and Edler, J. 2018. Demand, Challenges, and Innovation. Making Sense of New Trends in Innovation Policy. *Science and Public Policy* 45(4): 435–447.

Drejer, I. and Christensen, J. L. 2021. Chapter 4: The Danish regional innovation system in transition. In *Globalisation, New and Emerging Technologies, and Sustainable Development – The Danish Innovation System in Transition*, ed. Christensen, J. L., Gregersen, B., Holm, J. R. and Lorenz, E. L. Abingdon: Taylor & Francis.

Christensen, J. L. and Fagerberg, J. 2021. Chapter 1: The emergence of innovation Policy as a field: the international context and the Danish experience. In *Globalisation, New and Emerging Technologies, and Sustainable Development – The Danish Innovation System in Transition*, ed. Christensen, J. L., Gregersen, B., Holm, J. R. and Lorenz, E. L. Abingdon: Taylor & Francis.

Cohen, W. M. and Levinthal, D. A. 1990. Absorptive Capacity: A New Perspective on Learning and Innovation. *Administrative Science Quarterly* 35(1): 128–152.

Danmarks Forsknings-og Innovationspolitiske Råd (Danish Council on Research and Innovation Policy). 2016. *Viden i sammenhæng. Danmarks Forsknings-og Innovationspolitiske Råds årsrapport (Coherent Knowledge. Annual Report of The Danish Council for Research and Innovation Policy)*, 1–76. Copenhagen: Danmarks Forsknings-og Innovationspolitiske Råd.

Danmarks Forsknings- og Innovationspolitiske Råd/Danish Council on Research and Innovation Policy. 2019. *Innovationsmodne Virksomheder (IMV'er) – en ny Målgruppe for innovationsfremmeindsatsen 100.* Copenhagen: Uddannelses- og Forskningsministeriet.

Dosi, G., Llerena, P. and Labini, M. S. 2006. The Relationships between Science, Technologies and Their Industrial Exploitation: An Illustration Through the Myths and Realities of the so-called 'European Paradox'. *Research Policy* 35(10): 1450–1464.

Edquist, C., Zabala-Iturriagagoitia, J. M., Barbero, J. and Zafío, J. L. 2018. On the Meaning of Innovation Performance: Is the Synthetic Indicator of the Innovation Union Scoreboard Flawed? *Research Evaluation* 27(3): 196–211.

European Commission. 2001. *2001 Innovation Scoreboard: 56.* Brussels: European Commission.

European Commission. 2016. *European Semester Thematic Fiche. Skills for the Labour Market.* Bruxelles: European Commission.

European Commission. 2019. *Peer Review of the Danish R&I System: Ten Steps, and a Leap Forward: Taking Danish Innovation to the Next Level: 132.* Brussels: European Commission.

European Commission. 2020. *European Innovation Scoreboard 2020.* Brussels: European Commission.

Foray, D., David, P. A. and Hall, B. 2009. Smart Specialisation – The Concept. *Knowledge Economists Policy Brief* 9: 1–5. Brussels: European Commission.

Gallup. 2010. *Innobarometer 2010: Analytical Report, Innovation in Public Administration*, 1–196. Bruxelles: European Commission.

Gregersen, B., and Johnson, B. 2021. Chapter 13: The measurement and performance of the Danish innovation system in relation to sustainable development. In *Globalisation, New and Emerging Technologies, and Sustainable Development – The Danish Innovation System in Transition*, ed. Christensen, J. L., Gregersen, B., Holm, J. R. and Lorenz, E. L. Abingdon: Taylor & Francis.

Kuhlmann, S. and Rip, A. 2018. Next-Generation Innovation Policy and Grand Challenges. *Science and Public Policy* 45(4): 448–454.

Lindholm-Dahlstrand, Å., Andersson, M. and Carlsson, B. 2019. Entrepreneurial Experimentation: A Key Function in Systems of Innovation. *Small Business Economics* 53(3): 591–610.

Liu, J. S., Lu, W. M. and Ho, M. H. C. 2014. National Characteristics: Innovation Systems from the Process Efficiency Perspective. *R&D Management* 45(4): 317–338.

Mansfield, E. 1984. R&D and Innovation: Some Empirical Findings. In *R & D, Patents, and Productivity*, ed. Z. Griliches, 127–154. Chicago: University of Chicago Press.

OECD. 2017a. *Main Science and Technology Indicators*, Vol. 2017. Paris: OECD.

OECD. 2017b. *OECD Skills Outlook 2017: Skills and Global Value Chains*. Paris: OECD Publishing.

OECD. 2020. *Main Science and Technology Indicators*, Vol. 2020. Paris: OECD.

Økonomi- og Indenrigsministeriet. 2018. *Økonomisk Redegørelse (Maj 2018)*, 1–222. Copenhagen: Økonomi- og Indenrigsministeriet.

Pakes, A. and Griliches, Z. 1984. Patents and R&D at the Firm Level: A First Look. In *R&D, Patents, and Productivity*, ed. Z. Griliches, 55–71. Chicago: University of Chicago Press.

Regeringen. 2017. *Danmark - Klar til fremtiden. Regeringens mål for Dansk Forskning og Innovation*, 1–35. Copenhagen: Uddannelses- og Forskningsministeriet.

Robinson, D. K. R. and Mazzucato, M. 2019. The Evolution of Mission-Oriented Policies: Exploring Changing Market Creating Policies in the US and European Space Sector. *Research Policy* 48(4): 936–948.

Stamhus, J. and Nielsen, R. N. 2021. Chapter 7: Collaboration as a cornerstone in public sector – the case of Denmark. In *Globalisation, New and Emerging Technologies, and Sustainable Development – The Danish Innovation System in Transition*, ed. Christensen, J. L., Gregersen, B., Holm, J. R. and Lorenz, E. L. Abingdon: Taylor & Francis.

Styrelsen for Forskning og Innovation. 2017a. *FORSK2025 – fremtidens løfterige forskningsområder*, 1–224. Copenhagen: Ministry for Science and Education.

Styrelsen for Forskning og Innovation. 2017b. *FoU 2017. Erhvervslivets investeringer i forskning og udvikling i Danmark*, 1–59. Copenhagen: Styrelsen for Forskning og Innovation.

Styrelsen for Forskning og Innovation. 2017c. *Uddannelses- og Forskningspolitisk Redegørelse*, 1–436. Copenhagen: Uddannelses- og Forskningsministeriet.

Styrelsen for Forskning og Innovation. 2018. *Forskningsbarometer 2017. Årlig statistik og Analyse om Forskning og Innovation*, 1–96. Copenhagen: Styrelsen for Forskning og Innovation.

Styrelsen for Forskning og Innovation, & DASTI. 2019. *Self-Assessment of the Danish Knowledge-Based Innovation System*. Challenges to be addressed by the international peer review panel. Copenhagen: UFM and DASTI.

Vækstforum Nordjylland. 2016. *FremKom III: Fremtidens Nordjyske kompetencebehov*, 1–80. Aalborg: Vækstforum Nordjylland.

Weber, K. M. and Truffer, B. 2017. Moving Innovation Systems Research to the Next Level: Towards an Integrative Agenda. *Oxford Review of Economic Policy* 33(1): 101–121.

WIPO (World Intellectual Property Organization). 2018. *World Intellectual Property Indicators 2018*, 64. Geneva: World Intellectual Property Organization.

3 Entrepreneurship, experimentation and innovation

Future policy for innovative and growth-oriented entrepreneurs in Denmark

Kristian Nielsen, Michael S. Dahl, Bram Timmermans and Jesper Lindgaard Christensen

3.1 Introduction

Entrepreneurship is widely considered an engine of economic growth, innovation and prosperity, mainly, although not exclusively, based on its numerous economic contributions in the shape of new venture creation. First, and most applicable to the political domain, is the impact of entrepreneurship on job creation. This macroeconomic effect has topped the policy agenda ever since David L. Birch (1979) published his seminal work *The Job Generation Process*. This position has only intensified as empirical studies worldwide have repeatedly demonstrated that new businesses account for the majority of new jobs created (Haltiwanger et al. 2013; Ibsen and Westergaard-Nielsen 2011; Dahl et al. 2009). Second, new businesses can increase competition, which often keeps incumbent firms on their toes, thus increasing overall productivity, innovation and lower prices. New businesses entering the market with fresh ideas force existing firms to keep innovating. Over time, this strengthens the competitive advantage of all firms and, thus, the overall economy. An additional, third, argument relates to existing large businesses, which often have difficulties shifting focus to new ground-breaking innovations. Entrepreneurship is thus a vital component of technical change.

The founding of new businesses is thus key to the creation of innovative economies. More generally, entrepreneurship is considered an activity not easily separated from other systemic economic pursuits. For example, Acs et al. posit that:

> at the country level, entrepreneurship should be treated as a systemic phenomenon, similar to the way the literature on 'National Systems of Innovation' treats country-level infrastructures, policies, and institutions when considering factors that determine a country's ability to produce and take advantage of scientific discoveries and technological innovation.
>
> (Acs et al. 2014, p. 477)

The abovementioned benefits to the overall economy through the act of entrepreneurship follow the ideas of Joseph Schumpeter (1934; 1939), who argues that entrepreneurs are key drivers of economic change because they take risks and launch businesses based on (sometimes irrational) new ideas.

In economics, the view of entrepreneurship as an engine of innovation in capitalist economies has been promoted by scholars such as William J. Baumol (2010). In addition, entrepreneurial behaviour and actions among employees in established firms (i.e., intrapreneurship) are also promoted in innovation-driven economies as work tasks become more complex due to automation and the outsourcing of simple work tasks. Entrepreneurship is not only important for national economies because of the link to innovation. Busenitz et al. (2000) discuss entrepreneurship as a macro phenomenon, where the entrepreneurial orientation of countries can be classified (see also Acs et al. 2014).

Not surprisingly, these attributes have led to a strong political focus on stimulating entrepreneurship in Western economies. From the beginning of the 1980s, new businesses have grown more politically attractive following an increased focus from academics, the OECD and large organisations like the Kauffman Foundation in the US, but the attention to small firms and entrepreneurs was also stimulated by political discussions in Prime Minister Margaret Thatcher's UK and President Ronald Reagan's US. This represented a shift in attention from existing firms, often large businesses in clusters (the prime example being the Silicon Valley cluster in the US), to the role of entrepreneurs in the creation of economic growth and prosperity. Political interest in entrepreneurship was further stimulated by changes in production systems, where outsourcing increased the importance of the service industry and flexible production modes generally meant that the average size of firms decreased.

Entrepreneurship policy has also been a priority for many years in Denmark. One indicator of this is the significant increase in the number of students receiving education in creativity, innovation and entrepreneurship throughout the Danish education system, from elementary school to universities (Danish Foundation for Entrepreneurship 2019a). Another is the surge of university tech-transfer organisations and incubators as well as numerous mentoring, matchmaking and advisory programmes. Supporting entrepreneurs is regarded as an important driver of technological change and innovation, hence also important in the national innovation system.

In this chapter, we focus on measures that promote the increased entry of innovative, sustainable, knowledge-intensive and growth-oriented businesses by supporting and increasing experimentation both on behalf of the entrepreneur but also to treat policy-making as a purposeful experimental process. We review selected parts of the literature on entrepreneurship, innovation and entrepreneurial policy to establish the rationale for entrepreneurship policy. We map Danish entrepreneurship performance and the structure of the support landscape as well as the design of entrepreneurship policy in Denmark. Denmark is an interesting case through which to explore these questions as the policy process entails the heavy involvement of entrepreneurs, which is interesting in a policy context, and since Denmark generally fares well in the rankings for entrepreneurship framework conditions (see later in this chapter). The performance of Denmark could serve as an argument against changing current entrepreneurship policies. However, we argue that the COVID-19 crisis is likely to fuel a shake-out of current small businesses and decrease the creation of start-ups in the near future. In this scenario, it is expedient to think of alternative avenues for entrepreneurship policies. Based on the literature on entrepreneurship as an experimental process, we provide thoughts on how such alternative policies might take shape, which is of general interest beyond the Danish case.

3.2 The rationale behind entrepreneurship policies

3.2.1 The market failure argument and barriers to entrepreneurship

A common general argument for policy intervention is that market mechanisms fail to provide the socially optimal allocation of resources. In this vein, Sarasvathy (2004) discusses both market failures and general barriers to entrepreneurship. Regarding the former, the labour market for entrepreneurs is missing in contrast to the labour market for managers. For managers, or other occupations, the labour market will clear through the price (wage) mechanism due to an upward sloping supply curve and downward sloping demand curve. This will not be the case for entrepreneurs if this labour market does not exist. Moreover, an individual's decision to become an entrepreneur – rational or not – does not necessarily consider all the potential positive effects of this decision on society. In other words, there are positive externalities related to the previously introduced firm dynamics new ventures create. The remedy is an economic policy that increases the level of entrepreneurship.

Turning to the barriers to entrepreneurship, and going beyond market failures, Sarasvathy categorises these into six categories:

(i) property rights and the titling of untitled assets; (ii) governments that are not market-augmenting; (iii) lack of variety in types of risk capital; (iv) low levels of unemployment; (v) attitudes toward money and profit and (vi) entrenched decision processes in large corporations (Sarasvathy 2004, pp. 709–710).

In the following, we focus on those more relevant for Western economies, including Denmark. Starting with a lack of risk capital, entrepreneurs are often found to be capital restricted (Parker and Van Praag 2006), which can be related to the market imperfection of asymmetric information and the related problems of adverse selection and moral hazard (Shane 2003). Second, low levels of unemployment are also an acknowledged barrier to entrepreneurship (Sarasvathy 2004), but it is important to emphasise that low levels of unemployment are often accompanied by high levels of output in the economy, which increases opportunity-based start-ups in contrast to those that are necessity based. For example, Taylor (1996) finds that the probability of start-up creation is higher during economic upturns. This is also indicated in Denmark, where Gjerløv-Juel and Dahl (2013) note that the number of start-ups, and their survival rate, both decreased after the 2008 financial crisis, although the quality of the start-ups after the crisis increased overall. Third, recent entrepreneurship policies in Denmark have spurred the introduction of more formal entrepreneurship education, making the decision to become one's own boss part of an occupational choice set. Finally, the lasting imprint of work experience at large corporations on entrepreneurial behaviour is something worth exploring in a Danish context – considering its large public sector – as Özcan and Reichstein (2009) maintain that tenured employees are less likely to exit the public sector to engage in entrepreneurship, based on data from the US. In Denmark, however, there is a high degree of work autonomy (i.e., less bureaucracy) and room for intrapreneurship for employees compared to other countries (see Lorenz and Holm 2021, in this volume), which might also lower entrepreneurial propensities.

3.2.2 The selection argument: which entrepreneurs to support?

The entrepreneurial process is characterised by risk and uncertainty. It is therefore difficult, if not impossible, to assess ex ante the success of new entrants. As Nightingale and Coad state, 'the key issue is growth, which is hard (not easy), rather than market entry, which is easy (not hard)' (2013, p. 132). Furthermore, taking the point of departure from Schumpeter's arguments on how entrepreneurs affect the economy, entrepreneurial benefits do not only arise from average entrepreneurship activities but rather from innovative entrepreneurs (Van Praag and Versloot 2007; Stam and Wennberg 2009; Nightingale and Coad 2013). Bhidé (2000), however, finds that high growth start-ups in the US are often not based on an innovative idea or founded by highly educated or experienced individuals, referring to a sample of Incorporated 500 companies. Therefore, it can be questioned to what extent entrepreneurship policies that increase entry (targeted or not) are desirable at all (e.g., Dahl et al. 2009; Shane 2008; 2009; Lerner 2009; Nightingale and Coad 2013) as these efforts might lead to highly valuable firms but also a significant waste of resources given the high failure rate of new businesses.

If policies are designed with the sole purpose of attracting more entrepreneurs, those who create start-ups may not be drawn from the most capable among the population. This distribution is already highly skewed, as the majority of entrepreneurial firms can be classified as marginal, undersized and performing poorly rather than the much-desired gazelles (Nightingale and Coad 2013). Similarly, Scott Shane argues in *The Illusions of Entrepreneurship* (2008) that if the aim is to create societal value policies should be directed at specific entrepreneurs in terms of personal characteristics – the average entrepreneur is not innovative and has no growth ambition or comparative advantage (similar arguments in Baumol 2010). Based on a similar idea, Guzman and Stern (2016) use information on new ventures at the time of start-up to assess their quality based on predictive models, e.g., if the new firm has a patent at the time of start-up, then the firm is more likely to be observed later as a high-quality firm. This is then used to create an entrepreneurship index that takes into account the quality of new firms and not just their number.

Some entrepreneurship policy schemes are not meant to create innovative or high growth ventures (e.g., schemes that support start-ups by unemployed persons), whereas the policies that do have this objective focus on a small subset of entrepreneurs (Terjesen et al. 2016) such as academics (Nielsen 2015).

3.2.3 Avoiding failure

When comparing entrepreneurship failure rates in different countries, regions or cities, we arrive at two main stylised facts. On the one hand, failure rates are remarkably similar, while on the other hand they are consistently high. Most entrepreneurs fail within three to five years after founding the new firm; in the longer term, less than a third survive for more than seven to eight years. This has been shown not only for Denmark (Dahl and Reichstein 2007; Dahl et al. 2009; Dahl and Sorenson 2012) but for many other countries (Cooper et al. 1994; Santarelli and Vivarelli 2007). Low failure rates and prolonged survival may be key to a long-term effect of entrepreneurship.

Entrepreneurs take chances with their ideas and engage in projects that could damage their future financially, psychologically or socially, should the endeavour end in failure (Ucbasaran et al. 2013). But this relatively high failure rate is often underestimated by entrepreneurs (Cooper et al. 1988; Lowe and Ziedonis 2006). Studies suggest that entrepreneurs are risk-taking individuals who are overoptimistic about the prospects of their business and the quality of their business idea. Moreover, the theory of the liability of newness (Stinchcombe 1965) explains the failure of new businesses as a consequence of their organisational instability and legitimacy. New businesses need to establish their routines, organisation and communication patterns, which means that they are less effective than existing firms. Moreover, entrepreneurs must prove that their product or service is viable in the market in order to mobilise the necessary resources to run their businesses.

Some entrepreneurs tend to be more capable of dealing with these risks than others. In Denmark and similar countries, we know that serial entrepreneurs and entrepreneurs with industry experience are more likely to create businesses that will survive in the longer run (Dahl and Sorenson 2014; Dahl et al. 2009). They still fail to a large extent, but they do so at a significantly lower rate (Wright et al. 1997). They are argued to have better networks, skills and resources either themselves (Dahl and Sorenson 2012) or through the employees they recruit (Dahl and Klepper 2015; Bublitz et al. 2018), which enables them to limit the liability of newness or to be more realistic about their businesses. Founders with a university degree are also more likely to perform better in terms of survival and growth, both in stable and turbulent industries (Nielsen 2015).

3.2.4 Different types of entrepreneurship policies: can policy makers identify high-potential entrepreneurs ex ante?

Policy makers have a wide array of policy measures at their disposal. According to Verheul et al. (2002), such policy measures can be divided into five areas of intervention: (i) the demand side of entrepreneurship, which (in)directly impacts the type, number and accessibility of entrepreneurial opportunities; (ii) the supply side of entrepreneurship, which affects the pool or supply of potential entrepreneurs at the aggregate level; (iii) interventions that impact the availability of resources, skills and knowledge to potential entrepreneurs; (iv) interventions that affect the desire of individuals to become entrepreneurs and (v) measures that influence the decision-making process of individuals, i.e., potential entrepreneurs. These policy areas contain many different types of initiatives, varying from a more general aggregate level of policy making, primarily regarding demand- and supply-side interventions, to policies that specifically target entrepreneurship. Modern entrepreneurship policies range from the availability of venture capital, finance, the lowering of administrative tasks, direct advice and competence development. As elaborated later in this chapter, tax schemes, finance, advice and education are important policy initiatives that have been adopted in Denmark to increase the supply of entrepreneurs.

An important aspect of encouraging more (specific, high-skilled) entrepreneurs is what is often termed 'opportunity costs', e.g., do engineers with a university degree create more value for society at a start-up or in an R&D department at a large established firm? Similarly, does a professor of medicine add more value to society by establishing a private firm or through research and knowledge dissemination in a university position? Although these questions are hard to answer, this aspect is important to consider when formulating any entrepreneurship-focused policy.

The entrepreneurship policy question following this above reasoning is linked not only to eliminating barriers, but also selection. Entrepreneurs are selected by (i) self-selection, (ii) market developments (post start-up) and (iii) resource constraints. The latter entails a number of resources such as technology, finance and networks. Resource providers maintain public grants and other needed resources; hence, entrepreneurs are selected by several tiers of mechanisms. This creates a second-order selection problem: to pursue the most efficient and effective public policy, the selection process needs to be conducted in the best possible manner, which in turn requires that those individuals and organisations who select entrepreneurs worthy of support, should themselves be among the most skilful in doing so. In this setting, it has been argued that civil servants and public agencies are not set up to engage in and understand private business and entrepreneurship (Shane 2009). If true, this leaves the government with three possible strategies: (i) internal competence building and recruitment strategies, (ii) to co-invest with private actors who then act as lead investors and selectors and (iii) involve private actors in policy making and policy implementation to gain legitimacy and increase take-up rates of policy schemes. In practice, all three are used in the Danish context.

Selected parts of the entrepreneurship literature have pointed to the importance of institutions and the context in which entrepreneurship unfolds (Bruton et al. 2010), but it remains a subject that has received sparse attention. A recent work on the National System of Entrepreneurship (NSE) addresses this gap and points to how recommendations can be produced when mapping the performance of entrepreneurship systems in a specific manner. Based upon empirical benchmarks of countries, they operate with a bottleneck approach to provide policy advice. That is, countries are benchmarked by 14 'pillars', and their worst performing scores indicate where policy efforts would be most effective. Some of the authors in this tradition (Acs et al. 2014, 2016) posit that entrepreneurship studies have primarily focused on the individual, but as mentioned, say little about the role of the institutional and societal context regarding who starts new ventures, what type of venture is started, what strategies new ventures pursue and the results from these processes (Acs et al. 2016). Innovation studies, on the other hand, do address the impact of institutions and the context in which innovation processes unfold, but overlook individual agency. Some authors point out that the 'resource allocation system (is) driven by individual-level opportunity pursuit through the creation of new ventures' (Acs et al. 2016, p. 1). Hence, individual action is seen as the key driver of economic evolution. Furthermore, the NSE literature argues that a simple count of the number of firms, start-ups in an economy or opportunities in an economy do not provide insight into how the entrepreneurship system functions. Rather, it depicts how entrepreneurs access resources and transform them into productive use, pursuing opportunities that provide knowledge on how a system really works (Acs et al. 2014). More recently, and greatly inspired by innovation system thinking, there is a growing literature on entrepreneurial ecosystems (Mason and Brown 2014; Spigel 2017; Spigel and Harrison 2018), which emphasises the role institutional arrangements and resource endowments play in creating productive entrepreneurship (Stam and Van der Ven 2019). Following this, we return to the features of the Danish entrepreneurship system.

3.3 The Danish entrepreneurship system: performance, structure and policies

3.3.1 Danish entrepreneurship performance

Entrepreneurship performance in Denmark is relatively strong, evidenced by several indicators and rankings. Registered new firms in Denmark gradually increased from 17,647 in 2013 to 36,361 in 2018, followed by a drop to 25,288 in 2019 (Danish Chamber of Commerce 2020). The growth in the number of new companies is explained by the general growth of the economy in combination with a relaxation of regulations regarding establishment of new businesses in 2014, leading to a favourable environment for the conduct of business. When the Danish government abolished the private limited company (IVS) as a legal corporate entity in 2019, this partially resulted in the decline we observe in 2019.[1] In its 'Doing Business' analyses, where entrepreneurship framework conditions and performance are analysed, the World Bank ranks Denmark consistently high, for example as the fourth best country in the world in 2019 (World Bank 2015–2020). Similarly, Denmark leads the world and EU rankings in the digital economy and society index (DESI),[2] consistently appearing as number one every year from 2014 to 2018 and placing as a top four country in 2019 on a par with Finland, Sweden and the Netherlands.

The Global Entrepreneurship and Development Institute (GEDI)[3] produces the Global Entrepreneurship and Development Index (GEI), based on data from the World Bank and the Global Entrepreneurship Monitor, among others. According to their 2019 data, Denmark performed highly in entrepreneurship, placing consistently inside or close to the top five in the overall GEI world rankings across the years 2015 to 2019. Within the individual 'pillars', Denmark ranks number one in Entrepreneurial Abilities. Denmark also scores high on the Access to Finance index (first). In fact, Internationalisation seems to be the sole weakness in the Danish entrepreneurial system. Based on other statistics, growth-orientation might be another comparative weakness. According to Eurostat, growth-oriented firms (defined as firms with more than ten employees that grew by a minimum of 10% annually over the past three years) in Denmark amounted to between 3.4 and 3.7 per 10,000 inhabitants in the 2012–2015 period. In comparison, Norway and Sweden had between 5 and 6 growth-oriented firms per 10,000 inhabitants. Moreover, the share of wage earners in Denmark is the highest in the EU, with 92.5% of all employed in 2017 (Eurostat, Labour Force Survey 2017). Formal entrepreneurship education at all levels has also attracted attention, even if this has also increased significantly. The share of students who are taught entrepreneurship has increased from 12% in 2011–2012 to 26% in 2017–2018 (Danish Foundation for Entrepreneurship 2019b).

3.3.2 Support organisations in the Danish entrepreneurship landscape

A number of institutional arrangements, policies and agencies constitute the entrepreneurial system in Denmark. Technology Transfer Offices and entrepreneurship incubators at universities have received attention regarding their development and performance. Other important schemes and agencies include Vækstfonden, the Innovation Fund, seven approved technology institutes, four business incubators, 12 regional growth houses and the Danish Foundation for Entrepreneurship. Vækstfonden, the Danish state's innovation investment fund, was established in 1992 and is today a major player in the market for entrepreneurial finance and an important vehicle in the implementation of several policies in this area. Fund products include equity, loans and guarantees, which it invests together with private partners and Danish financial institutions. Angel investment is another important way for entrepreneurs to obtain financing. Crowdfunding is a relatively new phenomenon in general; its development in Denmark has been slow due to the fact that legislation has not been in place for equity crowdfunding specifically (Christensen 2019).

Denmark has four innovation incubators that offer a combination of traditional incubator services and early-stage gap funding for start-ups, some of which stem from university spin-offs or university knowledge. Even if they still exist and operate, they have now been phased out as part of the reorganisation of the business support system implemented in January 2019 (Drejer and Christensen 2021, this volume). The innovation incubators invested €10,000 in pre-seed funding for proof of business and a subsequent seed capital accompanied by counselling for entrepreneurs. The funding of approximately €25m (DKK 185m) annually was provided by the Danish Agency for Science, Technology and Innovation (DASTI).

3.3.3 Entrepreneurship policies in Denmark

Entrepreneurship policies have changed over the past few years, with the abovementioned reorganisation of the support system as the main event, where the regional tier has been abolished. In terms of the total government budget for entrepreneurship policies, obtaining an exact figure is complicated by several factors. One is that support of entrepreneurship stems from schemes under the Ministry of Business but also through tax policies. Moreover, the expenditures are grouped together in public accounts under 'Entrepreneurship and Innovation'. Fairly comparative figures show that expenditures for innovation and entrepreneurship programmes under the auspices of the Ministry of Business were 16.2% of total business support in 2017 and 17.1% in 2019. In 2019 the direct support from the Ministry of Industry, Business and Financial Affairs and the Ministry of Education was DKK 6bn (Ministry of Industry, Business and Financial Affairs, 2019) but as mentioned earlier, business support is also provided through the tax system (DKK 4.2bn in 2019).

The (former) government has generally strived for inclusive policies where entrepreneurs are invited into the policy making process. A prime example of this is the appointment in 2018 of a former entrepreneur as Minister of Higher Education and Science. Another example is that the former government established an advisory board, the Entrepreneurship Panel (Iværksætterpanelet), with the task of providing advice to the government on entrepreneurship policies. The panel consisted of 13 members, including nine entrepreneurs. Some of their initial recommendations spurred actual policy implementation, including tax incentives for investments in growth-oriented ventures, improved possibilities for shared ownership and increased educational efforts to promote talent within entrepreneurship, innovation and digitalisation programmes. These were later followed by another set of recommendations about access that focused on talent and enhanced entrepreneurship culture, but the group also suggested increased government-matched equity investments into firms during the early stages and better framework conditions and incentives for the commercialisation of research from universities. The implementation of some of these suggestions has proceeded whereas others are still in progress or under consideration.

It is noteworthy that both the 2017 Entrepreneurs Panel recommendations and subsequent recommendations have a strong element of enhancing entrepreneurial finance. The abovementioned bottleneck approach to entrepreneurship policies would not prescribe this focus, as the GEI index on entrepreneurial finance shows that Denmark is well above the average score in the index and that the variable 'risk capital' in the composite index contributes positively to the overall high rank of Denmark.

3.3.4 Danish entrepreneurship policies: development and the need for reorientation

In the early 1990s, Denmark promoted entrepreneurship through different schemes of direct financial support for prospective entrepreneurs. These largely targeted individuals with lower levels of financial resources, typically the longer-term unemployed. Dahl et al. (2009) study the performance of the recipients of these financial resources and find that their businesses had significantly lower performance and growth compared to other entrepreneurs. During the 2000s, especially from 2000 to 2006, additional regulations and strategies were implemented that focused more on highly educated entrepreneurs, especially university graduates. In 2006 the so-called globalisation strategy led to a more intense policy focus on entrepreneurial skills. This created a focus area on the role of the educational system in entrepreneurship. One of the measures to enhance entrepreneurship in education was to implement specific objectives on both this and spin-off companies in the development contracts between the ministry and universities. This created a significant increase in the entrepreneurship elements in university curricula as well as further offers for support infrastructure such as incubators, advisory services, mentoring programmes, matchmaking and business plan competitions. Still, the number of university spin-offs remains limited, around 80 in the 2013–2018 period, and it is argued by both the Entrepreneurship Panel and the international evaluation panel reviewing the Danish innovation system (see Section 3.3.3) that there is unutilised potential in transforming the top-performing research system in Denmark to more innovation and knowledge-based entrepreneurship.

As mentioned in the introduction to this chapter, the COVID-19 crisis is likely to cause many businesses to default and a virtual shake-out of small businesses is likely in many industries, as well as a decrease in the number of future start-ups. Faced with this situation, which challenges the high performance of the entrepreneurship system, calls for thinking about alternative entrepreneurship policies. In the following we therefore investigate literature on entrepreneurship as an experimental process to provide ideas on possible ways to redirect entrepreneurship policies.

3.4 Entrepreneurship as an experimental process: different frameworks

Considering the underlying features on how successful (innovative) entrepreneurs operate is a first crucial step in improving entrepreneurship policies. As mentioned, the entrepreneurial process is inherently random and involves degrees of unpredictable experimentation (Thomke et al. 1998; Thomke 2003). It involves a series of trial-and-error experimentations that requires many resources. Even for experienced incumbent firms and large multinationals, the innovation process is difficult and entails frequent mistakes and experimentation (Adner 2012). Even so, Per Davidsson (2008) argues that founders who want to imitate existing firms often end up with a different firm in the creative process, given that it is often impossible to copy an existing firm. That is, the process involves a high degree of creativity and the utilisation of the specific resources available, which could result in a different (innovative) firm.

Above we discussed the policy of selecting specific high-potential entrepreneurs. An alternative approach to entrepreneurship policy is to take the point of departure at experimentation. Given that (innovative) entrepreneurship is a stochastic, unpredictable and random process, policies according to this approach should not limit the number of start-ups and entrepreneurial attempts ex ante. Theoretical frameworks emphasise the importance of experimentation in the start-up process, including Kerr et al. (2014) who highlight that the experimental nature of entrepreneurship manifests itself on two different levels. First, experiments occur from a macro-economic Darwinian perspective, where entrepreneurs compete with incumbent forces resulting in either a successful entry of the entrepreneur, or an often quiet departure from the organisational landscape (Kerr et al. 2014). This experiment is solely market-based, which places some restrictions on the Darwinian notion of experiments as it is difficult to assess whether a venture or technology will succeed until investments have been made. The second reference frame looks at the act of entrepreneurship as a process of experimentation by the entrepreneur and their potential resource providers. In such a setting the decision to invest or shut down is taken by only a few individuals and is not the result of competition on the market as it occurs well before this process.

Bhidé (2000) discusses promising entrepreneurship in a profits-uncertainty-investments diagram with empirical cases from Incorporated 500 companies in the US. He argues that industries (or opportunities) with high mean profits (expected profits) and little profit deviation (uncertainty) between firms are attractive to enter, but these industries also require high investments. Therefore, these opportunities are exploited by established firms since entrepreneurs are found to be capital-constrained (Van Praag 2005; Van Praag et al. 2005; Parker and Van Praag 2006). Opportunities with high expected profits and investments but also high uncertainty require venture capital-backed entrepreneurship. The opportunities left are characterised by low expected profits and low investments and these opportunities cover both marginal entrepreneurship (if the deviation in profits is low) and promising entrepreneurship (if the deviation in profits is high). Thus, capital-constrained entrepreneurs are better at pursuing the latter opportunities given the chance of success. Moreover, these opportunities are unattractive to large firms and, in the event of failure, little money is lost.

Sarasvathy's (2009) dynamic model of effectuation also contains strong features of experimental behaviour by entrepreneurs (Chandler et al. 2011). In a world without uncertainty, it would be possible to predict expected profits from different opportunities by conducting thorough market research. Indeed, this has been the traditional way of teaching new venture formation: (i) conduct a market analysis, (ii) write a business plan with the goal of the business and (iii) obtain the necessary means for realising the goal. However, if the future is unpredictable, a more fruitful approach is: (i) the potential founder and individuals in the social network investigate the means available and (ii) set a goal based on the available means and change this along the way as new stakeholders (and, thus, new means) come on board (Sarasvathy 2009). The expert entrepreneur does not start with large investments but experiments at low costs by interacting and obtaining commitments from others. Indeed, the importance of the (social) network has been long recognised in the entrepreneurship literature (Aldrich and Zimmer 1986; Brüderl and Preisendörfer 1998; Davidsson and Honig 2003).

The benefits of pursuing the effectual approach to entrepreneurship as outlined are that in the case of failure, it is fast and cheap, which gives rise to the possibility of experimentation and increases the chance of introducing radical innovation since the goal is adaptable through the process and interaction with stakeholders. If entrepreneurship is about experimentation the question arises: who learns from experimentation? Nielsen and Sarasvathy (2016) explore this among Danish entrepreneurs and their findings suggest that learning from failure is not automatic but requires analytical skills, e.g., indicated by formal education. As a consequence, failure processing could be an important aspect of entrepreneurial education and training.

3.5 Rethinking the entrepreneurship policy approach in the context of experimentation

The experimental nature of the entrepreneurial process is not only for the entrepreneur to conduct but also exists in environmental conditions, which may lead to active participation. Such experimental behaviour concerning entrepreneurship has been linked to processes on how venture capital firms select and invest in entrepreneurship and innovation projects (Kerr et al. 2014). Kerr et al. (2014) stress the observation that successful venture capital firms are not merely profitable because they spread risks by building a portfolio of uncertain start-ups, but rather see this as a portfolio of tests. This perspective is also confirmed by interviews among venture capitalists conducted by Canales et al. (2019), where investors state that they invest in projects which they believe have market potential; however, up to the moment of investment this is not more than a hypothesis: it can only be tested after the first investments are made. A failure, i.e., not successfully introducing a product to the market, is not as much a disaster at large as it also might provide knowledge that there is no market for this particular product or that this opportunity should be organised differently (e.g., new ventures in general, or this new venture in particular, is not the vehicle by which this opportunity is best exploited). This knowledge can then be used in later investment opportunities. The potential learning from failure has begun to be both leveraged and recognised in policies.

The implication of the above approach would also be to reconsider how to treat entrepreneurial activities that are being supported. Policies that approach these entrepreneurial efforts as tests, similar to how venture capitalist firms treat their projects, may lead to the use of these test cases to generate a better understanding of the conditions that could foster future entrepreneurial success, either by the same entrepreneurs, other potential candidates or even other organisational forms. This would also mean that areas of experimentation should be placed more at the foreground compared to areas of selection. Thus, supporting living labs might be more fruitful compared to organising business plan (or business model) workshops, which is also highlighted to a large extent in the work by Sarasvathy (2009). How this arena should look is in itself an interesting form of entrepreneurial experiment.

Based on the idea of entrepreneurial experimentation in a broader setting, it might be useful to apply a systems approach as in Lindholm-Dahlstrand et al. (2019), where the interplay between new ventures and established firms and institutions creates system-wide entrepreneurial experimentation, which is important for creating, selecting and scaling up new technology and innovations. In this conceptual contribution, the authors argue that spin-off entrepreneurs from universities and large existing firms are important for the introduction of radical new technologies and innovations to the market given the inertia in these organisations and the lack of willingness to accept fundamental uncertainty (this is also in line with the framework of Bhidé (2000) outlined earlier). The process, however, does not end here since the new ventures often lack the finance and complementary resources needed to scale up, as highlighted earlier in this chapter. Therefore, the selection and scaling up of these new ventures through acquisition from large established firms becomes crucial at the later stage (Lindholm-Dahlstrand et al. 2019). The discussion of whether new firms or large firms are most important for innovation – and therefore should be the focus of entrepreneurship policy – is misleading in this systems framework. Instead, the main takeaway is that entrepreneurship policy should focus on removing barriers to experimentation in the three important phases related to entrepreneurship: creation, selection and scaling up. This could be done by looking at barriers to spin-off (e.g., non-compete agreements among employees) or acquisitions, which are the main micro-mechanisms discussed in Lindholm-Dahlstrand et al. (2019).

Accordingly, learning in such an experimental setting is not only limited to the entrepreneurs who are the first to attempt to create and exploit an entrepreneurial opportunity, but it also relevant for policy-makers who experiment with entrepreneurship policies related to the different parts of the entrepreneurial system of innovation. Whereas Danish entrepreneurship policies have allowed a certain degree of experimentation, there is also a plea for rigorous evaluations and the continuous monitoring of their costs and benefits. Moreover, one could intuitively argue that a systemic approach to entrepreneurship in itself contradicts experimentation. However, this is not necessarily the case. It is argued in both the Lindholm-Dahlstrand et al. (2019) approach and in the NSE literature mentioned above that even if experimentation is a key feature, it takes place within certain frames and trajectories that are determined by policies. A similar mindset is the cornerstone of the smart specialisation strategies now unfolding throughout Europe (Foray 2018). Entrepreneurial experimentation is explicitly designated the foundation of these strategies, but it is important to identify the potentially prosperous sectors where smart specialisation should take place.

This suggests an opening for the simultaneous experimentation and directionality of entrepreneurial policies. Current discussions on how nations pursue support of entrepreneurship and businesses generally address how states can themselves act in an experimental way, but at the same time provide directionality regarding the course of experimentation. Literature arguing for this approach includes the work of Mazzucato, her book *The Entrepreneurial State* (2013) being an important contribution. One of the strongest signals of directionality in this approach is government funding of research and development.

As indicated in the introductory chapter to this book, the economies of today face different challenges as well as an economic downswing caused by the COVID-19 crisis. The latter can potentially disrupt several types of industries but may also provide an opportunity for governments to think of how to design entrepreneurship policies that acknowledge the power of experimentation while also providing directionality for the future of business development.

Notes

1 https://em.dk/nyhedsarkiv/2019/februar/ivaerksaetterselskaber-afskaffes-og-kapitalkrav-for-anpartsselskaber-nedsaettes.
2 https://ec.europa.eu/digital-single-market/en/desi.
3 http://thegedi.org/.

References

Acs, Z. J., Audretsch, D. B., Lehmann, E. E. and Licht, G. 2016. National system of entrepreneurship. *Small Business Economics* 46(4):527–535.

Acs, Z. J., Autio, E. and Szerb, L. 2014. National systems of entrepreneurship: Measurement issues and policy implications. *Research Policy* 43(3):476–494.

Adner, R. 2012. *The wide lens: A new strategy for innovation*. Penguin UK.

Aldrich, H. E. and Zimmer, C. 1986. Entrepreneurship through social networks. In *The art and science of entrepreneurship*, 3–23. Ballinger, Cambridge, MA.

Baumol, W. J. 2010. *The microtheory of innovative entrepreneurship*. Princeton University Press.

Bhidé, A. 2000. *The origin and evolution of new businesses*. Oxford University Press.

Birch, D. G. 1979. *The job generation process*. MIT Program on Neighborhood and Regional Change.

Brüderl, J. and Preisendörfer, P. 1998. Network support and the success of newly founded business. *Small Business Economics* 10(3):213–225.

Bruton, G. D., Ahlstrom, D. and Li, H.-L. 2010. Institutional theory and entrepreneurship: Where are we now and where do wo need to move in the future? *Entrepreneurship: Theory & Practice* 34(3):421–440.

Bublitz, E., Nielsen, K., Noseleit, F. and Timmermans, B. 2018. Entrepreneurship, human capital, and labor demand: A story of signaling and matching. *Industrial and Corporate Change* 27(2):269–287.

Busenitz, L. W., Gomez, C. and Spencer, J. W. 2000. Country institutional profiles: Unlocking entrepreneurial phenomena. *Academy of Management Journal* 43(5):994–1003.

Canales, R., Regele, M., Grosberg, M. and Eftekhari, N. 2019. *Falling off the unicorn: The structural shortcomings of startup employment*. Working Paper, Yale School of Management.

Chandler, G. N., DeTienne, D. R., McKelvie, A. and Mumford, T. V. 2011. Causation and effectuation processes: A validation study. *Journal of Business Venturing* 26(3):375–390.

Christensen, J. L. 2019. *A critical view on equity crowdfunding*. Research paper for ISBE 2019 conference, Newcastle, UK, November 14–15.

Cooper, A. C. Gimeno-Gascon, F. J. and Woo, C. Y. 1994. Initial human and financial capital as predictors of new venture performance. *Journal of Business Venturing* 9(5):371–395.

Cooper, A. C. Woo, C. Y. and Dunkelberg, W. C. 1988. Entrepreneurs' perceived chances for success. *Journal of Business Venturing* 3(2):97–108.

Dahl, M. S. Jensen, P. G. and Nielsen, K. 2009. *Jagten på fremtidens nye vækstvirksomheder*. Jurist- og Økonomforbundets Forlag.

Dahl, M. S. and Klepper, S. 2015. Whom do new firms hire? *Industrial and Corporate Change* 24(4):819–836.

Dahl, M. S. and Reichstein, T. 2007. Are you experienced? Prior experience and the survival of new organizations. *Industry and Innovation* 14(5):497–511.

Dahl, M. S. and Sorenson, O. 2012. Home sweet home: Entrepreneurs' location choices and the performance of their ventures. *Management Science* 58(6):1059–1071.

Dahl, M. S. and Sorenson, O. 2014. The who, why, and how of spinoffs, *Industrial and Corporate Change* 23(3):661–688.

Danish Chamber of Commerce (Dansk Erhverv). 2020. https://www.danskerhverv.dk/si teassets/mediafolder/dokumenter/01-analyser/analysenotater-2020/3.-stort-fald-i-antal let-af-nyetableringer.pdf

Danish Foundation for Entrepreneurship (Fonden for Entreprenørskab). 2019a. *Entreprenørskab fra ABC til ph.d. Kortlægning af entreprenørskabsundervisning i det danske uddannelsessystem 2018/2019.*

Danish Foundation for Entrepreneurship (Fonden for Entreprenørskab). 2019b. *Iværksætterindblikket.* November.

Davidsson, P. 2008. *The entrepreneurship research challenge*. Edward Elgar.

Davidsson, P. and Honig, B. 2003. The role of social and human capital among nascent entrepreneurs. *Journal of Business Venturing* 18(3):301–331.

Drejer, I. and Christensen, J. L. 2021. The Danish regional innovation system in transition. In *Globalisation, new and emerging technologies, and sustainable development – The Danish innovation system in transition*, ed. Christensen, J. L., Gregersen, B., Holm, J. R. and Lorenz, E. L. Abingdon: Taylor & Francis.

Eurostat, Labour Force Survey. 2017. https://ec.europa.eu/eurostat/web/microdata/european-union-labour-force-survey (data extract).

Foray, D. 2018. Smart specialization strategies as a case of mission-oriented policy—a case study on the emergence of new policy practices. *Industrial and Corporate Change*, 27(5):817–832.

Gjerløv-Juel, P. and Dahl, M. S. 2013. *Den økonomiske krises betydning for opstart af nye vækstvirksomheder i Danmark: En rapport udarbejdet i samarbejde med tænketanken DEA.*

Guzman, J. and Stern, S. 2016. *The state of American entrepreneurship: New estimates of the quality and quantity of entrepreneurship for 32 US States, 1988–2014 (No. w22095).* National Bureau of Economic Research.

Haltiwanger, J., Jarmin, R. S. and Miranda, J. 2013. Who creates jobs? Small versus large versus young. *Review of Economics and Statistics* 95(2):347–361.

Ibsen, R. and Westergaard-Nielsen, N. 2011. *Job creation by firms in Denmark.* IZA Discussion Papers No. 5458. http://ssrn.com/abstract=1751440

Kerr, W. R., Nanda, R. and Rhodes-Kropf, M. 2014. Entrepreneurship as experimentation. *Journal of Economic Perspectives* 28(3):25–48.

Lerner, J. 2009. *Boulevard of broken dreams: Why public efforts to boost entrepreneurship and venture capital have failed - and what to do about it.* Princeton University Press.

Lindholm-Dahlstrand, Å., Andersson, M. and Carlsson, B. 2019. Entrepreneurial experimentation: A key function in systems of innovation. *Small Business Economics* 53(3):591–610.

Lorenz, E. and Holm, J. R. 2021. Workplace innovation and working conditions in Denmark. In *Globalisation, New and Emerging Technologies, and Sustainable Development – The Danish Innovation System in Transition*, ed. Christensen, J. L., Gregersen, B., Holm, J. R. and Lorenz, E. Abingdon: Routledge.

Lowe, R. A. and Ziedonis, A. A. 2006. Overoptimism and the performance of entrepreneurial firms. *Management Science* 52(2):173–186.

Mason, C. and Brown, R. 2014. *Entrepreneurial ecosystems and growth oriented entrepreneurship.* Final Report to OECD, Paris, 30(1):77–102.

Mazzucato, M. 2013. *The entrepreneurial state: Debunking public vs. private sector myths.* Anthem Press.

Ministry of Industry, Business and Financial Affairs (Erhvervsministeriet). 2019. *Redegørelse om erhvervsfremme og støtte 2019.* København, Oktober.

Nielsen, K. 2015. Human capital and new venture performance: The industry choice and performance of academic entrepreneurs. *The Journal of Technology Transfer* 40(3):1–22.

Nielsen, K. and Sarasvathy, S. D. 2016. A market for lemons in serial entrepreneurship? Exploring type I and type II errors in the restart decision. *Academy of Management Discoveries* 2(3):247–271.

Nightingale, P. and Coad, A. 2013. Muppets and gazelles: Political and methodological biases in entrepreneurship research. *Industrial and Corporate Change* 23(1):113–143.

Özcan, S. and Reichstein, T. 2009. Transition to entrepreneurship from the public sector: Predispositional and contextual effects. *Management Science* 55(4):604–618.

Parker, S. C. and Van Praag, C. M. 2006. Schooling, capital constraints, and entrepreneurial performance: The endogenous triangle. *Journal of Business & Economic Statistics* 24(4):416–431.

Santarelli, E. and Vivarelli, M. 2007. Entrepreneurship and the process of firms' entry, survival and growth. *Industrial and Corporate Change* 16(3):455–488.

Sarasvathy, S. D. 2004. The questions we ask and the questions we care about: Reformulating some problems in entrepreneurship research. *Journal of Business Venturing* 19(5):707–717.

Sarasvathy, S. D. 2009. *Effectuation: Elements of entrepreneurial expertise.* Edward Elgar Publishing.

Schumpeter, J. A. 1934. *The theory of economic development: An inquiry into profits, capital, credit, interest, and the business cycle* (Vol. 55). Transaction Publishing.

Schumpeter, J. A. 1939. *Business cycles*, Vol 1, 161–174. McGraw-Hill.

Shane, S. A. 2003. *A general theory of entrepreneurship: The individual-opportunity nexus.* Edward Elgar Publishing.

Shane, S. A. 2008. *The illusions of entrepreneurship: The costly myths that entrepreneurs, investors, and policy makers live by.* Yale University Press.

Shane, S. A. 2009. Why encouraging more people to become entrepreneurs is bad public policy. *Small Business Economics* 33(2):141–149.

Spigel, B. 2017. The relational organization of entrepreneurial ecosystems. *Entrepreneurship Theory and Practice* 41(1):49–72.

Spigel, B. and Harrison, R. 2018. Toward a process theory of entrepreneurial ecosystems. *Strategic Entrepreneurship Journal* 12(1):151–168.

Stam, E. and van de Ven, A. 2019. Entrepreneurial ecosystem elements. *Small Business Economics* 1–24.

Stam, E. and Wennberg, K. 2009. The roles of R&D in new firm growth. *Small Business Economics* 33(1):77–89.

Stinchcombe, A. L. 1965. Organizations and social structure. *Handbook of organizations* 44(2):142–193.

Taylor, M. P. 1996. Earnings, independence or unemployment: Why become self-employed? *Oxford Bulletin of Economics and Statistics* 58(2):253–266.

Terjesen, S., Bosma, N. and Stam, E. 2016. Advancing public policy for high-growth, female, and social entrepreneurs. *Public Administration Review* 76(2):230–239.

Thomke, S. H. 2003. *Experimentation matters: Unlocking the potential of new technologies for innovation.* Harvard Business Press.

Thomke, S. H., Von Hippel, E. and Franke, R. 1998. Modes of experimentation: An innovation process – and competitive – variable. *Research Policy* 27(3):315–332.

Ucbasaran, D., Shepherd, D. A., Lockett, A. and Lyon, S. J. 2013. Life after business failure the process and consequences of business failure for entrepreneurs. *Journal of Management* 39(1):163–202.

Van Praag, C. M. 2005. *Successful entrepreneurship: Confronting economic theory with empirical practice.* Edward Elgar Publishing.

Van Praag, C. M. and Versloot, P. H. 2007. What is the value of entrepreneurship? A review of recent research. *Small Business Economics* 29(4):351–382.

Van Praag, C. M., Wit, G. D. and Bosma, N. 2005. Initial capital constraints hinder entrepreneurial venture performance. *The Journal of Private Equity* 9(1):36–44.

Verheul, I., Wennekers, S., Audretsch, D. and Thurik, R. 2002. An eclectic theory of entrepreneurship: Policies, institutions and culture. In *Entrepreneurship: Determinants and policy in a European-US comparison*, 11–81. Boston, MA: Springer.

World Bank. 2015–2020. https://www.doingbusiness.org/en/doingbusiness (yearly reports).

Wright, M., Robbie, K. and Ennew, C. 1997. Serial entrepreneurs. *British Journal of Management* 8(3):251–268.

4 The Danish regional innovation system in transition

Ina Drejer and Jesper Lindgaard Christensen

4.1 Introduction[1]

This chapter analyses how different theoretically founded rationales have shaped Danish regional innovation policy since the turn of the millennium, with an emphasis on an innovation system perspective on two reforms implemented in 2007 and 2019, respectively. The reforms follow in the wake of a year-long debate on the relevance of the regional level for policies, which also includes a debate on which actors are relevant at different levels of aggregation. This debate is also ongoing in an international context (see e.g., Billing et al. 2019); hence, even if the chapter focuses on the Danish case, the discussions herein are relevant in other contexts as well.

Whereas we argue that the 2007 reform is influenced by a systems perspective and an explicit emphasis on place-specific characteristics, we find that the 2019 reform is shaped by a return to a more neo-classically inspired market failure perspective where the notion of place receives less attention. From a regional innovation systems perspective, place encompasses a specific institutional context as well as the importance of co-location and associated spatial proximity between actors for interactive learning. Thus, notions such as inter-firm relations, interpersonal connections, local learning and sticky knowledge are used to emphasise the importance of place (see e.g., Asheim and Isaksen 2002; Boschma and Lampooy 1999; Witt 2008). From a policy perspective, places can be defined from a functional point of view as 'regions in which a set of conditions conducive to development apply more than they do in larger or smaller areas' (Barca 2009, p. XI). Accordingly, the shifting trends in emphasis of place between the 2007 and 2019 reforms in Denmark are reflected in the type of policies promoted, as well as in the geographical levels at which policies are developed and implemented.

Stylised facts about the European development point towards the relevance of regional innovation policy. As summarised by Cornett (2017) using EC statistics, three trends stand out in the European Union development: (i) a long-term economic convergence between EU countries; a process that was halted by the financial crisis, which caused increased differences between northern and southern Europe; (ii) a trend towards increased disparities between metropole regions and other regions within countries; (iii) a trend towards increased disparities between rural areas and cities. Therefore, both the OECD (2018) and the European Commission (2017) point out that it is crucial how regions stimulate job creation and productivity growth. A similar development to what is generally is found across European Union countries has also taken place in Denmark, which, even though it is a small country, has had a political and policy-oriented focus on regional disparities since the 1950s (Illeris 2005). The development accentuates the relevance of regional innovation policy.

Although studies emphasise the relevance of a regional level in innovation policymaking (e.g., McCann and Ortega-Argilés 2013), the national and supranational policies continue to attract primary attention. Innovation systems literature was, at the outset, primarily focused on national innovation systems (Nelson 1993) and argued why the nation state still matters for innovation in a globalised world (Lundvall 1992), but a regional innovation systems branch of literature subsequently developed (e.g., Braczyk and Cooke 1998), and has continued to be an important theoretical and empirical guidance for innovation policy. Arguments for why a regional level is relevant for innovation policymaking are, e.g., based on the perception of innovation as a collective, cumulative and context-dependent process, which varies across actors, firms, industries and regions, and where interactions and exchange of knowledge are facilitated by proximity. Moreover, complexity in the innovation policy tasks is argued to require policymaking to be close to the target for policies and increasingly so (Feldman and Lowe 2018; Bianchi and Sandrine 2019). In turn, this trend in the innovation systems of today accentuates and motivates the focus in this chapter on the appropriate level of regionalism of innovation policies. The debate on regional innovation policies involves a general problem area around the appropriate level of aggregation at which regional policies are pursued. For example, the UK Regional Development Agencies (RDAs) existed from 1998–2010 (phased out through 2010–2012) as active operating entities for spurring regional development with a broad spectrum of means and responsibilities. In 2010 they were abolished and replaced by Local Enterprise Partnerships (LEPs). The LEPs were thought to be at a more appropriate regional level of aggregation as they were more geographically dispersed; 39 LEPs were formed from nine RDAs (BIS 2010). Simultaneously, a number of programmes were scrapped or centralised in order to achieve a simplification of the system. There is, though, a debate on whether the end result has in fact been a simpler system and whether the restructuring of the system has led to the desired effects (Bentley et al. 2010; Productivity Insights Network 2019). As will be evident, the problems discussed in the UK resemble those in Denmark. Moreover, despite arguments for the relevance of regional innovation policies, conflicting tendencies towards a stronger focus on improving general framework conditions while downplaying the attention to place-specific features can be observed across Europe. This chapter analyses these conflicting tendencies in more detail from the point of view of the Danish innovation and business promotion policy set-up.

Whereas this chapter takes its point of departure in a specific policy change, we also address the underlying theoretical rationale by comparing the content of the reforms to established theoretical rationales for policies at a regional level.[2] As will be evident below, these rationales have, though, been disputed and a theoretical consensus has not been established. In short, traditional neo-classical approaches make an appeal for market failures such as information deficiencies as the overarching argument for policy intervention, and regional differences are primarily ascribed to differences in factor endowments such as population growth and accumulation of physical capital. On the contrary, innovation system thinking argues that interactions between elements in the system are crucial and often better done when actors are in close proximity, facilitating the transfer of tacit knowledge. The latter approach renders a stronger focus and rationale for policies on alleviating system failures, and a stronger focus on the appropriate level where such interactions most often take place, arguably often at the regional level, or at least where proximity is high.

In the following section, we describe the Danish regional innovation and business promotion policy and set-up through the two major reforms implemented in 2007 and 2019, respectively. Despite the fact that a growing share of gross domestic expenditure on R&D (GERD) is allocated at the regional or local level in the period leading up to the latest reform, this drastically reduces the role of regional actors in innovation policy. Section 4.3 discusses the main underlying theoretical rationales behind the two reforms. As mentioned earlier, it is argued that different rationales have influenced different elements of the reforms, with the 2007 reform for example being influenced by a systems approach to innovation and business development, whereas a neoclassical-inspired market failure approach plays a more dominant role in the 2019 reform. The latter appears to reduce the scope of policies for regional actors, and to concentrate and centralise operational policy actors. Section 4.4 summarises the conclusions.

4.2 Regional innovation and business promotion policy in Denmark

4.2.1 The regional Danish business promotion system 2007–2018

In 2007, a major structural reform of the Danish local government system was implemented. The reform reduced the number of municipalities from 271 to 98, and five new regions replaced 13 counties. The regions vary in size, ranging from 0.6 to 1.6 million inhabitants. The main responsibility of the regions is health care, but they were also made responsible for regional development tasks (Vrangbæk 2010).

Prior to 2007, taking on responsibility for regional business promotion was a voluntary task for Danish counties and municipalities. With the 2007 reform, the national government delegated responsibility for regional business promotion activities to the regions (KL – Local Government Denmark 2005). The reform made it compulsory for the regions to dedicate financial resources to regional business development and to formulate regional growth strategies, which guided the implementation of the regional business promotion policy.

Regional growth forums were put in charge of the regional business promotion policy in each region and were set up with representatives from the business community, labour market organisations and knowledge institutions as well as members of the politically elected regional council (Cornett 2009). This is in line with the 'triple helix' approach (Etzkowitz and Leydesdorff 2000), which also has principles and procedures of involving participation. A central purpose of the growth forums was to promote increased regional coordination and collaboration for developing the regional conditions of growth (The Danish Government 2005).

The Business Promotion Act of 2005, which guides the work of the growth forums, included elements inspired by the OECD's (2001) analysis of growth drivers. The growth driver way of reasoning gained widespread recognition in policy circles after the OECD's 2001 analysis found that 70% of the productivity growth in Western OECD countries, also at the regional level, could be attributed to the growth drivers of innovation, entrepreneurship and human resources as well as the application of technology, in particular ICT. Among these, innovation and entrepreneurship were identified as the main drivers, whereas human resources and the application of technology were perceived as regional conditions of growth. The OECD's analysis is reflected in the activities, which the growth forums, according to the Danish Business Promotion Act of 2005, had the mandate to co-finance as a means of supporting regional business development. These activities could be related to (i) innovation, knowledge sharing and knowledge generation, (ii) the application of new technology, (iii) the founding of new businesses, (iv) the development of human resources, including the development of regional competences, as well as (v) growth and development in tourism and (vi) development activities in peripheral areas (Business Promotion Act 2005).

During the period 2007–2018, the Danish growth forums allocated approximately DKK 5bn to regional business promotion activities,[3] of which at least one third is estimated to have been dedicated to activities directly aimed at supporting innovation. At the local level, the regional growth forums were supplemented by a municipality-based business service system, which provided more basic services for businesses and entrepreneurs. At the national level, a National Growth Council and the Ministry of Economics and Business also had a mandate to initiate and fund activities that supported the national growth policy, as well as to co-fund regional initiatives.

Figure 4.1 illustrates that the regional and local share of funds allocated to total Danish public R&D funding has increased considerably (around 40%) over the last decade, especially in the 2011–2015 period, after which the share levels out and has a small drop from 2017 to 2018.

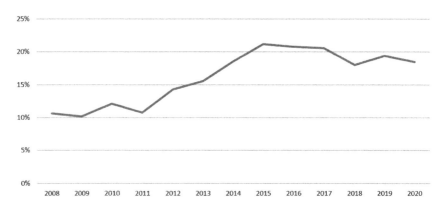

Figure 4.1 Regional and local share of government funds allocated for R&D 2008–2020. Source: Statistics Denmark. FOUBUD: Government Budget for Appropriations or Outlays for R&D by grant-awarding organisations and price unit.

This is just one indicator that the sub-national level gained increased importance in the past decade.

4.2.2 The 2019 reform of the Danish business promotion system

The growth forum set-up was changed by a new reform of how the business support system is organised in Denmark. This reform, implemented in January 2019, reorganises the business promotion system and reduces the regional tier substantially. Despite a rhetoric around enhancing tailor-made support and development outside large cities, the reform entails an element of centralisation of business support and advice through abandoning, by law, the regional tier in policy and administration of business support while strengthening the national level and reorganising the municipality level. Moreover, it significantly reduces the number of policy actors.

In order to understand why the new set-up of the business promotion system looks at is does, it is useful to look into how the political agreement behind the reform of the system came about.

There have been mixed opinions on the regional growth forums since their introduction in 2007. Although an evaluation in 2013 concluded that by and large the growth forums fulfilled their objectives (Ministry of Economic and Interior Affairs 2013), the growth forums have also been characterised as arenas of power struggles among different actors because the roles in relation to regional leadership were open for definition (Larsen 2017). Related to this, critics claimed that the growth forums were bureaucratic, they generated a plethora of actors and initiatives, and their efforts in terms of following up on and documenting effects of activities were deficient (e.g., Berlingske Tidende

2007; Wiegand 2010). In addition, there was no political consensus about the need for a regional government level in Denmark, and between 2007 and 2018, the continued existence of the regions was a major political theme in two national election campaigns.

A simplification of the business promotion system, based on a commissioned inspection report on the business promotion system (Landfall Strategy et al. 2016) was part of the government policy platform for the centre-right 'Trefoil Government' that came into power in Denmark in November 2016 (The Danish Government 2016), and a committee for simplifying the business promotion system was appointed in June 2017. The members of the committee counted seven representatives from the business community, a university rector and a principal from a university college. The mandate of the committee was to come up with a suggestion for a simpler organisation of the business promotion efforts (Ministry of Industry, Business and Financial Affairs et al. 2017), and their recommendations were to a large extent implemented in the 2019 reform. With the reform, the regional growth forums were abolished and the regions were, by law, prevented from having their own regional business promotion activities. Accordingly, the number of political levels responsible for business promotion activities has been reduced to two: a local (municipal) level, which is mainly responsible for providing introductory business counselling as well as referral to more specialised services, and a national level, which is responsible for the specialised services. As part of the reform, the budget for local business promotion activities was increased by DKK 180m (€24m) in 2019. In total, however, the public funds allocated to business promotion activities are reduced by DKK 100m annually.

At the national level, the Danish Executive Board for Business Development and Growth (EBBDG) is now responsible for ensuring that the decentralised business promotion initiatives are coherent across the state and municipal level. The board is given the task of drawing up a comprehensive strategy for the decentralised business promotion effort in Denmark from 2020 onwards. This strategy should take its point of departure in local and regional growth challenges and framework conditions and be coordinated with relevant national strategies.

Although there are only two political levels in the new structure, there are three types of actors at the decentralised level: (i) the Danish EBBDG, (ii) a set of six newly established cross-municipal business hubs, and (iii) the municipalities.[4] Complementing this, a digital platform is meant to provide a first, online, guidance to firms regarding simple questions, as well as indicating where in the support system they should direct their further enquiries. Figure 4.2 represents this framework with all its levels.

The above primarily focused on regional system *structures* in Denmark. In order to get deeper into a description of system *functions* we need to discuss further the rationales for regional policies.

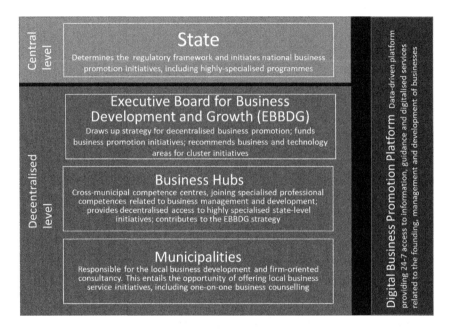

Figure 4.2 An overview of levels and actors in the 2019 version of the Danish Business Promotion System. Source: Ministry of Industry, Business and Financial Affairs (2019).

4.3 Theoretically founded rationales behind the regional innovation and business promotion policy in Denmark

4.3.1 Theoretical rationales behind the growth forum set-up 2007–2018

The OECD (2001) analysis, which is clearly reflected in the Danish Business Promotion Act of 2005, takes its point of departure in 'New Growth Theory', which emphasises innovation as the endogenous engine of growth. Furthermore, it challenges the classical economics assumption that 'the invisible hand' of the market will generate an efficient equilibrium growth path (Grossman and Helpman 1994) because innovation is associated with monopoly profits, and the existence of spill-overs will hamper full appropriation of returns from investments (ibid., p. 37). The policy lessons drawn from New Growth Theory are still primarily related to identifying and fixing market failures associated with e.g., technology transfer and appropriability of returns from investments in innovation as well as equipment (Crafts 1996).

However, the triple helix-oriented set-up of the regional growth forums deviates further from classical economics than simply acknowledging that markets are not always efficient, as it prescribes a more active role for policy. This policy is influenced by a systems approach[5] to business promotion policy, not least an innovation–driven business promotion policy. It should be noted that working with business promotion from a systems perspective in Denmark was not a completely new thing introduced with the 2007 reform. As shown in Christensen and Fagerberg (2021), elements of the systems approach have influenced national and regional business promotion policy since the mid-1990s.

While the systems approach to business promotion policy does not dismiss the existence of market failures, policies are to a larger extent substantiated by the existence of systems failures. The systems approach emphasises learning and the capacity to process different types of knowledge, not only focusing on scientific and technical knowledge, but also knowledge about, e.g., markets and organisational processes. The capacity to process knowledge is viewed from a dynamic perspective, implying that business promotion policy can have a long-term perspective of changing actors' ways of thinking, visions, organisational routines, etc. With reference to the need for a regional business promotion policy, innovation and business development are in the systems perspective perceived as collective, cumulative and context-dependent processes, which vary across actors, firms, industries and regions (Laranja et al. 2008).

The first innovation system studies primarily focused on the national level (Nelson 1993), but studies of regional innovation systems have become increasingly popular (e.g., Braczyk et al. 1998). A regional innovation system can be described as a system of (i) interacting public and private interests, (ii) formal institutions (knowledge and education institutions, financial institutions, public authorities etc.), (iii) other organisations that contribute to the generation, application and dissemination of knowledge, and (iv) informal institutions (e.g., Doloreux and Saeed 2005). Within the systems perspective, innovation and business development is assumed to occur in an interaction between actors at different levels, in a specific institutional context, and it is the actors and the context that defines the system in which innovations are developed. System failures occur when different elements of the system are missing or are insufficient to promote learning and development of new knowledge. Failures can, e.g., be in the form of missing links between different types of actors, such as firms and knowledge institutions (Carlsson and Jacobsson 1997), or missing information and/or competences to innovate and break free from locked-in development paths (Coenen et al. 2012). The system may also be fragmented in the sense that there is a lack of regional cooperation and trust among actors.

The purpose of business promotion policy from a systems perspective is to improve the performance of the system by increasing the capacity to overcome institutional inertia and supporting institutional structures that stimulate learning, alignment and interactions between the system's actors (Arnold 2004; Woolthuis et al. 2005). The primary role of business promotion agents according to this perspective is to act as organisers or facilitators of interactions between the actors in the system, as well as to define and coordinate the different roles and functions of the various actors (Laranja et al. 2008). Seen from a regional perspective, some regions are particularly well equipped to mend system failures and stimulate learning between the system's actors.

Accordingly, when Morgan (1997) refers to 'Learning Regions', he is inferring that regions do not only differ in terms of tangible resources and institutions, but also in terms of informal relations, norms and social capital – and it is the latter, which is the decisive factor in regions' ability to exploit and optimise learning from the fundamental processes associated to innovation.[6] Regional policy actors can – provided they have the necessary authority and financial means to develop and implement a regional business promotion policy – play a decisive role in terms of influencing the interactions in the regional innovation system towards supporting an unrestricted allocation of knowledge, competences and resources (Tödtling and Trippl 2005).

The notion of smart specialisation, which is a cornerstone of the European Commission's Europe 2020 strategy (Foray et al. 2009; McCann and Ortega-Argilés 2015; Foray 2018), is in its current form also to a large extent based on a regional innovation system logic, where not only technological and industrial competences, but also institutional characteristics and governance structures, are perceived as being strongly related to regional innovation potentials (McCann and Ortega-Argilés 2015). Smart specialisation processes are rooted in strategic interactions between public and private actors, with the aim of opening up new technological or market opportunities that take their point of departure in existing industrial assets and structures and involve a variety of actors in the system (Foray 2015, 2019). As such, these strategies are directional to a larger extent than prescribed by earlier regional innovation systems literature and based on new governance processes, in many cases denoted an 'experimental discovery process', involving 'quadruple helix actors', i.e., government, industry, university, civic society (ibid.). Two other characteristics of smart specialisation strategies are relevant in our context. First, they often imply the involvement of a wider range of policy areas and policy actors to create an adequate policy mix (Magro and Wilson 2019). Second, they explicitly emphasise the importance of place.

4.3.2 Theoretical rationales behind the 2019 reform of the business promotion system

As previously mentioned, the 2019 reform of the Danish business promotion system abolishes the regional growth forums and prevents the regions from having their own regional business promotion activities. The vocabulary in relation to the aim of policy has also undergone a change since the 2007 reform where regional coordination and collaboration was emphasised as an important factor shaping regional conditions of growth. In 2018, the committee for simplifying the business promotion system describes the main aim of public business promotion activities as meeting '…needs which are not sufficiently met by the private market. Possibly because such a market does not exist […], or because the market, due to market failures, does not work in an optimal way' (Committee for simplifying the business promotion system 2018, p. 15 – authors' translation). It is furthermore stated that a guiding principle behind the business promotion efforts should be that 'If a well-functioning private market exists, then there should not be a public business promotion effort' (ibid. p. 25 – authors' translation).

Markets and market failure are, thus, emphasised in the reasoning behind the new business promotion system. This reasoning has connotations of neoclassical economic theory, where it is a prevailing conception that the primary justification for public interventions is the correction of market failures. Analyses of market failures related to innovation are, e.g., based on basic characteristics of knowledge as being intangible and a public good that is only partly excludable in use; and investments in knowledge are associated with great uncertainty. Accordingly, market-based allocation and pricing mechanisms are hampered, and investments in knowledge will tend to be below what is societally optimal (Arrow 1962). Consequently, seen from a market failure perspective, public subsidies for investments in knowledge can be justified as a means to correct failures in mechanisms allocating private funds to investments in the development of new knowledge and the establishment of new, high-risk companies (Dodgson et al. 2011; Laranja et al. 2008).

The neoclassical perspective also has implications for the perceived need for a regional innovation – and general business promotion – policy. In neoclassical economics, it is traditionally assumed that growth occurs in a 'neutral' geographical space where contextual preconditions are not seen as decisive parameters influencing growth potentials. Rather, population growth and the accumulation of physical capital and technology are considered to be the main explanatory factors behind interregional differences in economic growth. This does not imply that contemporary neoclassical economics rejects that economic growth is geographically concentrated. Spatial autocorrelation, which is a statistical expression of spatial dependence, has, e.g., been used to explain geographical concentrations of wealth as a result of spill-over effects (Koch 2008).[7] Furthermore, New Economic Geography incorporates space into neoclassical models as a means to explain geographically uneven development (Wilson 2011). In New Economic Geography, distance between markets and, accordingly, transport costs are introduced as factors which make location matter, thereby implying that policy should promote trade and factor mobility, e.g., through infrastructure investments (ibid.).

4.3.3 Main differences between the systems and neoclassical perspectives on innovation

The neoclassical perspective can in general be characterised as an input-based understanding of innovation, which focuses on traditional 'hard' input factors such as physical investments and education-based human capital. This can to a large extent explain why context – and thereby place – tends to play a negligible role in this perspective since the 'hard' input factors tend to be less firm- and region-specific than social capital, networks, norms and culture, which will set their mark on the interactions that are emphasised in the systems-based perspective (Nauwelaers 2001). Accordingly, policy is also 'simpler' in a neoclassical framework, because it is much easier to measure the factors that are considered important for growth and economic development than is the case in a systems-based perspective, where the decisive factors tend to be more intangible and require long-term efforts to change (Metcalfe 1995; Wolfe 2019). In turn, this implies that the number of actors need not be as large as prescribed by a systemic perspective. Hence, the role that regional policymakers are expected to play according to the systems perspective, prescribes an active role as a facilitator and partner, rather than a provider of inputs. In a systems-based policy set-up, the policy actors themselves are part of the system, and therefore also become targets for execution of policy (Nauwelaers 2001; Feldman and Lowe 2018).

We conclude this section with a specific example of how a policy has been changed as a result of the 2019 reform. The example illustrates how the role of place and regional embeddedness has been drastically reduced in the formulations of cluster policies.

4.3.4 An example: Danish cluster policies before and after the 2019 reform

Cluster policies have been a well-established policy field at both national, regional and municipal level in Denmark since the 1990s (Drejer et al. 1999). The Danish cluster policies were influenced by the writings of e.g., Michael Porter (Porter 1998, 2000), which emphasise how geographical proximity is an important part of why firms in clusters perform better than firms outside clusters – something the Danish ministry has also found and promoted in evaluations of clusters in Denmark (Ministry of Education and Research 2017). Accordingly, clusters in Denmark have traditionally been regionally embedded and had a relatively narrow field of specialisation. Although the national cluster programmes already became less focused on regional development aims when three programmes – Regional Technology Centres, High-Technology Networks and Regional ICT Centres – were connected in the Innovation Network Denmark programme in 2008, the reduced focus on the regional dimension in the national cluster programme received little political attention at the time. This might be ascribed to the fact that the, at that time newly established, regions had their own regional development funds, and had begun supporting regional clusters (Thomsen 2020).

With the abandonment of the regional tier in business policy, the ambition in the 2020 Cluster Programme of identifying technological strongholds at a national level of aggregation only, is expected to have a considerable effect on the Danish cluster landscape. According to the Cluster Excellence Denmark association, there were approximately 50 clusters in Denmark in 2020, which were certified under the European Cluster Excellence Initiative and/or supported as Innovation Networks by the Danish Ministry of Education and Research.[8] The Danish EBBDG's strategy for business promotion in Denmark for the period 2020–2023 states that each of the 13 pre-identified clusters areas should have only one, national base and support (The Danish Executive Board for Business Development and Growth 2020). In addition to securing funding for the cluster organisations, becoming certified as one of the 13 'official' clusters in Denmark also opens the door to funding from state-financed research and development activities as well as support from the budget of the Danish EBBDG – thereby making the 13 national clusters strong centres of business development.

Although the process of identifying clusters under the 2020 Cluster Programme does involve the regions, the final decision is made by the Danish EBBDG. The previously regionally-based clusters are likely to face difficulties in becoming included in the national support scheme if they leverage intensively and primarily on regional resources, rather than on national partners. Alternative public sources of funding for sub-national cluster initiatives are not a part of the post-2019 business promotion system, except in the form of strictly local initiatives, which may still be supported by a municipality.

4.4 Conclusions, policy assessment and perspectives

The substantial differences in the policy approaches between traditional neoclassical thinking and system-oriented policies are closely related to fundamental differences in the basic understanding of how the innovation process unfolds and whether proximity and place-specificity play a role in this. Whereas factors related to the place-specific historical, structural and institutional conditions for coordinating and allocating resources play a crucial role in the systems perspective, they are in general not considered in a neoclassical market failure frame of reference (Dodgson et al. 2011). This, we argue, leads to a focus on respectively market failures and system failures as the primary targets for policies in the two policy set-ups studied in this chapter.

In Denmark, there has, since the late-1990s, generally been a recognition of system perspectives of business promotion policies, and, adhering to not only the national but also the regional innovation system approach, there has been an increasing attention on the importance of the regional level in business development. This is also reflected in the funding set-up, where this chapter has demonstrated that the share of regional public R&D expenditures as a share of total public R&D in Denmark has increased by 40% over the past decade.

It is therefore remarkable that the policy reform of 2019 appears to centralise how business support is provided and also to possibly decouple some of the already established systemic links between actors. Although the new business promotion policy set-up in Denmark does acknowledge that the decentralised business promotion effort should take a point of departure in local and regional growth challenges and framework conditions, there is a clear move towards simplification in organisation and actors, as well as in policy means, which is in accordance with a neoclassical economics logic. The focus on promoting a range of growth drivers is replaced by an emphasis on increasing productivity in firms. There are no references to needs for improving connections between different types of actors; now attention is solely on the firms and how their challenges and needs can be met by a business promotion system that is described as efficient, simple, easy to grasp and with no overlapping activities (The Danish Executive Board for Business Development and Growth 2019). How the new system will work in practice is too early to tell. Possible reduced costs of running the new system may come at the expense of some firms not finding the support they need, most likely those with a demand for specific and specialised competences, firms that are likely to be among the highly innovative firms.

Consequently, the assessment of the 2019 reform presented in this chapter is by no means an evaluation, and it is generally too soon to go far into an assessment of the specific consequences. The sceptical tone we apply when presenting the reform is grounded in a claim that the reform contrasts the abovementioned principles of how to stimulate innovation systems as it reduces proximity between actors. This does not rule out that there are other types of benefits that may surface with the new system. Another issue with the reform concerns the number and types of actors in the system. The reform intended to reduce the number of different types of actors. Even if this has also been the result, it does not necessarily lead to reduced complexity of the system. The effective number and types of actors in the system is a balance between the needs of users, the specialisation of the suppliers of the support, and the coordination costs involved in providing the support. When firms' problems and needs for advice get still more complex and the pace of change increases (Iammarino and McCann 2013), increased demand for differentiated types of providers of support is likely. On the other hand, surely a too segmented and complex system will challenge the users' ability to use the system and, again, we do not rule out that the new set-up has advantages in serving certain segments of firms.

Hence, it still remains to be seen if the current set-up of the business support system is able to provide adequate support for the majority of users. Nonetheless, we do point to crucial problem areas in this respect, regarding both the actors and the links between these as earlier literature (The Danish Council for Research and Innovation Policy 2017; Cooke 2001) has emphasised the importance of the connectivity of innovation systems. In any case there are inevitably costs and coordination problems in a transition phase towards the new organisation of the system as well as substantial loss of accumulated experiences. Again, to balance the critical stance on the system change, we propose that there are no accurate prescriptions regarding the most effective number and types of actors in the system. In principle, the number of instruments used for policies has a clear correlation with the number of objectives of the policies. This is also known as the Tinbergen assignment theorem (Tinbergen 1967). According to this design principle, the number of policy programmes should be guided by the number of objectives, and the number of instruments fixed by the number of market failures potentially occurring at the market. The inherent risk for government in following this is to produce instruments that are not used and are too costly to deliver. On the other hand, this needs balancing against unintentionally not targeting the weakest links of the system, which is inexpedient as this is likely to determine the overall performance of the system (Acs et al. 2014). We posit though that this is a question that needs to be addressed in specific contexts. This means that taking 'place' seriously in policy also means considering the likelihood of certain instruments being more or less effective and efficient in different regional contexts. The same policy instrument can have different effects in two different geographical contexts. Indeed, different policy mixes may have developed over time in specific contexts because they demonstrate effectiveness, and this questions the general Tinbergen design principle of policies (Magro and Wilson 2019).

More generally, this chapter also pointed to the importance of going beyond the national level of aggregation when analysing innovation systems. This implies not only analysing political-administratively defined regions within national borders but also considering what is the appropriate geographical level of aggregation and definition of policy instrument and regional context. Even innovation systems, as such, may span across established geographically defined boundaries such as nation states. The following chapters in this volume do not all take an explicit geographical perspective, but they do consider what the relevant system boundaries and definitions are.

Notes

1 The chapter builds in some sections on Christensen and Drejer (2018), which deals more extensively with the theoretical rationales behind regional policy.
2 In this chapter we operate with three different tiers of policies: the state, regional and local levels. The latter mainly refers to the municipality level in Denmark. When we use the term 'region' in relation to the Danish regional innovation and business promotion policy in Denmark, we refer to administrative regions.
3 These funds were supplemented by funds from the European Union's Structural Funds as well as private co-funding.
4 https://em.dk/media/12908/strategi-for-decentral-erhvervsfremme-2019.pdf
5 The innovation systems vocabulary has been quite widely applied in relation to the Danish growth forums. An example of this is OECD (2012), which, in a Review of Regional Innovation in Central and Southern Denmark, e.g., talks about the 'functional role of different innovation system actors' (p. 26), the role of universities as nodes as well as global gateways in the innovation system (p. 27), and in relation to policy specifically states that 'The RIS [Regional Innovation Systems] lens highlights the variety of regions within countries, the different dynamics of innovation, and the interactions across institutions in a given system. Policies or brokering institutions can reinforce those systemic relations' (p. 39). The individual growth forums also adhere to the innovation systems rhetoric and way of thinking (see e.g., Growth Forum Zealand 2012; Growth Forum North Denmark 2012).
6 Storper (1995) labels this 'untraded interdependencies', which to a large degree are regionally bound.
7 Neoclassical and evolutionary economics have different perspectives on spill-overs; Whereas spill-overs in neoclassical economics are assumed to occur automatically, e.g., in the form of a positive effect of being located close to a capital-intensive company or region, the assumption in evolutionary economics is that spill-over processes do not occur spontaneously, but need to be actively enforced by economic agents (Audretsch and Keilbach 2004, Metcalfe 1995; Witt, 2008).
8 www.clusterexcellencedenmark.dk accessed April 30, 2020.

References

Acs, Z. J., Autio, E. and Szerb, L. 2014. National systems of entrepreneurship: Measurement issues and policy implications. *Research Policy*, 43: 476–494.

Arnold, E. 2004. Evaluating research and innovation policy: A systems world needs systems evaluations. *Research Evaluation* 13(1): 3–17.

Arrow, K. J. 1962. The economic implications of learning by doing. *The Review of Economic Studies* 29(3): 155–173.

Asheim, B. and Isaksen, A. 2002. Regional innovation systems: The integration of local 'sticky' and global 'ubiquitous' knowledge. *The Journal of Technology Transfer*, 27(1): 77–86.

Audretsch, D. and Keilbach, M. 2004. Entrepreneurship and regional growth: An evolutionary interpretation. *Journal of Evolutionary Economics* 14(5): 605–616.

Barca, F. 2009. *An agenda for a reformed cohesion policy - A place-based approach to meeting European Union challenges and expectations*. Independent report prepared at the request of Danuta Hübner, Commissioner for Regional Policy.

Bentley, G., Bailey, D. and Shutt, J. 2010. From RDAs to LEPs: A new localism? Case examples of West Midlands and Yorkshire. *Local Economy* 535–557.

Berlingske Tidende. 2007. *Debat: Vækstfora er uproduktive*. 15 October.

Bianchi, P. and Sandrine, L. 2019. Regional industrial policy for the manufacturing revolution: Enabling conditions for complex transformations. *Cambridge Journal of Regions, Economy and Society* 12: 233–249.

Billing, C., McCann, P. and Ortega-Argilés, R. 2019. Interregional inequalities and UK sub-national governance responses to Brexit. *Regional Studies* 53(5): 741–760.

BIS. 2010. *Local growth: Realising every place's potential*. White paper published by the British Government.

Boschma, R. and Lampooy, J. G. 1999. Evolutionary economics and economic geography. *Journal of Evolutionary Economics* 9(4): 411–429.

Braczyk, H.-J., Cooke, P. and Heidenreich, M. (eds). 1998. *Regional innovation systems: The role of governances in a globalized world*. London: University College London.

Business Promotion Act. 2005. Lov nr. 602 af 24/06/2005 (Lov om erhvervsfremme).

Carlsson, B. and Jacobsson, S. 1997. In search of useful public policies: Key lessons and issues for policy makers. In *Technological systems and industrial dynamics*, ed. Carlsson, B., 299–316. Dordrecht: Kluwer Academic Publishers.

Christensen, J. L. and Drejer, I. 2018. Er det regionale niveau relevant for erhvervspolitikken?, *Økonomi og Politik*, No.4.

Christensen, J. L. and Fagerberg, J. 2021. Chapter 1: The emergence of innovation policy as a field: The international context and the Danish experience. In *Globalisation, new and emerging technologies, and sustainable development – The Danish innovation system in transition*, ed. Christensen, J. L., Gregersen, B., Holm, J. R. and Lorenz, E. L. Abingdon: Taylor & Francis.

Coenen, L., Moodysson, J. and Martin, H. 2012. Path renewal in old industrial regions: Possibilities and limitations for regional innovation policy. *Regional Studies* 49(5): 850–865.

Committee for Simplifying the Business Promotion System. 2018. *Fokuseret og Fremtidssikret. (Focused and future-proof)*. Report with the committee's recommendations, April.

Cooke, P. 2001. Regional innovation systems, clusters, and the knowledge economy. *Industrial and Corporate Change* 10(4): 945–974.

Cornett, A. P. 2009. Aims and strategies in regional innovation and growth policy: A Danish perspective. *Entrepreneurship and Regional Development* 21(4): 399–420. doi:10.1080/08985620903020078

Cornett, A. P. 2017. Inter- and intra-regional balance: Drivers of change and development. In *Geographies of growth: Innovations, networks and collaborations*, ed. Karlsson, C., Andersson, M. and Bjerke, L., 70–95. Cheltenham: Edward Elgar Publishing.

Crafts, N. 1996. Post-neoclassical endogenous growth theory: What are its policy implications?. *Oxford Review of Economic Policy* 12(2): 30–47.

Dodgson, M., Hughes, A., Foster, J. and Metcalfe, S. 2011. Systems thinking, market failure, and the development of innovation policy: The case of Australia. *Research Policy* 40(9): 1145–1156.

Doloreux, D. and Saeed, P. 2005. Regional innovation systems: Current discourse and unresolved issues. *Technology in Society* 27: 133–153.

Drejer, I., Kristensen, F. S. and Laursen, K. 1999. Cluster studies as a basis for industrial policy: The case of Denmark. *Industry and Innovation* 6(2): 171–190.

Etzkowitz, H. and Leydesdorff, L. 2000. The dynamics of innovation: From national systems and 'Mode 2' to a triple helix of university-industry-government relations. *Research Policy* 29: 109–23.

European Commission. 2017. *My region, My Europe, our future: The seventh report on economic, social and territorial cohesion*. Commission Staff Working Document 2017/0330.

Feldman, M. and Lowe, N. 2018. Policy and collective action in place. *Cambridge Journal of Regions, Economy and Society* 11(2): 335–351.

Foray, D. 2015. *Smart specialisation. Opportunities and challenges for regional innovation policy*. London: Routledge.

Foray, D. 2018. Smart specialization strategies as a case of mission-oriented policy – a case study on the emergence of new policy practices. *Industrial and Corporate Change* 27(5): 817–832.

Foray, D. 2019. On sector-non-neutral innovation policy: Towards new design principles. *Journal of Evolutionary Economics* 29: 1379–1397.

Foray, D., David, P. A. and Hall, B. 2009. *Smart specialisation: The concept. Knowledge for growth. Prospects for science, technology and innovation*. Selected papers from Research Commissioner Janez Potočnik's Knowledge for Growth Expert Group, November.

Grossman, G. M. and Helpman, E. 1994. Endogenous innovation in the theory of growth. *Journal of Economic Perspectives* 8(1): 23–44.

Growth Forum North Denmark. 2012. *Regional vækstredegørelse*. Aalborg: North Denmark Region.

Growth Forum Zealand. 2012. Order of business February 8th, 2012, item 4, 'Udvikling af det regionale innovationssystem'. https://www.regionsjaelland.dk/Politik/vaekstforum -sjaelland/dagsordener%20og%20materialer/2012/2012-02-08%20VF%20dagsorden.p df. Accessed February 8, 2020.

Iammarino, S. and McCann, P. 2013. Introduction: Multinational enterprises, innovation and geography in today's globalized world. In *Multinationals and economic geography: Location, technology and innovation*, ed. Iammarino, S. and McCann, P., 1–29. Cheltenham: Edward Elgar Publishing.

Illeris, S. 2005. *Egnsudvikling - egnsudviklingens historie i Danmark*. Copenhagen: Dansk Byplanlaboratorium.

KL - Local Government Denmark. 2005. *En sammenhængende erhvervsfremme – de nye regionale vækstfora*. Copenhagen: Kommuneinformation A/S.

Koch, W. 2008. Development accounting with spatial effects. *Spatial Economic Analysis* 3(3): 321–342.

Landfall Strategy, Damvad Analytics, Struensee & Co., McKinsey & Company. 2016. *Eftersyn af Erhvervsfremmeindsatsen (Inspection of the business promotion effort)*. Report, November.

Laranja, M., Uyarra, E. and Flanagan, K. 2008. Policies for science, technology and innovation: Translating rationales into regional policies in a multi-level setting. *Research Policy* 37(5):823–835.

Larsen, P. W. 2017. Delineating partnerships from other forms of collaboration in regional development planning. *International Planning Studies* 22(3): 242–255.

Lundvall, B-Å. ed. 1992. *National systems of innovation: Towards a theory of innovation and interactive learning.* London: Pinter Publishers.

Magro, E. and Wilson, J. R. 2019. Policy-mix evaluation: Governance challenges from new place-based innovation policies. *Research Policy* 48: 103612.

McCann, P. and Ortega-Argilés, R. 2013. Modern regional innovation policy. *Cambridge Journal of Regions, Economy and Society* 6: 187–216.

McCann, P. and Ortega-Argilés, R. 2015. Smart specialization, regional growth and applications to European Union Cohesion policy. *Regional Studies* 49(8): 1291–1302.

Metcalfe, J. S. 1995. The economic foundations of technology policy: Equilibrium and evolutionary perspectives. In *Handbook of industrial innovation*, ed. P. Stoneman, 409–511. London: Blackwell Publishing.

Ministry of Economic and Interior Affairs. 2013. *Evaluering af kommunalreformen (Evaluation of the municipal reform).* Copenhagen: Ministry of Economic and Interior Affairs.

Ministry of Education and Research, Styrelsen for Institutioner og Uddannelsesstøtte. 2017. *Effekter af virksomheders deltagelse i klynger og innovationsnetværk.* Copenhagen: Ministry of Education and Research.

Ministry of Industry, Business and Financial Affairs. 2019. *Strategi for decentral erhvervsfremme 2019 (Strategy for decentral business development 2019).* Copenhagen: Ministry of Industry, Business and Financial Affairs.

Ministry of Industry, Business and Financial Affairs, Ministry of Education and Research, Ministry of Foreign Affairs, Ministry Economic and Interior Affairs, Ministry of Finance. 2017. *Kommissorium for forenkling af erhvervsfremmeindsatsen (Mandate for simplifying the business promotion effort).* June. Copenhagen: Ministry of Industry, Business and Financial Affairs.

Morgan, K. 1997. The learning region: Institutions, innovation and regional renewal. *Regional Studies*, 31(5): 491–503.

Nauwelaers, C. 2001. Path-dependency and the role of institutions in cluster policy generation. In *Cluster policies – cluster development?*, ed. Mariussen, Å., Vol. 2. Nordregio Report.

Nelson, R. R. 1993. *National systems of innovation: A comparative study.* Oxford: Oxford University Press.

OECD. 2001. *The new economy: Beyond the hype.* Final report on the OECD Growth project. Paris: OECD Publishing.

OECD. 2012. *OECD reviews of regional innovation: Central and southern Denmark.* Paris: OECD Publishing.

OECD. 2018. *Productivity and jobs in a globalised world. (How) can all regions benefit?* Paris: OECD Publishers.

Porter, M. 1998. Location, clusters and the 'new' microeconomics of competition. *Business Economics* 33(1): 7–17.

Porter, M. 2000. Location, competition and economic development: Local clusters in a global economy. *Economic Development Quarterly* 14(1): 15–34.

Productivity Network Insights. 2019. https://productivityinsightsnetwork.co.uk/publicat ions/

Storper, M. 1995. The resurgence of regional economics, ten years later: The region as a nexus of untraded interdependencies. *European Urban and Regional Studies* 2(3): 191–221.

The Danish Council for Research and Innovation Policy. 2017. *Viden i sammenhæng: Danmarks Forsknings- og Innovationspolitiske Råds Årsrapport 2016.* København: Danmarks Forsknings- og Innovationspolitiske Råd.

The Danish Executive Board for Business Development and Growth. 2019. *Strategi for decentral erhvervsfremme.* Draft report.

The Danish Executive Board for Business Development and Growth. 2020. *Erhvervsfreme i Danmark 2020–2023.* Silkeborg: Danish Business Authority.

The Danish Government. 2005. *Regionalpolitisk redegørelse 2005 – Regeringens redegørelse til Folketinget.* Copenhagen: Ministry of Interior Affairs and Health.

The Danish Government. 2016. *Towards a freer, richer and safer Denmark.* Government Platform, The Marienborg Agreement.

Thomsen, M. S. 2020. *Fra regionale vækstmiljøer til nationale styrkepositioner.* RegLab Report.

Tinbergen, J. 1967. *Economic policy: Principles and design.* Chicago: Rand McNally & Company.

Tödtling, F. and Trippl, M. 2005. One size fits all? Towards a differentiated regional innovation policy approach. *Research Policy* 34(8): 1203–1219.

Vrangbæk, K. 2010. Structural reform in Denmark, 2007–09: Central reform processes in a decentralised environment. *Local Government Studies* 36(2): 205–221. doi:10.1080/03003930903560562

Wiegand, B. 2010. Manglende opfølgning hæmmer regional vækstindsats. *Mandag Morgen,* 16.

Wilson, J. 2011. Colonising space: The new economic geography in theory and practice. *New Political Economy* 16(3): 373–397.

Witt, U. 2008. What is specific about evolutionary economics? *Journal of Evolutionary Economics,* 18(5): 547–575.

Wolfe, D. A. (2019). Innovation by design: Impact and Effectiveness of Public Support for Business Innovation. *Annals of Science and Technology Policy* 3(3): 258–347.

Woolthuis, R. K., Lankhuizen, M. and Gilsing, V. 2005. A system failure framework for innovation policy design. *Technovation* 25(6): 609–619.

Part II

Value chains, innovation and inter-organisational relations

5 Supplier firms in transition – the case of Denmark

Poul Houman Andersen, Ina Drejer and Christian Richter Østergaard

5.1 Introduction

Inter-firm relations, including user–producer interactions, play an important role in structuring a national innovation system (Lundvall 2016). However, increasing internationalisation changes the framework for relations between firms. This chapter focuses on how supplier firms in Denmark, like suppliers in other high-cost countries, may face challenges in maintaining their value proposals to local customers as manufacturing activities in these countries decline. Iris Group (2015) reports that employment in manufacturing declined by approximately 500,000 people in the Nordic countries during the period 1991–2013, and a similar trend is seen in other high-cost Western countries. In the 1990s, suppliers frequently enjoyed being close to their customers' production activities (Andersen 1999). Now, digitalisation has improved possibilities for global coordination of value chains and improved conditions for doing business in a wide range of low-cost countries (Holmström and Partanen 2014). Thus, the dominant reason for offshoring from high-cost countries is lower costs (Stehrer et al. 2012). This has contributed to a global shift in the centre of manufacturing from highly industrialised high-cost countries to low-cost countries (Quah 2011). Figures 5.1 and 5.2 clearly illustrate the relocation of activities in the industry sector from Denmark and other high-cost countries to low-cost countries. Supplementary calculations of value added per employee in industry shows that this has increased most rapidly in the East Asia region.[1]

The concerns about survival of suppliers in high-cost countries has spurred a large number of studies that either argue for suppliers' need to relocate or focus on how to improve the framework conditions for supplier firms through industrial policy (e.g. Molnar et al. 2007). However, a relocation of suppliers to low-cost countries in order to improve their competitiveness might have adverse effects on the national competitiveness of the high-cost countries in general. Traditional perspectives on the drivers of national competitiveness often take an atomistic perspective on competitiveness and tend to overlook the innovation dynamics on a system level, as they are described in the innovation system literature and other literature on system level innovation dynamics (Porter 1990; Lundvall 1992; Nelson 1993). According to this approach,

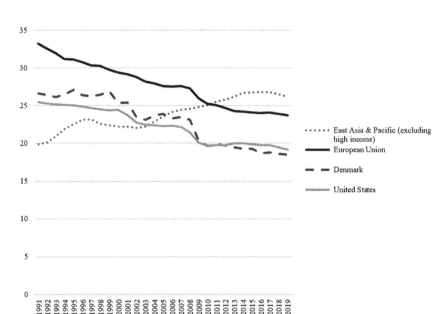

Figure 5.1 Development in industry employment across regions (% of total employment).
Source: Calculations based on own survey data.

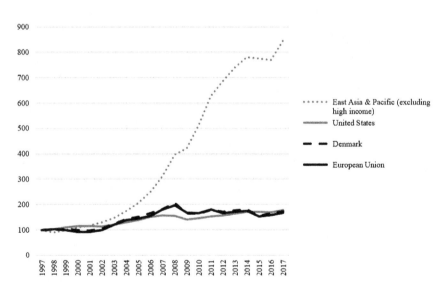

Figure 5.2 Development in value added across regions (current US$, index 1997 = 100).
Source: Calculations based on own survey data.

cooperation and learning benefits accrued through interaction in user–producer relationships is at the heart of an innovation system's international competitiveness (Lundvall 1985; Christensen et al. 2008). Suppliers' development of value-creation activities to maintain customer relationships can be seen at the centre of this dynamic, which is also the focus in this chapter.

Taking a supplier's perspective, the main purpose of this chapter is to deepen our understanding of the value creation activities pursued by suppliers in Denmark in a context of increasing global competition and production relocation. The analysis explores the avenues that suppliers in Denmark have followed in order to continue to maintain and develop relationships with their most important customers.

The analysis is based on a survey of 980 supplier firms in Denmark carried out in 2014, combined with register data on firm characteristics.[2] The survey reveals that although manufacturing is shrinking in Denmark, the share of industrial firms that serve as suppliers has remained relatively stable since a similar survey was carried out in 1994. But the function that suppliers fulfil in relation to their most important customers has changed considerably. As mentioned above, suppliers in high-cost countries face challenges and, accordingly, suppliers in Denmark have been considered to be a relatively vulnerable group of firms. However, when analysing the suppliers further, the vulnerability appears to be exaggerated – at least for the suppliers that have survived the transition – as many suppliers have developed strong ties to their most important customers (Drejer et al. 2015). This chapter presents a data-driven typology of supplier firms in Denmark based on their value creation activities towards their main customers, and discusses this in light of overall characteristics of how firms in the Danish innovation system typically interact. In this sense, we follow in the footsteps of a well-grounded innovation research tradition dating back to Pavitt (1984).

5.2 The changing role of suppliers – a review of the literature

Since the 1990s, manufacturers in Denmark and other high-cost countries have increased their international sourcing activities and established supply chains in low-cost countries (Coucke and Sleuwagen 2008; Statistics Denmark 2008). This development has led to a debate with respect to the implications and future prospects for the manufacturing suppliers in high-cost countries (Scott and Storper 2003). Already in the 1980s and 1990s, there was a growing concern about the competitive decline of firms in high-cost economies due to loss of internal capabilities (Bettis et al. 1992). In turn, both offshoring decisions of customers and the competitive threat from low-cost country suppliers affect domestic suppliers' ability to maintain customer relationships. High-cost country suppliers have experienced that customers strip out standardised components from the most sophisticated activities and in essence move manufacturing activities to low-cost country suppliers (Mudambi and

Venzin 2010). Increasing internationalisation may change the internal cohesiveness of a national innovation system. From a national innovation system perspective, the interaction and corresponding flow of activities between the system elements is a core element for explaining the system's ability to create and maintain innovations (Edquist and Hommen 2008). Notably, user–producer interaction is a central element for generating novelty and innovation, because it can communicate information about technological opportunities as well as user needs and, in some instances, also involve joint problem-solving activities (Lundvall 2016, p. 122). As also discussed by Kringelum et al. (2021, this volume), trust and commitment increase the mutual benefits and general effectiveness of user–producer interactions, which implies that not all relations between suppliers and their users/customers can be prioritised equally, and there may be a tendency to value local relations. It is, however, not a new observation that national innovation systems have become 'leakier', and that internationally oriented firms act as vehicles for internationalisation of innovation systems (Carlsson 2006). However, the emphasis in the national innovation systems literature has been on the *national* elements, and there has been less focus on the international influences on the systems, including on understanding how the accelerating globalisation of value chains and possible erosion of conventional proximity advantages impacts the positioning of suppliers in high-cost country systems. Suppliers from high-cost countries that seek to create value propositions that are attractive to customers in a globally competitive market face the immediate challenge of matching direct cost differentials offered by low-cost country suppliers, but also face challenges with respect to bandwagon effects, as there seems to be a strong consensus among manufacturers about the benefits of sourcing from low-cost countries (Kotabe and Mol 2006). Low-cost country suppliers are increasingly well placed to compete in producing more high value-added types of production. This has been in response to rising wages in several manufacturing sectors (Lee and Ki 2017; Safdar and Gevelt 2020). However, the value propositions of low-cost country suppliers are not necessarily superior (Horn, Schiele and Werner 2013). They may be matched and challenged by high-cost country suppliers.

High-cost country suppliers' ability to initiate, maintain and develop value propositions that differentiate them from their rivals is central to their value chain position. For a supplier, creating a value proposition in a customer relationship comes with choice, since no firms are equally good at providing all forms of value propositions. A supplier must configure a set of activities that is considered valuable by customers while also being resource-coherent and profitable for the supplier.

Our focus in this contribution is on identifying profiles of the supplier firms in Denmark which managed the transition to expand their value proposition towards customers and survive despite the increasing competition from suppliers in low-cost countries. The following sections unfold that data and the methods applied in the analysis.

5.3 Data

The analysis is based on a unique cross-industry dataset on suppliers' relations with their most important customers. This dataset is based on a non-mandatory survey, carried out in 2014, of the total population of 4196 firms in Denmark with at least ten employees (excluding micro firms) in manufacturing industries, as well as a few selected business services industries (see Table 5.1). The survey takes a supplier perspective focusing on the relations and deliveries to the most important customer. The suppliers' deliveries to their most important customers can comprise physical products, components and different types of services.

CEOs and CTOs from 980 firms answered the questionnaire, resulting in a response rate of 23.4%. The survey, which was carried out by Statistics Denmark on behalf of Aalborg University, covered issues such as the location of the customers, the duration of the relationship between the supplier and customer, the customers' economic importance, suppliers' involvement in customers' development projects, type and content of main deliveries, the supplier firms' competencies and statements on the extent of various types of interactions and relations with their most important customers. The survey data are matched with register data from Statistics Denmark on firm size, industry affiliation, employee background and economic performance.

The survey is inspired by a similar survey carried out in Denmark in 1994, thereby allowing the identification of possible changes in general patterns of suppliers' relations with their most important customers between 1994 and 2014.

A comparison of the two surveys (see Table 5.2) shows that suppliers continue to have an important role in the manufacturing sector of Denmark. However, important changes can be found with respect to both the length and the scope of suppliers' collaboration with their most important customers (Drejer et al. 2015).

We have taken a cautious approach in comparing the findings from the 1994 and 2014 surveys, by only counting the suppliers which responded that a specific type of relationship existed to some or to a high extent. Also including suppliers in the 2014 survey which acknowledged that these types of relationships existed to 'a minor extent' would have shown an even more dramatic change. Although the comparisons in Table 5.2 are coarse, they portray a significant change suggesting that relationships between suppliers in Denmark and their most important customers have become closer than arm's length in orientation. It tells a story of a dramatic increase in the scope of buyer–supplier exchange relationships, including both development and production activities. Furthermore, the proportion of contractually governed customer relationships have doubled. This suggests long-term relationship governance rather than adverse competitive regimes in supply chains (Wathne and Heide 2004). It implies that suppliers configure customer relationships in order to maintain strategic positions vis-á-vis their customers. Furthermore, it has become the

Table 5.1 Industries included.

	No. and percentage of firms in population		No. and percentage of firms in respondent group	
Mfr. of food products, beverages and tobacco products	390	9.3%	66	6.7%
Mfr. of textiles, wearing apparel, leather and leather products	79	1.9%	20	2.0%
Mfr. of wood and products of wood and cork, except furniture	104	2.5%	25	2.6%
Mfr. of paper and paper products	60	1.4%	17	1.7%
Printing or reproduction of recorded media	118	2.8%	20	2.0%
Mfr. of coke and refined petroleum products, chemicals and chemical products, basic pharmaceutical products and pharmaceutical preparations	95	2.3%	24	2.4%
Mfr. of rubber and plastic products	188	4.5%	57	5.8%
Mfr. of other non-metallic mineral products	122	2.9%	25	2.6%
Mfr. of basic metals, fabricated metal products, except machinery and equipment	665	15.8%	179	18.3%
Mfr. of computer, electronic and optical products	161	3.8%	42	4.3%
Mfr. of electrical equipment	115	2.7%	32	3.3%
Mfr. of machinery and equipment not elsewhere classified	511	12.2%	112	11.4%
Mfr. of motor vehicles, trailers and semi-trailers and other transport equipment	86	2.0%	15	1.5%
Mfr. of furniture	142	3.4%	28	2.9%
Other manufacturing	81	1.9%	24	2.4%
Repair and installation of machinery and equipment	152	3.6%	29	3.0%
Computer programming, consultancy and related activities	606	14.4%	122	12.4%
Architectural and engineering activities, technical testing and analysis	381	9.1%	106	10.8%
Scientific research and development	87	2.1%	24	2.4%
Specialised design activities	53	1.3%	13	1.3%
Total	*4196*	*100.0%*	*980*	*100.0%*

Table 5.2 Comparing findings from two surveys on Danish suppliers' collaboration with their most important customers.

Supplier survey 1994*		Supplier survey 2014**	
Customers provide components or raw materials to be processed by supplier	18%	Suppliers process materials supplied by customers	25%
Customers frequently exchange new product ideas with suppliers	42%	Customer and supplier collaborate on the development of products and services	81%
Joint R&D activities between customers and suppliers	22%		
Supplier involved in customers' product development	43%		
Customers involved in suppliers' product development	29%		
Products are typically developed based on the customers' technical specifications	45%	Products are developed based on technical specifications	78%
		Products are developed based on customers' specifications	84%
Supply governed by contractual arrangements with customers	34%	Supply governed by long-term contractual arrangements with customers	67%

* The percentage of firms which answered that the specific type of relation existed vis-á-vis the most important customers.
** The percentage of firms which answered that the specific type of relation existed to some or a high degree vis-á-vis the most important customers.

rule rather than the exception that suppliers participate actively in their customers' product and service development activities, testifying a move from arm's length exchange towards more engaged forms of collaboration with customers.

These observations imply that contemporary suppliers in Denmark – taking a more passive role in the past – now actively configure customer relationships in order to maintain strategic positions vis-á-vis their customers, while at the same time being pressured on delivering both cost and value optimisation by their customers. This observation from Denmark is in accordance with findings by Lindgreen et al. (2013), seen from the purchasing perspective of US companies. Furthermore, although the applied data do now provide information on work organisation, the findings of the recent survey are in accordance with other innovation system-related studies that include firm-level data for Denmark, such as Lorenz (2015) and the chapter by Lorenz and Holm (2021, this volume), who find that Denmark together with other Nordic countries has the highest proportion of employees working in industry or service sector firms characterised by a form of work organisation assumed to promote inter firm cooperation.

5.4 Method

In order to identify the different value creation activities that Danish firms pursue in their customer relations, principal factor and cluster analyses are performed on the supplier firms' responses to 24 statements regarding their relations with their most important customers (see Table 5.3). Due to item non-responses, the cluster analyses are carried out on responses from 663 supplier firms.[3] The suppliers are asked to indicate the degree to which they engaged with their key customers in each of the 24 activities expressed in the statements. The engagement is measured on a four-point scale, ranging from 'to a large extent' to 'not at all'. Respondents can also reply 'do not know', but such answers are treated as non-responses in the analyses. Because several of the 24 variables based on the statements are highly correlated, the analyses are carried out in two steps. First, a principal factor analysis is carried out based on the polychoric correlation between the 24 variables. Five factors are retained in the principal factor analysis.[4] The factor loadings of the variables associated with the 24 statements are illustrated in Table 5.3.

Factor 1 relates to *Inter-Organisational Integration* in terms of the degree to which organisational structures and processes are aligned across the organisational interface. Differences in the extent to which employees are exchanged, joint collaboration on new products, the establishment of cross-organisational teams, joint training, etc., all contribute to this notion.

Factor 2 reflects *Openness* in terms of information-sharing activities in the buyer–supplier relationships and indications of the willingness to share information across the organisational interface in terms of, among other things: joint purchasing arrangements, cost reduction sharing and open calculations.

Factor 3 reflects *Commitment* as expressed by customer-specific investments and other obligations taken on by the supplier in the buyer–supplier relationship, such as product responsibilities.

Factor 4 concerns the *Formalisation* of exchange in terms of the extent to which procedures guide interactions. Here, formalisation covers the role of specifications and agreeing to terms of an order.

Finally, factor 5 concerns suppliers' *Standardisation* of products and services in customer relationships. This factor covers items such as supplier specification or adaptation of standard products and services.

In the second step of the analysis, the factor loadings are used as input to a k-means cluster analysis, where a solution with three clusters is chosen as the most stable (Table 5.4). The identified clusters of firms are interpreted as expressions of different value creation activities pursued by suppliers with regards to relations with their most important customers.

Each supplier firm is exclusively associated with one cluster. However, the negative value of the cubic clustering criterion statistic[5] (-3.382), which is a measure of within-cluster homogeneity relative to between-cluster heterogeneity (Ketchen and Shook 1996), indicates a large heterogeneity in the data

Table 5.3 Principal factor analysis – rotated factor pattern.

		Factor 1	Factor 2	Factor 3	Factor 4	Factor 5
1	Collaborates on the development of new products/services	**0.40195**	0.10809	0.29930	0.23852	0.21913
2	Exchanges/posts of employees	**0.59010**	0.16188	-0.17450	0.23839	0.02513
3	Establishes cross-organisational teams	**0.77765**	0.11002	0.07531	0.10765	0.02346
4	Carries out joint training/education	**0.63368**	0.04507	-0.01724	-0.04707	0.16208
5	Cooperates on the optimising of processes	**0.52208**	0.20726	0.13672	0.31664	0.01030
6	Supplies products/services produced according to technical specifications	0.15046	0.22709	**0.44057**	**0.47822**	-0.01586
7	Guarantees certification or other types of documentation or approval	0.04761	0.14389	**0.57978**	0.13918	0.10169
8	Functions as an extra production capacity	0.13734	**0.63236**	-0.02049	0.15880	-0.00694
9	Makes adaptions to materials/intermediate goods supplied by the customer	-0.02600	**0.68575**	0.04275	0.24714	-0.03178
10	Supplies products/services, that are sold under the trademark of the customer	-0.05176	**0.55344**	0.30389	-0.13566	0.06598
11	Uses open calculations	0.35499	**0.51326**	0.08424	0.04946	-0.12036
12	Engages in joint co-operation with approved technical service institutions or universities	**0.49753**	0.14521	0.23207	-0.08314	0.03629
13	Agrees on prices and conditions of delivery per order	0.05303	-0.00446	-0.04847	**0.52347**	0.04513
14	Shares the achieved cost reductions	0.23724	**0.47070**	**0.40275**	-0.02286	-0.09631
15	Enters into long-term contracts	0.38405	0.03667	0.36138	-0.05038	0.02546
16	Integrates technology from other suppliers to the customer	**0.54633**	0.07877	0.23290	0.34096	0.08172
17	Provides advice on customers' technologies or materials	**0.45336**	0.04628	0.26073	**0.41897**	0.06933
18	Engages in joint purchasing	0.35843	**0.57368**	0.19053	-0.03621	0.03583
19	Invests in customer-specific technology, machinery or equipment	0.24634	0.38684	**0.41984**	0.05778	0.06799
20	Supplies products/services according to the customers' specifications	0.03559	0.37940	0.32277	**0.57020**	0.10600
21	Specifies products/services for the customers	0.26968	-0.02980	0.20027	**0.43190**	**0.47335**
22	Adapts standard products/services to the requirements of the customers	0.17637	0.06133	0.13947	0.23698	**0.74814**
23	Supplies standard products/services to the customers	0.00498	-0.12736	-0.01377	-0.12488	**0.70357**
24	Takes on product responsibility for components or systems that are integrated in the products/services of the customer	0.04028	0.10515	**0.42016**	0.15291	0.36277
	Variance explained by each factor	*3.2158*	*2.5141*	*1.8009*	*1.7702*	*1.5584*

Table 5.4 K-means clustering – cluster means.

Cluster	Factor 1	Factor 2	Factor 3	Factor 4	Factor 5
1	−.2072	−.3915	−.6408	−.8131	−.0585
2	0.5290	0.9689	0.1490	−.0651	0.1915
3	−.1630	−.2695	0.2598	0.4431	−.1694

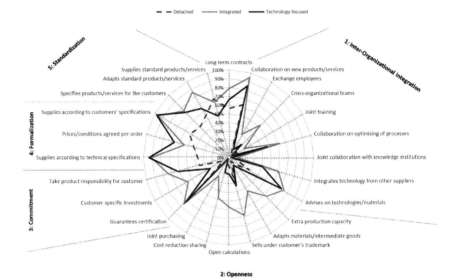

Figure 5.3 Visual overview of value creation activities pursued by the three types of supplier.
Source: Calculations based on own survey data.

with possible outliers. The clusters should thus not be perceived as very stable types of supplier firms, but rather as a grouping of the main types of supplier behaviours towards their most important customers.

The first cluster consists of firms that are characterised by engaging very little with their customers, reflected in the negative mean values of all five factors for this cluster. Accordingly, this cluster is labelled *Detached Suppliers*. The second cluster consists of firms with high means for factors 1, 2 and 5, reflecting suppliers with a wide scope of engagement with customers. These can be labelled as *Integrated Suppliers*. The third cluster consists of firms with high means for factors 3 and 4, reflecting suppliers with a strong emphasis on technical and technology-related aspects in their engagements with customers. This cluster can be labelled *Technology-focused Suppliers*.

Figure 5.3 provides a visualisation of the three identified types of value creation activities in terms of the extent to which each supplier type takes on each of the 24 different activities in the buyer–supplier relationships. The 24 activities are grouped into the five factors identified in the principal factor analysis based on the correlation between the variables explaining each factor.

It is apparent from Figure 5.3 that there are many similarities between the *Integrated* and the *Technology-focused* supplier types. Both types of suppliers engage closely with customers. However, there is a decisive difference in the scope of activities provided. The *Integrated* suppliers generally seek to align as many types of activities as possible. *Technology-focused* suppliers, on the other hand, adapt fewer types of activities to their customers. The activities that *Technology-focused* suppliers adopt are mainly linked to the provision of technology inputs to their customers. The limited area outlined for the *Detached* suppliers in Figure 5.3 illustrates that this type of supplier mainly provides standard offerings and in general is involved in a few different types of activities with their customers. The following sections provide more detailed characteristics of the three identified supplier types.

5.5 Supplier types in Denmark: characterising the different approaches followed by suppliers

Combining the survey data with register data on industry affiliation, financial accounts and employee information allows for a comparison of characteristics between the firms in the three identified types of supplier firms. Table 5.5 shows the industry and size distribution of firms across the three types of supplier firms, the share of firms that import and export, as well as the location of the most important customer, while Table 5.6 provides a more detailed characteristic of the firms assigned to each type. Table 5.7 presents the results of a multiple logistic regression model of supplier types, which allows for a detailed comparison of firms' likelihood of being classified as an Integrated supplier or Technology-focused supplier relative to being a detached supplier. The data presented in the three tables is now discussed in detail during the description of the three types.

5.5.1 Detached suppliers

The detached suppliers account for the smallest share of analysed firms (19%). Of those, 36% have fewer than 20 employees and 80% have fewer than 50 employees. Moreover, 35% of the firms are in services, which in the current analysis includes five service subsectors assumed to be closely related to manufacturing (see Table 5.1), and 36% are low-tech manufacturing firms. Responses show that 87% of the detached suppliers report that their most important customer is located in Denmark or one of the three neighbouring countries, Sweden, Norway and Germany.

Table 5.6 reveals that the detached suppliers' mean number of 19 employees is substantially lower than the integrated suppliers.

Table 5.5 Industry and size distribution of the different supplier types, as well as location of the most important customer.

		Detached	Integrated	Technology-focused
Share of analysed firms		19%	35%	46%
High-tech manufacturing		4%	7%	3%
Medium-/high-tech manufacturing		16%	23%	21%
Medium-/low-tech manufacturing		14%	30%	24%
Low-tech manufacturing		36%	21%	23%
Services		35%	20%	29%
Fewer than 20 employees		36%	28%	38%
20–49 employees		44%	38%	38%
50–99 employees		12%	17%	14%
100+ employees		8%	18%	10%
Export		71%	83%	67%
Import		71%	79%	74%
Location of the most	Denmark	74%	67%	71%
important customer	Germany	5%	7%	5%
	Sweden	5%	5%	3%
	USA	5%	3%	3%
	Norway	3%	3%	3%
N (weighted)		130	237	315

Note: Weighted according to the size and industry distribution of the population.
Source: Own calculations based on survey and register data.

The detached suppliers are characterised by supplying standard products or services to their main customers, including customised standard products or services. They also frequently supply products or services that are specified by their customers. The detached suppliers also often enter long-term contracts with their customers, but as Table 5.6 shows, the mean duration of the most important customer is 16 years, which is only slightly higher than the Integrated suppliers. The detached suppliers are characterised by a much more limited extent of interactions with their main customers than the other two supplier types. Figure 5.3 shows that, typically, the detached suppliers do not collaborate with their main customers on organisational and employee-related areas such as exchange of employees or using cross-organisational teams. In general, they score low on the factors reflecting inter-organisation integration and openness. This could potentially limit their importance for user-producer type of innovation collaboration with their main customers. However, most of the detached suppliers also collaborate with their main customers on the development of new products and services. This might seem at odds with the low extent of interaction with their customers compared to the other supplier types, but the detached suppliers have the highest share of highly educated employees (12%). Thus, it seems that the detached suppliers rely on a relatively highly skilled workforce and automation.

Table 5.6 Characteristics of the different supplier types.

	Detached		Integrated		Technology-focused	
	Mean	Median	Mean	Median	Mean	Median
Employees (FTE)	49	22	100	33	51	22
Share of highly educated employees	0.12	0.04	0.09	0.03	0.11	0.04
Most important customer's share of turnover	22	15	31	25	23	17
Duration of relationship with most important customer (years)	16	12	15	14	16	14
Growth in FTE 2012–2015	0.07	0.10	0.06	0.04	0.004	0.05
Value added per FTE 2015 (DKK)	654,212	575,713	690,048	621,337	697,416	646,536
Growth in value added per FTE 2012–2015	0.11	0.07	0.04	0.06	0.15	0.08
N (weighted)	118		231		297	

Note: Outliers are removed in the calculations of growth rates. The average growth in FTE in 2012–2015 is calculated by the following formula in order to avoid problems of high growth in very small firms distorting the results: (FTE 2015 − FTE 2012)/((FTE 2015 + FTE 2012/2)). A similar method is used for value added growth measures.
Source: Own calculations based on survey and register data.

Table 5.7 Multiple logistic regression model of supplier types.

Parameter	Benchmark: Detached	Integrated			Technology-focused		
		Estimate	Standard error	Pr > ChiSq	Estimate	Standard error	Pr > ChiSq
Intercept		−2.089	0.610	0.001	−0.389	0.559	0.486
Employees, FTE (log)		0.422	0.138	0.002	0.147	0.135	0.279
Share of highly educated employees		0.096	1.044	0.927	0.923	0.908	0.309
Most important customer's share of turnover		0.026	0.006	0.000	0.003	0.006	0.657
Duration of relationship with most important customer (years)		−0.018	0.010	0.070	−0.000	0.009	0.973
Value added per FTE 2015		0.000	0.000	0.678	0.000	0.000	0.173
Export (yes/no)		0.565	0.329	0.085	−0.406	0.285	0.154
Import (yes/no)		−0.068	0.330	0.838	0.323	0.298	0.278
Industry: benchmark services	Low-tech manufacturing	−0.108	0.420	0.797	0.038	0.374	0.919
	Medium-/low-tech manufacturing	1.185	0.455	0.009	0.972	0.422	0.021
	Medium-/high-tech manufacturing	0.553	0.458	0.227	0.613	0.421	0.145
	High-tech manufacturing	0.873	0.600	0.146	−0.543	0.664	0.413
N (weighted)							641
R^2							0.14

The detached suppliers appear to be very different from the standard suppliers with an arms-length relationship that was the dominant supplier type in Denmark in the early 1990s (Andersen and Christensen 1998). The detached supplier type has a higher level and extent of interaction with their most important customer – which may explain why the detached suppliers are no less inclined than the Integrated and Technology-focused suppliers to identify customers located in relative geographical proximity as the most important ones[6] – and also have a highly-educated workforce. Furthermore, they are not in any apparent financial distress or decline. The detached suppliers have had the highest growth in full-time equivalent (FTE) during 2012–2015 and also a high growth in value-added per FTE. They do, however, still have a slightly lower than average level of value added per FTE in 2015 compared to the other two supplier types.

5.5.2 *Technology-focused suppliers*

Technology-focused suppliers comprise the largest group of firms in the sample (46%). Table 5.7 reveals that they are more likely to be found in medium-/low-tech manufacturing compared to the detached suppliers. The average firm size is 51 employees, which is less than the Integrated suppliers, and approximately the same average size as the detached suppliers. Responses show that 82% of the technology-focused suppliers identify Denmark, Norway, Sweden or Germany as the location of their most important customer.

The technology-focused suppliers have the highest average value-added per FTE of the three supplier types and also the highest growth in value added per FTE during 2012–2015. The median growth rate of FTE during 2012–2015 is 5%, but the average growth is barely positive, since some firms have declined. The technology-focused suppliers are in general characterised by a broader extent of interaction with their main customers compared to the detached suppliers, but less than the integrated suppliers. Most of technology-focused suppliers are collaborating with their main customers on the development of new products or services. They provide their customers with advice on materials, and guarantee certification or provide other types of documentation of products or services. They also score high on the formalisation factor by supplying according to customers' specifications or technical specifications. The majority of the technology-focused suppliers take on product responsibility for components or systems that are integrated into the customers' products or services. They have a higher share of highly educated employees (11%) than the integrated suppliers. The characteristics of the technology-focused suppliers to some extent fit with the profile of the development orientated type of suppliers that accounted for 34% of the firms in Denmark in 1994 (Andersen and Christensen 1998). However, in addition to participating in the customers' development activities and entering long-term contracts with the main customer, the development-oriented suppliers also invested in customer-specific specific technology and machinery. Only a minority of the technology-focused suppliers do that.

5.5.3 Integrated suppliers

The integrated suppliers account for 35% of the analysed firms. The integrated supplier firms are more likely to be found in medium-/low-tech manufacturing compared to the detached supplier type. On average, the firms employ 100 people, and the average share of highly educated employees is 9%. The most important customers' share of turnover accounts for 31% on average, which is higher than for the other supplier types. The main characteristic of the Integrated suppliers is the broad scope of collaboration with their main customers. They score high on the factors related to inter-organisational integration and openness. Nearly all collaborate with their main customers on the development of new products and/or establish cross-organisational teams with their main customers. They also collaborate with the main customers on process optimisation and advice on technology as well as integrating technology from other suppliers. They also score high on commitment in terms of taking product responsibility and invest in customer-specific technology, machinery or equipment. In contrast, they also adapt standard products and services to the requirements of the customer, as well as supplying standard products and services and acting as extra production capacity for the customers.

The integrated suppliers are characterised by a broad scope and a high degree of customer-specificity in their value creation activities. One the one hand, they are very active in knowledge sharing activities and contribute to the main customers' innovation activities, but on the other hand, they are also involved in a range of activities related to standardisation and formalisation. Thus, they offer a broad spectrum of activities. This capacity to engage widely with customers is probably related to the Integrated suppliers' larger average size. It is worth noticing, that despite the close integration with the most important customers, the Integrated suppliers have the lowest share of firms (although 82% is still a high proportion) reporting that the most important customer is located in Denmark or in one of the three neighbouring countries.

5.6 Concluding discussion

This chapter has described three contemporary – and by all accounts also viable – strategies for interaction with and activities provided for important customers, followed by Danish supplier firms. The Danish innovation system has for decades been characterised as interaction-oriented (e.g., Christensen et al. 2008). Nonetheless, the analyses presented in this chapter, when compared to similar analyses based on data from the 1990s, indicate that inter-firm interactions – at least when looking at customer–supplier interactions – has evolved further, to the extent that strong ties between suppliers and their most important customers are now characteristic of the two most dominant types of supplier firms' value-creating activities towards their main customers. And even the most detached type of supplier strategy involves selected elements of close interaction. The Danish innovation system has become more international with distributed innovation activities, relocation of production, increasing participation in global value chains and exports/imports. However, the suppliers participate in a larger extent in user–producer interaction activities. The national innovation system literature tends to focus on national interactions and knowledge flows, which is also important for the Danish suppliers as between two-thirds and three-quarters of the suppliers have their most important customer in Denmark. However, the integrated suppliers who have the greatest scope of interaction with their customers, are the type of supplier that are most likely to export and have their most important customers outside Denmark more frequently than the other types.

We have analysed this transition in supplier activities towards the most important customers in the wake of the increasing internationalisation and global relocation of manufacturing activities, which is facilitated by digitalisation-supported coordination opportunities. This could have been detrimental to the 'Danish way' of inter-firm interaction and, accordingly, altered the structure of the Danish innovation system. However, this does not seem to have been the case, even when it comes to the types of firms that have been assumed to be most vulnerable in the global competitive game, namely the typical relatively small suppliers to the manufacturing sector, which are facing strong price competition from suppliers in low-cost countries. The proportion of manufacturing jobs has declined in Denmark, just as is the case in other high-cost countries; and some Danish supplier firms have without doubt been outperformed by international competitors. One of the limitations of this chapter's analysis is that we are not able to systematically follow which supplier firms have gone out of business over the last couple of decades and which firms have been able to transform and adjust to the changing conditions. But the Danish supplier firms have not been wiped out, nor are there any indications of them having entered into a race-to-the-bottom competition with suppliers in low-cost countries. On the contrary, it seems as if the surviving supplier firms have extended their collaborative activities with their main customers with point of departure in what has been considered one the traditional strengths of the Danish innovation system, and thereby been able to continue the further development of this particular trait of the system. One aspect that has been discussed in relation to this is the link between the doing, using and interacting (DUI) mode in innovation systems and innovation and learning in buyer–supplier relationships (Jensen et al. 2007). A possible mechanism for explaining the persistence of Danish suppliers' relationships to key customers in spite of global competitive pressure from low-cost countries can be proposed in the linkage between the changing scope of collaboration and its ability to support a more varied and broader spectrum of innovation and learning forms. A further exploration of this question is a task for future research.

Notes

1 Calculations are based on estimated data from the World Bank Database and the International Labour Organisation's ILOSTAT database. Over the period 1997 to 2006, the increase in the East Asia and Pacific (excluding high income) region has exceeded the increase in the European Union, Denmark and the United States by a factor of at

least 2.5. This indicates that even if increased automation can explain some of the declining employment in industry in high-cost countries, this is more than out-weighed by the catching up of countries in the East Asia and Pacific region.

2 Because of incomplete responses to the survey, as well as missing data for some firms in the register data, our analyses are generally based on fewer than 980 observations.

3 With the exception of the proportion of suppliers that process materials supplied by customers, which is only 17% for the firms included in the principal factor and cluster analysis, compared to 25% for all respondents in the survey, these firms have a distribution similar to all respondents in terms of the aspects of collaboration with their most important customers, which are shown in Table 5.2.

4 In principal factor analysis, it is quite common with negative eigenvalues because the data do not fit the common factor model perfectly. This causes the cumulative proportion of variance explained to exceed 1 for several factors. According to the guidelines provided by SAS Institute Inc. (2013), the cumulative proportion of variance explained by the retained factors should in these cases be approximately 1 for principal factor analysis. This criterion has been applied in the decision to retain five factors.

5 As a rule of thumb, a value of the cubic clustering criterion statistic greater than 2 indicates 'good' clusters; values between 0 and 2 indicate potential clusters that should be used with caution; and large negative values can indicate outliers in the data.

6 The detached suppliers are in fact the supplier type that most frequently identify Denmark, Sweden, Norway or Germany as the location of the most important customer.

References

Andersen, P. H. and Christensen, P. R. 1998. *Den Globale Udfordring: Danske Underleverandørers Internationalisering*. Erhvervsministeriet: Erhvervsfremme Styrelsen.

Andersen, P. H. 1999. Organizing international technological collaboration in subcontractor relationships: an investigation of the knowledge-stickiness problem. *Research Policy*, 28(6), 625–642.

Andersen, P. H., Drejer, I., Østergaard, C. R., Søberg, P. V. and Wæhrens, B. V. 2019. Supplier value creation configurations in high-cost countries. *Journal of Global Operations and Strategic Sourcing*, 12(3), 429–448.

Bettis, R. A., Bradley, S. P. and Hamel, G. 1992. Outsourcing and industrial decline. *Academy of Management Perspectives*, 6(1), 7–22.

Carlsson, B. 2006. Internationalization of innovation systems: A survey of the literature. *Research Policy*, 35(1), 56–67.

Christensen, J. L., Gregersen, B., Johnson, B., Lundvall, B. and Tomlinson, M. 2008. An NSI in transition? Denmark. In *Small Country Innovation Systems – Globalization, Change and Policy in Asia and Europe*, ed. Edquist, C. and Hommen, L. E. Cheltenham: Edward Elgar, 403–441.

Coucke, K. and Sleuwaegen, L. 2008. Offshoring as a survival strategy: Evidence from manufacturing firms in Belgium. *Journal of International Business Studies*, 39(8), 1261–1277.

Drejer, I., Andersen, P. H., Østergaard, C. R., Wæhrens, B. V., Johansen, J., Park, E. and Søberg, P. V. 2015. *En kortlægning af underleverandører i Danmark*. Copenhagen: Industriens Fond.

Edquist, C. and Hommen, L. 2008. Comparing national systems of innovation in Asia and Europe: Theory and comparative framework. In *Small Country Innovation Systems. Globalization, Change and Policy in Asia and Europe*, eds. Edquist, C. and Hommen, L. E. Cheltenham: Edward Elgar, 1–28.

Holmström, J. and Partanen, J. 2014. Digital manufacturing-driven transformations of service supply chains for complex products. *Supply Chain Management: An International Journal*, 19(4), 421–430.

Horn, P., Schiele, H. and Werner, W. 2013. The "ugly twins": Failed low-wage-country sourcing projects and their expensive replacements. *Journal of Purchasing and Supply Management*, 19(1), 27–38.

Jensen, M. B., Johnson, B., and Lorenz, E. 2007. Forms of knowledge and modes of innovation. *Research Policy*, 36(5), 680–693.

Ketchen, D. J. and Shook, C. L. 1996. The application of cluster analysis in strategic management research: An analysis and critique. *Strategic Management Journal*, 17(6), 441–458.

Kotabe, M. and Mol, M. J. 2006. International sourcing: Redressing the balance. In *Handbook of Global Supply Chain Management*, eds. Mentzer, J. T., Myers, M. B. and Stank, T. P., London: Sage Publications, 393–406.

Kringelum, L. B., Gjerding, A. N. and Taran, Y. 2021. Collaborative business models in innovation systems: the case of physical infrastructures. In *Globalisation, New and Emerging Technologies, and Sustainable Development – The Danish Innovation System in Transition*, eds. Christensen, J. L., Gregersen, B., Holm, J. R. and Lorenz, E. Abingdon: Routledge.

Lee, K., and Ki, J. H. 2017. Rise of latecomers and catch-up cycles in the world steel industry. *Research Policy*, 46(2), 365–375.

Lindgreen, A., Vanhamme, J., van Raaij, E. M. and Johnston, W. J. 2013. Go configure: The mix of purchasing practices to choose for your supply base. *California Management Review*, 55(2), 72–96.

Lorenz, E. 2015. Work organisation, forms of employee learning and labour market structure: Accounting for international differences in workplace innovation. *Journal of the Knowledge Economy*, 6(2), 437–466.

Lorenz, E. and Holm, J. R. 2021. Workplace innovation and working conditions in Denmark. In *Globalisation, New and Emerging Technologies and Sustainable Development – The Danish Innovation System in Transition*, eds. Christensen, J. L., Gregersen, B., Holm, J. R. and Lorenz, E. Abingdon: Routledge.

Lundvall, B.-Å. 1985. *Product Innovation and User-Producer Interaction*. IKE research report.

Lundvall, B.-Å. 1992. User-producer relationships, national systems of innovation and internationalisation. In *National Systems of Innovation: Towards a Theory of Innovation and Interactive Learning*, ed. Lundvall, B.-Å., Pinter Publishers, 45–67.

Lundvall, B.-Å. 2016. National systems of innovation: Towards a theory of innovation and interactive learning. In *The Learning Economy and the Economics of Hope*, ed. Lundvall, B.-Å., 85–106. London: Anthem Press.

Molnar, M., Pain, N. and Taglioni, D. 2007. *The Internationalisation of Production, International Outsourcing and Employment in the OECD*. OECD Economics Department Working Papers, No. 561, OECD Publishing. doi:10.1787/167350640103

Mudambi, R. and Venzin, M. 2010. The strategic nexus of offshoring and outsourcing decisions. *Journal of Management Studies*, 47(8), 1510–1533.

Nelson, R. R. (ed.). 1993. *National Innovation Systems: A Comparative Analysis*. New York: Oxford University Press.

Nordic Council of Ministers (Norden)Iris Group. 2015. Digitalisation and automation in the Nordic manufacturing sector – Status, potentials and barriers. *TemaNord*, 2015, 578.

Pavitt, K. 1984. Sectoral patterns of technical change: Towards a taxonomy and a theory. *Research Policy*, 13, 343–373.

Porter, M. E. 1990. *The Competitive Advantage of Nations*. New York: Free Press

Quah, D. 2011. The global economy's shifting centre of gravity. *Global Policy*, 2(1), 3–9.

Safdar, M. T. and Gevelt, T. V. 2020. Catching up with the 'Core': The nature of the agricultural machinery sector and challenges for Chinese manufacturers. *The Journal of Development Studies*, 56(7), 1349–1366.

SAS Institute Inc. 2013. *SAS/STAT® 13.1 User's Guide*. Cary, NC: SAS Institute Inc.

Scott, A., and Storper, M., 2003. Regions, globalization, development. *Regional Studies*, 37(6–7), 579–593.

Statistics Denmark. 2008. *International Sourcing*. Copenhagen: Statistics Denmark.

Stehrer, R., Borowiecki, M., Dachs, B. et al. 2012. *Global Value Chains and the EU Industry*. Verein 'Wiener Inst. für Internat. Wirtschaftsvergleiche' (WIIW).

Wathne, K. H. and Heide, J. B. 2004. Relationship governance in a supply chain network. *Journal of Marketing*, 68(1), 73–89.

6 Collaborative business models in innovation systems – the case of physical infrastructure

Louise B. Kringelum, Allan Næs Gjerding and Yariv Taran

6.1 The role and importance of modern ports in regional innovation systems

Modern ports are spatial settings that hold great potential for regional development (Pettit and Beresford 2009; Hall and Jacobs 2010; Cahoon et al. 2013; De Martino et al. 2013; Sakalayen et al. 2016). The potential comprises the development of existing economic activities as well as the innovative development and attraction of new economic activities. Most importantly, ports are hubs for agglomeration economies and locational advantages where companies within the port perimeter and the port hinterland tap into global and national logistics and value chains. In effect, ports are instrumental in creating both direct and indirect effects on value creation and employment growth in regional systems of innovation. As will be shown later in this chapter the contribution of ports evolves along the same lines by which economic spaces or industrial districts contribute to national systems of innovation.

In Denmark, where almost 80% of all foreign trade depends on the inbound and outbound activities within industrial ports (Port Transformation 2018), the direct and indirect effects of ports have been monitored since mid-2000s.[1] While only 1200 jobs can be associated directly with the operation of industrial ports, around 10% of total Danish employment is indirectly associated with activities within the port perimeter and the port hinterland. The indirect effects vary considerably across industrial ports, in the range 5–15%. When regarding the five largest ports in Denmark they are similar in terms of traditional maritime activities but differ by developing distinct areas of specialisation and hinterland engagement. While the Port of Aarhus on the east coast of Jutland specialises in containerised logistics, the Port of Esbjerg on the west coast of Jutland specialises in fishery, offshore coal and gas and offshore wind. The Port of Copenhagen has merged with the Port of Malmö in Sweden to create a logistics hub for shipping activities in the Baltic Sea area. The Port of Odense has become a hub of national importance for research and production in robotics and the Port of Aalborg (henceforth referred to as PoAa) is specialising in developing sustainable hinterland activities by attracting companies and cooperating with knowledge institutions, including the nearby Aalborg University.

The common denominator for these different patterns of specialisation is the need for the management of industrial ports to engage with a variety of firms, companies, knowledge institutions and authorities. The recurrent monitoring of the direct and indirect effects of ports reflects an increasing political interest in the role of ports in the regional and national economy, which has led to various national policy schemes on maritime industrial and technological development. Furthermore, Danish ports are entwined in local and regional innovation and industrial policies where local and regional political influence is secured by a significant portion of politicians at the board of directors. In effect, the management of ports, referred from hereon as 'port authority',[2] increasingly find themselves in a position where they proactively take part in establishing new innovative lines of economic activities within the port perimeter and the hinterland.

In the following, we analyse the implications of this development by exploring the role of port authorities in promoting collaborative business models in a regional innovation system development context. First, we discuss the role of modern ports in innovation systems at a more general level, and we argue that the proactive role of port authorities can be analysed in terms of collaborative business models of value creation. Second, we describe the evolution of modern ports and how this evolution is associated with value creation. Third, we apply a case study of the PoAa to dig further into the role of the modern port. The case study illustrates that modern ports are evolving into local and regional innovation systems, where value creation depends on the institutionalisation of economic behaviour and collective learning (Lundvall 2010; Asheim 2012; Doloreux et al. 2019). Finally, we discuss our findings, and propose scholarly and managerial implications.

6.1.1 The systemic role of modern ports in innovation systems

Modern ports are increasingly becoming an important arena for the co-evolution of firms, institutions and other types of organisations in ways that contribute to the dynamics of regional and national systems of innovation (Hall and Jacobs 2010; Cahoon et al. 2013; De Martino et al. 2013; Sakalayen et al. 2016). While asset specificities and economies of scale remain important properties of competitive advantage in ports, collaborative value creation and capture among actors within port systems is increasingly being identified as the nexus for not only port competitiveness, but also competitiveness of actors within port systems (De Martino et al. 2019).

Innovation systems, whether at the national or regional level, can be understood as 'constituted by a network of nodes and linkages between various actors, agencies and organisations, which contribute to promoting innovation in societies', and where an 'innovation system contains a core as well as a wider setting' (Asheim 2019, p. 11). The role of modern ports in innovation systems can be understood at two levels of aggregation. First, ports are part of the national and international infrastructure that support the exchange of final goods and intermediaries across markets and industries. Second, ports are part of innovation networks that contribute to regional development (Cahoon, Pateman and Chen 2013) by creating collaborative governance across value chains and logistic interfaces which facilitates clustering of organisational actors (Haugstetter and Cahoon 2010).

In this latter respect, ports over time have increasingly become systems of concerted action among organisational actors, which rely on relational or 'social' capital in the sense of trust, commitment and shared understandings supporting knowledge exchange and cooperation (Kale et al. 2000; Welbourne and Pardo-del-Val 2009; Fukuyama 1995; Putnam 1995). For these reasons, modern ports can be understood in terms of an industrial space (Scott and Storper 1988) in which, as emphasised by Doloreux et al. (2019, p. 1168) in their analysis of territorial innovation models, *'social capital plays a significant role in territorial cohesion'*. How cohesion among organisational actors comes about depends on the style of governance and the type of innovation, as we show in the case analysis in Section 6.3.

6.1.2 Collaborative business models as vehicles of concerted action

The tendency to establish concerted action within ports implies that economic activities are not only being coordinated, but also come about as co-operation on, and co-creation of, value and value capture across business models (Kringelum and Gjerding 2018). We call these phenomena *collaborative business models*, where 'collaborative' implies that economic actors share resources in pursuit of mutual and/or individual goals. However, in order to do so, the economic actors in question must engage in qualitative change of the institutional setup of economic activities by dissolving the boundaries of existing business models. In order to understand this phenomenon, two important aspects must be considered.

First, a collaborative business model is an institutional arrangement between two or more actors that need to coordinate activities. In consequence, collaborative business models are organisational forms which are neither market, nor hierarchy, but something in between depending on appropriate forms of governance such as partnerships, portfolios of relationships, and networks (Powell 1990; Håkansson and Ford 2002; Wilkinson and Young 2002; Ritter et al. 2004).

Second, a collaborative business model implies *innovation* in that current activities across a set of collaborating partners are being changed or even replaced in order to improve the collaborators' position at the market. Moreover, collaboration implies that the analysis of business models focuses on how firms co-create and evolve new ways of value creation and capture, which challenge the traditional notion of firm-centric value creation and capture (Zott et al. 2011).

Thus, the transformation of ports and the creation of new collaborative business models are considered co-evolutionary phenomena with an inherent dialectical relationship. As port authorities are adjusting to a new competitive landscape, business models across the port system are changing and likewise, the expectations of port authority business models are changing (Kringelum 2019). One way of managing these interrelationships and changes is by developing collaborative business models.

6.1.3 Value creation across port generations

European ports are often described as developing across a number of successive port generations (UNCTAD 1992; Beresford et al. 2004). These generations represent a sequence of qualitative change in policy, strategy, scope and organisational arrangement of port activities. When developing from one generation to another, port authorities are radically changing their value creation and value capture, which reflects a process of taking on new business models. However, the process of evolving by managing and mastering the value creation of existing and new generations at the same time (Gjerding and Kringelum 2018) is rarely described, and the complexity inherent in the process is not explicated. Just like the most advanced of ports will have remnants from previous generations (Beresford et al. 2004), there appears to be no determinism as to whether a port *must* proceed to advance to the next generation. As evident in the competitive nature of port landscapes, different generations and specialisations within generations of ports co-exist with each fulfilling their strategy based on a business model that is in alignment with the need of the hinterland and economic actors in the specific port system.

According to the United Nations Conference on Trade and Development (UNCTAD), the first generation of ports were 'merely the interface locations for cargo between land and sea transport' (1992. p. 13) characterised by low value-added activities governed by informal relationships between the port and its users (Beresford et al. 2004. p. 95). During the 1960s, the scope of port activities gradually became larger with an increasing focus on the improvement of value added, and the relationship between the port and its users became closer and more formalised. While the labour/capital ratio had been a decisive factor in the activities of first-generation ports, access to capital became more dominant in second-generation ports. Third-generation ports that emerged in the 1980s are characterised by a strong position in international value chains, diversity of services offered and knowledge-intensive production methods. Thus, while capital is still a decisive factor, technology and know-how aimed at guiding information flows and improving activities have become more important as drivers for growth and increasing scope of activities. At the same time, ports have become vehicles for industrial agglomeration, contributing widely to local and regional development.

This evolution of ports has changed the system of *governance* from one of loose coordination between the port, its users, and the local and regional authorities, to one of closer integration between port authorities, user strategies, and public policies for industrial and economic change. These changes have interacted with industrial, technological and social *innovation* aimed at creating a diversity of knowledge-intensive production and services contributing both to commercial activities and to the development of local and regional industrial districts through agglomeration and interfaces between business models.

Theoretically and practically, this development has induced a discussion on what the next generation of ports may look like. In 1999, UNCTAD (1999) proposed that fourth-generation ports may become horizontally integrated by common operating and administrative activities (Kaliszewski 2018). Nevertheless, the fourth-generation port concepts fall short of grasping most contemporary challenges in port development including logistics integration and trade systems and security (Lee et al. 2018). In addition, it overlooks technological and non-technological innovations that are necessary (De Martino et al. 2013), expectations of supporting sustainability both environmentally and socially (de Langen and van der Lugt 2006) and adjusting to a more commercial customer-centric community focus (Flynn et al. 2011; Lee and Lam 2016) as a part of becoming a fifth-generation port.

In fifth-generation ports, port authorities are increasingly expected to manage multiple interlinked business models that create value for various port users and stakeholders that hold various expectations and requirements. In consequence, port authorities need to be aware of the interdependence of the dual and often triple foci underlying the various business models in order to manage the challenges of business model innovation inherent in developing ports towards the next generation (Kringelum 2019).

Based on the introduction of ports as part of both national and regional innovation systems, we argue that managing port generation shifts presupposes both the implicit and explicit development of not just the focal business model of the port authority but also the challenge of developing collaborative business models to create value for and with customers and stakeholders across the port system. The change process is illustrated in Sections 6.2 and 6.3 through a case study of the PoAa, which in the past five years, has attempted to organise to create value as a third- and potentially fourth-generation port. As exemplified in the case study, the development of collaborative business models presupposes a transformation and innovation of the value creation logic of port authorities, as well the interaction with and role of port actors in the port ecosystem. This, in turn, presupposes development of relation capital within the port system (Vale et al. 2017; Gjerding and Kringelum 2018).

6.2 The port of Aalborg – case study

As ports progress from one generation to another complexity increases, causing many challenges to port authorities, which need to adopt and amend their managerial, governance and administrative processes and behaviour, so they fit the profile of the new port generation characteristics. The challenges for port authorities are thus threefold:

Firstly, from a port innovation perspective, port authorities face challenges in: 1) understanding what is the right timing for initiating a generation shift, 2) developing new capabilities that will stimulate the growth of the new intended port generation, 3) leading and running successfully the actual transition process and 4) sustaining and ensuring that the new evolving port generation will run efficiently and effectively alongside the existing activities that co-exist from previous generations.

Secondly, from an inter- and intra-firm perspective, port authorities must adopt a systemic approach to establishing relational capital through collaboration, thus developing relational capabilities in structures of value co-creation and co-capture is of an increasing demand (Gjerding and Kringelum 2018).

Thirdly, from a broader perspective, given that an increasing number of stakeholders are involved through generation shifts, it is also important to learn what is the expected role of port authorities and their affiliation to their external environment, e.g., regional/national innovation systems, clusters and/or business ecosystems.

Combining these three challenges together indicates that port authorities need to rethink not only their own organisational roles, but also the structures and business models of all stakeholders involved in that transition process, given that each generation is demanding increasing connectivity, but also co-dependency, between different stakeholders. The case study of the PoAa exemplifies one way of managing a complex web of value creation within a medium-sized port authority through collaborative business model innovation, as a part of organising the value creation for the next generation port.

6.2.1 Case description

The PoAa is an inland port located in the largest and most important municipality in northern Jutland and is currently the fifth largest port in Denmark. The port authority[3] that manages the value creation processes of the PoAa is a municipality-owned private limited company. Due to rising competitive pressure on logistics, in recent years the PoAa has focused on developing the local area as an industrial park with joint initiatives in both logistics and sustainability for regional growth. With less than a quarter of the revenue stemming from ship and goods tax, the need for capturing value through services, building rental and infrastructure development is essential for the port authority. In addition, being a municipality-owned private limited company requires a continuous focus on facilitating development, growth and employment regionally.

In order to manage the value creation of the PoAa towards a third and potentially a fourth-generation port, in 2013 the port authority developed a strategic vision to become 'The Intelligent Port of Aalborg'. According to the port's annual report this involved:

> the transformation from being an infrastructure port, attending to the industrial business to be a modern port attending to a society, where value creation is based on knowledge in and around products and processes to … work with operations, ideas and solutions which combine the needs of

companies and society, in a way that creates value, knowledge and development in both the business community and society.

(Aalborg Havn 2013)

This vision encompasses various dimensions of value creation due to the multiplicity of customer segments and stakeholders for which the PoAa provides services. Currently, 117 companies are located at the port area of which many are small and medium sized. They compete in a diverse range of industries with a few informal clusters of, e.g., wind energy and cement production.

To translate the vision into a viable strategy while making it more tangible for both employees and stakeholders, the strategy was structured around three intertwined organisational roles of the port authority (Aalborg Havn 2015; Gjerding and Kringelum 2015; Gjerding and Kringelum 2016):

(1) The role as a *firm* managing inward and outward-bound logistics on a commercial basis with the aim of generating profit for the shareholders and accumulating capital for future investments to ensure growth through self-sufficient investments.
(2) The role as a *frame* for firms operating within the spatial boundaries of the port perimeter. This entails providing, servicing and actively managing the framework of trade within the port system as a competitive advantage for firms located at the area with the potential for collective business development and regional employment growth.
(3) The role as an *integrator* of cooperation and clustering through the establishment of networks of firms, knowledge institutions and authorities or directly through cooperation with single firms. The aim of this role is to stimulate long-term economic and social development within the local, regional and national community.

The three roles represent interconnected logics of value creation within the PoAa and the value capture inherent in the various roles, depending on the scope and objectives. It is therefore argued that the three organisational roles are representative of interdependent business models within the organisation, existing at various dimensions in the value network of the port system. Below we elaborate how the need for collaborative business models arises as the port authority takes on the challenge of evolving from a second- towards a fourth-generation port and the implications for the port system as a whole.

6.2.2 *Data collection and analysis*

Through an exploratory case study (Yin 2014), the empirical setting of the PoAa allows us to explore the complex set of intra- and inter-organisational activities that constitute the PoAa. Data were collected through a process of engaged scholarship (Van de Ven 2007) in the organisation from 2013 to 2017, see Table 6.1. In addition, the intra-organisational strategic development was followed by a

Table 6.1 Data collection.

Data type	Time, place/participants	Data format
Engaged scholars	Port of Aalborg 2014–2020	Observational notes
Strategy presentations, external	2014–2018	PowerPoint, pdf
Semi-structured interviews	CEO Middle managers 2015–2016	Recorded sound files
Facilitating internal strategy seminars	Top management teams Strategic business units 2015–2017	Observational notes Copies of presentations Written output
Semi-structured interviews	Port actors 2015–2020	Recorded sound files and written notes

research team through extensive interaction with the organisation at both operational and top management levels through semi-structured interviews with the CEO of the PoAa and central private actors within the port area. This has been supplemented by secondary data, such as archival data, annual reports, company presentations and press releases, to substantiate the empirical observations (Yin 2014). Furthermore, collaborative initiatives with external port actors have been followed both through participation in meetings and semi-structured interviews. Applying multiple qualitative methods has enabled continuous attention to ensure both validity and reliability throughout the abductive process of identifying parameters of collaborative business models in the case study.

To ensure contingent validity and encompassing the contextual aspects of the phenomena under study, data triangulation has been done in terms of both data sources and respondents to include the perspectives of various port actors. The analytical validity (Healy and Perry 2000) of the findings is founded in the learning potential derived from the single case study (Flyvbjerg 2006). Reliability is strengthened through multiple researcher engagement both in data collection and analysis (Bryman 2012).

6.3 Analysis

In the PoAa, the definition of three organisational roles (cf. Section 6.1), has served as a way of distinguishing the independent but interlinked objectives that underlie the value creation by the port authority. The challenges of being a publicly owned firm with a spatial connection to the city, various environmental constraints and requirements for being proactive in regards to sustainability initiatives, as well as meeting societal expectations of regional growth, are continuously interwoven with the day-to-day operations and the threshold requirement of maintaining an asset-heavy infrastructure.

The interplay of organisational roles occurs within multiple business models which creates implications for obtaining both economic, ecological and societal value that are inherent in the strategic aim of the PoAa. These challenges reflect the constraints experienced in the PoAa when attempting to manage the value creation of the next-generation port and moving beyond the goal of port sustainability towards building collaborative advantage as a network leader. This, however, requires the port authority to engage in collaborative business model innovation with central actors within the port system that presupposes both institutional changes in the relations across organisational boundaries as well as changes within the participating firms in order to adjust to exogenous expectations and new forms of governance.

The ability to create collaborative business model innovation as a part of evolving from one port generation to another is affected by asset specificity, proximity, relational capital, governance and the degree of innovation. These parameters are explored in relation to the development of the PoAa in the following and summarised in Table 6.2.

6.3.1 Asset specificity

As a firm, the role of the port authority explicates the value created for port users and leaseholders. This value created is dependent on the port's function as a logistics centre, with a reasonable amount of cargo coming from within the perimeter and the hinterland making it of interest to shipping lines as a port of call. Thus, the role as a firm is founded on the threshold assets and

Table 6.2 Parameters affecting the development of collaborative business models (CBMs).

Parameters of CBMs \ Port authority roles	The role as a firm managing inward- and outward-bound logistics	The role as a frame for firms operating within the spatial boundaries of the port perimeter	The role as an integrator of cooperation and clustering
Port generation	2	3	4
Asset specificity	High asset specificity	High asset specificity	Low asset specificity
Proximity	Spatial	Spatial–Institutional	Cognitive–Organisational
Relational capital	Low	Medium	High
Governance	Transactional	Coordination	Collaboration
Degree of innovation	Exploitation	Exploitation/ exploration	Exploration
Examples in the PoAa	Crane and quay investments (2015)	Environment++ (2016–2020)	Green Hub Denmark (initiated 2020)

capabilities of developing a port. As argued by Van den Berg et al. (2012), port authorities must be willing to undertake fundamental investments such as the construction of quays and bulwarks and the implementation of safeguards against potential terrorist attacks as well as multi-modal facilities to provide the foundation for the port as a transportation and logistics centre. The asset specificity entails that the port authority manages investments for an efficient logistics system, and even when evolving towards newer port generations, this infrastructure remains a central part of the port value creation. The struggle of managing a large infrastructure while adjusting to a value creation logic that is less dependent on the physical infrastructure is, nevertheless, a challenge. As emphasised by the CEO (see Table 6.1 for interview details):

> We have a large 'body' but not a large 'brain'. Currently, we are a big elephant. CEO, PoAa

An example of trying to escape the role of a big elephant is the first attempt of the PoAa to create collaborative capabilities through joint investments in crane capacity. Following heavy investment in crane capacity in 2015, the PoAa went on to create inter-organisational coordination with private actors operating their own crane capacity. The purpose of this coordination was to achieve synergy, that would increase the overall crane capacity of the port system, thus representing the most basic form of collaborative business model.

As the port authority moves towards a role as an integrator of cooperation and clustering, the degree of asset specificity becomes less significant as there is greater reliance on processes where the port authority does not have a hierarchical control of assets. For the third role to come into existence, asset specificity must be scaled back so port actors are able to create joint value that is not necessarily embedded in a single organisation but evolves in the ecosystem of the port. In one example, where the port authority entered into a strategic alliance with a private logistics operator at the port perimeter, asset specificity became an inter-organisational phenomenon as they embarked on an exploration process to create a joint value proposition. Another example is the role of the port authority in developing Green Hub Denmark, which is a public-private collaboration on a platform for green growth to become a sustainable version of Silicon Valley in northern Jutland.

6.3.2 Proximity

The 108 companies that are located at the industrial area at the PoAa are connected indirectly through interwoven supply chains and activities. Based on the spatial confinement of a port system, port authorities have the potential to facilitate interaction between companies. In the PoAa the process of facilitating interaction between companies to increase productivity or implement sustainability initiatives has nevertheless proved quite challenging as the port system is impeded by low trust and isolated companies working beside each other instead of together. The high degree of asset specificity discussed previously further substantiates the low degree of trust. For this reason, collaboration between port actors is a central challenge for the port authority both as a frame and an integrator.

Geographical proximity is also central as a foundation for other types of proximity to develop that can support learning and knowledge sharing (Boschma 2005). As a frame for creating collective business development, the port authority is dependent on both spatial and institutional proximity between port actors. As argued by Hall and Jacobs (2010), the spatial proximity can facilitate the absorptive capacity of organisations, which means that the port actors become more likely to absorb new knowledge obtained through inter-organisational relations as they exist within the same regional conditions and contingencies. In addition, institutional proximity is necessary for port actors to create a culture of shared trust as a foundation for obtaining learning and, potentially, innovation. However, close coupling between organisations within a similar spatial and institutional context provides the risk of path dependence or lock-in that can impede the development of new and innovative collaborative business models (Laudien and Daxböck 2015). For this reason, the port authority has been focusing on how to attract firms to the region, to create spatial proximity, by understanding the business model of the firms and thus emphasising where potential value can be developed between firms:

> [we] are a group of loosely coupled organizations, there must be triggers that say it must be located in Aalborg. When potential arises, there must be a system that captures it, so we get it in place … and we know the business model, we each know what to do.
>
> CEO, PoAa

Exploiting the spatial proximity has been especially evident in the development of the strategic initiative 'Environment[++]', where the port authority together with partners in the hinterland and researchers from Aalborg University have developed sustainable business models through industrial symbiosis (Mortensen et al. 2020). While the PoAa has maintained a role as a transport and logistics centre in this project, the attention towards sustainability in the port area represents one of the seeds evident in the sustainability initiative and port-city symbiosis found in future port generations.

However, the initial focus is increased through the third role of becoming an integrator of cooperation and clustering which can provide new areas of development for both the port and port actors. As this role moves beyond the value created within existing supply chains and the spatial confinements of the port areas, it means that taking on this role requires both cognitive proximity through a shared knowledge and organisational proximity as a relational aspect to be developed between the actors (Boschma 2005).

6.3.3 Relational capital

When focusing on the role as a firm managing inward and outward-bound logistics the dependency on port actors is low, and the interaction is mostly transactional for which reason the need for relational capital is also low. However, when evolving towards becoming a frame that both provides services and creates strategic collaboration, the port authority is faced with a need for developing relational capital that can support the interaction between organisations.

> The port cannot deliver it all. And that is why we say, in the frame, that is where we must build new competencies. CEO, PoAa

As complexity increases in the value created by the port authority, the need for relational capital increases to reduce the risk of opportunistic behaviour between port actors. As the port system is notoriously filled with mistrust and suspicion concerning the profit maximising behaviour of partners, the PoAa approached this through various activities. First, the port authority created a strategic vision that was broadly communicated to ensure transparency and open communication. Second, they entered into dialogue with strategic port actors to search for potential areas of coordination to ensure efficiency and productivity. These initiatives were put in place to address the central concern of the CEO:

> How do we start activating collaboration with firms so we can create more trust, so a greater intuitive exchange and openness can be created… CEO, PoAa

It remains a challenge for the port authority to develop relational capital in and beyond the port system due to suspicion of opportunistic behaviour. Thus, the greater the complexity of value creation inherent in the role of the port authority the more important the creation of relational capital through mutual trust, communication and commitment becomes (Blomqvist and Levy 2006; Gjerding and Kringelum 2018).

6.3.4 Governance

As the roles of the port authorities develop, the classification of value creation changes and different modes of governance become of relevance (De Martino et al. 2015). As a firm, the port authorities manage arms-length transactions based on market mechanisms that can only be moderated to a small extent.

When the port authority becomes a frame for firms within the spatial boundaries of the port, the mode of governance changes towards an internal coordination of activities to potentially create collective business development. Thus, as a frame, the value creation potential becomes dependent on the openness of port actors to engage more or less proactively in the development of the port as an industrial area, e.g., as ecosystem development (Jacobides et al. 2018). As the focus shifts from pure market transactions, the need for control of the interaction process shifts as well, as emphasised by the CEO of the PoAa:

> We have no desire for ownership, we desire control – control with development, control with creating growth and places of employment, control with creating tax bases, control with attracting companies to the area.
>
> CEO, PoAa

As an integrator, the mode of governance shifts towards collaboration for value creation. While the implications might appear minor, there is an immense change in the impact on value creation and especially value capture. For the port authority, the aim of creating regional long-term economic and social development reflects how the value capture is not confined to the organisational goal of profit maximisation. Rather, it is directed towards societal value capture which the PoAa pursues in its capacity as a community-centred driver.

In sum, the ambition of the port authority becomes one of creating port clusters as:

> … a set of interdependent firms engaged in port related activities, located within the same port region and possibly with similar strategies leading to competitive advantage and characterized by a joint competitive position vis-à-vis the environment external to the cluster.
>
> (Haezendonck 2001, p. 136)

6.3.5 Degree of innovation

The value creation of the PoAa as a frame has been focused on the establishment of strategic partnerships with companies at the port perimeter including both exploitation and exploration in the spatial frame. This has proved successful in at least two instances in projects carried out between 2013 and 2017. The first project included a reduction of costs and an increase of efficiency in the container terminal by scrutinising and questioning existing processes by coordinating with the terminal operator. The second project entailed entering into a strategic collaboration with a global heavy-lifting and logistics company with the aim of attracting 'heavy industries' both nationally and internationally. The joint value creation evolved by entering into dialogue with firms that were interlinked with the activities of the port authorities with an aim of developing and extending the current activities and thereby managing the frame more efficiently and effectively. The intention was to initiate bilateral partnerships that could expand to include multiple actors as networks within the port system along the way. For this reason, the port authority has moved between different contexts of both exploitation and exploration in their collaborative endeavours (Kringelum and Gjerding 2018).

> The scary thing is that we can end up saying that we must use all of our money as an integrator and get someone else to operate the port.
>
> CEO, PoAa

However, as indicated by the CEO in this statement, the third role represents a new type of value creation and extensive exploration of new potential, which requires significant investment in the capabilities of the port authority. Due to the scope of value creation, such investment is not necessarily reflected in the turnover of the organisation. For this reason, the value captured within the third business model is measured by the production value generated within the port perimeter and employment effect on the regional development. Thus, initiatives such as Green Hub Denmark extend beyond the scope of the port perimeter entailing a need for both organisational and especially cognitive proximity to create a community for exploring potential value co-creation.

6.4 Discussion and conclusion

As illustrated by the case study of the PoAa, managing port generation shifts presupposes both implicit and explicit development of collaborative business models. However, as illustrated in Table 6.2, the development of collaborative business model is challenged by various parameters in the process.

The competitive advantage of ports has, traditionally, been created by assets and economies of scale (Cahoon et al. 2013). However, the evolution of ports implies that value creation is, increasingly, an outcome of inter-organisational agency that involves multiple actors (De Martino et al. 2019) within a context where the development of ports and regions are co-dependent (Sakalayen et al. 2016). For this reason, the creation of new collaborative business models is often a co-evolutionary phenomenon that occurs, because business models with the port system must change as ports are changing, and ports are changing because the business models within the port systems are changing.

The collaborative nature of business models represents both an impetus and a challenge to governance across organisational boundaries. While collaboration opens new avenues for resource endowment and positioning at the marketplace, it rests upon certain properties of agency. The pursuit of mutual benefits among actors depends on a combination of intrinsic motivation and trust between the actors (Miles et al. 2005), and structures of coordinated agency must be in place in order to support and maintain motivation and trust. This requires that concerted action is undertaken, both in terms of the alignment of interests and actions, commitment, and some degree of integration and formalisation across the collaborating actors (Todeva and Knoke 2005;

Thomson et al. 2009; Gulati et al. 2012). In effect, organisational innovation is a prerequisite as well as an emerging property of collaborative business models, and this implies the occurrence of inter-organisational learning and coordination through processual, organisational and network level changes (Heikkilä and Heikkilä 2013) based on the establishment of shared values (Breuer and Lüdeke-Freund 2017). This becomes evident as the shift towards new port generations requires a higher degree of relational capital.

The evolution of inter-organisational trust, learning and coordination is sensitive to the spatial, technological, social and cognitive proximity among the collaborating actors (Asheim 1999; Morgan 2004; Boschma 2005; Nooteboom et al. 2007; Molina-Morales and Martínez-Fernández 2010; Ooms et al. 2018; Werker et al. 2019). Due to its effect on trust, commitment and the formation of shared understandings among actors, proximity creates favourable conditions for establishing collaborative business models. Conditions of close proximity are to a high extent present in modern ports, and as most modern ports exhibit a large variety of organisations, industries and activities, we expect modern ports to be conducive to the establishment of collaborative business models across industries and sectors. As evident in the case of the PoAa, shifting towards new generations will naturally broaden the scope of development and innovative activities from within a small circle of maritime-oriented organisations towards the whole hinterland and regional area. Furthermore, since the occurrences of collaborative business models are becoming more frequent, and since modern ports are important arenas for co-evolutionary contributions to regional and national systems of innovation, we expect that modern ports to an increasing degree will contribute to the emergence of collaborative business models as vehicles for innovation system dynamics. This is highly relevant when considering the degree of specialisation found in Danish ports. Each port plays a part in the physical infrastructure of the national system of innovation and provides potential paths of collaborative development based on specificity and the exact position on the ladder of generations from which the port is evolving.

From a managerial point of view, the increasing complexity associated with the evolution of modern ports implies that port authorities must devote strategic and operational attention to three important challenges.

First, port authorities must develop new capabilities suitable for the next generation of the port and identify the right timing for initiating a generation shift. The development of new capabilities must take into account that existing activities must be carried out effectively alongside a smooth transition process. This means that the most important strategic capability is the ability to combine short-term operations with long-term strategic activities. Second, port authorities must conceive themselves as important nodes for inter-organisational coordination. It becomes paramount to adopt a systemic approach to establishing relational capital through collaboration with the purpose of developing and facilitating value co-creation and co-capture (Gjerding and Kringelum 2018). Third, port authorities must be proactive in pursuing politi cal ambitions on local and regional development and take part in orchestrating the external environment, e.g., targeting how clusters and ecosystems within the port perimeter and the hinterland can be supported and developed.

Notes

1 This has been undertaken by a cooperation between University of Southern Denmark, the Danish Centre for Regional and Tourism Research (CRT), and Danske Havne (Danish Ports) which is a trade association for Danish industrial ports. The research in direct and indirect effects are based on the SAM-K/LINE model which combines the Social Accounting Matrices for Danish municipalities developed by Statistics Denmark (SAM-K) and the Local INtersectional and interregional Economic model (LINE) developed by CRT.
2 In the following, we use the term 'port authority' instead of 'management of ports'. Port authority is the established term in the field of port research, e.g., as can be seen in leading journals like *Maritime Policy & Management* and *Research in Transportation Business and Management*. See also Endnote 3.
3 A port authority is defined as 'the entity, which whether or not in conjunction with other activities, has as its objective under national law or regulation, the administration and management of the port infrastructures, and the co-ordination and control of the activities of the different operators present in the port' (Verhoeven 2010: 251; Commission of European Communities 2001).

References

Aalborg Havn, P. A. 2013. *Annual Report 2013*. Aalborg.
Aalborg Havn, P. A. 2015. *Den Intelligente Havn Strategirapport 2015*. Aalborg.
Asheim, B. 1999. *Innovation, Social Capital and Regional Clusters: On the Importance of Co-Operation, Interactive Learning and Localised Knowledge in Learning Economies*. European Regional Science Association 39th European Congress, Dublin, 23–27 August.
Asheim, B. 2012. The changing role of learning regions in the globalizing knowledge economy: A theoretical re-examination. *Regional Studies* 46(8):993–1004. doi:10.1080/00343404.2011.607805.
Asheim, B. 2019. Smart specialisation, innovation policy and regional innovation systems: what about new path development in less innovative regions? *Innovation: The European Journal of Social Science Research* 32(1):8–25.
Beresford, A. K. C. et al. 2004. The UNCTAD and workport models of port development: evolution or revolution?. *Maritime Policy & Management* 31(2):93–107. doi:10.1080/0308883042000205061.
Blomqvist, K. and Levy, J. 2006. Collaboration capability – a focal concept in knowledge creation and collaborative innovation in networks. *International Journal of Management Concepts* 2(1):31–48. doi:10.1504/IJMCP.2006.009645.
Boschma, R. 2005. Proximity and innovation: A critical assessment. *Regional Studies* 39(1):61–74. doi:10.1080/0034340052000320887.
Breuer, H. and Lüdeke-Freund, F. 2017. Values-based network and business model innovation. *International Journal of Innovation Management* 21(3):1–35.
Bryman, A. 2012. *Social Research Methods*. 4th ed. Oxford: Oxford University Press.
Cahoon, S., Pateman, H. and Chen, S. L. 2013. Regional port authorities: Leading players in innovation networks? *Journal of Transport Geography* 27:66–75.
Commission of European Communities 2001. *Reinforcing Quality Services in Sea Ports – A Key for European Transport*. COM (2001) 35 Final.

Doloreux, D. et al. 2019. Territorial innovation models: to be or not to be, that's the question. *Scientometrics* 120(3):1163–1191. Netherlands: Springer. doi:10.1007/s11192-019-03181-1.

Flynn, M., Lee, T. and Notteboom, T. 2011. The next step on the port generations ladder: Customer-centric and community. In *Current Issues in Shipping, Ports and Logistics*, ed. Notteboom, T., 497–510. Brussels: Academic and Scientific Publishing.

Flyvbjerg, B. 2006. Five misunderstandings about case-study research. *Qualitative Inquiry* 12(2):219–245. doi:10.1177/1077800405284363.

Fukuyama, F. 1995. *Trust: The Social Virtues and the Creation of Prosperity.* New York: Free Press.

Gjerding, A. N. and Kringelum, L. B. 2015. *Innovating Through Collaborative Business Models.* Paper presented at the DRUID15 Conference Rome on the Relevance of Innovation, Rome, Italy.

Gjerding, A. N. and Kringelum, L. B. 2016. *Strategic Collaboration on Business Model Innovation. A Transaction Cost Perspective.* Paper presented at the EURAM Conference, France, Paris. doi:10.1017/CBO9781107415324.004.

Gjerding, A. N. and Kringelum, L. B. 2018. Systemic coordination of organizational roles: The importance of relational capital in port governance. *Research in Transportation Business and Management* 28. doi:10.1016/j.rtbm.2018.10.002.

Gulati, R., Wohlgezogen, F. and Zhelyazkov, P. 2012. The two facets of collaboration: cooperation and coordination in strategic alliances. *Academy of Management Annals* 6:531–583.

Haezendonck, E. 2001. *Essays on Strategy Analysis for Seaports.* Leuven: Garant.

Håkansson, H. and Ford, D. 2002. How should companies interact in business networks? *Journal of Business Research* 55(2):133–139. Available at: https://www.sciencedirect.com/science/article/pii/S014829630000148X (Accessed 14 February 2020).

Hall, P. V. and Jacobs, W. 2010. Shifting proximities: the maritime ports sector in an era of global supply chains. *Regional Studies* 44(9):1103–1115. doi:10.1080/00343400903365110.

Haugstetter, H. and Cahoon, S. 2010. Strategic intent: Guiding port authorities to their new world? *Research in Transportation Economics* 27(1):30–36. Elsevier Ltd. doi:10.1016/j.retrec.2009.12.005.

Healy, M. and Perry, C. 2000. Comprehensive criteria to judge validity and reliability of qualitative research within the realism paradigm. *Qualitative Market Research: An International Journal* 3(3):118–126. doi:10.1108/13522750010333861.

Heikkilä, M. and Heikkilä, J. 2013. *Collaborative Business Model Process for Networked Services Innovation.* Paper presented at the International Conference on Electronic Commerce. Berlin, Heidelberg, Springer.

Jacobides, M. G., Cennamo, C. and Gawer, A. 2018. Towards a theory of ecosystems. *Strategic Management Journal* 39(8):2255–2276. doi:10.1002/smj.2904.

Kale, P., Singh, H. and Perlmutter, H. 2000. Learning and protection of proprietary assets in strategic alliances: Building relational capital. *Strategic Management Journal* 21(3):217–237. doi:10.1002/(SICI)1097-0266(200003)21:3<217::AID-SMJ95>3.0.CO;2-Y.

Kaliszewski, A. 2018. Fifth and sixth generation ports (5GP, 6GP) – the evolution of the economic and social role of ports. *Studies and Materials of the Institute of Transport and Maritime Trade* 14:93–123.

Kringelum, L. B. 2019. Reviewing the challenges of port authority business model innovation. *World Review of Intermodal Transportation Research* 8(3):265. doi:10.1504/WRITR.2019.102371.

Kringelum, L. B. and Gjerding, A. N. 2018. Identifying contexts of business model innovation for exploration and exploitation across value networks. *Journal of Business Models* 6(3):45–62.

de Langen, P. W. and van der Lugt, L. M. 2006. Governance structures of port authorities in the Netherlands. *Research in Transportation Economics* 17(06):109–137.

Laudien, S. and Daxböck, B. 2015. Path dependence as a barrier to business model change in manufacturing firms: insights from a multiple-case study. *Journal of Business Economics* 86(6):611–645. doi:10.1007/s11573-015-0793-1.

Lee, P. T.-W. and Lam, J. 2016. Developing the fifth generation ports model. In *Dynamic Shipping and Port Development in the Globalized Economy. Volume 2: Emerging Trends in Ports*, 186–210. Palgrave Macmillan. doi:10.1057/9781137514233_8.

Lee, P. T. W. et al. 2018. Developing the fifth generation port concept model: An empirical test. *International Journal of Logistics Management* 29(3):1098–1120. doi:10.1108/IJLM-10-2016-0239.

Lundvall, B. Å. 2010. Scope, style, and theme of research on knowledge and learning societies. *Journal of the Knowledge Economy* 1(1):18–23. US: Springer. doi:10.1007/s13132-009-0007-6.

De Martino, M. et al. 2013. Logistics innovation in seaports: An inter-organizational perspective. *Research in Transportation Business and Management* 8:123–133.

De Martino, M., Carbone, V. and Morvillo, A. 2015. Value creation in the port: opening the boundaries to the market. *Maritime Policy & Management* 42(7):682–698.

De Martino, M., Magnotti, F. and Morvillo, A. 2019. Port governance and value creation in the supply chain: The case of Italian ports. *Case Studies on Transport Policy*, 1–10. Elsevier. doi:10.1016/j.cstp.2019.10.004.

Miles, R. E., Miles, G. and Snow, C. C. 2005. *Collaborative Entrepreneurship: How Communities of Networked Firms Use Continuous Innovation to Create Economic Wealth*. Stanford CA: Stanford University Press.

Molina-Morales, F. X. and Martínez-Fernández, M. T. 2010. Social networks: effects of social capital on firm innovation. *Journal of Small Business Management* 48(2):258–279.

Morgan, J. Q. 2004. *The Role of Regional Industry Clusters in Urban Economic Development: An Analysis of Process and Performance*. Ph.D. dissertation, Raleigh: North Carolina State University.

Mortensen, L., Kørnøv, L., Lyhne, I., and Raakjaer, J. 2020. Smaller ports' evolution towards catalysing sustainable hinterland development. *Maritime Policy & Management* 47(3):402–418. https://doi.org/10.1080/03088839.2020.1711978

Nooteboom, B., Haverbeke, W. V., Duysters, G., Gilsing, V. and van den Oord, A. 2007. Optimal cognitive distance and absorptive capacity. *Research Policy* 36(7):1016–1034.

Ooms, W., Werker, C. and Caniëls, M. 2018. Personal and social proximity empowering collaborations: the glue of knowledge networks. *Industry and Innovation* 25(9):833–840.

Pettit, S. J. and Beresford, A. K. C. 2009. Port development: from gateways to logistics hubs. *Maritime Policy & Management* 36(3):253–267. doi:10.1080/03088830902861144.

Port Transformation. Havnepolitisk Redegørelse. 2018 *Port Policy Statement 2018*. Copenhagen.

Powell, W. 1990. Neither market nor hierarchy: network forms of organization. *Research in Organizational Behavior* 12:295–336. doi:10.1590/S1415-65552003000200016.

Putnam R. D. 1995. Bowling alone: America's declining social capital. *Journal of Democracy* 6(1):65–78.

Ritter, T., Wilkinson, I. F. and Johnston, W. J. 2004. Managing in complex business networks. *Industrial Marketing Management* 33(3):175–183. Elsevier. doi:10.1016/j.indmarman.2003.10.016.

Sakalayen, Q. M. H., Chen, P. S. L. and Cahoon, S. 2016. Investigating the strategies for Australian regional ports' involvement in regional development. *International Journal of Shipping and Transport Logistics* 8(2):153–174. doi:10.1504/IJSTL.2016.075012.

Scott, A. and Storper, M. 1988. *New Industrial Spaces: Flexible Production, Organization and Regional Development in North America and Western Europe.* London: Pion.

Thomson, A. M., Perry, J. L. and Miller, T. K. 2009. Conceptualizing and measuring collaboration. *Journal of Public Administration Research and Theory* 19(1):23–56. doi:10.1093/jopart/mum036.

Todeva, E. and Knoke, D. 2005. Strategic alliances and models of collaboration. *Management Decision* 43(1):123–148. doi:10.1108/00251740510572533.

UNCTAD. 1992. *Port Marketing and the Third Generation Port, TD/B C.4/AC.7/14.* Geneva.

UNCTAD. 1999. *Technical Note – The Fourth Generation Port.* Geneva.

Vale, J., Ribeiro, J. A. and Branco, M. C. 2017. Intellectual capital management and power mobilisation in a seaport. *Journal of Knowledge Management* 21(5):1183–1201. doi:10.1108/JKM-01-2017-0043.

Van de Ven, A. H. 2007. *Engaged Scholarship: Creating Knowledge for Science and Practice.* Oxford: Oxford University Press.

Van den Berg, R., de Langen, P. W. and Costa, C. R. 2012. The role of port authorities in new intermodal service development; the case of Barcelona Port Authority. *Research in Transportation Business and Management* 5:78–84.

Verhoeven, P. 2010. A review of port authority functions: towards a renaissance? *Maritime Policy & Management* 37(3):247–270.

Welbourne, T. M. and Pardo-del-Val, M. 2009. Relational capital: strategic advantage for small and medium-size enterprises (SMEs) through negotiation and collaboration. *Group Decision and Negotiation* 18(5):483–497. Springer.

Werker, C., Korzinov, V. and Cunningham, S. 2019. Formation and output of collaborations: the role of proximity in German nanotechnology. *Journal of Evolutionary Economics* 29(2):697–719.

Wilkinson, I. and Young, L. 2002. On cooperating: firms, relations and networks. *Journal of Business Research* 55(2):123–132. Elsevier. doi:10.1016/S0148-2963(00)00147-8.

Yin, R. K. 2014. *Case Study Research Design and Methods.* 5th ed. California: SAGE.

Zott, C., Amit, R. and Massa, L. 2011. The business model: Recent developments and future research. *Journal of Management* 37(4):1019–1042. doi:10.1177/0149206311406265.

7 Collaboration as a cornerstone in public sector innovation – the case of Denmark

Jørgen Stamhus and René Nesgaard Nielsen

7.1 Introduction

In 2007, the Danish government issued the so-called Quality Report on how to improve quality and efficiency in the public sector (The Government 2007). One central strategic element of the report was the recommendation to increase focus on user-driven innovation to enhance the innovative capacity of the public sector. This strategic initiative to promote collaborative innovation has for years been augmented by initiatives to increase public–private innovation partnerships. Danish governments, regions and municipalities have established public–private agencies like Welfare Tech and Center for Offentlig Innovation (Centre for Public Sector Innovation), to support and disseminate what could be labelled external collaborative innovation. Within the public sector, both municipalities and regions have a long tradition of collaboration on many issues, which also extends to innovation. Often their collaborations are facilitated and supported by their respective interest organisations: Local Government Denmark and Danish Regions. Hence, collaborative innovation in the public sector has been on the policy agenda in Denmark for a long time. The question is, however, if all governmental strategic and local authorities' initiatives have translated into actual collaborative innovation at the workplace level. In this chapter, we explore this and related questions, such as who is initiating collaborative innovation and who are collaboration partners, by exploiting data from a survey on public sector innovation conducted in 2016.

The concept of innovation originated from studies of the private sector, and most studies on innovation have focused on the private sector. The concept of innovation has, however, also entered the public sector agenda and increasingly attracted academic interest (De Vries et al. 2016; Duivenboden and Thaens 2008; OECD 2015). Given the focus on cooperation and interaction, the collaborative perspective on innovation in the public sector relates to the literature on networked government (Agranoff 2007; Moore 2009). It is also inspired from and comparable to innovation theory developed primarily concerning the private sector, for example, Chesbrough's open innovation perspective (Chesbrough 2003) and Von Hippel's democratic innovation perspective (Von Hippel 2005), as well as systems of innovation approaches (see e.g., Lundvall 1992, 2011) when it comes to the generation, implementation and diffusion of innovations.

In light of the economic importance of the public sector, increased interest in innovation is natural. Furthermore, public sector innovation is an integrated part of the national innovation system, and thus a better understanding of this will contribute to increasing the overall knowledge of the innovation system. This is particularly relevant in the case of Denmark given its extended public sector with tax-funded welfare services (health, education, social security, pension, etc.), demanding a public workforce of 29% of all employees (OECD 2017) and public expenditures amounting to 51% of GDP in 2018 (OECD 2020).

Innovation is a key factor in the Danish public sector because it can increase public value through better quality and increased efficiency in the public sector. Furthermore, innovation is increasingly needed for the strategic agenda of the public sector to deal with significant challenges in the future (Torfing et al. 2014). Such challenges include scarce resources, demographic changes, technological development, environmental problems, citizens' demand for better service and the politicians' ambition to display effective and timely solutions to societal problems in a dynamic context.

The Danish public sector consists of three connected levels: state, regional and municipality with one state, five regions and 98 municipalities. Earlier studies found that regardless of the level of aggregation (state, region, municipality) the public sector in Denmark is characterised by a high share of innovation, according to the Danish Innovation Barometer survey of 2017 (Lykkebo et al. 2018). The survey showed that approximately 80% of public sector workplaces responded that they have introduced at least one innovation in the period 2015–2016. The numbers on frequencies of innovation are significantly higher than corresponding figures from the private sector. Given the rather high share of innovation in the Danish public sector, and related, the high share of collaboration for innovation in the Danish public sector, this chapter will explore and examine the following questions:

- What are the perceived advantages of collaborative innovation, and what explains the high share of collaboration for innovation in the public sector in Denmark?
- Are there similarities and/or differences between the three administrative levels of the Danish public sector?
- What are the patterns in the collaboration for innovation? Is it internal collaboration and/or external collaboration?

Furthermore, we want to explore to what extent and how employees are involved in collaborative innovation? In both the public and private sectors, employee-driven innovation is an important supplement to top-down driven activities, which is often overlooked (Holmquist and Johansson 2019). Frontline staff are valuable assets in innovation as they both on their own and through interaction with users, citizens and suppliers generate knowledge and innovative ideas to improve efficiency in the workplace. We investigate to what extent this transmits into collaborative innovative activity and we extend much-needed research on the issue of employee involvement in innovation.

The remainder of the chapter will proceed in the following way. In Section 7.2 we present a brief review of the literature on collaborative innovation in the public sector. In Section 7.3 we introduce our data from the Danish Innovation Barometer survey of 2017 and present an overall empirical analysis of collaborative public sector innovation. In Section 7.4 we look into the systemic foundations for innovation collaboration. Section 7.5 features a special empirical analysis of the role of employees in collaborative innovation. Finally, in Section 7.6 we summarise and discuss our findings and state our proposals for further research.

7.2 Collaborative innovation in the public sector

There has been a growing interest in how to spur innovation in the public sector, and recent research points to multi-actor collaboration as a key driver of public innovation (Torfing 2019). This is an innovation driver that complements more hierarchical and competitive strategies for innovation or may even be seen as superior to both hierarchy and competition when it comes to generating and implementing innovative solutions (Roberts 2000).

A collaborative perspective on innovation in the public sector is based on the fact that there is a multitude of different actors that are at least potentially relevant for generating, implementing and diffusing innovations in the public sector. These are actors such as politicians, public leaders, employees, citizens, other public organisations, private firms and non-profit organisations, i.e., actors internal and external any given public organisation. Through collaboration, actors can pool their relevant knowledge, ideas, creativity and resources to develop and diffuse innovations (Bommert 2010).

> the exchange of different experiences, ideas and opinions tend to disturb the established practices and their cognitive and normative underpinnings, thereby triggering transformative learning processes while simultaneously building joint ownership over new and bold solutions.
>
> Torfing (2019, p. 4)

The collaborative perspective on innovation is, following this, based on a relational and interactive perspective on innovation; a perspective that at the same time may also challenge and complement more unilateral perspectives.

The collaborative perspective on innovation encompasses both politicians, public sector managers and employees as potentially relevant actors in generating, implementing and diffusing innovations in the public sector. Borins (2002) distinguishes between a *top-down* and a *bottom-up* perspective on initiating and developing innovations in the public sector. The *top-down* perspective constitutes a more formal and conventional perspective based on the fact that politicians in general are those who are responsible for and have the ultimate decision-making power in the public sector. Therefore, it is the politicians who, together with or through the top managers in the public sector, can and must initiate and implement what they find valuable based on a democratic mandate. The *bottom-up* perspective suggests that middle managers, as well as employees without management responsibilities in the public sector, can initiate and contribute to innovation processes in the sector. These groups can contribute to innovation because they often have very concrete and applicable knowledge and a thorough understanding of the problems as well as opportunities in and around the organisations in which they are employed.

A number of different types of collaboration partners have been outlined. The question of which actor is the more important one, if any, may very well depend on the given context and situation. Equally important as the partner is the degree to which an organisation pursues open innovation processes.

7.3 Collaborative innovation in the public sector in Denmark

There is an established tradition for collaboration in the public sector in Denmark. An obvious reason for a high degree of collaboration is that many public sector workplaces face the same challenges and tasks, and competition issues are limited.

In this section, we provide descriptive statistics on the frequencies of collaborative partnerships of innovation by exploiting data from the latest Danish Innovation Barometer survey. Our aim is primarily to extract new knowledge on the extent of collaboration, and on which actors' public sector workplaces most frequently engage in partnerships.

Lykkebo et al. (2018, p. 240) document the data behind the Innovation Barometer in detail. From a population of 15,102 workplaces a random sample of 4766 public workplaces was drawn, and 2363 responded (50%), with the questionnaire directed at top-level management. The survey stratifies workplaces by size (3–49, 50–99, 100–249, and 250+ employees), region, sector (municipality, region and state) and branches. The responding workplaces' sectoral distribution is as follows, with representativeness as a percentage of the population in parentheses: municipalities 1771 (13%), regions 164 (31%) and state 428 (30%). The survey follows the guidelines for innovation statistics of the Oslo Manual (OECD/Eurostat 2005). Accordingly, innovative activity divides into four types: process- and organisational, communicative, service and product innovation. Tables 7.1 and 7.2 report the overall innovation activity and the distribution of the different types in each sector. We present data in unweighted format.[1]

Table 7.1 shows that innovative activity is quite high in all parts of the public sector, with only marginal differences between the sectors. The total

Table 7.1 Percentage of workplaces which have implemented at least one type of innovation in 2015–2016 (unweighted).

Sector	Percentage	N
State	86	369
Region	84	137
Municipality	81	1436
Total	82	1942

Source: Data provided by Centre for Public Sector Innovation, Innovation Barometer 2017.

Table 7.2 Types of innovation by sector, 2015–2016 (%).

Sector	Product*	Service	Process	Communication	N
State	44	52	75	56	427
Region	44	53	76	46	163
Municipality	39	47	70	46	1771

* Product innovations in the public sector include e.g., medical instruments, rehabilitation equipment and elderly care appliances. Source: Data provided by Centre for Public Sector Innovation, Innovation Barometer 2017.

percentage of workplaces with at least one type of innovative activity amounts to 82%.

In Table 7.2 we report the distribution of the different types of innovation in each sector. Process innovation, which also encompasses new ways of organising work, is the most common type of innovative activity in each sector; with 70–76% of workplaces having implemented some kind of innovative change in this respect. Workplaces at the state and regional level engage in this type of innovation more so than workplaces at the municipality level. Otherwise, sectoral differences are small. The shares of process innovation are generally well above the three other innovation types.

The survey asked participants to state if and with whom they collaborated on their latest innovation. The overall picture is that collaborative partnerships related to innovation are pervasive throughout the Danish public sector and that the predominant partnership is with a workplace at the same sectoral level (i.e., municipal, regional and state). To go into more detail, we look at each level.

Starting with the municipal workplaces, Table 7.3 shows that a large majority of innovation activity (80%) happens with collaboration. This often involves other municipal workplaces (55%) within their 'own' municipality. It is worth noting that this percentage includes all combinations where intra-municipality workplaces are involved, as the questions allow for more than one answer. We further analyse the data to find the three most frequent combinations of collaborative partnerships (not shown here). These are: other intra-municipal

Table 7.3 Public sector workplaces: did your workplace collaborate with one or more of the following during the development of your latest innovation?

Collaborative partnerships	Municipality N = 1436		State (N = 363)		Region (N = 369)	
	Frequency	%	Frequency	%	Frequency	%
1. Other intra-municipality/state/region workplaces	789	55	163	44	71	52
2. Other external municipality/state/region workplaces	285	20	34	9	26	19
3. State workplaces, non-higher education and research institutions	64	4	76	21	3	2
4. Higher education and research institutions	201	14	37	10	17	12
5. Regional/state/municipality workplaces	56	4	63	17	24	18
6. Citizens	313	22	40	11	38	28
7. Voluntary organisations	179	14	29	8	11	8
8. Private firms and organisations	328	23	145	39	37	27
9. Foundations	55	4	26	7	6	4
10. Foreign collaborators	25	2	29	8	10	7
11. No collaboration	289	20	69	19	14	10

Note: More than one answer allowed. Source: Data provided by Centre for Public Sector Innovation, Innovation Barometer 2017.

workplaces alone (20%), private firms alone (6%), other intra-municipality workplaces combined with citizens (4%) equal to the combination of other intra-municipality workplaces combined with private firms. Although much collaboration happens with other intra-municipality workplaces, external collaboration on innovation is widespread.

In state sector workplaces, the results shown in Table 7.3 above indicate an overall similar level of collaboration as in the municipalities, but with stronger involvement of private firms as these are involved in 39% of innovations compared to 23% in municipal workplaces and 27% in regional workplaces. One can only guess about the explanations for the differences here. Maybe state level innovations in general revolve around larger innovation projects, which demand external knowledge from private firms, while innovation at the municipal and regional level has a more incremental character and less scope for public–private collaboration. More detailed insight from actual state level innovation projects is needed to explain this difference in collaborative patterns.

In accordance with the results for the municipality workplaces, around 80% of innovations at the state level include collaboration, which by any means is a clear-cut indication of the importance of collaboration to achieve innovative solutions in the public sector.

The most frequent collaborative partnership combinations (not shown in Table 7.3) with state sectoral workplaces are with other government agencies alone (17%), solely with private firms (12%) and other intra-state workplaces together with private firms (5%).

In Denmark, the regional level is politically responsible for major parts of the health service, including hospitals. Traditionally, these are highly innovative workplaces for several reasons e.g., medical staff engaged in R&D, budgetary pressures and ongoing workplace interaction with private firms to provide new and better medical solutions. Some of this interaction, although it is unclear how much, takes place in special innovation units provided by hospitals in each region to promote and develop innovative ideas as a part of the Danish innovation system.

Only 10% of the latest innovations were made without collaboration. Citizens are more often involved at the regional level than at the state and municipal level, which might be due to frequent staff/citizen interaction at hospitals dealing with different kinds of treatments, technologies and administrative issues. Otherwise, there is not much deviation from the municipal level where workplaces and tasks are somewhat more comparable than at state level. Further analysis reveals that the most frequent combinations of collaborations are with other intra-regional workplaces solely (16%), private firms solely (10%) and private firms combined with other intra-regional workplaces (8%), a pattern resembling the results from the two other sectors. Overall, the results show a prominent collaborative involvement in the innovation of regional workplaces with both citizens and firms as external actors.

7.3.1 International comparisons

Country-specific empirical data comparable to the recent Danish data has, until 2019, been lacking. Fortunately, national surveys for the Nordic countries were conducted in 2018. These allow for cross-Nordic comparisons by using similar methodologies and definitions as the Danish Innovation Barometer survey. Data from the surveys, now reported and explored in Lykkebo et al. (2019), show a similarly high level of innovation activity in other Nordic public workplaces. Regarding collaborative innovation, the overall level is close to 80% in all countries, but the types of innovation collaborators differ to some degree between the countries. For example, collaboration with citizens is more common in Sweden (31%) than in Denmark (21%) (Lykkebo et al. 2019, p. 22). Further research is needed to explain the differences in the collaborative patterns, but apparently Swedish workplaces have adopted a more open stance to the involvement of citizens. How this has been institutionalised differently than in Denmark is an interesting question.

Outside the Nordic countries, the European Commission Innobarometer 2010 survey offers some data-based findings on external collaboration as analysed by Arundel and Hollanders (2011). Regarding the development of service innovations, external collaboration amounted to 62.5%, 41.4% and 35.9% for other public organisations, private businesses and not-for-profit organisations, respectively. These findings are not directly comparable to the Nordic surveys, but in general support the findings here of an important role for external collaboration in public sector innovation. Even more interesting is the observation that these numbers surpass the equivalent Danish figures for all three sectors. Interpreted with considerable caution, this indicates, surprisingly, that civil society innovation is higher in Europe compared to Denmark.

To our knowledge, there is not much additional data available on the issue. Research copying the Nordic Innovation Barometer surveys would be helpful and welcome to allow for investigative research on systemic differences between countries.[2] That said, it is important to emphasise that even the Nordic countries differ in the organisational structure of their public sectors.

7.4 Systemic foundations for innovation collaboration

While quantitative data on collaborative innovation in the public sector is limited, there is a large number of case studies that generally report the positive effects of collaboration (see Torfing 2019 for an overview).

The indications of high innovation activity in general and extended collaborative innovation specifically beg the question if public sectors in Denmark and other Nordic countries have favourable systemic foundations for innovation. All five countries have larger-than-average public sectors, which might spur more innovation. Related, there is a general trend of increased demand for public sector services without budgets increasing correspondingly. Furthermore, there has even been a general 2% reduction in public sector institutions' yearly budgets, resulting in an expected increase in workplace productivity. This kind of budgetary pressure together with rising demand and quality expectations will certainly demand innovative efforts. Another explanation related especially to collaborative innovation might be that public workplaces in the Nordic countries are quite open to external ideas and bottom-up type innovations. We have selected data from three questions from the Danish Innovation Barometer survey, to shed some light on this. We present the frequency distributions of each question from the respondent managers in Table 7.4.

The first question presented in Table 7.4 is included to present management views on their workplace facilitation of internal collaboration. A large majority (77%) totally or partly agree that they do not experience any problems with crosswise collaboration, while 22% partly or totally disagree with this proposition. This figure indicates that workplace collaboration is not frictionless in all cases. Several papers discuss how to overcome these frictions or obstacles to collaborative innovation inside public agencies. Smith et al. (2012) identify leadership support, employee autonomy and organisational culture favouring development as important. Wihlman et al. (2014) stress the importance of the formation of a continuous learning process and the exchange of ideas inside the organisation. Crosby and Bryson (2010) support this view, focusing on the importance of the creation of procedures to problem identification, overcoming power imbalances, and tracking of innovation processes. In general (see also Bason 2010), the literature highlights the importance of organisational design to foster an innovation culture and supportive leadership.

The next question in Table 7.4 focuses on the openness to external collaboration with citizens and firms. Results show that 75% of managers totally or partially agree that they work systematically to include citizens (in some cases they are obliged to do so, according to the law) or firms' perspectives in relation to the workplace. Although not directly related to innovation activity, it at least gives a clear indication that public sector workplaces in Denmark include

Table 7.4 To what degree do you agree or disagree with the following statements concerning your workplace? (%).

	Totally agree	Partly agree	Partly disagree	Totally disagree	Not relevant/ do not know
We do not experience any problems with crosswise collaboration at the workplace	32	45	19	3	2
We work systematically to include citizens or firms' perspectives	29	46	15	2	8
We work systematically to find and reuse others new solutions	15	52	21	5	7

Source: Data provided by Centre for Public Sector Innovation, Innovation Barometer 2017. N = 2361.

external ideas and influence, even if responses might be biased, as it cannot be expected that managers disagree with the question.

Willingness to include new solutions from other actors and/or organisations is another indication of openness. From Table 7.4 we find that 52% of managers partly agree and 15% totally agree that they work systematically to include and reuse other new solutions. At the municipality level in Denmark there is a tradition for extensive municipal collaboration on several issue and task areas. As documented in a survey by the interest organisation of the municipalities, Local Government Denmark (2018), this collaboration also extends to innovative activity. Municipalities working together on joint and new solutions is a tradition in Denmark and quite systematic, sometimes supported and/or initiated by the aforementioned interest organisation, as well as several different policy initiatives.

To summarise, we find a high degree of external collaborative innovation activity in public sector workplaces in Denmark, which is similar to what is found in other Nordic countries. We found collaboration to be a cornerstone of public sector innovations, as only between 10 to 20% of innovations in Denmark are non-collaborative. Collaborations most frequently take place between other state level, regional or municipality workplaces, but a significant share includes the private sector, citizens and firms. We find that public sector managers state an openness to external collaboration, which to some extent explains the high collaboration frequencies, but more explorative knowledge is needed to explain this apparent openness.

7.5 Employees as collaborative innovative agents

In the previous section, we focused on the extent of external collaboration to foster public sector innovation. In the following, we turn our attention to employees and their importance as an innovative resource. Employees gain knowledge rooted in everyday practices and the contact between the frontline worker and the user of the public service. This interaction can result in so-called employee-driven innovation. (Høyrup 2010, 149) defines this as:

> … innovative practices, contributed by any employee (outside the boundaries of his/her primary job responsibilities), at all levels of the organization. Innovation is driven by employees' resources: ideas, creativity, competence, and problem-solving abilities. These innovative activities are embedded in employees' daily work activities – often in working teams – based on their experience and on-the-job learning.

The utilisation of the innovative capabilities of employees relies on organisational and managerial support. Collaboration between employees and management on ideas brought forward by employees either individually or in a group is crucial for developing and implementing innovation in public sector organisations. Furthermore, employees could be important in the facilitation of external collaborative innovation, also labelled as co-initiated innovation

(Sørensen and Torfing 2018) through their interaction with citizens, firms, not-for-profit organisations and other public institutions and organisations.

In this section, we provide documentation on the collaborative involvement of employees in the initiation of the latest innovation of public workplaces to get an overall impression of their importance for driving the overall innovation activity in the public sector in Denmark. In the Danish case, several factors support the involvement of employees as collaborative innovative agents. The country has an extensive public sector with open access for citizens and firms to frontline staff. The interaction is both formal and informal. Furthermore, staff are well skilled and operate in work organisations with a high degree of autonomy and rather informal hierarchical structures. All in all, barriers to employee co-initiated innovation should be low, making Denmark a benchmark case for public sector innovation.

In general, empirical data and evidence are lacking regarding the extent of the collaborative involvement of employees in the initiation of innovation of public workplaces, not just from Denmark. Sørensen and Torfing (2018) provide some case-specific Danish findings regarding co-initiation in collaborative innovation processes but this study presents data from the latest Danish Innovation Barometer survey to draw up the broader picture. The Innovation Barometer Survey includes a question asking respondents to state who or what initiated the latest innovation. From these answers we extract the number of cases where employees solely initiated innovation, including instances where changes in legislation, budgetary conditions and technology prompted the initiation, and more importantly here, cases where employees in collaboration with other actors (citizens, management, private firms, political leadership, voluntary organisations and universities) initiated innovation. We report the findings in Table 7.5 distributed by type of innovation.

As seen in the second row, employees are involved in collaborative initiation of approximately a quarter of any type of the latest innovative activity at the workplace. The first row reports incidences where employees solely initiate innovation, which is the case in around 10% of innovations, indicating that

Table 7.5 Employee involvement in the initiation of the latest innovation.

	New or significantly changed products	New or significantly changed service	New or significantly changed processes or ways of organising work	New or significantly changed ways of communicating with the outside world
Employees solely, %	11	9	9	10
Employees in collaboration with other actors, %	29	27	25	27
N	491	701	1415	712

Source: Data provided by Centre for Public Sector Innovation, Innovation Barometer 2017.

employee-driven innovation as a sort of bottom-up driven innovation happens quite often.

The type of innovation does not significantly affect employees' involvement in initiation. Although it is difficult to have any prior expectation to which type of innovation employees would be more frequently involved, this is still somewhat puzzling. However, it emphasises that employees should not be disregarded as actors in the public innovation process.

To provide more detail on with whom employees collaborate, Table 7.6 reports the most frequent collaborative partnerships. As the questionnaire allows for more than one response, there are several combinations, so we have opted, for the purpose here, only to extract the most frequent combinations. Also, note that the populations in Tables 7.5 and 7.6 diverge simply because they are constructed from different questions in the survey.

Table 7.6 shows that the combinations of employees and managers are by far the most frequent partnerships of co-initiation of innovation (53.7%) where employees are involved. This is hardly surprising as these actors are the prime stakeholders of the workplace and know the challenges fostering innovative initiatives. The employee–manager partnership is quite often (7.4%) supplemented with either one or more of the following: private firms, political leadership, voluntary organisations or universities. Even more pronounced is the co-initiation with citizens in different combinations with employees, managers and others. In total, combining the second, fourth and sixth row in Table 7.6, citizens and employees' share of co-initiation amounts to 23.8%. This clearly indicates an openness to including citizens' ideas into the innovation process of Danish public workplaces. Apparently, citizens are more important collaborative actors than the other external actors encompassed by the survey. It raises an interesting research question as to how and why this seems to be the case. As consumers of public services and as clients, citizens certainly have an indirect influence, but this does not necessarily lead to direct collaboration on innovation. We previously hinted at some explanations for citizens' role as

Table 7.6 Ranking of most frequent collaborative partnerships between employees and other actors.

	N	%
Employees with managers	268	53.7
Employees and citizens	65	13.0
Employees and managers combined with others (excl. citizens)	37	7.4
Employees, managers and citizens	36	7.2
Employees and either one or two of the following: private firms, political leadership, voluntary organisations or universities	29	5.8
Employees, citizens and others (excl. managers)	18	3.6
Total (including less frequent collaborations not shown above)	499	

Note: Others includes either private firms, political leadership, voluntary organisations or universities.
Source: Data provided by Centre for Public Sector Innovation, Innovation Barometer 2017.

co-innovators, one further important institutional influence worth mentioning could be the formation, for years, of user councils throughout the public sector in Denmark (hospitals, schools, elderly care, etc.). This is an example of a continued political and governance-constituted move in Denmark since 2007, from a perception of citizens as clients towards the role of co-producer/co-creator (Agger and Lund 2017). In any case, the influence of citizens in public sector innovation is certainly an area which calls for more research (see Hartley 2014: Agger and Lund 2017 for further discussion).

The data presented above points towards a small role for private firms to engage in collaboration with public sector employees on the initiation of innovation, at least not without management involvement. One possible explanation is less informal access to public sector institutions and workplaces compared to that of citizens. Another more general explanation is that the public and private sectors operate by two different logics. Whereas the former abides by laws and rules to provide common goods, the latter operates according to the logic of profit maximisation. This leaves less room for collaboration without some kind of institutionalisation as constituted by public-private innovation partnerships programmes, which entail rules, regulations and guidelines. In Denmark, it is governed by The Danish Business Authority.

To sum up this part of the chapter, we find that employees often initiate innovation, but more often co-initiate. This finding is valid across all types of innovation. The most frequent collaborative partnership is between managers and employees, showing the importance of inter-organisational facilitation and managerial support for the inclusion of innovative ideas from front-line staff. The data presented in this section also shows that employees often collaborate with citizens and other external actors on the initiation of innovation, which documents that employees can be an important channel for the extraction of new solutions from users of public sector services.

7.6 Conclusion and discussion

In national systems of innovation, the public sector is essential, not only because it makes up a substantial proportion of most Western economies, but also because it produces innovations and is a key player and partner in development of innovation in the private sector. In 2007, the former Danish government launched a strategy for public sector innovation. The vision is, then and now, that the public sector should work more systematically to drive innovation. A key tool in the strategy is collaboration and exploitation of knowledge across public workplaces, private firms, citizens and knowledge institutions. Some 13 years later the question is to what degree collaborative innovation has unfolded in public sector workplaces.

The findings provided in this chapter indicate that collaboration is a cornerstone of public sector innovation in Denmark. Regardless of whether the collaborative partnerships are between internal actors, i.e., managers and employees, or extended to external agents like citizens and firms, the data from the Danish Innovation Barometer survey presented in this study demonstrate the importance of collaborative and co-initiated innovation, as around 80% of all innovation activities include collaborative partnerships. We also document the importance of employees as significant initiators of innovation. Most often employee-driven innovation takes place in collaboration with managers, but they also act as agents of innovation transferring ideas from other citizens, firms and non-profit organisations to innovative initiatives inside the workplace. This highlights the importance of both managerial support of employee-driven innovation and institutional design.

Following Torfing (2019, p. 3), the argument for collaborative public sector innovation rests upon the foundation that a collaborative innovation strategy enhances knowledge, competences and ideas between relevant actors. This facilitates mutual learning and problem-solving capacity inside public sector workplaces. In turn, this increases productivity and quality in delivering public services. Furthermore, it may champion top-down driven hierarchical innovation strategies in creating feasible solutions and successful implementation.

The extensiveness of collaborative innovation in Denmark raises the question if this constitutes a special Danish feature and how and why this has developed. We call for further research on these questions. We document similar frequencies of collaboration in the other Nordic countries, which might indicate a Nordic model. These countries also report high workplace innovation activity. This hints at the size of the public sector as an explanatory variable. As budgetary pressures develop and demand for public services increases, public sector workplaces seek new solutions inside and outside their organisations to make ends meet. Although this is likely to be a part of the explanation, there is room for further research into how the collaborative model has developed.

The Danish version of the Nordic innovation surveys fills a gap in providing quantitative data on public sector innovation activity. It would be very interesting to see similar surveys from other countries with differently sized and organised public sectors, and this would enable investigations of the question if the Danish model is something special, or if collaboration is more generally a common feature to public sector innovation.

This chapter has not scrutinised how the collaborations unfold. Concerning this, we need more research to gain more knowledge of the specific roles of the actors involved. Are external actors merely superficially involved, and how do they contribute to the innovation process? These are just a couple of questions which the findings provided in this chapter beg to ask.

Notes

1 Test for difference between weighted and unweighted distributions shows only very marginal differences.
2 Denmark is heading the work on statistical information on public sector innovation by the development of the Copenhagen Manual, which will set common guidelines for public innovation barometers across countries. At present 19 countries take part in a co-creation process leading to a common base for producing better statistics.

References

Agger, A. and Lund, D. H. 2017. Collaborative innovation in the public sector – new perspectives on the role of citizens? *Scandinavian Journal of Public Administration* 21(3): 17–37.

Agranoff, R. 2007. *Managing Within Networks: Adding Value to Public Organizations*. Washington, DC: Georgetown University Press.

Arundel, A. and Hollanders, H. 2011. *A Taxonomy of Innovation: How Do Public Sector Agencies Innovate?* Results of the 2010 European Innobarometer Survey of Public Agencies.

Bason, C. 2010. *Leading Public Sector Innovation*. Bristol: Policy Press.

Bommert, B. 2010. Collaborative innovation in the public sector. *International Public Management Review* 11(1): 15–33.

Borins, S. 2002. Leadership and innovation in the public sector. *Leadership & Organization Development Journal* 23(8): 467–476.

Chesbrough, H. W. 2003. *Open Innovation – The New Imperative for Creating and Profiting from Technology*. Boston, MA: Harvard Business School Press.

Crosby, B. C. and Bryson, J. M., 2010. Integrative leadership and the creation and maintenance of cross-sector collaborations. *Leadership Quarterly* 21(2): 211–230.

De Vries, H., Bekkers, V. and Tummers, L. 2016. Innovation in the public sector: A systematic review and future research agenda. *Public Administration* 94(1): 146–166.

Duivenboden, H. V. and Thaens, M. 2008. ICT-driven innovation and the culture of public administration: A contradiction in terms? *Information Polity* 13(3–4): 213–232.

Government. 2007. *Bedre velfærd og større arbejdsglæde – regeringens strategi for høj kvalitet i den offentlige service*, Copenhagen: Danish Government.

Hartley, J. 2014. New development: Eight and a half propositions to stimulate frugal innovation. *Public Money & Management* 34(3): 227–232.

Holmquist, M. and Johansson, A. 2019. Employee-driven innovation: An intervention using action research. *Technology & Innovation Management Review* 9(5): 44–53. http://doi.org/10.22215/timreview/1240

Høyrup, S. 2010. Employee-driven innovation and workplace learning: Basic concepts, approaches and themes. *Transfer* 16(2): 143–154. https://doi.org/10.1177%2F1024258910364102

Local Government Denmark 2018. *De samarbejdende kommuner*. København. Retrieved from: https://www.kl.dk/ImageVaultFiles/id_85175/cf_202/De_samarbejdende_kommuner.PDF/

Lundvall, B.-Å. (ed.) 1992. *National Systems of Innovation – Towards a Theory of Innovation and Interactive Learning*. London: Pinter Publishers.

Lundvall, B.-Å. 2011. Økonomisk innovationsteori: Fra iværksættere til innovationssystemer. In *Samarbejdsdrevet Innovation i den offentlige sektor*, ed. Sørensen, E., and Torfing, J., 41–57. København: Jurist- og Økonomforbundets Forlag.

Lykkebo, O. B., Jakobsen, N. and Sauer, P. 2018. *Innovationsbarometeret: Nyt sammen bedre*. Center for Offentlig Innovation & Dansk Psykologisk Forlag A/S.

Lykkebo, O. B., Munch-Andersen, M. and Jacobsen, N. (eds) 2019. Measuring new Nordic solutions: Innovation barometer for the public sector. *Innovationbarometer.org*, Retrieved from https://www.innovationbarometer.org/nordic-publication/

Moore, M. H. 2009. Networked government: Survey of rationales, forms, and techniques. In *Unlocking the Power of Networks: Keys to High-Performance Government*, ed. Goldsmith, S., and Kettle, D., 190–228. Washington, DC: Brookings Institution Press.

OECD. 2015. *The Innovation Imperative in the Public Sector: Setting an Agenda for Action.* Paris: OECD Publishing.

OECD. 2017. *Government at a Glance 2017.* Paris: OECD Publishing. https://doi.org/10.1 787/gov_glance-2017-en.

OECD. 2020. *General Government Spending (Indicator).* doi: 10.1787/a31cbf4d-en (Accessed on May 22, 2020).

OECD/Eurostat. 2005. *Oslo Manual: Guidelines for Collecting and Interpreting Innovation Data.* Paris: OECD Publishing. https://doi.org/10.1787/19900414

Roberts, N. C. 2000. Wicked problems and network approaches to resolution. *International Public Management Review* 1(1): 1–19.

Smith, P., Ulhöi, J. P. and Kesting, P. 2012. Mapping key antecedents of employee-driven innovations. *International Journal of Human Resources Development and Management* 12(3): 224–236. http://dx.doi.org/10.1504/IJHRDM.2012.048629

Sørensen, E. and Torfing, J. 2018. Co-initiation of collaborative innovation in urban spaces. *Urban Affairs Review* 54(2): 388–418. https://doi.org/10.1177/1078087416651936

Torfing, J. 2019. Collaborative innovation in the public sector: The argument. *Public Management Review* 21(1): 1–11. doi:10.1080/14719037.2018.1430248

Torfing, J., Sørensen, E. and Aagaard, P. 2014. Samarbejdsdrevet innovation i praksis: En introduktion. In *Samarbejdsdrevet Innovation i praksis*, ed. Aagaard, P., Sørensen, E., and Torfing, J., 15–36. København: Jurist- og Økonomforbundets Forlag.

Von Hippel, E. 2005. *Democratizing Innovation.* Cambridge, MA: MIT Press.

Wihlman, T., Hoppe, M., Wihlman, U. and Sandmark, H. 2014. Employee-driven innovation in welfare services. *Nordic Journal of Working Life Studies* 4(2): 159–180. https://doi.org/10.19154/njwls.v4i2.3869

Part III

Technology, employee learning and the labour market

8 The impact of robots and AI/ML on skills and work organisation

Jacob Rubæk Holm, Edward Lorenz and Jørgen Stamhus

8.1 Introduction

A large amount of high-quality research has been undertaken on the consequences of the diffusion of robotics for wages, for income distribution and for employment (Autor et al. 2003; Goos and Manning 2007; Goos et al. 2014; Brynjolfsson and McAfee 2015; Acemoğlu and Restrepo 2018; OECD 2017; Graetz and Michaels 2018). Such studies often use relatively aggregate and dated data in the interest of obtaining high coverage and high-quality data. Few studies are able to take into account the significant recent changes that have emerged along with collaborative robots (cobots) and the integration of robots with artificial intelligence (AI) and machine learning (ML), or the more recent diffusion of AI and ML more generally in the economy. There is thus a need to expand the study of robots with micro level data (as also pointed out by Seeman and Raj 2018). Furthermore, as pointed out by Brynjolfsson et al. (2018), there is a need to study ML intensively, as it is becoming a general-purpose technology, and its impact on job redesign and task bundles will be widespread.

Like ML, the diffusion of robots is picking up pace. According to data from the International Federation of Robotics (IFR) the number of industrial robots (automatically controlled, reprogrammable multipurpose manipulator programmable in three or more axes, ISO 8373) sold worldwide exceeded 400,000 for the first time in 2018 (IFR 2019a). Most of these (65%) have been installed in the automotive, electrical/electronics, metal and machinery industries. This suggests broader diffusion of robots, and so does the rapid increase in sales of professional service robots (perform useful tasks for humans or equipment excluding industrial automation applications, ISO 8373) which increased by 60% from 2017 to 2018, when worldwide sales were 111,000, and this yearly growth rate is expected to continue (IFR 2019b). In Denmark, the share of private sector firms using robots increased from 10 to 12% from 2018 to 2019, while the increase in firms using AI or ML was from 5 to 6% (DST 2020). In relative terms, this is a 20% increase for both robotics and AI/ML in one year.

The increased rate of automation both within and across sectors and industries has certainly contributed to boost productivity, although with diminishing gains (Graetz and Michaels 2018), but has also raised concerns regarding job losses, job polarisation and income inequality (Brynjolfsson and McAfee 2015; Acemoğlu and Restrepo 2018; OECD 2017). The acceleration of automation is posing new demands for skill formation on firms and at the national level (Pinzone et al. 2017; World Economic Forum 2018). To achieve the full productivity potential of robots and AI/ML, the workforce must be equipped with necessary skills supported by changing modes of work organisation. This creates both opportunities and challenges for the national innovation system. New opportunities emerge to develop, produce, install and maintain such new technologies, and other challenges emerge in terms of the effects on workers. New technologies require adaptation of the skills of the workforce which can be facilitated by labour market policy and the training and education system (Nielsen et al. 2021). This aspect of the so-called Industry 4.0 revolution has been somewhat neglected in the literature compared to the number of contributions focusing on the aforementioned negative ramifications.

Against this background, the purpose of this chapter is to strengthen knowledge on how automation technology has affected the skills of employees and work organisation. The case of Denmark could be especially interesting in this regard for at least a couple of reasons. Firstly, because Denmark is a leading country outside Asia in the development and dissemination of robot technology (Graetz and Michaels 2018), which might have contributed to furthering the dissemination and adaptation of skills. Secondly, a positive stance exists among Danish employer and employee organisations towards adopting robots and AI/ML to exploit the potential in the new technologies. This collaborative approach among labour market organisations may potentially have led to a more rapid spread of technologies and skills in the Danish labour market by mitigating the fears of job losses and restructuring. As an example of labour unions positively embracing technological change, one could mention that the Danish Metalworkers Union has proposed a robot strategy (Dansk Metal 2019) with a number of suggestions as to how this technology could be applied to strengthen productivity and competitiveness. The Danish case thus contains some systemic characteristics, which makes it especially interesting.

As described in more detail, the analysis in this chapter uses new data from the Danish TASK Survey 2019, which consists of employee survey data on skills, work organisation and the use of robots, AI and ML at work for a representative stratified sample of the Danish workforce. Our new and unique data give us the opportunity to review key issues of policy importance. It allows us to go deeper into the effects of robotics for individual workers than previous studies, and it allows us to compare the effects of robotics with the effects of AI and ML.

The chapter is structured as follows. In Section 8.2, we provide a detailed account of the TASK Survey data and use cluster analysis to develop a taxonomy of forms of work organisation. Section 8.3 presents the dissemination of working tasks involving robot technology as well as AI/ML, supplemented by a mapping of related skill gaps and their causes. We then proceed in Section 8.4 to shed light on the predictors of diffusion and skill gaps for workers utilising the two types of technologies in a series of logistic regression models. Finally, in Section 8.5, we conclude and discuss the implications for general educational policies as well as policies for continued education and training.

8.2 Data: the TASK survey

We use data from a Danish survey on technologies and skills (TASK) undertaken in the spring of 2019. The survey was carried out by researchers from the IKE group at Aalborg University together with Statistics Denmark.[1]

The TASK survey covered individual employees in Denmark. Registry data from November 2018 covering the entire population of Denmark was used to delimit the relevant population and for the sampling frame. The main paid job of each individual was identified and only wage earners were included in the population. People employed at workplaces with less than five full time equivalent employees (FTEs) or at workplaces with a sectorial (NACE)[2] code for public sector administration were excluded. The result was a population of 2,076,617 employees in Denmark and from this population a stratified sample of 3117 employees was drawn. The sample was stratified in ten strata defined by the five geographical (NUTS2)[3] regions of Denmark and whether the workplace of the employees had fewer than 50 FTEs or 50+ FTEs. In the population, close to half of all individuals are in workplaces with 50+ FTEs and half are in workplaces of fewer than 50 FTEs. However, as the questions explored in the survey – in particular work organisation and the use of robots and other advanced technologies – were assumed to be more relevant for larger workplaces, and workplaces in Denmark are relatively small, larger workplaces were oversampled. Thus, two thirds of the sample are in the five strata of 50+ FTEs.

The survey was initially administered through the platform for digital communication used in communication between the Danish public sector and the public (e-Boks), and followed up by phone interviews to boost the response rate. The result was 1244 full responses or a response rate of 39.9% and an additional 145 partial responses. Statistics Denmark finally produced post stratification weights to make the data representative by each of the ten strata according to gender, age, wage and education, and to correct for the oversampling of employees at large workplaces.

In addition to the responses from the TASK survey the dataset created by Statistics Denmark contains a handful of variables copied from the registry data: industry of workplace (ten groups), wage (four groups), age (three groups) and education (three groups).

8.2.1 Work organisation in Denmark

Earlier work (Lorenz and Valeyre 2005; Holm et al. 2010; Holm and Lorenz 2015) used data from the European Working Conditions Survey (EWCS) to study the characteristics of work organisation. To build further on this work the TASK survey included the same questions on work organisation as the EWCS, with only minor necessary changes identified in the pilot survey, and with additional retrospective questions regarding changes in work organisation over time.

For the analysis presented here we make use of 14 of these questions. In the survey the respondents are asked how often they experience each work organisation characteristic on a five-level scale, from which we create binary variables taking the value 1 when the respondent experiences the characteristic 'always' or 'often'. The 14 binary variables are then subjected to a multiple correspondence analysis (MCA) and the first two factors are used to identify distinct forms of work organisation. Table 8.1 lists the 14 characteristics and reports the share of respondents experiencing the characteristic by work organisation cluster.

The interpretation of the clusters builds directly on Lorenz and Holm (2021). Clustering based on the first two factors of the MCA yields a three-cluster solution representing stylised forms of work organisation. The shares of employees grouped in the first and second clusters are both above the population average on work organisation characteristics, indicating continuous learning on the job. This means learning new things, having complex tasks and engaging in problem solving. However, in the second cluster, this is combined with above average presence of constraints on the work pace or rate. This includes horizontal, norm-based, automatic and hierarchical constraints, while in the first cluster high rates of learning are combined with below average constraints and also with relatively high levels of autonomy in setting the work

Table 8.1 Work organisation clusters.

Variables	DL	Lean production	Simple organisation	Average
Discretion in fixing work methods	73.7	62.2	19.0	55.8
Discretion in fixing work pace	73.4	49.5	30.2	56.7
Learning new things at work	72.3	76.2	20.7	58.1
Problem solving activities	93.4	91.5	65.4	84.9
Complexity of tasks	73.6	76.3	25.5	60.1
Responsibility for quality control	90.3	90.4	72.1	85.0
Respect for quality norms	69.3	95.7	87.1	79.2
Teamwork	62.8	80.8	32.3	57.3
Job rotation	58.0	81.9	38.2	56.6
Repetitiveness of tasks	18.8	55.3	49.9	34.4
Horizontal constraints on work rate	26.7	74.2	31.2	36.6
Norm-based constraints on work rate	28.2	89.9	34.3	41.1
Automatic constraints on work rate	2.9	48.7	23.7	17.2
Hierarchical constraints on work rate	4.3	37.3	15.0	13.3
Total	53.0	18.1	28.9	100.0

Percentage experiencing each characteristic.

pace and choosing work methods. The second cluster captures jobs character-ised by learning but in a relatively tightly structured mode. We refer to this as *lean* work organisation. The first cluster captures jobs characterised by learning, autonomy and few constraints. We refer to this as *discretionary learning* (DL) work organisation. The third and final cluster is located in between the first two clusters when considering constraints in the jobs. Workers in the third cluster also tend to score low on variables indicating autonomy and continuous learning in the job. This corresponds to relatively traditional jobs with limited skill development in the job and a combination of autonomy and constraints depending on the specific task in question. We refer to this as *simple* work organisation.

According to the TASK survey, roughly half (53%) of the employees in Denmark have DL forms of work organisation, 18% have lean work organisa-tion and the remaining 29% have simple work organisation. These numbers are not directly comparable with the earlier studies based on EWCS data which were restricted to private sector establishments. The analysis here using the TASK survey data has a broader coverage including both the education and health sectors.[4]

8.3 Describing new technology use

When describing new technology use in jobs in Denmark five questions on the TASK survey are central. These all ask the respondent to indicate how often their job involves specific tasks:[5]

1. delivering input or receive output such as raw materials, final goods or semi-manufactured to or from a robot
2. starting, monitoring and stopping a robot to accomplish a specific task
3. making use of information compiled automatically for you by a computer or by computerised machinery for making decisions or for advising clients or customers
4. receiving orders or directions generated automatically by a computer or by computerised machinery
5. using a computer or computerised machinery that has the ability to auto-matically learn and improve from experience.

The first two tasks relate to robots and the final three tasks relate to AI and ML. In the detailed analysis later in the chapter, we distinguish between all five tasks but initially we present a simple overview indicating the share of workers using robots or AI/ML in some manner in their job. We thus initially collapse the first two into one indicator for using robots and the final three into one indica-tor for using AI/ML. While this has the advantage that our robot indicator, for example, captures the use of robots in a broad sense, it has the disadvantage of ignoring differences in the ways robots may be used in a firm. This is amended in the later econometric analysis.

An employee uses robots (AI/ML) if he/she performs at least one of the first two (final three) tasks at least weekly. In addition to whether an employee has performed a task or not in 2019, we are also interested in whether he/she has experienced an increase in the frequency of the task since 2016, whether they have the necessary skills for the task and the main mechanism used for acquiring skills for the task.

An employee has seen an increase in tasks related to robots (AI/ML) if he/she reports an increase in at least one of the first two (final three) tasks over the last three years. An employee has a skill gap for robots (AI/ML) if he/she does not have the skills for performing at least one of the first two (final three) tasks 'to a high extent', conditional on performing the task. The TASK survey allows the respondent to indicate one main mechanism for acquiring skills for each task that he/she performs. The possible mechanisms are formal training, peer learning and self-taught. An employee has used one mechanism for acquiring skills related to robots (AI/ML) if he/she reports have used only that mechanism for the first two (final three) tasks conditional on performing the task. If he/she indicates different mechanisms on the first two (final three) tasks, then the mechanism for acquiring skills is 'a combination'.

8.3.1 The use of robots

Figure 8.1 shows according to occupation, sector and the form of work organisation the relative proportion of employees that use robots, the relative proportion that experience a skill gap and the relative proportion that have seen an increase in the use of robots over the preceding three years. The proportions are relative to the national average so that a value of 2 indicates twice the national average. At the national level, 8.27% of employees use robots, of these 50.04% have a skill gap and 5.22% have seen an increase in the use of robots from 2016 to 2019.

The left-hand side shows the use of robots by occupation, the centre shows the distribution by industry and the right-hand side shows the distribution

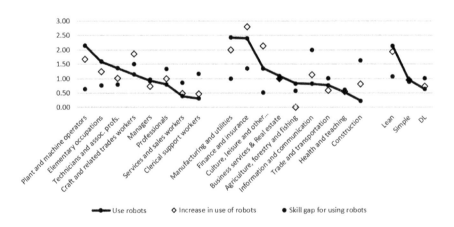

Figure 8.1 Robot use in Denmark. Source: Calculations based on own survey data.

by work organisation. For example, the left-hand side shows that the use of robots by plant and machine operators is slightly over twice the national average of 8.27%. The other two occupations with relatively high penetrations of robot use are also occupations often associated with manufacturing: elementary occupations and technicians. However, as opposed to manufacturing as a whole, these three groups have below average skill gaps.

Unsurprisingly, the centre shows that robots are most commonly used in the manufacturing industry where the diffusion is more than twice the national average of 8.27% as shown by the dots connected with a solid line. Notice that the groups are ordered in descending order by robot use. The increase in robot use in manufacturing is twice the national average (cf. the diamonds) and the skill gap is at the national average (cf. the dots), which is, however, a seemingly high 50%.

A curious finding is that the finance industry seems to have robot penetration at the same level as manufacturing and an even stronger increase than manufacturing, but this is likely to result from a measurement error as AI-based computer programmes are typically referred to as 'robots' in the finance industry. A more interesting observation is that craft workers have both the largest skill gaps and the largest increase in robot use, although the increase only brings them up to the national average. Relatedly, the construction industry is simultaneously the industry with the lowest robot penetration and one of the largest skill gaps, which probably reflects that robots are poorly adapted to the varied and changing physical conditions of worksites in the construction industry. It could also indicate that craft workers are insufficiently trained for using robots and that this is hampering the diffusion of robots in construction.

Some interesting but largely unexplainable results stand out. The culture and leisure industry has seen a large increase in robot use and employees in this industry have very low skill gaps, while the ICT industry is where the largest skill gaps are found. These results will be pursued further in the multivariate analysis that follows.

While learning at work is one of the main differences between the forms of work organisation, there does not seem to be any relationship between work organisation and the proportion of workers that report skill gaps in using robots in their work. Robot use and the increase in robot use are both particularly high for employees with the Lean form of work organisation and low for employees with DL work organisation. It thus appears that the major difference lies in constraints at work: employees who work more often with robots have more constraints. These constraints are, however, also combined with both learning and complexity, which can mean that using robots at work makes the job more intrinsically gratifying.

8.3.2 The use of AI/ML

Figure 8.2 is similar to Figure 8.1 but describes the use of AI/ML rather than robots. At the national level 25.57% use AI/ML, of which 50.75% have a skill gap and 11.27% have seen an increase in the use of AI/ML from 2016 to 2019.

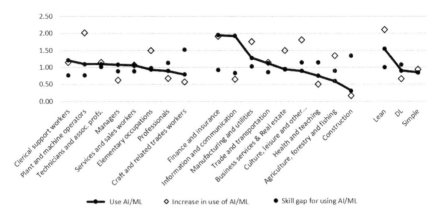

Figure 8.2 AI/ML use in Denmark. Source: Calculations based on own survey data.

The diffusion of AI/ML by occupational groups shows that the technologies are evenly diffused (cf. the left graph in Figure 8.2). The share of employees using AI/ML is close to the national average in all groups. Interestingly, there is an almost perfect inverse relationship between the share that uses the technologies and the share that experiences a skill gap for the technologies when considering the occupational groups (cf. the steady increase in the bold dots when going left to right across occupational groups). A somewhat similar pattern seems to hold across the industry groups in the central part of Figure 8.2. Either this implies a sort of externality where employees more often feel that they do not have sufficient skills for a technology when the technology is relatively exotic in their industry, or diffusion of the technology is hampered by a lack of skills among employees. Again, craft workers and the construction industry stand out as the occupational group and the industry group with particularly low diffusion and large skill gaps.

Not surprisingly, AI/ML is relatively widely diffused in the finance and ICT industries while increase in the use of AI/ML is seen across a wide range of industries. Interestingly, increase in AI/ML use by occupation is highest in occupations that are not traditionally considered highly skilled: plant and machine operators and elementary occupations. However, neither group reports particularly high skill gaps for using AI/ML. This does not mean that there is no room for improvement as the national average for the skill gap is 50.75%.

Regarding work organisation it can be observed again that both the greatest diffusion and the greatest increase in diffusion of AI/ML is seen for Lean work organisation. As with the use of robots, this can imply that AI/ML technologies at work substitute the dull tasks and leave employees with more interesting jobs characterised by continuous learning, while also imposing constraints on work. However, the opposite direction of causality is in principle also possible which would imply that employees with Lean forms of work organisation have jobs that are relatively susceptible to automation with robots or AI/ML and thus that such employees necessarily must be adaptable or risk losing their jobs.

The differences by occupation, industry and work organisation described in Figures 8.2 and 8.3 are likely to be correlated. For example, employees in construction may no longer have above average probability of a skill gap after correcting for the fact that many employees in construction are craft and related trades workers. Before using regression analysis to disentangle these effects, we describe the relationships between skill gaps, training mechanisms and job security.

8.3.3 Mechanisms for acquiring skills

Figure 8.3 shows the learning mechanisms used for the five questions on the use of new technology in work. The figure shows the percentage of employees using each mechanism as the main mechanism for skill acquisition by technology task, and the shares when considering only employees with a skill gap for the task. The two points are connected by a line segment and the slope of the line thus illustrates whether the learning mechanism is relatively more or less common among workers with a skill gap. If a learning mechanism is relatively less common among workers with a skill gap (negative slope), then the mechanism appears to mitigate skill gaps, and vice versa.

The solid line is the top line for all tasks except ML tasks which means that peer learning is the main mechanism for skill acquisition in all other cases. For controlling robots, the share reporting peer learning as the main mechanism for skill acquisition is around 85%. Peer learning is generally used more often for acquiring robot-related skills than for acquiring AI-related skills. For all five skills the least used mechanism for skill acquisition is formal training (dotted line). At the same time, it seems that formal training is reported less often as the most important mechanism for employees with a skill gap (i.e., the dotted lines all have negative slopes). This indicates that relying on formal training as

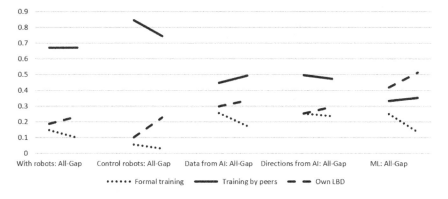

Figure 8.3 Learning mechanisms. Source: Calculations based on own survey data.

the main mechanism for skill acquisition is associated with the absence of skill gaps. Correspondingly, the dashed lines for the skill acquisition mechanism own 'learning-by-doing' (LBD) consistently has a positive slope indicating that employees with a skill gap relatively often have had own LBD as the main mechanism for skill acquisition. This pattern, of course, only indicates that own LBD is associated with skill gaps when own LBD is the main mechanism for skill acquisition. Own LBD may very well still be a good complement to other training forms.

The most pervasive learning mechanism – training by peers – seems to have varying associations with skill gaps. Training by peers is associated with less likelihood of skill gaps for controlling robots and for taking directions from AI (i.e., the slope is negative) but associated with a higher likelihood of skill gaps for using data from AI and for using ML. In Nielsen et al. (2021), it is emphasised that experience-based learning is important when employees face novel technologies and the descriptive results here partially contradict this by showing a positive relationship with formal training. However, it must be emphasised that Figure 8.3 focuses on the 'main' mechanism, and that the figure only reports a bivariate relationship. Learning mechanisms are not context free; what works in manufacturing may not work very well in the finance industry. The result is thus likely to change in the multivariate analysis.

8.4 Regression analyses

In this section we report two sets of five logistic regressions. The first five models are based on the full dataset and predict, respectively, whether or not the employee has one of the five technology related tasks: working alongside robots, controlling robots, using data from AI, taking directions from AI and using ML. In all five cases 'using' means using at least weekly. The next five models rely on subsets of the data, as they seek to predict skill gaps for the five tasks, and skill gaps can only be defined for employees actually having the relevant task. Having a skill gap is a binary variable taking the value 1 if the respondent reports to only have the necessary skills for the task to 'some' degree or less.

In all regressions, we use the weights supplied by Statistics Denmark for the TASK survey and we cluster the standard errors by the strata of the survey. In all regressions, we have only categorical regressors. We use weighted effect coding instead of the more common reference coding as we are not interested in the difference between each category and a specific reference category, but rather in the difference relative to the average observation, as in Figures 8.1 and 8.2.[6]

8.4.1 *Using technologies*

The five variables for having tasks at work involving the use of robots, AI or ML, are regressed on the variables from Figures 8.2 and 8.3: occupation, industry and work organisation. In addition, we control for age as a proxy for experience, wage as a proxy for position in the organisational hierarchy, employment level at the workplace and region. The results are presented in Table 8.2 and show that four of the five tasks are positively associated with Lean work organisation. Thus, the positive association between AI/ML and Lean in Figure 8.2 is reproduced but the positive relationship between robots and Lean in Figure 8.1 only pertains to controlling robots. The results are consistent with both robotics technologies and AI/ML technologies involving new knowledge acquisition (learning) but also intensification of work pace.

There is no statistically significant difference in work organisation for people working alongside robots. Similarly, the strong associations between industry and robots, and occupation and robots only pertain to controlling robots. It thus seems like working alongside robots is more broadly diffused than controlling robots. This can be explained by workers in diverse sectors working alongside service robots rather than industrial robots.

Except for clerks using data from AI relatively often, the result that AI/ML technologies are evenly diffused across occupational groups is reproduced in Table 8.2. The differences by industry are, however, more detailed as compared to Figure 8.2. AI appears to be relatively widespread in the manufacturing sector hinting at the growing integration of robotics and AI. While Figure 8.2 shows equally high diffusion rates for AI/ML technologies in ICT and in finance, Table 8.2 shows that there is a large difference: all three types of AI/ML tasks are relatively common in finance while in ICT it is only the task of using data from AI that is common. ICT firms may of course often be involved in developing AI/ML technologies, but this does not necessarily mean that such firms also use these technologies. The positive relationship with using AI-generated data can reflect that specific ICT firms with online business models such as social media firms use AI/ML intensively. Workers in culture and leisure use AI/ML technologies often but only in the sense that they take directions from AI. This may potentially include platform-based personal services where customers are connected to independent contractors by AI, cultural facilities such as libraries where AI systems determine the organisation of books and other materials, or betting and gambling firms where AI is used intensively.

No relationship between the size of the workplace and technology-related tasks is found. This may be because our only available measure of size is relatively crude (above or below 50 FTE), or because the size measure is based on employment, which may in principle be decreased when automation technologies are diffused. Neither age nor wage has much effect on the likelihood of having tasks that include robots, AI or ML. This implies that there are no systematic differences in the hierarchical level or work experience of employees using these technologies. Finally, a number of regional controls are significant indicating that our variable for industry does not capture all regional heterogeneity in diffusion, or that regional differences in diffusion reflect more than just regional differences in industry structure. In particular, both robotics and AI are used relatively

Table 8.2 Models for using technologies.

| | Dependent variable: Work with.... | | | | |
	With robots	Controls robots	AI data	AI instr.	ML
DL	−0.224	−0.360	−0.035	−0.191	−0.083
	0.384	0.392	0.166	0.217	0.200
Lean	0.653	1.014**	0.713***	0.977***	0.682*
	0.544	0.510	0.272	0.368	0.370
Simple	0.054	0.108	−0.372	−0.216	−0.255
	0.601	0.716	0.286	0.396	0.406
Size 50+ FTE	0.070	0.036	0.065	0.111	0.048
	0.207	0.187	0.104	0.140	0.152
Size 5–49 FTE	−0.161	−0.083	−0.148	−0.254	−0.111
	0.474	0.429	0.239	0.320	0.348
Managers	0.489	2.259	−0.200	−0.191	−0.049
	1.679	1.591	0.338	0.760	0.745
Professionals	0.038	1.064*	−0.051	−0.245	−0.103
	0.526	0.595	0.241	0.286	0.285
Assoc. profs and techs	0.289	2.151***	−0.251	0.122	−0.132
	0.718	0.533	0.248	0.330	0.332
Clerical support	−0.907	−14.825***	0.854**	0.250	−0.191
	1.151	0.850	0.380	0.581	0.569
Service and sales	−1.221	0.900	0.124	0.150	0.653
	3.790	1.409	0.681	0.676	0.563
Craft and related trades	0.750	2.416**	0.305	−0.473	0.043
	1.153	0.956	0.646	0.742	1.107
Plant and machine operators	0.757	2.443**	−0.077	0.656	0.108
	0.908	1.015	0.621	0.737	0.474
Elementary occupation	0.276	2.779**	−0.549	0.442	0.114
	2.051	1.349	0.633	0.972	0.803
Agriculture and fishing	−0.178	−15.358***	−1.452	0.496	−13.596***
	1.685	0.720	1.022	1.356	0.565
Manufacturing and utilities	1.189*	2.707***	0.566*	0.798**	0.386
	0.658	0.598	0.291	0.374	0.321
Construction	−1.633	−15.824***	−1.562	−1.803	−0.990
	2.745	0.683	1.713	2.160	1.450
Trade and transportation	0.015	1.266	0.472	0.266	−0.257
	1.263	1.458	0.417	0.513	0.550
ICT	0.337	−14.819***	1.727***	−0.314	0.915
	1.487	1.231	0.573	0.892	1.103

(*Continued*)

Table 8.2 Continued

	Dependent variable: Work with….				
	With robots	*Controls robots*	*AI data*	*AI instr.*	*ML*
Finance and insurance	1.551★	2.840★★★	1.274★★★	1.431★★★	1.432★★
	0.834	0.886	0.376	0.510	0.707
Business services	0.513	1.307	−0.381	0.697	0.200
	0.809	0.892	0.336	0.487	0.407
Teaching and health	−0.717	1.254★★	−0.450★	−0.687★	−0.056
	0.905	0.582	0.231	0.367	0.231
Culture, leisure and other	0.702	1.995★★	0.038	1.447★★	0.781
	3.514	0.979	1.237	0.627	0.528
Lowest wage quartile	−0.290	−0.623	−0.326	−0.129	−0.038
	1.425	1.272	0.816	0.505	0.635
Second wage quartile	0.485	0.737	−0.021	0.491	0.173
	0.903	0.559	0.255	0.328	0.260
Third wage quartile	0.292	−0.049	0.274	0.197	0.005
	0.449	0.571	0.327	0.452	0.330
Top wage quartile	−0.517	−0.368	0.049	−0.561★	−0.163
	0.570	0.794	0.300	0.316	0.346
Age 18–39	0.211	0.177	−0.105	0.130	−0.183
	0.677	0.801	0.251	0.379	0.349
Age 40–59	−0.071	0.064	−0.002	−0.121	0.082
	0.316	0.384	0.116	0.185	0.173
Age 60+	−0.128	−0.487	0.179	0.159	0.048
	1.171	1.081	0.260	0.372	0.338
Copenhagen City	0.167	−0.945	−0.033	−0.238	−0.395
	0.770	0.815	0.307	0.394	0.547
Copenhagen Surroundings	0.157	0.380	−0.364	−0.016	−0.192
	0.461	0.567	0.347	0.400	0.415
North Zealand	1.034	0.526	0.447	0.436	1.019★★
	0.718	0.566	0.489	0.706	0.501
Bornholm	−13.916★★★	1.308	0.351	1.247★★	0.759
	1.892	1.328	2.567	0.558	0.875
East Zealand	1.570★★	1.582★	1.532★★★	1.470★★★	0.332
	0.740	0.943	0.500	0.476	0.620
West and South Zealand	0.162	−0.216	0.050	0.297	0.054
	1.541	0.772	0.452	0.514	0.671
Funen	−0.310	−0.412	−0.386	0.102	0.041
	0.759	0.855	0.495	0.810	0.536

(*Continued*)

Table 8.2 Continued

| | Dependent variable: Work with.... | | | | |
	With robots	Controls robots	AI data	AI instr.	ML
South Jutland	0.440	0.253	−0.083	0.120	−0.187
	0.406	0.691	0.331	0.638	0.328
West Jutland	−0.353	0.566	−0.037	−0.851	−0.384
	2.843	2.398	0.515	0.810	0.616
East Jutland	−0.532	−0.138	−0.103	−0.635★	0.330
	0.560	0.506	0.570	0.383	0.538
North Jutland	0.268	0.093	0.424	0.766★	0.028
	1.350	0.771	0.384	0.453	0.501
Constant	−3.369★★★	−6.843★★★	−1.726★★★	−2.570★★★	−2.206★★★
	0.468	0.350	0.205	0.209	0.172
Observations	1061	1062	1061	1057	1058

Note: ★p < 0.1; ★★p < 0.05; ★★★p < 0.01.

intensively in the region of East Zealand, which is an area just outside the capital city of Copenhagen, well known for the concentration of large multinational companies (MNCs). North Zealand is another region just outside Copenhagen and here it seems that a disproportionate share of employees uses ML in their job. While East Zealand is characterised by many MNCs in general, North Zealand tends to be the location of pharmaceutical and chemical MNCs such as Bavarian Nordic, Chr. Hansen, ALK–Abelló and Coloplast.[7]

8.4.2 Skill gaps

Skill gaps would ideally be regressed on the same variables as used in the previous section and, in addition, the training mechanisms of Figure 8.3 and an indicator for the frequency of technology use. The frequency of technology use is relevant as the descriptive figures earlier suggested that, at the industry level, there is an inverse relationship between technology use and skill gaps. However, the number of observations for the models for skill gaps is limited by the fact that employees who do not use a given technology in their job cannot have a skill gap for that technology relative to the job's requirement. It has therefore been necessary to construct the models stepwise and exclude variables that do not contribute to explaining skill gaps. Both the individual t-tests and the joint F-test were considered when dropping variables, and the same set of regressors has been used in both models for comparability.

Industry and region are therefore excluded in the five models for skill gaps presented in Table 8.3. We are left with a model consisting of occupation, work organisation, frequency of the relevant task, learning mechanism for acquiring skills for the relevant task, wage and age.

Table 8.3 Models for skill gaps.

	Dependent variable:				
	Skill gap for...				
	With robots	Controls robots	AI data	AI instr.	ML
Formal training	−1.056	−2.719**	−0.731	0.014	−0.955**
	−0.811	−1.063	−0.465	−0.412	−0.464
Peer learning	0.038	−0.456	0.302	−0.044	0.019
	0.220	0.278	0.203	0.323	0.297
Own LBD	0.518	5.577★★	0.147	0.069	0.516
	0.630	2.333	0.283	0.668	0.341
Daily	−0.637*	0.116	−0.391**	−0.303	−0.459***
	−0.364	−0.576	−0.182	−0.315	−0.132
Weekly	0.730	−0.884	0.300	0.244	0.870★
	0.726	1.306	0.371	0.628	0.475
Monthly	1.125	0.420	0.646★	0.457	0.824★★
	0.864	1.481	0.351	0.529	0.387
DL	−0.174	−0.220	0.004	0.060	0.177
	−0.524	−0.626	−0.208	−0.246	−0.236
Lean	0.299	0.858	0.217	−0.124	−0.291
	0.927	1.071	0.399	0.586	0.470
Simple	0.171	−0.083	−0.143	−0.046	−0.182
	0.955	1.209	0.407	0.418	0.466
Managers	−0.167	−3.863**	−0.520	−0.675	−0.167
	−2.293	−1.813	−0.468	−0.780	−0.840
Professionals	0.569	−0.858	0.378	0.657	0.388
	0.859	0.988	0.267	0.425	0.359
Assoc. profs and techs	−0.673	1.124	0.213	0.328	0.347
	0.828	0.873	0.332	0.434	0.392
Clerical support	−1.566	−0.542	−0.389	−0.693	−0.094
	3.341	1.727	0.629	0.872	0.829
Service and sales	0.332	2.002	0.100	−0.958	−0.798
	1.090	2.271	0.733	1.245	0.922
Craft and related trades	2.477★★	3.248★★	1.505	1.029	−0.584
	1.200	1.499	0.947	0.866	2.021
Plant and machine operators	−0.557	0.896	−1.363	−0.354	−0.295
	1.573	1.203	0.833	0.662	0.630
Elementary occupation	−0.663	1.144	−1.606	−1.513	−0.601
	0.932	1.604	1.506	1.585	0.556
Lowest wage quartile	−0.793	−0.015	−0.121	0.036	1.089
	−1.613	−1.061	−0.632	−0.814	−0.710
Second wage quartile	0.0004	−0.129	0.145	0.111	0.602
	0.703	0.895	0.376	0.554	0.381

(*Continued*)

Table 8.3 Continued

	Dependent variable:				
	Skill gap for...				
	With robots	*Controls robots*	*AI data*	*AI instr.*	*ML*
Third wage quartile	−0.460	−3.745	0.152	0.127	−0.552
	0.910	2.592	0.551	0.486	0.614
Top wage quartile	0.767	2.477*	−0.173	−0.218	−0.951***
	0.873	1.297	0.254	0.501	0.343
Age 18–39	0.677	−0.329	0.078	−0.244	−0.535
	−0.936	−0.963	−0.325	−0.475	−0.559
Age 40–59	−0.213	0.498	−0.079	0.184	0.234
	0.726	1.142	0.184	0.258	0.305
Age 60+	−0.453	−0.989	0.115	−0.164	0.159
	3.271	4.552	0.288	0.450	0.512
Constant	−0.115	−1.296	−0.33	−0.246	0.263
	0.677	1.724	0.235	0.271	0.210
Observations	85	68	252	151	157

Note: The variables for frequency of use and for training methods differ across the models. In each model the variables refer to the task as indicated by the dependent variable. *$p < 0.1$; **$p < 0.05$; ***$p < 0.01$.

The descriptive analysis of Figure 8.3 suggested that formal training is associated with a lower likelihood of skill gaps and this result is reproduced for two of the five tasks: formal training is associated with lower likelihood of skill gaps for controlling robots, and for using ML but not for the remaining three tasks. Based on Figure 8.3 it was also expected that own LBD would be positively associated with skill gaps, but this is only found for the task of controlling robots. While the training mechanism thus plays a role in skill formation for controlling robots, it is found that frequency of the task is an important predictor for skill gaps when working alongside robots, using data from AI or using ML. In all three cases, daily frequency is negatively associated with skill gaps while monthly frequency is positive for the last two. No statistically significant effects are found for work organisation indicating that, while work organisation does differ for workers with different tasks as shown earlier, this is not reflected in skill gaps. In particular, workers with technology-related tasks are broadly more likely to have Lean work organisation but this does not affect their proficiency for the technology-related task.

There are only a few significant relations between occupations and skill gaps. In particular, it seems that craft workers tend to have skill gaps for both working alongside robots and for controlling robots. As craft workers are also more likely than the average worker to control robots as part of their job, this appears unfortunate.

Workers in crafts and related trades are more likely than average to have a skill gap for working alongside robots or for controlling robots but with the exception of managers, no occupational group is less likely than average to have a skill gap for using robots. Workers in occupational groups that are more likely to use robots (plant and machine operators, and elementary occupation – cf. Model 1) are just as likely to be adequately or inadequately trained as the average worker.

The weak effects for age and wage indicate that there is no relationship between workers' skill gaps and their job experience or their position in the organisational hierarchy.

For AI/ML the results show that workers who use the technology daily tend not to have a skill gap. The result cannot determine whether this is because only the most capable employees work regularly with these technologies or because the experience workers gain through regular use of the technology contributes to reducing any skills gap, they may have had.

8.5 Discussion

The analysis shows that there are significant differences between robot technologies and AI/ML technologies. Less than one in ten workers in Denmark use robots weekly and the use of robots varies significantly with the occupation of the worker and with the worker's position in the organisational hierarchy (as captured by the worker's wage). However, a quarter of all workers use AI/ML at least weekly and this is independent of job function and hierarchy. Thus, even though robotics has been around for decades it has only diffused to relatively specific occupations, while the more recent AI/ML has rapidly become pervasive across the economic system. In other words, AI/ML has uses throughout the economic system while robots are used more specifically. This supports the argument by Brynjolfsson et al. (2018) that AI may be a new general-purpose technology, and it implies that the adoption of AI and ML may pose a broader and more systematic challenge in terms of labour market restructuring and the need for investments in new skills than the use of robots.

Reducing skill gaps is nevertheless important for dissemination and utilisation of both robotics and AI/ML technologies. These seem to be quite pervasive among workers regardless of technology. Approximately 50% of workers in the TASK survey reported experiences of skill gaps. These are largest in manufacturing and construction and seem unrelated to the type of work organisation. We find an interesting inverse relationship between the share that uses AI/ML and the share that reports a skill gap. This might indicate a hampering of diffusion of these technologies because of a lack of skills.

Regarding skill acquisition, the data show that the main mechanism is peer learning, while formal training seems of lesser importance, but it must be emphasised that the data refer only to the main mechanism. The fact that peer learning is most often the main mechanism for skill acquisition does not mean that formal training is not used to support peer learning. Policies aiming to manage the supply of skills mainly work through formal training so the effectiveness of policies for managing skills in the workforce may hinge on the use of formal training for skill acquisition. The importance of formal training is supported by our analysis which shows that in general, using formal training as the main mechanism for skill acquisition is associated with fewer skill gaps. There might be important interactions in skill formation between peer learning and formal training, but in any circumstance, we recommend further discussion as to how the educational and vocational systems could play a more pronounced role for skill acquisition in the future.

As mentioned earlier, work organisation has no statistically significant relationship with skill gaps, while workers using new technologies are more likely to have Lean work organisation. Thus, firms adopting new technologies find ways to cover skill formation regardless of their choice of work organisation. Other research has found that work organisation along the lines of DL organisation makes firms more innovative and workers more satisfied (Lorenz and Holm 2021), and our results suggest that such work organisation can be promoted without compromising skill sufficiency.

The results presented in this chapter show that the use of robots is confined to a relatively narrow set of industries and occupational groups in the Danish NSI (national system of innovation) while AI and ML are more widely diffused. AI and ML are also more diffused in absolute terms compared to robots. The results indicate that these technologies are impacting firms and workers more pervasively than robotics at the aggregate level. Thus, while employees, as represented by unions, have embraced robotics and to some degree facilitated employers' adoption of robotics for automation, AI and ML have diffused much more widely without such explicit support. While robotics has for decades been a productivity-enhancing technology that allows manufacturing firms to remain cost competitive in globalised competition, it remains to be seen whether AI and ML will have the same role over coming decades for more or less all industries and occupations in the economy. Our results show that using AI or ML technologies is strongly associated with Lean work organisation, suggesting that adoption of AI or ML is either easier with Lean work organisation, or leads to a Leaner form of work organisation. However, if Lean facilitates the adoption of AI and ML then Lean work organisation should also be associated with fewer skill gaps, which we do not find. Hence, as Lean is elsewhere found to be associated with less innovation and less job satisfaction compared to specific other forms of work organisation, there may be some voluntarism in the way AI and ML are diffused in the Danish national system of innovation so as to foster forms of work organisation that tend to enhance innovative performance and to assure a higher quality of working life (Lorenz and Holm 2021; Nielsen et al. 2021).

Notes

1 TASK was funded partially by the Obel Family Foundation through the ReDy project and partially by the talent programme for young researchers at the faculty of social sciences, Aalborg University.
2 NACE refers to the Statistical Classification of Economic Activities in the European Community and is derived from the French term Nomenclature statistique des Activités Economiques.
3 NUTS refers to the Nomenclature of Territorial Units for Statistics or NUTS and is derived from the French term Nomenclature des Unités Territoriales statistiques. There are three levels and NUTS2 refers to the second or regional level.
4 The analysis based on EWCS for 2015 excluding health and education in Lorenz and Holm (2021) in this volume shows a share for the DL forms very close to the estimate based on TASK.
5 The TASK survey uses a definition of robots that combines the IFR's definitions of service robots and industrial robots into one broad definition 'a programmable and movable machine, which performs tasks in manufacturing or services. Robots can be stationary using an arm for example doing welding, assembling or packing, or they can be mobile robots for example doing cleaning, maintenance or warehouse work'.
6 Effect coding still entails leaving out one category to avoid perfect multicollinearity when estimating but the estimate for this category can be derived from the estimates for the included categories. Alternatively, a second regression can be undertaken leaving out a different category. We report estimates for all categories including the category originally left out.
7 See Holm et al. (2017) for an analysis of MNCs in Denmark.

References

Acemoğlu, D. and Restrepo, P. 2018. The race between man and machine: Implications of technology for growth, factor shares, and employment. *American Economic Review* 108(6): 1488–1542. doi:10.1257/aer.20160696

Autor, D. H., Levy, F. and Murnane, R. J. 2003. The skill content of recent technological change: An empirical exploration. *The Quarterly Journal of Economics* 118: 1279–1333.

Brynjolfsson, E. and McAfee, A., 2015. Will humans go the way of horses? Labor in the second machine age. *Foreign Affairs* 94(4): 8–14.

Brynjolfsson, E., Mitchell, T. and Rock, D., 2018. What can machines learn, and what does it mean for occupations and the economy? *AEA Papers and Proceedings* 108: 43–47. doi:10.1257/pandp.20181019

Dansk Metal. 2019. *Behov for robotter i dansk erhvervsliv: Dansk Metals anbefalinger til en robotstrategi, der kan forbedre Danmarks konkurrenceevne*, Copenhagen.

DST. 2020. *Statistik Banken, Table ITAV7*. https://www.statistikbanken.dk/ITAV7. Last accessed 20 January 2020.

Goos, M. and Manning, A. 2007. Lousy and lovely jobs: The rising polarization of work in Britain. *Review of Economics and Statistics* 89: 119–133.

Goos, M., Manning, A. and Salomons, A. 2014. Explaining job polarization: Routine-biased technological change and offshoring. *American Economic Review* 104: 2509–2526.

Graetz, G. and Michaels, G. 2018. Robots at work. *The Review of Economics and Statistics* 100(5): 753–768.

Holm, J. R. and Lorenz, E. 2015. Has "Discretionary Learning" declined during the Lisbon Agenda? A cross-sectional and longitudinal study of work organization in European nations. *Industrial and Corporate Change* 24: 1179–1214.

Holm, J. R., Lorenz, E., Lundvall, B.-Å. and Valeyre, A. 2010. Organizational learning and systems of labor market regulation in Europe. *Industrial and Corporate Change* 19: 1141–1173.

Holm, J. R., Timmermans, B. and Østergaard, C. R. 2017. *The Impact of Multinational R&D Spending Firms on Job Polarization and Mobility*. JRC Technical Report, JRC108560. Luxembourg: Publications Office of the European Union.

IFR. 2019a. *World Robotics 2019: Industrial Robots*. https://ifr.org/free-downloads/. Last accessed 20 January 2020.

IFR. 2019b. *World Robotics 2019: Service Robots*. https://ifr.org/free-downloads/ Last accessed 20 January 2020.

Lorenz, E. and Holm, J. R. 2021. Workplace innovation and working conditions in Denmark. In *Globalisation, New and Emerging Technologies, and Sustainable Development – The Danish Innovation System in Transition*, ed. Christensen, J. L., Gregersen, B., Holm, J. R. and Lorenz, E. London: Routledge.

Lorenz, E., and Valeyre, A. 2005. Organisational innovation, HRM and labour market structure: A comparison of the EU-15. *Journal of Industrial Relations* 47: 424–442.

Nielsen, P., Holm, J. R. and Lorenz, E. 2021. Work policy and automation in the fourth industrial revolution. In *Globalisation, New and Emerging Technologies, and Sustainable Development – The Danish Innovation System in Transition*, ed. Christensen, J. L., Gregersen, B., Holm, J. R. and Lorenz, E. London: Routledge.

OECD 2017. *Better Use of Skills in the Workplace: Why It Matters for Productivity and Local Jobs*. Paris: OECD Publishing.

Pinzone, M., Fantini, P., Perini, S., Garavaglia, S., Taisch, M. and Miragliotta, G. 2017. *Jobs and Skills in Industry 4.0: An Exploratory Research*. In *IFIP International Conference on Advances in Production Management Systems*, ed. Lödding et al., 282–288. Springer.

Seeman, R., and Raj, M. 2018. *AI, Labor, Productivity and the Need for Firm-Level Data*. NBER Working Paper Series. Working paper 24239.

World Economic Forum. 2018. *The Future of Jobs Report 2018*. Geneva.

9 Work organisation, innovation and the quality of working life in Denmark

Edward Lorenz and Jacob Rubæk Holm

9.1 Introduction

The impact of the 'transformed workplace' on company performance and on employee outcomes is the subject of a vast literature in the field of human resource management (HRM) practices. The debate on this topic has its roots in the rising interest in Japanese-style management practices from the 1980s and 1990s which were perceived to supersede more hierarchical Taylorist forms of work organisation adapted to large scale mass production, especially in the automobile and consumer electronics industries. One branch of this literature, often referred to as 'high-performance work systems' (HPWS), is distinctive for arguing not only that there are strong complementarities between work organisation and specific HRM practices affecting pay and careers, but that such transformed workplaces offer mutual gains and serve to enhance both company performance and employee satisfaction and wellbeing at work (e.g., Appelbaum et al. 2000; Black et al. 2004; Freeman and Kleiner 2000; Young et al. 2010; Van De Voorde and Beijer 2015). The view that employees benefit from new forms of work organisation has not been without its critics, however, and several scholars have argued that the benefits workers may derive from the transformed workplace are outweighed by the disadvantages due to higher stress and a higher risk of workplace injury (e.g., Ramsay et al. 2000; Askenazy et al. 2002; Godard 2001; Guest 2017; Jensen et al. 2013; Ogbonnaya et al. 2017).

Innovation scholars have intermittently shown some interest in the role of work organisation and organisational design as important components of innovation systems. Freeman (1987), in his classic study of the Japanese innovation system, identified the characteristics of the Japanese firm as an innovative organisation arguing that the factory was used as a laboratory for innovation. In his 1995 paper on globalisation and innovation systems, he went on to argue that the success of innovations depends on more than formal R&D and that incremental innovations in particular came from production engineers, technicians and the shop floor, and were strongly related to different forms of work organisation (Freeman, 1995, p. 10). Subsequently, however, as Lundvall (2013) observed, innovation studies scholars have given relatively little attention to the role of workers and work organisation in innovation processes and the emphasis has rather been on the role of formal R&D.[1]

A notable exception to the tendency to ignore the role of workers and work organisation in innovation studies research was the DISKO project undertaken by members of the IKE group at Aalborg University in 1995–1996.[2] The project included a major survey of private sector firms in Denmark and the framework was designed to capture not only the firm's innovation performance but also the characteristics of interactive learning processes both within the firm and between the firm and external organisations. An underlying hypothesis was that innovation would be enhanced by adopting a 'learning organisation' design with work organisation and managerial practices designed to increase opportunities for employees at all levels of the organisation to learn and explore new knowledge in their daily work activity. Many of the features and work practices identified in the survey were the same ones that were emphasised in the HPWS literature. The results from the 1996 and subsequent rounds of the DISKO survey provided the basis for a number of highly cited publications that uniquely explore the interconnections between product and process innovation on the one hand, and forms of interactive learning both within and between firms on the other (e.g., Laursen and Foss 2003; Nielsen and Lundvall 2007; Jensen et al. 2007; Vinding 2006).

This chapter follows in the path of the DISKO project with its focus on the relationship between organisational forms and innovation performance. It extends the research based on the DISKO survey in several respects. First, the analysis situates Denmark in an internationally comparative context, comparing the frequency with which private sector establishments in Denmark adopt different organisational forms with the frequencies of adoption for establishments in other European nations. To do this, we use the 2013 round of the European Company Survey (ECS) which covered the EU27. The questionnaire design for the 2013 ECS drew some of its inspiration from the DISKO survey and there is considerable overlap in the indicators of forms of work organisation used in the two surveys.

Secondly, we also explore the relation between the adoption of different forms of work organisation in Denmark and indicators of the quality of working life. To do this we use a separate survey carried out at the employee level in 2015, the European Working Conditions Survey (EWCS). The EWCS, which has been carried out every five years since 1995, includes several indicators of work organisation, as well as a vast array of indicators of employee outcomes including job satisfaction and stress linked to work intensification. Using the results of the EWCS, we are able to both compare over time the adoption of different forms of work organisation in Denmark in relation to other EU member countries between 2005 to 2015, and to analyse the relation of the forms of work organisation adopted in Denmark to the quality of working life as measured by various indicators of employee outcomes.

Following this section, the chapter is structured as follows. Section 9.2 describes how indicators based on the employer-level ECS are used to map the relative importance of the different organisational forms adopted by enterprises in Denmark and across the EU27. Logit regression analysis is used to estimate the relative impact of adopting a learning organisation design on enterprise innovation performance. Section 9.3 uses the employee-level EWCS data to generate a similar mapping of forms of work organisation and traces changes in the frequency of learning forms of work organisation between 2005 to 2015. Logit regression analysis is used to estimate the relative impact of learning forms of work organisation on different indicators of the quality of working life. Section 9.4 compares the results from the two mappings and Section 9.5 concludes.

9.2 Mapping enterprise organisational forms with the European Company Survey

The third ECS was carried out by Eurofound in 2013 in the EU28, the Republic of North Macedonia, Iceland, Montenegro and Turkey. The target respondents were senior managers in charge of personnel in establishments with ten or more employees in all sectors excluding agriculture, forestry and fishing, the activities of households and the activities of extraterritorial organisations and bodies.[3] The analysis presented in this chapter is restricted to private sector establishments in the EU27 and excludes establishments in education, health and in public administration and defence.

The focus of the 2013 round of the ECS is on work organisation, workplace innovation, HR practices, employee participation and social dialogue. Table 9.1 presents the results of factor and cluster analysis used to identify groups of establishments with different organisational forms or designs. The factor analysis method used is multiple correspondence analysis which is adapted for categorical variables. Clustering is done on the first three factors, accounting for 36.8% of the total variance of the dataset, using Ward's method of hierarchical clustering. This allowed for the identification of three distinct classes or groups of establishments, the learning organisation, the HRM hybrid and the simple organisation.

The first column of Table 9.1 lists the indicators from the ECS used as a basis for identifying the three distinct forms of establishment organisation. The choice of indicators was based in part on a reading of literature on HPWS referred to earlier, as well as the literature on the relationship between organisational design and innovation performance associated with Burns and Stalker (1961) and Mintzberg (1983). Mintzberg (1983), within the context of the broad distinction between bureaucratic and organic organisations made by Burns and Stalker, identifies two types of organic organisation with a high capacity for adaptation: the operating adhocracy and the simple organisation. The forms of work organisation and types of work practices that characterise these two organic forms are quite different. The simple form is quite rudimentary in terms of managerial hierarchies and typically relies on direct supervision by one individual (typically a manager). A classic example of this type of organisation

Table 9.1 Establishment organisational forms in 2013: EU27.

	Percentage of establishments by organisational cluster reporting each variable			
Variables	*Learning organisation*	*HRM hybrid*	*Simple organisation*	*Average*
Work organisation				
Employee normally has or shares responsibility for planning and execution of tasks	**87.4**	10.1	38.5	45.9
Teamwork				
Employees decide on the allocation of tasks	**45.7**	0.9	10.8	19.5
Superior usually decides on the allocation of tasks	36.3	**64.0**	**57.4**	52.5
Some employees rotate tasks	66.2	**72.6**	60.0	66.4
Employees document and record good work practices or lesson learned	**69.1**	66.1	45.4	60.5
Establishment monitors quality	76.3	**83.1**	68.7	76.1
Employee involvement and consultation				
Suggestion schemes	**52.3**	42.1	27.1	40.8
Regular staff meetings open to all	**78.7**	88.0	9.8	59.4
Regular meetings between employees and supervisor	**98.7**	99.8	55.9	85.2
Training and incentives				
On-the-job training during last 12 months★	**53.2**	41.3	22.4	39.3
Group performance pay	**31.7**	21.6	20.6	24.8
Performance appraisal once a year★	**77.7**	**58.9**	33.7	57.2
All sample	34.4	33.2	32.4	100.0

Source: 3rd ECS, 2013 (weighted data). ★40% or more of employees.

is the small service sector firm. The operating adhocracy tends to prevail in high technology sectors such as software, electronics and biotechnology. Work is typically organised through temporary project teams and the organisational design is 'flat' with little top-down decision-making. Coordination is achieved through what Mintzberg refers to as 'mutual adjustment' and decision-making power is closely tied to the persons with the necessary expertise.

The first six variables capture the core work organisation practices identified in the HPWS literature including employee involvement in operational decision-making, the use of autonomous teams, task rotation and the documenting of good working practices as a basis for benchmarking and continuous improvement. Communication across services and teams is promoted through the use of regular staff meetings and meetings between employees and their immediate supervisors. Employee involvement is also measured through an indicator of the use of suggestion schemes. Skills development is measured through an indicator of the importance of on-the-job training, and incentives for employees to participate and contribute to company performance are captured through indicators of group performance pay and annual performance appraisal.

Columns 2, 3 and 4 of Table 9.1 show the frequencies with which the establishments in the population use the various practices for the learning organisation, HRM hybrid and simple organisation clusters respectively. For example, the figures in the table show that in 87.4% of the establishments grouped in the learning organisation cluster, employees normally have or share responsibility for the planning and execution of their tasks. Column 5 shows the frequencies for the entire population of enterprises.

The first cluster or organisational group described in column 2 accounts for a little over a third of the entire population. It is distinctive for the decentralisation of decision-making. The involvement of employees in the planning and execution of tasks is almost twice the population average and the use of autonomous teams is more than twice the rate of use for the population average. The first group is the only one of the three characterised by high levels of employee control over how tasks are carried out and by high levels of employee responsibility for planning and execution of tasks. The share of establishments in this class that use HPWS practices such as job rotation and monitoring quality is at average or above average levels, and the share in which employees document and share information on good working practices is above the average. The measures of employee involvement and consultation are above the population average. The establishments in the first class make the highest use of on-the-job training for skills development and have the highest use of incentive devices that can encourage greater effort and involvement. For these reasons we refer to this class as the learning organisation.

The second organisational class described in column 3 presents a mixed situation. Employee control over work activity and decision making is very low while the use of HPWS practices job rotation and quality monitoring are at above average levels. Teamwork is used but almost exclusively in a hierarchical mode with superiors fixing the allocation of tasks. This group of firms makes as high or higher use of consultation practices than the first group and the provision of on-the-job training and the use of annual appraisal are somewhat above the population average. The characteristics of this class, which makes up about 32% of the population, when compared to the first makes it clear that HPWS practices can be adopted in a way that preserves hierarchical control. Due to this combination, hierarchical control and high use of new forms of work organisation and consultation, we refer to this class as the HRM hybrid organisation.

The degree of hierarchy in the establishments grouped in the third class is at intermediate levels with slightly under 40% of the establishments organising work so that employees have or share responsibility for the planning and execution of tasks. The use of the other formal practices identified in the HPWS literature are below the population average. For this reason, we refer to this organisational class as the simple organisation.

Table 9.2 shows the ranking of the EU member nations in terms of the frequencies of the three organisational forms. The Nordic countries are distinctive for the high frequencies of the learning organisation form. The results show that slightly under 62% of enterprises in Denmark use a learning organisation design, somewhat below the shares in Finland and Sweden. The adoption of the learning organisation is somewhat over the population average in the UK

Table 9.2 Establishment organisational forms across the EU27 in 2013.

Country	Learning organisation	HRM hybrid	Simple organisation	Total
Continental Europe				
Austria	57.15	18.37	24.48	100.00
Belgium	27.95	33.55	38.50	100.00
Germany	47.14	23.59	29.27	100.00
France	29.08	33.56	37.36	100.00
Luxembourg	33.46	29.16	37.38	100.00
Netherlands	39.59	35.60	24.81	100.00
North				
Finland	66.49	13.51	20.00	100.00
Denmark	61.76	21.68	16.56	100.00
Sweden	69.72	20.88	9.41	100.00
South				
Italy	21.73	39.21	39.06	100.00
Greece	28.78	39.18	32.04	100.00
Spain	26.94	36.39	36.67	100.00
Portugal	18.96	39.32	41.72	100.00
West				
Ireland	37.26	41.79	20.95	100.00
UK	41.09	32.80	26.11	100.00
East				
Bulgaria	24.58	47.41	28.01	100.00
Czech Republic	22.12	54.73	23.15	100.00
Hungary	25.28	43.76	30.95	100.00
Poland	26.21	25.30	48.49	100.00
Slovenia	50.70	29.16	20.14	100.00
Slovakia	18.55	59.66	21.79	100.00
Romania	24.89	47.34	27.77	100.00
North-east				
Estonia	36.30	26.32	37.39	100.00
Latvia	26.38	32.00	41.62	100.00
Lithuania	29.84	31.01	39.15	100.00
South-east				
Cyprus	35.04	36.21	28.75	100.00
Malta	26.34	35.29	38.37	100.00
EU27	34.43	33.24	32.32	100.00

Source: 3rd ECS, 2013 (weighted data).

and Ireland and in all the continental European countries except for France. There is a low rate of adoption of the learning organisation forms in the southern European countries and they also tend to be underrepresented in most of the central and eastern European countries. The notable exception is Slovenia where the results show that about 50% of the population of enterprises use a learning organisation design.

9.2.1 Organisational forms and innovation performance

In this section we use logit regression to investigate the relation between the establishment's organisational form and its innovation performance. We make use of a binary measure of product innovation based on the Oslo Manual definitions: 'whether or not the establishment has introduced onto the market over the last three years a new or significantly improved product or service'. Columns 1 and 2 in Table 9.3 show the results for the EU27 with and without controls for sector of activity and establishment size, and columns 3 and 4 show the results for the case of Denmark.

The results for the EU27 show that learning organisations are more likely to develop new products and service compared to establishments with the HRM hybrid form. Establishments with the simple organisation form are less likely to innovate. These results are robust to the introduction of sector and establishment size controls. For the case of Denmark, the regression results also show that learning organisations are more likely to introduce new products or services onto the market than establishments with the HRM hybrid form of organisation. In terms of odds, the regression with controls shows that the odds of a learning organisation in Denmark innovating a new product or service are 1.8 times the odds of an HRM hybrid. Unlike the EU27 on average, there are no statistically significant differences between the simple and HRM hybrid forms for the case of Denmark.

9.3 Mapping forms of work organisation with the European Working Conditions Survey

The EWCS has been carried out every five years since 1995. The survey has retained the same core set of indicators since 1995 while periodically adding additional ones. As discussed here, the results of the survey provide the basis for measuring how the frequencies of specific forms of work organisation have changed over time within EU member nations, and in this chapter we focus on the decade from 2005 to 2015. The EWCS has covered the EU27 plus several other countries including Switzerland, Norway, Croatia and Turkey since the 2005 round. The target population is all residents of the countries covered aged 15 or older (16 or older in Bulgaria, Norway, Spain and the UK) and in employment at the time of the survey.[4] The analysis here focuses on the EU27 and is restricted to employees working in private sector establishments with ten or more employees excluding agriculture, forestry and fishing, the activities of

Table 9.3 Logit regressions predicting product or service innovation.

Variable	(1)	(2)	(3)	(4)
	Product/service innovation			
	EU27		*Denmark*	
Learn	0.174★★★	0.152★★	0.591★★	0.571★
	(3.31)	(2.82)	(2.60)	(2.42)
HRM Hybrid (reference)				
Simple	-0.313★★★	-0.316★★★	-0.0697	0.113
	(-5.74)	(-5.70)	(-0.23)	(0.37)
10–49 employees				
50–249 employees		0.364★★★		0.334★
		(7.80)		(2.08)
>249 employees		0.599★★★		0.849★★
		(7.78)		(2.83)
Industry				
(Reference)				
Construction		-0.757★★★		-0.700
		(-8.86)		(-1.77)
Wholesale, retail food,		0.0900		0.201
accommodation		(1.58)		(0.82)
Transport		-0.731★★★		-1.380★★
		(-7.00)		(-2.66)
Financial services		-0.425★★★		0.0113
		(-3.46)		(0.03)
Other services		-0.118		-0.0229
		(-1.87)		(-0.09)
cons	-0.350★★★	-0.282★★★	-0.198	-0.227
	(-9.46)	(-5.57)	(-1.02)	(-0.89)
N	21004	20818	838	828

T statistics in parentheses. Robust standard errors and weighted data. ★ $p < 0.05$, ★★ $p < 0.01$, ★★★ $p < 0.001$.
Source: 3rd ECS, 2013.

the household, and the activities of extraterritorial organisations and bodies. The sector and establishment size coverage, then, are the same as that for the analysis based on the ECS.

In order to identify distinct forms of work organisation from the employee's perspective, we use the same statistical methods described earlier, performing first a multiple correspondence analysis on 15 variables measuring work organisation for the 2005 round of the EWCS and then doing a hierarchical clustering with Ward's method using the factor scores on the first four factors, each of which account for an above average proportion of the total variance of the dataset. As in Lorenz and Valeyre (2005) and Holm et al. (2010), this allows us to identify four distinct classes or groups, the discretionary learning, lean, Taylorist and simple forms of work organisation. Following the procedure used in Holm and Lorenz (2015), we use the weights form the 2005 cluster analysis to allocate employee observations from the 2010 and 2015 rounds of the EWCS to one of the four classes or groups. This allows us to measure the change in the shares of the four work organisation classes over time from the perspective of the structural conditions in 2005. The results are shown in Table 9.4.

The first column in Table 9.4 lists the 15 indicators used from the EWCS to capture forms of work organisation. The variables are designed to capture differences in the amount of learning and problem-solving activity that employees are involved in their daily work activity as well as the degree to which they have control over how they perform their tasks. The premise is that it is the combination of having opportunities for learning and problem solving at work and exercising autonomy in how work is carried out that is a defining feature of a learning organisation. Employee discretion in how work is carried out increases the scope for employees and teams to explore novel solutions to the problems they face and, in this way, can increase the capacity of the organisation to learn. As in the case of the analysis based on the ECS, the variables are also chosen to capture some of the specific managerial and work organisation practices associated with the HPWS or Japanese forms of work organisation including quality control, respect for quality norms, job rotation and teamwork. The measures of monotony and repetitiveness in work provide a basis for assessing the extent to which more traditional and hierarchical forms of work organisation associated with Taylorist principles are being used. The final four indicators provide further insight into the degree to which employees exercise control over their work activity, notably by capturing cases where work pace is driven by the speed at which the equipment is operated or by production targets imposed by the management.

The first cluster, which we refer to as the discretionary learning (DL) forms, accounts for 38.1% of the total population in 2005. Work organisation in this cluster is distinctive for the way high levels of autonomy in work are combined with high levels of learning, problem-solving and task complexity. The variables measuring constraints on work pace and monotony are underrepresented. The use of teamwork is near to the average for the population and job rotation is somewhat underrepresented. Work organisation in this cluster corresponds rather closely to that found in Mintzberg's (1979) 'operating adhocracy'.

The second cluster, referred to as lean production, accounts for about 25% of the population in 2005. Compared to the first cluster, work organisation in the second cluster is characterised by lower levels of employee discretion in setting work methods. The use of job rotation and teamwork, on the other hand, are higher than in the first cluster, while work effort is more constrained by quantitative production norms and by the collective nature of work organisation. Respect for quality norms in work and employee responsibility for quality control are the highest across the four clusters. These features point to a more structured or bureaucratic style of organisational learning that corresponds

Table 9.4 Frequencies of forms of work organisation for the EU27: 2005, 2010 and 2015.

Forms of work organisation	Discretionary learning			Lean production			Taylorist forms			Simple forms			Total		
	2005	2010	2015	2005	2010	2015	2005	2010	2015	2005	2010	2015	2005	2010	2015
Discretion in fixing work methods	89.9	87.0	87.3	58.9	59.3	61.5	8.6	8.6	8.5	56.2	49.8	46.9	60.3	58.2	62.0
Discretion in fixing work pace	81.1	82.7	84.8	62.5	60.2	66.2	29.1	25.8	28.1	61.3	55.5	59.2	63.3	61.2	66.4
Learning new things in work	90.2	89.7	90.8	86.4	86.4	88.2	31.9	33.0	36.6	34.5	33.5	32.5	68.2	68.2	71.1
Problem solving activities	97.4	98.1	96.7	93.5	94.3	95.4	42.1	46.7	47.1	57.8	58.6	59.8	78.9	80.2	82.0
Complexity of tasks	83.2	84.0	84.7	81.7	79.1	80.7	27.8	26.5	27.8	25.6	19.5	21.0	61.9	60.0	63.2
Responsibility for quality control	83.6	86.0	84.4	91.6	91.8	92.3	49.5	52.7	54.7	31.9	31.8	34.7	69.7	71.2	73.2
Respect for quality norms	79.9	81.7	78.2	96.2	96.7	96.3	87.8	83.9	85.6	39.0	36.3	36.2	77.8	77.5	76.6
Teamwork	66.8	63.9	64.4	81.0	85.3	82.5	58.7	58.4	46.8	32.3	36.4	27.3	62.4	63.4	59.7
Job rotation	49.1	45.9	47.3	70.6	70.9	73.0	43.6	45.6	46.7	23.0	27.5	28.4	48.6	49.0	50.6
Repetitiveness of tasks	21.7	22.2	25.2	68.6	71.7	74.9	71.0	73.4	74.4	33.4	43.2	41.2	44.6	48.7	49.0
Monotony of tasks	7.6	11.7	8.0	48.1	51.1	46.2	39.3	48.3	36.6	16.2	20.7	16.0	25.1	30.6	24.1
Horizontal constraints on work rate	42.6	36.4	37.5	83.1	79.7	78.1	61.5	59.7	56.2	21.6	19.6	15.8	52.2	49.0	47.2
Hierarchical constraints on work rate	27.9	29.3	26.8	73.8	69.7	68.6	64.3	60.1	59.6	27.1	23.2	22.1	45.9	44.5	42.1
Norm-based constraints on work rate	45.7	48.5	45.2	80.4	78.8	79.4	66.0	66.0	69.4	14.3	14.5	15.9	52.2	53.4	52.6
Automatic constraints on work rate	5.0	6.8	6.8	53.0	48.3	50.9	57.0	55.7	58.6	3.7	5.5	5.2	26.2	26.6	26.2
Total	38.1	36.3	39.6	25.1	26.4	26.7	18.3	18.5	15.2	18.7	18.7	18.5	100	100	100

Source: EWCS 2005, 2010, 2015 (weighted data).

rather closely to the characteristics of the Japanese or 'lean production' model (Lam 2000; MacDuffie and Krafcik 1992; Womack et al. 1990). Much as in the case of the comparison between the HRM hybrid and the learning organisation based on the ECS, the characteristics of the lean forms of work organisation compared to the DL forms make it clear that the use of HPWS practices can be used in a relatively hierarchical manner.

The third class, which groups about 18% of the population in 2005, corresponds in most respects to a classic characterisation of Taylorism. The work situation is in most respects the opposite of that found in the first cluster, with low discretion and low level of learning and problem-solving. The use of teams and job rotation are at about average levels, implying that the use of these practices is a highly imperfect indicator of the transition to new forms of work organisation involving high levels of learning and problem-solving. The characteristics of this cluster draw attention to the importance of what some authors have referred to as 'flexible Taylorism' (Cézard et al. 1992; Linhart 1997).

The fourth cluster groups a little less than 19% of the population in 2005. All the variables are underrepresented. The frequencies of the two variables measuring the use of quality norms and individual responsibility for quality control are lowest among the four types of work organisation and there are few constraints on the work pace. This class presumably groups traditional forms of work organisation where methods are for the most part informal and non-codified. We refer to it in terms of the simple forms of work organisation.

Table 9.5 shows the frequencies of the different work organisation classes for the member states of the EU27 between 2005 and 2015. The Nordic countries rank high in the adoption of the DL forms of work organisation although this is less so for Finland than for Denmark and Sweden. The continental European nations have above average levels of adoption of the DL forms and in the case of the Netherlands the levels are quite close to those of the Nordic countries. Rates of adoption of the DL forms are also well above the population average in Malta. The highest rate of adoption of the lean forms are found in the UK and Ireland and in the eastern European nations of Estonia, Lithuania and Romania. The Taylorist forms tend to be overrepresented relative to the population average in the southern European nations and in several eastern European countries including Bulgaria, Romania, Slovakia and Hungary.

9.3.1 Inequality in access to learning opportunities in work between 2005 and 2015

As the figures in Table 9.5 show, while the patterns of change over the decade in the frequencies of the four work organisation forms are diverse across nations, on average for the EU27 there is a decline in the DL forms between 2005 and 2010 followed by an increase in 2015 to above the 2005 level. The lean forms increase slightly over the decade and the Taylorist forms decline

Table 9.5 Frequencies of the four forms of work organisation across the member states of the EU27.

Country	Discretionary learning			Lean production			Taylorist forms			Simple forms		
	2005	2010	2015	2005	2010	2015	2005	2010	2015	2005	2010	2015
Continental Europe												
Austria	47.8	47.4	48.4	20.5	23.0	21.5	17.6	16.9	16.7	14.0	12.7	13.3
Belgium	48.6	**43.6**	47.6	18.6	**26.7**	23.8	16.4	13.8	12.9	16.4	15.8	15.8
Germany	40.3	44.0	**45.3**	20.3	22.4	**14.3**	16.6	17.1	**13.6**	22.8	**16.4**	**18.9**
France	46.1	**30.0**	**43.0**	22.2	**27.5**	**32.2**	16.5	19.9	**12.1**	15.3	**22.7**	**12.7**
Luxembourg	48.0	**38.8**	**43.1**	24.1	31.2	**40.9**	12.9	16.5	**5.4**	15.0	13.5	10.6
Netherlands	57.3	58.6	56.0	18.3	16.1	17.7	11.8	11.4	9.4	12.6	13.9	16.9
North												
Finland	48.8	**43.8**	**56.3**	28.6	**37.8**	**22.1**	11.1	7.0	9.5	13.4	11.4	12.1
Denmark	60.0	60.2	**53.5**	21.9	18.7	**29.4**	7.3	7.2	4.9	10.8	13.9	12.2
Sweden	70.3	**59.2**	61.8	11.0	20.9	17.9	4.8	**11.2**	7.5	13.8	8.6	**12.7**
South												
Italy	34.4	35.7	41.5	24.6	23.2	**15.9**	23.6	19.7	22.1	17.4	21.4	20.5
Greece	25.3	22.0	**15.4**	30.7	33.1	**29.3**	27.8	**36.5**	**28.5**	16.2	18.4	**26.9**
Spain	17.5	**27.3**	25.4	30.7	33.8	**44.1**	23.1	18.5	18.4	28.7	**20.5**	**12.0**
Portugal	24.9	25.6	29.7	20.5	**27.9**	30.3	17.6	**26.1**	21.2	14.1	16.5	18.9
West												
Ireland	42.9	**27.3**	**36.7**	23.5	**39.4**	36.0	10.2	**21.4**	**13.4**	23.4	**11.9**	**13.8**
UK	34.0	29.9	**38.2**	30.6	**38.8**	35.9	17.6	19.1	**13.0**	17.9	**12.2**	12.9
East												
Bulgaria	21.8	17.8	**22.8**	28.3	29.0	31.1	16.3	**30.0**	29.1	30.0	**23.3**	**17.1**
Czech Republic	28.9	31.7	26.0	25.2	25.9	27.8	23.6	22.6	18.7	22.3	19.8	**27.5**

Hungary	35.4	34.4	**33.9**	18.6	21.4	**14.6**	22.7	**30.2**	31.7	23.3	**14.0**	**19.8**
Poland	35.3	36.1	**28.8**	31.0	**20.4**	**32.6**	15.6	**19.2**	15.1	18.1	**24.3**	23.5
Slovenia	38.3	40.6	43.8	28.0	30.6	**26.1**	19.5	**15.1**	13.8	14.2	13.7	16.4
Slovakia	29.2	28.0	**24.0**	21.8	**28.3**	**20.8**	30.4	**23.6**	25.9	18.6	20.1	**29.3**
Romania	25.0	25.7	22.2	33.5	33.8	36.7	27.0	21.7	24.0	14.5	**19.8**	17.1
North–east												
Estonia	40.0	36.8	**44.9**	32.6	**31.6**	**32.5**	11.5	8.9	10.4	16.0	12.8	12.2
Latvia	33.2	**48.4**	**27.9**	33.5	**25.5**	**16.9**	16.4	**9.8**	**19.1**	16.9	16.3	**36.1**
Lithuania	17.8	**26.5**	28.0	30.3	**36.2**	34.7	26.6	**22.2**	19.1	25.3	15.2	18.3
South–east												
Cyprus	23.8	**33.6**	12.3	26.8	**17.8**	**29.0**	24.3	25.3	25.4	25.9	23.3	25.3
Malta	43.4	**51.6**	**55.7**	32.4	28.2	32.8	9.2	**5.6**	**2.4**	14.9	14.6	**9.2**
EU27	**38.1**	**36.3**	**39.6**	**25.1**	**26.4**	**26.7**	**18.3**	**18.5**	**15.2**	**18.7**	**18.7**	**18.5**

Source: EWCS 2005, 2010, 2015 (weighted data).

after 2010. In relation to this average trend for the EU27, Denmark stands out for the sharp decline in the share of workers having access to DL forms of work organisation after 2010 and the big increase in the share involved in the lean forms. The increasing importance of the lean forms in Denmark after 2010 indicates that employees in Denmark are working to tighter constraints on their work pace and with less control over their work activity.

There is also evidence pointing to increasing inequality in access to learning opportunities across occupational categories in Denmark. To support this, we adopt the procedure used in Lundvall et al. (2008) and distinguish between 'managers' and 'workers' where the manager group is composed of managers, technicians and professionals, and the worker group is composed of the other lower-level occupational categories: sales and service workers and skilled, semi-skilled and unskilled manual workers. We expect the share of the manager group having access to the DL forms of work organisation will be higher than the worker group. Table 9.6 presents a simple index of inequality by dividing the share of 'workers' having access to DL by the share of 'managers' and subtracting this ratio from 1. Lower values of the index, which can vary between 0 and 1, indicate less inequality. The results of this exercise show a sharp increase in inequality in Denmark between 2005 and 2010 with the index rising from 0.36 to 0.49. Inequality declines somewhat between 2010 and 2015 but at 0.42 remains above the level in 2005.

9.3.2 The impact of work organisation on employee outcomes

While access to the DL forms has declined in general in Denmark over the decade from 2005 to 2015 and there is a trend towards greater inequality in access, it is reasonable to ask: does it really matter? In this section, using logistic regression, we use the results from the EWCS to show that workers in Denmark on average are more satisfied with the DL forms compared to the lean forms, that they experience less stress in work and that they are less likely to work at high speeds and to tight deadlines. These results, combined with those in Section 9.2.1 identifying a positive impact of adopting a learning organisation design on innovation performance, provide support for the view that learning forms of organisation offer mutual gains for employers and for employees.

Table 9.6 Inequality in access to learning opportunities in work in Denmark: 2005, 2010, 2015.

	2005	2010	2015
Share of 'managers' with access to DL	77.8	84.8	72.1
Share of 'workers' with access to DL	50.0	43.4	42.3
Inequality Index	0.36	0.49	0.42

Source: EWCS 2005, 2010, 2015 (weighted data).

Table 9.7 presents the results of a logit regression predicting the likelihood that the employee is very satisfied with his or her main paid job, experiences stress in work all or most of the time, works to tight deadlines all or most of the time and works at high speeds all or most of the time. The regressions control for establishment size, occupational category, industrial sector and gender. In terms of odds, an employee in the DL forms in Denmark has odds of being very satisfied that are 1.74 times those of an employee engaged in the lean forms of work organisation. Compared to an employee in the lean forms of work organisation, the odds for an employee in the DL forms experiencing stress in work all or most of the time are 61% less, and the odds of working to high speeds and working to tight deadlines all or most of the time are respectively 63% and 81% lower. Interestingly, none of the coefficients on the occupational controls are statistically significant, implying that after taking into account the form of work organisation, differences in the employee's position

Table 9.7 Logit regressions predicting the likelihood of employee outcomes in Denmark, 2015.

Variables	(1)Very satisfied	(2)Stress all or most of time	(3)High speed all or most of time	(4)Tight deadlines all or most of time
Learning	0.554*	-0.952**	-1.107***	-1.672***
	(2.08)	(-2.77)	(-3.89)	(-6.17)
Lean		reference		
Taylor	-0.533	0.632	0.408	-0.613
	(-0.90)	(1.12)	(0.77)	(-1.24)
Simple	0.708	-0.690	-0.814	-1.533**
	(1.87)	(-1.08)	(-1.66)	(-3.19)
Managers		reference		
Professionals	-0.208	-0.275	0.166	0.694
	(-0.46)	(-0.39)	(0.29)	(1.13)
Technicians	-0.0583	-0.656	-0.134	0.0761
	(-0.13)	(-0.91)	(-0.23)	(0.12)
Clerks	0.206	-0.585	0.0226	0.269
	(0.42)	(-0.79)	(0.04)	(0.41)
Service workers	0.255	-0.884	0.301	0.418
	(0.45)	(-0.98)	(0.45)	(0.59)
Craft workers	-0.850	-0.332	1.104	1.104
	(-1.62)	(-0.92)	(-0.49)	(1.65)
Plant operators	-0.833	0.218	0.774	0.774
	(-1.44)	(-1.05)	(0.33)	(1.16)
Elementary trades	0.227	-0.797	-0.582	0.638
	(0.43)	(-0.93)	(-0.83)	(0.91)
N	450	450	450	450

T statistics in parentheses. * p < 0.05, ** p < 0.01, *** p < 0.001.
Regressions include controls for sector, establishment size and gender.

in the occupational hierarchy are not statistically significant predictors of the level of satisfaction or the level of stress experienced in work.

9.4 The relation between the employee-level and employer-level cluster analyses

The results from the EWCS-based cluster analysis provide an employee-level perspective on the adoption of the forms of work organisation characteristic of a learning organisation. Employees are well placed to identify the detailed characteristics of the work they perform, including whether they are involved in problem-solving and have control over their work methods and pace of work. While employers can provide an overall characterisation of how the establishment is organised, their responses to the ECS questionnaire can at best identify whether workers in general use specific work practices or provide estimates of the percentages of the workforce that do so. There may well be a gap between what the employer perceives and what workers experience on the shop floor. Despite these differences, it can be argued that at the aggregate national level both analyses provide measures of the extent to which establishments are organised in ways that provide employees with significant opportunities for engaging in learning and problem-solving activities in their daily work with a degree of influence or control over how work is organised. On this basis we could expect that the national rankings of the adoption of learning organisations based on the ECS and the rankings of the adoption of the DL

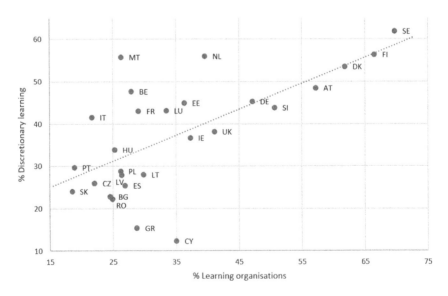

Figure 9.1 The relationship between learning organisations and discretionary learning.
Source: 3rd ECS, 2013 and EWCS, 2015.

forms of work organisation based on the EWCS shown in Tables 9.2 and 9.5 respectively would be similar.

Figure 9.1 below shows this to be the case. It shows the relation for the EU27 of the ranking of nations in 2015 based on the EWCS clustering to the ranking based on the ECS clustering in 2013. The Spearman's rank correlation of 0.64 points to a quite strong positive and statistically significant relation between the two ranking variables. The relation is somewhat stronger for countries with a higher GDP per capita. If we restrict our attention to countries with a GDP per capita of €30,000 or more in 2015, the Spearman's rank correlation increases to 0.77.

9.5 Conclusions

The analysis in this chapter has shown that the transformed workplace can provide mutual gains for employers and for employees. The employer-level results for Denmark show that when establishments are organised so as to provide employees with opportunities for taking or sharing responsibility for the planning and execution of their tasks combined with regular consultation and the use of incentives for employee involvement, the chances of introducing new products or services onto the market increase. The employee-level results show that when employees' work activity involves learning and problem-solving in combination with control over their methods and pace of work, satisfaction tends to be higher and there is less stress in work.

The results help to shed light on the debate over the impact of HPWS practices on employee outcomes. The employee-level analysis shows that HPWS practices such as teams, job rotation and employee responsibility for quality control can be used in different ways, with significantly different effects on employee outcomes. Where such practices are combined with considerable employee control over work methods and work pace, satisfaction tends to be higher and stress lower. Where these practices are combined with low levels of employee control over their work methods and with tight constraints on work pace, stress tends to increase, and satisfaction is lower. In short, neither the proponents of HPWS practices nor their detractors are entirely justified. The effects will depend on the extent to which these practices are used in ways that allow employees to regulate their work pace and have control over their work methods.

The comparative analysis shows that the Danish national innovation system ranks high within the EU in terms of the adoption of learning forms of organisation seen both from the employer's and the employee's perspectives. At the same time, there is evidence that the frequency with which employees in Denmark have access to the DL forms of work organisation has declined between 2010 and 2015, and there also is evidence of an increase in inequality of access to learning opportunities at the workplace. Given the evidence of potential mutual gains from the adoption of a learning form of organisation, acting to reverse this trend and increase the opportunities for employee learning in Danish workplaces is arguably one of the important challenges faced by the Danish system of innovation.

This raises the question of whether policies can be implemented to favour the adoption of work practices that increase opportunities for employee learning and involvement in workplace decision-making. Policy intervention in this sense is often criticised on the grounds that it fails to address firm heterogeneity assuming 'one size fits all', and constitutes an unacceptable infringement on the employer's prerogatives, who in any case is in a better place than the policymaker to know what works best in his or her workplace. Such arguments are belied, however, by the successful use of policy measures to promote workplace innovation in the other Nordic nations. Alasoini, (2006, 2009) in reviewing workplace innovation policies across Europe, highlights the programmes implemented in Sweden, Finland and Norway, describing them as 'generative projects' that fund workplace innovation proposals submitted by individual firms or networks of firms on a competitive basis.[5] Since the projects are initiated by the employers and are tailored to the specific needs of the firms involved, they override the criticisms noted above.

Up to now Denmark has not implemented national level policies to support workplace innovation. While the traditional strong emphasis on skills development at the workplace supported in part through the Danish system of active labour market policy measures no doubt has favoured the adoption of learning forms of work organisation, the recent trend suggests that this 'supply-side' approach may not be enough. In this context, there are good reasons to argue that Denmark can benefit by looking to the experiences of its Nordic neighbours and drawing lessons with respect to implementing policies to support employee learning at the workplace.

Notes

1   For a further discussion of the limited attention given to work organisation in the innovation studies literature, see Lorenz (2013)
2   For an overview of the DISKO project, see Lundvall and Christensen (1999).
3   For details on sampling design of the survey, see 3rd European Company Technical Report, European Foundation for the Improvement of Living Conditions, Dublin.
4   For details on the sampling design, see 6th European Working Conditions Survey: Technical Report. https://www.eurofound.europa.eu/sites/default/files/ef_survey/fie ld_ef_documents/6th_ewcs_-_technical_report.pdf
5   Some of the most highly cited examples of this type of policy initiative include the TEKE (1996–2003) and TEKES (2004–2009) programmes in Finland (Alasoini 2019), the Competent Workplace Programme (2007–2011) in Sweden which involved funding from VINNOVA, the Swedish research and innovation agency (Döös and Larsen 2008), and the Enterprise Development Programme (1994–2001) and its successor the Value Creation Programme (2001–2010) in Norway (Gustavsen 2007).

References

Alasoini, T. 2006. In search of generative results: A new generation of programmes to develop work organization. *Economic and Industrial Democracy* 27(1): 9–37.

Alasoini, T. 2009. Strategies to promote workplace innovation: A comparative analysis of nine national and regional approaches. *Economic and Industrial Democracy* 30(4): 614–642.

Alasoini, T. 2019. *The Promotion of Workplace Innovation in Finland: Policy Developments and Outlook for the Future.* Report to the Finnish Institute of Occupational Health. Finnish Institute of Occupational Health, Helsinki.

Appelbaum, E., Bailey, T., Berg, P. and Kalleberg, A. L. 2000. *Manufacturing Advantage: Why High-Performance Work Systems Pay Off.* Ithaca, NY: Cornell University Press.

Askenazy, P., Caroli, E. and Marcus, V. 2002. New organizational practices and working conditions: Evidence from France in the 1990's. *Recherches Economiques de Louvain/ Louvain Economic Review* 68(1–2): 91–110.

Black, S., Lynch, L. and Krivelyova, A. 2004. How workers fare when employers innovate. *Industrial Relations: A Journal of Economy and Society* 43(1): 44–66.

Burns, T. E. and Stalker, G. M. 1961. *The Management of Innovation.* University of Illinois at Urbana-Champaign's Academy for Entrepreneurial Leadership Historical Research Reference in Entrepreneurship.

Cézard, M., Dussert, F. and Gollac, M. 1992. Taylor va au marché. Organisation du travail et informatique. *La Lettre d'Information du CEE* 26: 1–8.

Döös, M. and Larsen, P. 2008. Den kompetenta arbetsplatsen – Forskning om kompetens i arbetsplatsens relationer. Programkatalog. *Vinnova Information* VI: 16. Vinnova, Stockholm.

Freeman, C. 1987. *Technology, Policy, and Economic Performance: Lessons from Japan.* London: Pinter Publishers.

Freeman, C. 1995. The 'National System of Innovation' in historical perspective. *Cambridge Journal of Economics* 19(1): 5–24.

Freeman, R. B. and Kleiner, M. M. 2000. Who benefits most from employee involvement: Firms or workers? *American Economic Review* 90(2): 219–223

Godard, J. 2001. High performance and the transformation of work? The implications of alternative work practices for the experience and outcomes of work. *ILR Review* 54(4): 776–805.

Guest, D. E. 2017. Human resource management and employee well-being: Towards a new analytic framework. *Human Resource Management Journal* 27(1): 22–38.

Gustavsen B. 2007. Work organization and the Scandinavian model. *Economic and Industrial Democracy* 28(4): 650–671.

Holm, J. R. and Lorenz, E. 2015. Has "Discretionary Learning" declined during the Lisbon Agenda? A cross-sectional and longitudinal study of work organization in European nations. *Industrial and Corporate Change* 24(6): 1179–1214.

Holm, J. R., Lorenz, E., Lundvall, B.-Å. and Valeyre, A. 2010. Organizational learning and systems of labour market regulation in Europe. *Industrial and Corporate Change* 19(4): 1141–1173.

Jensen, J. M., Patel, P. C. and Messersmith, J. G. 2013. High-performance work systems and job control: Consequences for anxiety, role overload, and turnover intentions. *Journal of Management* 39(6): 1699–1724.

Jensen, M. B., Johnson, B., Lorenz, E. and Lundvall, B. Å. 2007. Forms of knowledge and modes of innovation. *Research Policy* 36(5): 680–693.

Lam, A. 2000. Tacit knowledge, organizational learning and societal institutions: An integrated framework. *Organization Studies* 21(3): 487–513.

Laursen, K. and Foss, N. J. 2003. New human resource management practices, complementarities and the impact on innovation performance. *Cambridge Journal of Economics* 27(2): 243–263.

Linhart, D. 1997. Travail: Défaire, disent-ils. *Sociologie du Travail*, 39(2): 235–249.

Lorenz, E. 2013. Innovation, work organisation, and systems of social protection. In *Innovation Studies: Evolution and Future Challenge*, ed. Fagerberg, J., Martin, B. and Andersen, E. S. Oxford: Oxford University Press: 71–89.

Lorenz, E. and Valeyre, A. 2005. Organisational innovation, human resource management and labour market structure: A comparison of the EU-15. *Journal of Industrial Relations* 47(4): 424–442.

Lundvall, B. Å. 2013. Innovation studies: A personal interpretation of the state of the art. In *Innovation Studies: Evolution and Future Challenges*, ed. Fagerberg, J., Martin, B. and Andersen, E. S. Oxford: Oxford University Press: 21–70.

Lundvall, B. Å. and Christensen, J. L. 1999. *Extending and Deepening the Analysis of Innovation Systems: With Empirical Illustrations from the DISCO-Project.* (No. 99–12), Department of Industrial Economics and Strategy, Copenhagen: Copenhagen Business School.

Lundvall, B. Å., Rasmussen, P. and Lorenz, E. 2008. Education in the learning economy: A European perspective. *Policy Futures in Education* 6(6): 681–700.

MacDuffie, J. P. and Krafcik, J. 1992. Integrating technology and human resources for high-performance manufacturing: Evidence from the international auto industry. In *Transforming Organizations*, eds. Kochan, T. and Useem, M., Oxford: Oxford University Press: 209–226.

Mintzberg, H. 1979. *The Structuring of Organizations: A Synthesis of the Research*. University of Illinois at Urbana-Champaign's Academy for Entrepreneurial Leadership Historical Research Reference in Entrepreneurship.

Mintzberg, H. 1983. *Structure in Fives: Designing Effective Organisations*. Englewood-Cliffs, NJ: Prentice Hall.

Nielsen, P. and Lundvall, B. Å. 2007. Innovation, learning organisations and relations. In *Working It Out?*, 65–83. Budapest: Hungarian Academy of Science.

Ogbonnaya, C., Daniels, K., Connolly, S. and van Veldhoven, M. 2017. Integrated and isolated impact of high-performance work practices on employee health and well-being: A comparative study. *Journal of Occupational Health Psychology* 22(1): 98.

Ramsay, H., Scholarios, D. and Harley, B. 2000. Employees and high-performance work systems: Testing inside the black box. *British Journal of Industrial Relations* 38(4): 501–531.

Van De Voorde, K. and Beijer, S. 2015. The role of employee HR attributions in the relationship between high-performance work systems and employee outcomes. *Human Resource Management Journal* 25(1): 62–78.

Vinding, A. L. 2006. Absorptive capacity and innovative performance: A human capital approach. *Economics of Innovation and New Technology* 15(4–5): 507–517.

Womack, J., Jones, D. T. and Roos, D. 1990. *The Machine That Changed the World: Massachusetts Institute of Technology*. New York: Rawson Associates

Young, S., Bartram, T., Stanton, P. and Leggat, S. G. 2010. High performance work systems and employee well-being. *Journal of Health Organization and Management*, 24(2): 182–199.

10 Work policy and automation in the fourth industrial revolution

Peter Nielsen, Jacob Rubæk Holm and Edward Lorenz

10.1 The labour market in Denmark and technological change

With technological change comes social change, as technological change affects production, distribution and power in society. Studies of earlier waves of technological change suggest that each wave is associated with a 'structural crisis of adjustment' which can be identified empirically by the social conflicts. These social conflicts emanate in the labour market from increasing job insecurity, downward pressure on wages, and uncertain career prospects, and they may spill over into the political system as, typically, hostility towards immigration (Freeman and Louçã 2001, see especially section C.3). Labour market policy can mitigate the risk of social conflict by facilitating an inclusive labour market. Labour market policy in Denmark is closely connected to the Danish labour market model. The core of this model is primacy to the social partners concerning the wages and employment system (Marsden 1999). This model is the foundation of the flexicurity system, which is an important lubricator in situations of structural change in the labour market. Together with the active labour market policy, it constitutes the so-called 'golden triangle' (Madsen 2003) of flexicurity. The institutional and organisational relations between the social partners and the state form preconditions of acting as an inclusive part of the national innovation system, shaping the social and economic consequences of what has been called the fourth industrial revolution in the labour market.

Currently, there are at least four significant driving forces that affect the future of work and thus structural developments in the labour market in a forward-looking perspective. These are globalisation, technological development, demography and climate change (Dølvik and Steen 2018; ILO 2018). Technological development is special as a driving force, as it can directly or indirectly moderate or enhance the influence of the other drivers on the labour market imbalances. In this way, technological development is of particular interest when considering the labour market of the future and the political opportunities to handle structural challenges.

Technological change often has a limited influence on specific segments in the labour market. However, some technological innovations are universal in such a way that they diffuse broadly in the labour market as part of new production processes, market relationships and skills requirements of the workforce. The electric motor and electrification of industrial production are good examples of the abovementioned technological innovations. Here, new ways of organising the work processes (Taylorism) meant that the demand for skills in the labour force was significantly reduced. Freeman and Perez (1988) call the above phenomenon a techno-economic paradigm shift. The development of Information and Communication Technology (ICT) and in particular technological innovations in the form of Artificial Intelligence (AI), robotics and the Internet of Things (IOT), meets the conditions for a techno-economic paradigm shift. These technologies have been termed as drivers of a fourth industrial revolution, which consists of the diffusion and application of digital technologies making production increasingly interconnected, adaptable and automatic. This is expected to have a significant impact on changes in the structure of the labour market, not least changes in the requirements for the skills of the labour force and the competences to be used in production. Although the technologies are important drivers, they cannot be described as determining the development of the labour market. The labour market is unique in the way that stakeholder relationships and the influence of agents at different levels play a major role in implementing market mechanisms. An essential thesis in this chapter is thus that there is a scope of voluntarism present in the connection between the technological possibilities of digitisation and the processes surrounding job development. This means that the effect technological change has on the task contents of jobs and on the number of jobs is not exogenous but depends on the simultaneous choices made by managers, workers and policy makers. In this chapter we focus on the policy for mitigating structural and social imbalances created by technological change. This naturally leads us to focus on policy for workers who are forced to adapt, often because they lose their jobs. Such workers are often mid-skilled and play a central part in the national system of innovation by constituting the source of continuous incremental innovations on the shop floor (Lundvall 1999). They thus complement the role of the more highly educated workers, as studied in e.g., Eriksen and Holm (2021).

10.1.1 Technologies destroy jobs

A number of studies have found that technological change will replace jobs in the near future. Frey and Osborne (2013) find for the US that jobs highly likely (70% chance or greater) to be automated include almost half (47%) of total employment. Bowles (2014) extended the analysis and found that the figure for Denmark is 49.5%. This result is based on expert assessments of the degree to which tasks in general can be automated with big data and deep learning and does not take into account, for example, differences in task characteristics for the same occupation across firms of different sizes or across firms with a different product mix. Frey and Osborne focus in on the industrial use of machine learning in the form of deep neural networks which they observe opens up new automation possibilities and in particular allows for the automation of tasks, like identifying component defects with image classification or predictive maintenance using machine vibration data that depend on auditory and perceptual skills that were traditionally considered beyond the scope of automation.[1]

Frey and Osborne also note that this process is accelerated by the tendency of modern organisations to focus on measurability. When tasks or tasks' results have to be made measurable, the tasks are typically repeated and standardised which, all else being equal, makes it easier to apply deep learning methods.[2] Moreover, the increasing focus on measurability means that the increasing amounts of data needed to train neural nets exists. This process is further enhanced by the development of more accurate and cheaper sensors for data collection and processing.

Frey and Osborn's analysis is highly speculative and it has received a great deal of criticism. In an analysis of whether the individual tasks and not occupational categories are automated, Arntz et al. (2016) find that only 9% of jobs in the US are at high risk of being fully automated, against Frey and Osborn's 47%. Arntz and colleagues' analysis is based on Frey and Osborn's general assessment of the types of tasks that are most susceptible to automation, but they combine it with individual level data on workers' abilities and tasks. This radically different result has been reached with an almost identical analysis, where the main difference is moving the focus from occupational job categories to detailed tasks.

There are not many studies yet on the microeconomic effects of automation, but the results in Dauth et al. (2017), Holm et al. (2020) and Bessen et al. (2019) show some of the effects for companies and workers. Bessen and colleagues focus on what happens to the people who are subjected to automation in the workplace. The interesting result is that the substitution from humans to machines is a process over a number of years. At the time of investment in automation, no immediate effect is seen on the workforce, but in subsequent years the employees have increased likelihood of leaving the workplace. This indicates that automation is a process where the employer over time learns which employees can and will adapt, and who can be dispensed with. At the same time, the workers learn whether they can and will adapt or prefer to leave the workplace. Dauth et al. (2017) find a similar result and both studies to some extent show that increased automation makes it harder for young workers to find stable employment, as automating firms tend not to expand the workforce, but rather let the workforce contract as older workers leave the firm. Holm and colleagues focus on the company level in their study of the effects on the composition of the workforce. They show how technological and organisational change affect the composition of the workforce, including how technological change is associated with changed work organisation, which places new demands on employees' competencies. Both Holm et al. (2020) and Bessen et al. (2019) thus show the importance of adapting compe tences among the employees.

Some studies show that the net effect of automation is not uniformly nega-tive. As robots substitute for labour there will be a negative gross effect on equilibrium employment but spill-overs from income effects and complemen-tary innovations counteract the gross decline (Acemoglu and Restrepo 2017, 2018). Empirical tests of the equilibrium prediction suggest that the effect of trade on its own is not sufficient to create a positive net effect on equilibrium employment (Acemoglu and Restrepo 2017). On the other hand, empirical studies of the substitution effect by robots in manufacturing suggest that sub-stitution is more than offset by new jobs in services, although often at a lower wage (Dauth et al. 2017; Graetz and Michaels 2018; Gregory et al. 2019). This result can also be obtained in a broader analysis studying growth in total fac-tor productivity and not just the addition of new robots (Autor and Salomons 2018). However, underneath the net effect, a structural displacement exists. Jobs with many routine tasks are substituted, and expanding output creates jobs with fewer routine tasks. In addition, it should be noted that most analyses are undertaken at a more or less aggregate level, and a more disaggregate level of analysis of specific technologies can reveal net effects on jobs that are negative.

Although there is evidence that the overall impact is neutral or even posi-tive, it is very different jobs that are created and displaced. Jobs that are dis-placed are primarily routine jobs in industries for tradable goods. These are typically jobs with an intermediate salary level. New jobs are also created in the same industries, but these are jobs with low routine content and typically high or low wage levels. At the same time, jobs are created in industries for non-tradable goods.

10.1.2 The room for voluntarism

Holm et al. (2020) demonstrate the relationship within firms between changes in work organisation and management practices, and the occupational compo-sition of the workforce. The results are important in relation to the voluntarist thesis. The fact that the company level is important for the understanding of the dynamic labour market effects is also consistent with the analysis in Arntz et al. (2016). The results of Arntz et al. (2016) show that the occupational composition of firms' workforces varies, which indicates that the occupational composition is not static, but can be adjusted in line with the technological development. The fact that firms can adjust their workforce and the task con-tent of jobs can be adjusted so that the substitution effect is reduced, and labour productivity is increased along with the new technology is a key element of the voluntarist thesis.

The prerequisite for the voluntarist thesis, however, is that the labour force can develop the qualifications and competencies that incorporate new technol-ogy complementing tasks. Thus, in general, it becomes both a matter of devel-oping jobs' task content, which complements technological development, and a matter of workers acquiring the skills and competences needed to perform the new tasks that complement technological development. The task content of jobs will depend on which technologies are adopted and the manner in which they are adopted. Adopting robots, for example, may mean adopting the traditional industrial robots that perform the same task endlessly and operate fenced off from workers, or adopting collaborative robots that work closely together with workers and can be frequently and inexpensively reprogrammed. Even for a given 'robot' the work organisation of the firm will shape the effects on the workforce. If workers have a high degree of discretion and regularly must develop new competencies, then the addition of a robot will entail new programming and monitoring tasks for the production worker. Whereas in a more hierarchical form of work organisation, it can be expected that the addition of a robot leads to a division of labour where technicians perform the programming, and the production worker is reduced to more mundane monitoring. Voluntarism thus entails that there is both a choice of what technology to adopt and a degree of malleability in how it is adopted. The challenge is that the technology develops at considerable speed, so it is difficult to determine tasks and skills needs in the future. In addition, the development takes place within the companies, which makes it necessary to focus on this level.

The Danish labour market has good developmental preconditions for the development and modification of the dynamic voluntarist triangle of change: task content, job organisation and applied technologies. This dynamic triangle is an important element of the Danish national system of innovation as it facilitates the diffusion of new technologies in the economy, but the triangle can be challenged when technological change creates structural imbalances. Business personnel application surveys show a significant use of moving staff between different tasks, in order to ensure that corporate personnel resources meet the needs. Naturally, there will be challenges in managing the change processes, both for the internal relations of the companies and, not least, the relations with the structure of the labour market policy. This is a theme we will look into in the later section on the labour market policy challenges. First, we need to look more closely at how both labour market policy and the Danish labour market have changed in recent years.

10.2 Changes in the Danish labour market

The Danish labour market is often related to the flexicurity system, defined as an integrated strategy with the aim to improve flexibility and security at the labour market (European Commission 2007). The flexibility side of the system has become more or less synonymous with numerical flexibility to and from companies and the security side with the unemployment benefits. This dimension of flexicurity is certainly important, but the concept of flexicurity embraces more than numerical regulation by hiring and firing (Bredgaard and Madsen 2015). Functional flexibility thus relates to employees' change of functions and tasks inside the company. Working time flexibility concerns regulation of working time. Organisational flexibility promotes learning and organisational change and wage flexibility aims at wage regulation. Complementary to these forms of flexibility, job security, employment security and income security make up the security side of the multidimensional flexicurity system. A survey from 2010 of private sector companies (GOPA) shows that nearly 70% of companies use functional flexibility to a high or some extent and a similar measurement in 2006 (DISKO) shows that the proportion using functional flexibility to a high or at some degree is 60% of the companies. The surveys thus document that the staff in Danish companies largely have routines for flexible tasks. More recent survey data from the 2019 TASK[3] survey show that over a period of just three years, 29% of all continuously employed employees had changed either employer, occupation or both. Of the 29%, 25% have changed employer while 4% have remained with the same employer but have a new occupation. This shows considerable flexibility in the Danish labour market but also functional flexibility within firms (Table 10.1).

While employees are thus required to be continuously flexible, the qualification instrument of Danish labour market policy has received continuously less emphasis in recent years.[4] Figure 10.1 shows the number of full-time equivalent students enrolled in the public Labour Market Education (AMU) programme in Denmark per employed person. The number is naturally sensitive

Table 10.1 Labour market flexibility.

Occupation	Employer		Total
	Different	*Same*	
Different	10	4	15
Same	15	71	85
Total	25	75	100

Percentage of respondents in representative sample. Occupations are defined at the four-digit ISCO-08 level. Source: the TASK survey.

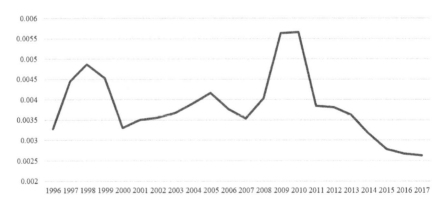

Figure 10.1 FTE AMU/employment. Source: Statistics Denmark. www.statistikbanken.dk; VEUAMU1, VEUAMU10, RAS93, RAS07 and RAS309.

to the business cycle and the 2008 crisis clearly stands out. Enrolment decreases during economic expansions and it is clear that enrolment was much lower in the latest expansion from 2013 compared to the previous expansion leading up to the 2008 crisis.

The recent decline in the emphasis on labour market training means that firms have had to find other ways of training their workers to use new technologies. Data from the TASK survey show that formal training only plays a small role in acquiring the skills to work with robots, while formal training is still somewhat important for acquiring skills to work with machine learning and artificial intelligence. The main mechanism for skill acquisition is peer learning in the workplace, which reflects the importance of hands-on experience when developing competencies for working with new technologies (Table 10.2).

The importance of peer learning and learning by doing reflect the importance of learning in the current job, and thus also demonstrates the difficulties related to helping the unemployed acquire the competencies for working with new technologies.

Peer learning in the workplace is of course only available to persons who already have a job, while formal training must necessarily be more important for the unemployed. However, many of the skills that are needed can only be acquired though problem-solving activity in the workplace. Thus, training for the unemployed should also include a workplace activity component. In the TASK survey of 2019, only 10% of the unemployed report that their skills are obsolete, but simultaneously 65% do not agree that they receive the necessary continuing education for finding a job (Table 10.3).

The descriptive statistics document both the importance and the decline of the qualification instrument of labour market policy in Denmark. In parallel with the decline of the qualification instrument there has been an increase in the emphasis on the motivation instrument in Danish labour market policy. (See the appendix for details on the qualification and motivation instruments.) This is primarily seen in a decreasing level of unemployment benefits. Figure 10.2 shows income from unemployment benefits as a share of total household income in Denmark. While this time series is naturally sensitive to the business cycle it is also obvious that there has been a continuous decline.

Table 10.2 Source of competencies in 2019.

Main source of competences	*Task*				
	Work alongside robot	*Control robot*	*Use data from AI*	*Receive instructions from AI*	*Use computer or machine with ML*
Formal training	15	5	25	25	25
Peer learning	67	84	45	50	33
Learning by doing	18	10	30	25	42

Percentage of respondents in representative sample. AI: Artificial Intelligence. ML: Machine Learning. Source: the TASK survey.

Table 10.3 Skills among the unemployed: 2019.

	Percentage who agree or strongly agree
My skills are obsolete compared to the jobs being offered.	10
I receive the necessary continuing education such that I can fill the jobs being offered.	35
My union helps me acquire the skills required for me to find employment again.	22
Government assistance helps me acquire the skills necessary for me to find employment again.	24

Percentage of respondents in representative sample. Source: the TASK survey.

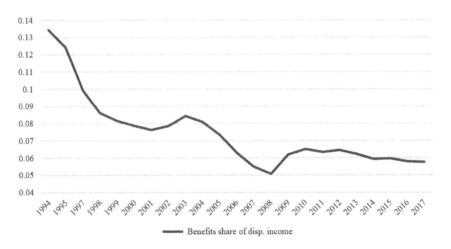

Figure 10.2 Benefits/income. Source: Statistics Denmark. www.statistikbanken.dk; INDKF112.

Looking closer at the rate of compensation, the variation between occupational groups is substantial. Social and health assistants have an average compensation grade of 70% while engineers have an average compensation rate of 50% (Dagpengekommisionen 2015).

The increasing emphasis on the motivation instrument has primarily been effectuated as an effort to make the relatively generous unemployment benefits less accessible, and thus moving the unemployed to other and less generous benefit schemes. Over recent decades, the period where one can receive unemployment benefits has been shortened, the amount of paid work required to again be eligible for unemployment benefits has increased, and the requirements one must submit to while receiving unemployment benefits have increased. For example, before 1993 a person could

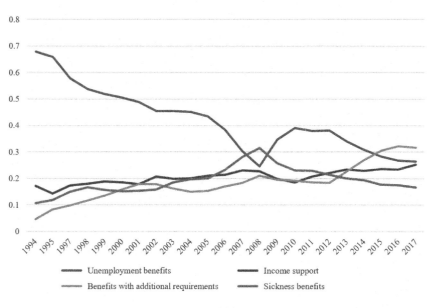

Figure 10.3 Composition of benefits. Source: Statistics Denmark. www.statistikbanken.dk; INDKF112.

in practice receive unemployment benefits indefinitely. After 1993 the period was restricted to seven years. Then from 1995 it was five years, from 1998 it was four years, and since 2008 the period has been only two years (Arbejdsmarkedskommissionen 2009).

The increasing inaccessibility of unemployment benefits has entailed that unemployment benefits have declined from almost 70% of all benefits in household sector income in 1994 to less than 30% in 2017. Instead, people out of work have been shifted to alternative benefits such as sickness benefits and other benefits with additional requirements, or the much lower level of income support, which is at the time of writing is only available after a person has spent all savings, sold all assets and if there is no partner to support the person. This is seen in Figure 10.3.

The decreasing emphasis on the qualification instrument and the increasing emphasis on the motivation instrument arguably entails that Danish labour market policy requires some adjustments in order for the Danish labour market to meet the challenges posed by recent technological change.

10.3 Labour market policy and current challenges from technological change

The technological developments at the company level challenge the current labour market policy significantly. Both the employed and unemployed need to develop new skills and competences that can ensure that they can continuously interact productively with technological change. In relation to this, it is essential that job dynamics in the labour market play out without major structural imbalances. Labour market policy can be defined as public regulation of labour market structures and functions. Motivation and qualification instruments have been dominant tools in Danish labour market policy. The motivation instruments aim to encourage the unemployed workforce to take up vacancies, and the tools are availability commitments, a period of unemployment benefits and mobility provisions. The qualification instruments consist of tools to build up the 'human capital' of the workforce through vocational and labour market education, continuing education and lifelong learning. Historically, the qualification instruments have been important tools in periods of relatively rapid structural change (Nielsen 1979). This includes an explicit objective to remove economic and social barriers for workers with shorter education when upgrading to better employment opportunities (Jørgensen 2006/7) which also promote economic equality. A significant recognition was that it was appropriate to mix the unemployed and employed in adult education. This allowed the unemployed to form network contacts and socialise for the job. However, as also described in the appendix, the motivation instruments have also been used successfully in combination with the qualification instruments to tackle high unemployment in periods of fiscal austerity (Bredgaard et al. 2011).

The above-mentioned phenomenon is most clearly seen in the labour market reform from 1993, which is often referred to as the start of the active labour market policy in Denmark. The reform included both motivation measures and qualification initiatives as tools aimed at both the unemployed and employed in a comprehensive activation line for solving structural problems. This policy also managed to reduce the relatively high unemployment rate at the time. The fundamental principle was a transitional understanding of the labour market, where employment could alternate with upgrading in a more needs-adapted pattern of working life.

The crucial question is thus whether the labour market education system manages to meet the challenges posed by the workforce's qualification and competence development in order to complement an automated production apparatus that is continuously being renewed. The question is crucial because labour market policy in the period since the turn of the millennium and especially since the financial crisis has been dominated by the motivational instruments. This means that the so-called 'work first' principle has been the driving force in the period. The principle implies that the effort focuses on motivation in order to get the unemployed into jobs as quickly as possible and thus supporting the quantitative labour supply. This means that economic incentives to work, activation programmes and work testing are the dominant policy tools (see also the parallel argument in Jørgensen 2020). Qualification initiatives are downplayed as they are not perceived as serving to get the unemployed quickly into jobs. During this period, the labour market policy has developed a relatively short-term and narrow supply-creating horizon. Analyses (e.g., Jørgensen et al. 2017) indicate a significant erosion of the qualification function in labour market policy, which is reflected in a declining level of activity in the public labour market training programmes, among other things, as a result of cutting the economic framework conditions. The level of activity has thus fallen to less than half in the AMU programmes since the financial crisis and these are increasingly regarded as educational policy rather than labour market policy instruments. In addition, it has become difficult for companies to use AMU and at the same time limit their opportunity costs in connection with the activity. This creates a self-reinforcing effect that reduces the supply of courses in contrast to the increasing use of tertiary level continuing education (Eriksen and Holm 2021, this volume). The declining level of activity goes beyond the opportunities of the under-educated in the labour market, which means that education-conscious companies organise their own tailor-made educational initiatives. Key elements of the labour market's education system are thus not only neglected for a long period but tend towards a decoupling from the labour market policy. Such a decoupling implies a narrow labour market policy, which, in the present form, hardly manages to promote skills development and mobility sufficiently as a lubricant to address the structural challenges of automation in the labour market. However, since the tripartite agreement on continuing education in 2017, the trend reversed, and a small increase is observed. This is due to the aims of increasing activity, motivation, transparency and coherence.

Future-proofing skills and competence development must be based on how tasks are exposed to automation (Nielsen and Holm 2020). Content and scope of tasks are related to the job design resolved at company level and to the industrial relation between the parties in the labour market through the delimitation of occupations as trades in collective agreements, etc. In general, it can be said that the more routine tasks are displaced by more varied, problem-solving and knowledge-based tasks. How the occupations evolve is not only unambiguously determined by the new digital technology but is resolved at corporate level by how new tasks replace obsolete tasks in work organisation and functional flexibility. This makes it necessary to focus on the company level in order to understand the challenges that lie ahead for the active qualification instrument of labour market policy. Labour market education has traditionally contributed to equipping workers with skills that are geared towards narrowly defined subjects or job category skills. Competences, however, equip employees with capacity to utilise learned qualifications for the performance of tasks in the work situation (Høyrup and Petersen 2002). Competence development will thus be the continuous development of knowledge, skills, influence, capacity for action and responsibility in relation to the employees' tasks (Nielsen 2004). Competence development is closely linked to tasks and the organisation of tasks at the company level.

As decisions on automation take place at company level, the actors and their actions at this level become essential to whether routine intensive occupations evolve with new, more varied and problem-solving tasks that complement new technology, or are displaced. A recent Danish study shows that employees are often involved in technology development and work organisation (Nielsen 2015), which supports that voluntarism exists at the workplace level. Employees of all skill levels are involved in idea development, negotiations, decision making and implementations of changes. The same study finds that about a quarter of employees experience that their professional organisation, trade union or collaborative committee participates in the phases of change. Therefore, it would be appropriate if the influence of companies and their employees' involvement is coordinated through the established stakeholder system.

Within the vocational education and training system there is a tradition for involving the social partners of the labour market in central and local boards and educational committees, and to have the social partners involved in implementation of labour market policy. There is thus an established cooperation and governance structure, known as 'the Danish model' to build on if the qualification instrument is to be related to the agents at the company level and their ongoing competence and occupational development. When practice and theory are part of the same integrated education and training programme, for example when practice training at the company level is supplemented with formal vocational training and courses, the knowledge element in learning is strengthened for the benefit of problem solving and functional flexibility (Tidemand and Lindström 2003; Nielsen 2004).

The structural challenges associated with new automation technologies mean that the qualification instrument must be realigned, but in a completely new design of the policy. Central to this design will thus be the level of the company, including the employees' and labour market parties' involvement and participation in the companies' technological development, change of work and functional development of occupations. With the company level's central guiding role for competence development and qualification needs, active work policy becomes a more precise term than active labour market policy and at the same time the answer to the automation challenges' structural challenges.

10.3.1 Can qualification and competence development be future-proofed?

There is some evidence that skill development at the company level has been in decline recently. Lorenz and Holm (2021, this volume) study recent trends in work organisation and find that employees in Denmark have been experiencing a decline in on-the-job skills development. Labour market education and training could potentially be developed so that they support the development of skills at the company level. A recent Danish government commissioned report (Ekspertgruppen for voksen- efter- og videreuddannelse 2017) emphasises that it can be advantageous to create a national competence panel, which, overall, must analyse and monitor the entire adult, after-school and further education system. As an experimental scheme, the report recommended to establish collaboration with 3–4 competence clusters, in order to develop and test models for how close the cooperation between the companies in the competence clusters and the education system can be organised, so that the educational institutions are able continuously to develop qualification offers that match companies' competence needs; beyond employer involvement in setting the curriculum to the development of integrated work learning schemes.

In the same way, partnerships between educational institutions and relevant regional actors are to be established in order to coordinate the regional and local efforts for continuing education. For all employees, the report recommended that, through a personal education account, they should be entitled to upgrade their education, and that competences acquired through the performance of work functions (real skills) must be recognised as further education. This can be interpreted as a suggestion for strengthened coordination of the efforts in close interaction with companies that are leading the way in technology development. It is coupled with a desire that the upgrading of skills must capture the workforce broadly through individual educational accounts, and that competences acquired in the companies are recognised in the education system. At the same time, it is a dynamic effort, which is partly based on analysis and monitoring activities, and partly on a collaboration with a number of competence clusters that must be assumed to be leading technology. The social partners have an important role in monitoring and supervising proactive planning of education and training. The partners are also expected to finance part of the individual educational accounts within their collective agreements. At the firm level, the management and employee representatives have a role of screening for basic competences and acting as agents in a demand-driven vocational education and training system (Ekspertgruppen for voksen- efter- og videreuddannelse 2017).

For a large part of the workers, problem-solving and continuous learning are part of work (Nielsen 2015). When it comes to formal education, there may be challenges for many unskilled workers who perceive education as negative and demotivating. If the teaching is linked to the knowledge and skills of practical problem solving in their work situation, learning becomes close to reality and motivating. A company survey (Fremkom 2016) thus shows that the ability to use what is learned through courses and education in practice is given high priority by a majority of companies. Another study (DEA 2015) shows that a large number of the unskilled workers actually perform work functions at a higher level than their formal (lack of) education appears to qualify them for, and that it is the AMU programmes that help to maintain them at this level. The AMU thus turns out to be of importance for how the formally least skilled often manage to perform work functions at a higher level in the companies. The unemployed, however, must be handled differently in relation to qualification development. The specific competencies are primarily developed in the companies, and therefore the motivation instrument has been increasingly used to get unemployed people to work as soon as possible and let the upgrading work take place in interaction with the companies.

It is beyond doubt that there is an important role for employers in skills development for the unemployed both through integrated work learning schemes and workplace activities. However, there is no strong evidence that forced participation based on the threat of forfeiting unemployment benefits ensures the participation or active involvement of the unemployed. Such policies are more likely to make agents focus on short term arrangements to ensure income than to participate in skills development programmes. Relatedly, the application of technology and the organisational design are, as mentioned, developed to be very company-specific, so that a general qualification is very difficult to develop from the top down. The training of workers, both unemployed and employed, must therefore only focus to a certain extent on concrete competences, but first and foremost on competences to develop competences. The more specific competencies must be continuously developed in the companies in interaction with development in the organisation and use of the technology.

10.4 Conclusions

An important part of a national system of innovation is the diffusion of new technologies in the economy. Such diffusion is facilitated by a workforce with both numerical and functional flexibility, but such requirements may also lead to structural imbalances. This chapter has focused on the challenges faced by labour market policy from technological change, including the demands made on the skills of the labour force. With this focus, we have discussed the structure of labour market policy and how this can be developed into an active work policy, in which qualification and competence development are continuously future-proofed.

An account of recent research contributions to the understanding of how technological change can be expected to affect the future labour market structure (and vice versa) shows that a significant share of jobs or tasks are vulnerable to automation. The research results are somewhat sensitive to the methodology of the studies, but all studies tend to find some automation potential. The crucial point here is that it is not jobs that are automated but tasks in jobs. Frequently, it will only be some of the tasks that are automated, thereby freeing the worker to take care of other tasks. With the importance of the tasks in the automation analyses, very different estimates of the effect of automation on employment appear. The methodological insight, however, gives the opportunity to continuously relate critically to the difference in the results. A few studies focus partly on company level and partly on the individual level. They show how technological and organisational changes affect the composition of the workforce and show the adaptation of the workforce as a result of automation in the workplace. These studies are interesting as they emphasise the importance of adaptation and development among workers. Similarly interesting, are studies that examine the dynamic effects of automation. Overall, substitution, output and spill-over effects entail that automation creates more jobs than it destroys. However, the potential of automation depends entirely on the occupations' content in terms of tasks.

The data presented in this chapter documents the recent evolution of labour market policy in Denmark, and also includes new data showing the importance of different mechanisms for competence acquisition among workers in Denmark. It was documented that over recent decades, Danish labour market policy has been increasingly emphasising the motivation instrument while the qualification instrument has been neglected. However, recent political changes suggest that the qualification emphasis is currently receiving renewed attention. The data also documented the importance of learning at the workplace versus formal training, and that, while the unemployed do not themselves consider their current competencies obsolete, they struggle to upgrade their competencies with the options available to them.

Based on research on the effect of automation on the structure of the labour market, and on our data on Danish labour market policy and Danish workers' acquisition of competence, we then discussed the labour market policy challenges. The qualification instrument has been a decisive tool in earlier periods of structural change. However, developments over the past decade also show how the qualification instrument is eroded in the policy, so that the result is a narrow operational labour market policy.

If the qualification and competence development is to be future-proofed, the qualification instrument must be linked to labour market policy, but with a bottom-up perspective, with the inclusion of both unemployed and employed. Thus, the company level must be the basis for competence development in relation to tasks that develop in parallel with technological change. At the company level, decisions on productivity-enhancing technology development and job organisation take place. However, the agents at the company level have a widespread practice of involvement and participation in the decisions about technological change and job organisation.

Correspondingly, the companies and other agents of the labour market have practical experience for a collaboration that involves the labour market social partners. The key point, however, is whether vocational and labour market training can develop and maintain a broad and dynamic understanding of competences. This understanding should be based on analysis and collaboration with competency clusters of companies and focus on the development of skills that enable employees to apply and continuously develop the skills that are essential for the management of knowledge and problem-oriented work functions. This applies to all categories of education. A boost of skills in reading, maths, collaboration and digital problem-solving must form the basis. The crucial thing is that the programmes must focus on building higher-order competencies, i.e., developing the competences-to-develop-competences of the labour force, while the companies must focus on the fact that the specific task-related competence development takes place continuously for all employees.

Notes

1 For a clear discussion of machine learning see Chollet (2018). According to Chollet, in traditional 'symbolic' programming, programmers input rules or a programme and data to be processed by the programme in order to arrive at an answer. In contrast, in machine learning the data engineer inputs data and the expected outcome and the system by means of a feedback loop typically over several thousands of iterations 'learns' the rules or mapping between inputs and outputs. This involves optimising the values for often several millions of weights or parameters. The mapping can then be used with new data to predict new outcomes.

2 For a useful discussion of what kinds of tasks are most open to automation with machine learning, see Brynjolfsson, et al. (2018).

3 See Holm, Lorenz and Stamhus (2021) for details on the TASK survey.

4 Recent reports suggest a more favourable development since 2017 with a small expansion in enrolment but these data are at present not yet systematised by Statistics Denmark, and the suggested increase in enrolment is very limited – i.e., 2019 enrolment at the level of 2015 enrolment. See for example Højlund (2019).

References

Acemoglu, D. and Restrepo, P. 2017. *Robots and Jobs: Evidence from US Labour Markets*. NBER Working Paper, (w23285).

Acemoglu, D. and Restrepo, P. 2018. The race between man and machine: Implications of technology for growth, factor shares, and employment. *American Economic Review* 108(6): 1488–1542.

Arbejdsmarkedskommissionen. 2009. *Velfærd Kræver Arbejde, Arbejdsmarkedskommissionens anbefalinger – Analyserapport*. Copenhagen. http://www.amkom.dk

Arntz, M., Gregory, T. and Zierahn, U. 2016. *The Risk of Automation for Jobs in OECD Countries: A Comparative Analysis*. OECD Social, Employment and Migration Working Papers. No., 189. Paris: OECD Publishing.

Autor, D. H. and Salomons, A. 2018. *Is Automation Labour-Displacing. Productivity Growth, Employment, and the Labour Share*. NBER Working Papers 24871, National Bureau of Economic Research.

Bessen, J., Goos, M., Salomons, A. and van den Berge, W. 2019. *Automatic Reaction – What Happens to Workers at Firms That Automate?* L and Economics Series Paper No. 19-2. Boston, MA: Boston University School of Law.

Bowles, J. 2014. *The Computerization of European Jobs*. Brussels: Bruegel.

Bredgaard, T., Jørgensen, H., Madsen, P. K. and Rasmussen, S. 2011. *Dansk Arbejdsmarkedspolitik*. Copenhagen: Jurist- og økonomforbundets Forlag.

Bredgaard, T. and Madsen, P. K. 2015. *Dansk Flexicurity – Fleksibilitet og sikkerhed på arbejdsmarkedet*. Copenhagen: Dansk Arbejdsmarkedspolitik.

Brynjolfsson, E., Mitchell, T. and Rock, D. 2018. What can machines learn, and what does it mean for occupations and the economy? *AEA Papers and Proceedings* 108: 43–47.

Chollet, F. 2018. *Deep Learning with Python*. Shelter Island, NY: Manning Publications.

Dagpengekommisionen. 2015. *Kompensationsgraden i Dagpengesystemet*. Working Paper, Ministry of Labour, Copenhagen.

Dauth, W., Findeisen, S., Südekum, J. and Woessner, N. 2017. *German Robots-The Impact of Industrial Robots on Workers*. IAB Discussion Paper 30/2017. Nürnberg: Institut für Arbeitsmarkt- und Berufsforschung (IAB).

DEA. 2015. *Super ufaglærte og Super faglærte – kompetenceløft gennem efteruddannelse*. DEA Rapport.

Dølvik, J. E. and Steen, R. J. 2018. The Nordic future of work – drivers, institutions and politics. *TemaNord,* 2018: 555.

Ekspertgruppen for voksen- efter- og videreuddannelse. 2017. *Nye kompetencer hele livet - Fremtidens voksen-, efter- og videreuddannelse,* Ministry of Employment, Copenhagen.

Eriksen, J. and Holm, J. R. 2021. Firm innovation and tertiary continuing education. In *Globalization, New and Emerging Technologies, and Sustainable Development – Therapie Danish Innovation System in Transition,* eds. Christensen, J. L., Gregersen, B., Holm, J. R. and Lorenz, E. London: Routledge.

European Commission. 2007. *Mod fælles principper for Flexicurity – Flere og bedre job ved hjælp af fleksibilitet og sikkerhed,* Brussels.

Freeman, C. and Louçã, D. 2001. *As Time Goes by: From the Industrial Revolutions to the Information Revolution.* Oxford: Oxford University Press.

Freeman, C. and Perez, C. 1988. *Long Waves and Changes in Employment Patterns, in Structural Change and Labour Market Policy.* Stockholm: ALC.

Fremkom. 2016. *Fremtidens kompetencer i Nordjylland.* http://fremkom.dk/

Frey, C. B. and Osborne, M. 2013. *The Future of Employment.* Oxford: Oxford Martin Programme on Technology and Employment.

Graetz, G. and Michaels, G. 2018. Robots at work. *Review of Economics and Statistics* 100(5): 753–768.

Gregory, T., Salomons, A. and Zierahn, U. 2019. *Racing with or Against the Machine? Evidence from Europe.* IZA Institute for Labour Economics Discussion Paper Series No. 12063.

Højlund, N. 2019. Rygterne om AMUs snarlige død er stærk overdrevet. *A4nu,* 22 October. https://www.a4nu.dk/artikel/rygterne-om-amu-s-snarlige-doed-er-staerkt -overdrevne. Accessed: 21 April 2020.

Holm, J. R., Lorenz, E. and Nielsen, P. 2020. Work organization and job polarization. *Research Policy* 49(8): 104015.

Holm, J. R., Lorenz, E. and Stamhus, J. 2021. The impact of robots and AI/ML on skills and work organization. In *Globalisation, New and Emerging Technologies, and Sustainable Development – The Danish Innovation System in Transition,* eds. Christensen, J. L., Gregersen, B., Holm, J. R. and Lorenz, E. Abingdon: Routledge.

Høyrup, S. and Pedersen, K. 2002. Lærings- og kompetencebegreberne i arbejdslivsforskningen. In *Udspil om læring i arbejdslivet,* red. Illeris, K. Roskilde: Roskilde University Press.

ILO. 2018. *Inception Report for the Global Commission on the Future of Work.* Geneva.

Jørgensen, H. 2006/7. *Arbejdsmarkedspolitikkens fornyelse – Innovation eller trussel mod dansk "Flexicurity".* Bruxelles and Aalborg.

Jørgensen, H. 2020. Arven fra Rehn-Meidner-modellen: Idégrundlag og erfaringslære for aktiv arbejdsmarkedspolitik. In *Aktiv arbejdsmarkedspolitik: Etablering, udvikling og fremtid,* eds. Klindt, M. P., Rasmussen, S. and Jørgensen H. Copenhagen: Djøf Forlag.

Jørgensen, H., Klindt, M. P., Pedersen, V. H., Lassen, M. S., Buchholt, P. 2017. *Et udfordret AMU system – mod revitalisering og fornyelse.* Report, Aalborg University, Aalborg.

Lorenz, E. and Holm, J. R. 2021. Work organisation, innovation and the quality of working life in Denmark. In *Globalisation, New and Emerging Technologies, and Sustainable Development – The Danish Innovation System in Transition,* eds. Christensen, J. L., Gregersen, B., Holm, J. R. and Lorenz, E. Abingdon: Routledge.

Lundvall, B.-Å. 1999. *Det Danske Innovationssystem.* Copenhagen: The Danish Development Council.

Madsen, P. K. 2003. *The Danish Model of Flexicurity Experiences and Lessons to Learn.* Paper to ETUI Conference, Brussels.

Marsden, D. 1999. *A Theory of Employment Systems.* Oxford: Oxford University Press.

Nielsen, P. 1979. Beskæftigelsespolitikken i 60'erne og 70'erne. Baggrund – Interessemodsætninger – Konsekvenser. *Økonomi og Politik* 53(3): 209–258.

Nielsen, P. 2004. *Personale i vidensøkonomien – Innovation, vidensorganisationer og kompetenceudvikling I det nye årtusinde.* Aalborg: Aalborg Universitetsforlag.

Nielsen, P. 2015. *Arbejde i forandring – Udviklingslinjer i private og offentlige arbejdsrelationer.* bookboon.com, London, UK.

Nielsen, P. and Holm, J. R. 2020. Arbejdsmarkedspolitik i automatiseringens tidsalder. In *Aktiv arbejdsmarkedspolitik: Etablering, udvikling og fremtid,* eds. Klindt, M. P., Rasmussen, S. and Jørgensen H., Copenhagen: Djøf Forlag.

Tidemand, F. and Lindstrøm, P. 2003. *Arbejder der Uddanner.* Copenhagen: Confederation of Danish Industry.

Appendix

In this appendix we explain the basic ideas and give practical examples of the motivation and qualification instruments in Danish labour market policy.

Since its foundation in the early 1960s, labour market policy in Denmark has related to two basic principles: the active principle meaning that the policy instruments should affect the dynamics, behaviour and resources of the target groups and the corporatism principle meaning that the social partners should be involved at various levels of the policy process. The influence of the two principles has been oscillating and, at times, narrow and weak. However, the principles have always been important in order to understand the potential of the policies in solving the labour market challenges. The motivation and the qualification instruments have been developed and applied in periods with various structural and functional challenges. A first period started in the early 1960s where the AMU institution was founded. The social partners were present in the boards at national and local school level. The first task of these qualification instruments was to transform labour from agriculture to manufacturing and building industry. The qualification instruments contributed greatly to this major restructuring being carried out with significant productivity growth both in agriculture, but especially in the manufacturing and building sectors as a result (Nielsen 1979). The policy showed how the active and corporatist labour market policy could solve major structural challenges. In the following period, starting at the beginning of the 1970s, the public labour exchange (AF) was founded, and the unemployment insurance (A-kasserne) was partly public financed. It was a period where women increasingly entered the labour market. The public labour exchange contributed to transparency and mobility, matching increasing labour supply to job openings. Together with a public financed unemployment allowance it became part of the institutional foundation for motivation instruments related to the flexicurity model. Later in the 1970s unemployment was increasing and selective work offers (ATB) with economic support became important instruments fighting the long term and youth unemployment. An early retirement scheme (Efterlønsordningen) was established to reduce the labour supply. The 1980s was a decade dominated by structural challenges at the labour market (Bredgaard et al. 2011). An economic upturn showed bottleneck problems, which gave rise to an active surveillance and job matching. The ATB were supplemented by financially supported training arrangements (UTB) and AMU was expanded. Nevertheless, the so-called natural rate of unemployment was estimated at 6%. This rate of natural unemployment represented the lower limit for increasing wage and inflation pressure on the economy. In 1993 the unemployment rate was 12% when a comprehensive labour market reform was implemented. The purpose of the reform was to overcome the structural problems. The labour market reform combined motivational measures, i.e., a cancellation of the vesting period on unemployment benefit when in a supported work offer, with a significant and broad focus on qualification measures (Bredgaard et al. op cit.) i.e., educational and training arrangements, job rotation and educational leave. This reform of the active labour market policy stimulated both reductions of unemployment and employment growth, which rose significantly towards the turn of the millennium. From around 2000 onwards, labour market policy has increasingly been dominated by a 'work first' principle using control and sanctions. The motivation instruments have thus predominantly become threat instruments. Reduction of social protection (and the security side of flexicurity) is part of this regime of increasing the supply of labour. In Denmark there is a relatively weak tradition for policy focusing on the demand side, compared to, for example, initiatives like the Finnish workplace development programmes. Such programmes are more or less unknown in Denmark. Fundamentally, labour market policy in Denmark has been mainly a supply-side policy. However, there is a recent political discussion on the limits of the supply policy with contributions from some of the leading neoclassic Danish economists.

11 Firm innovation and tertiary continuing education

Jesper Eriksen and Jacob Rubæk Holm

11.1 Introduction

The continuing education and training system has been considered an important part of the national system of innovation (NSI) since the earliest part of the NSI literature (see e.g., Lundvall 1992, pp. 14–15). The most commonly pursued formal continuing education (CE) was short-term labour-market-oriented CE in the 1990s, which aimed at providing low-skill workers with specific human capital skill upgrades supporting both the worker and their firm (Gregersen and Holek 1996). In the first empirical analysis of the role of CE in the Danish National Innovation System, Voxsted (1998) studied how Danish manufacturing firms used these short-term CE programmes to prepare their firms for incremental innovation through innovation, communication protocols and quality control. Even today, these programmes continue to serve as a tool to help employees achieve desirable employment outcomes (Nielsen et al. 2021, this volume). Starting in the 2000s, however, many firms began to provide their workers with longer and more knowledge-intensive Master's and Diploma-level tertiary CE that emphasise management skills. The increased use of tertiary level CE arguably reflects a change in the role of CE in the National Innovation System and the increased importance of human capital and networks in the innovation process.

Several prior studies have linked initial education levels and diversity, two measures of firms' human capital base, to firm innovation (see e.g., Audretsch et al. 2018; D'Este et al. 2014; Schubert and Tavassoli 2020; Østergaard et al. 2011), but CE has received less attention. CE provides firms with human capital upgrades of particular skills after the participants have earned the initial degrees that are most often emphasised in the levels and diversity studies. This type of upgrade is particularly relevant in the face of technological change (Holm et al. 2021, this volume).

While a few studies have linked short-term labour-market CE to incremental product and process innovation in firms (Bauernschuster et al. 2009; Børing 2017; Dostie 2018; Voxsted 1998), none, to the best of our knowledge, have studied the relation between tertiary CE and firm innovation. Like short-term CE, tertiary CE provides post-initial education skill upgrades. It differs from short-term CE as it gives access to a specific type of human capital, managerial skills, as opposed to applied skills such as how to use specific welding equipment. Tertiary CE programmes are also often longer (up to two part-time years compared to an average of four days in short-term programs) and taken at a more intense pace measured in the number of hours per year. The differences between CE and initial education, and short-term and tertiary CE, makes it particularly relevant to empirically study the role of CE in the national innovation system.

The main hypothesis of this study is that when a firm's employees participate in tertiary level CE, the firm becomes more likely to innovate because the firm gains the managerial skills necessary to support the innovation process.

We contrast the hypothesis of the internal use of managerial skills with a network hypothesis to test alternative explanations for tertiary CE and innovation relationships. Recent studies of MBA participants (a form of tertiary CE) have shown that network influences are important determinants of participants' subsequent behaviour (Shue 2013; Hacamo and Kleiner 2020). One type of network effect which we can test with our available data is networks linking firms and universities. Such relations have been linked to having a higher likelihood of successfully innovating (Cohen et al. 2002; Jaffe 1989). To test if managerial skills are likely to work internally or are based purely in network effects, the second hypothesis, we first test whether employee participation in tertiary CE predicts collaboration with universities for innovation purposes, and secondly whether this channel fully explains any relation between tertiary CE participation and firms' likelihood of innovating.

The empirical study is based on three types of Danish administrative data and a descriptive and instrumental variable identification approach. The datasets contain information on spells of tertiary CE participation at the individual level, worker and firm characteristics, as well as linked Danish Research, Development and Innovation (RDI) surveys with information about a representative sample of firms' R&D inputs, and whether the firms have product innovated (put a new product on the market), or process innovated (changed internal organisational routines).

We show that firms with employees who received tertiary CE training within the last two years are more likely to innovate new products and processes than firms without. We also confirm that the effects are plausibly causal using an instrumental variables strategy, relying on changing distances to nearest tertiary CE education institutions as instruments. Also, having former tertiary CE participants in the firm is positively associated with collaborating with universities as would be suggested under our second hypothesis. However, collaboration with universities does not fully explain the effect of tertiary CE on innovation. Tertiary CE appears to have causal effects on innovation through a collaboration channel but also through other channels that we cannot investigate in this paper.

Our study has importance from a policy perspective. Policies intending to improve the competitiveness of firms through their likelihood of innovating can readily focus on tertiary CE. Increasing access to tertiary CE, either through opening more programmes or lowering participation costs, is likely to lead to higher rates of innovation in firms constrained by their managerial skills which are an input in the innovation process.

The chapter proceeds as follows. In Section 11.2 we discuss earlier literature and the theory linking CE to firm-level innovation outcomes, and we provide a brief introduction to the Danish tertiary CE programmes, contrasting the programme with the short-term CE programmes. Section 11.3 contains a description of data sources used for the chapter and our empirical strategy to estimate the effects of tertiary CE on firms' likelihood of innovating. Section 11.4 contains our empirical findings. Finally, Section 11.5 concludes the chapter.

11.2 Continuing education and innovation

In this section, we first describe the existing research linking human capital and particularly short-term CE to innovation, as well as prior studies on individual and firm-level effects of tertiary CE participation. We then discuss theoretical foundations that describe why upskilling already highly educated tertiary CE participants may lead to an increased likelihood of successful innovation.

11.2.1 Existing studies

The education level and composition of firms' workforces have often been used as a measure of human capital in innovation studies, and are found to be an important input to the innovation process (e.g., Audretsch et al. 2018; Østergaard et al. 2011; D'Este et al. 2014; Schubert and Tavassoli 2020). The term human capital describes the embodied productive characteristics of an individual (Becker 1993). While often related to educational attainment at the primary, high school and post-secondary level, experience and in-firm training (Bhuller et al. 2017; Lemieux 2006), it is also used to capture broader sets of characteristics, such as training, attitudes, motivation and job satisfaction, and has been linked to innovation within firms (Lenihan et al. 2019; McGuirk et al. 2015).

A few prior studies have investigated the relation between short-term CE and innovation.[1] Bauernschuster et al. (2009) use German IAB establishment surveys from 1997 to 2001 to estimate the relation between training support (either financial or through paid time off for training) and the likelihood the firm product innovates. Dostie (2018) and Børing (2017) use similar Canadian and Norwegian surveys to show that having employees with short-term training is positively related to the likelihood of incremental product innovation. The only Danish study of the relationship between short-term CE and innovation is Voxsted (1998), who used the Danish DISKO survey data from a sample of Danish manufacturing firms to investigate firms' use of training. Voxsted found that among the participating firms, 25% had used the public labour market education programmes to upskill their workers to prepare the firm for process innovations. In general, these studies suggest some effect of increasing the skills of the least educated on incremental product and process innovations.

Studies of tertiary CE are scarcer than the studies on short-term training, and to the best of our knowledge none directly investigate tertiary CE and innovation links. Several authors have studied individual financial returns to, and behaviour in, tertiary CE programmes (e.g., Altonji and Zhong 2020; Bertrand et al. 2010; Boneva et al. 2019). Bolvig et al. (2017) investigate wage returns to tertiary CE in a Danish context, finding no income returns from tertiary CE in Denmark. A small literature on US tertiary CE MBA participants have also investigated firm-level outcomes from hiring tertiary CE participants. These studies typically focus on the effect of peer networks on firm policies among firms hiring MBA programme peers, e.g., on top management salaries, acquisitions, investment strategies and the likelihood of successful entrepreneurship (Ahern et al. 2014; Lerner and Malmendier 2013; Shue 2013).

In summary, while there is a large set of studies linking various forms of human capital and the likelihood of innovation, few have investigated CE effects on innovation. The existing studies also tend to focus on short-term CE, leaving no empirical evidence directly on the effects of tertiary CE.

11.2.2 Theoretical links from tertiary CE to innovation

Tertiary CE differs from initial education in that participants already have high levels of education, and substantial work experience. Like short-term CE it allows firms to upgrade their employees' skills beyond what can be learned in the firm through learning-by-doing given the existing internal knowledge base of the firm.[2] This external skill acquisition becomes increasingly important as firms will have to adapt to technological change, which may force firms and workers to grapple with new technologies and innovation opportunities and demands (Holm et al. 2021; Nielsen et al. 2021). Tertiary CE also differs from the short-term CE in that it focuses not on specific applied skills, but rather on more general skills and in particular managerial skills.

The importance of managerial skills is emphasised in the Strategic Management literature. In the 'Resource-Based View of the Firm' (e.g., Barney 1991; Peteraf 1993), firms gain competitive advantages when their managers effectively utilise (valuable) resources idiosyncratic to the firm. The more recent Dynamic Capabilities literature (e.g., Teece 2007; Teece et al. 1997, Winter 2003) focus on long-run adaptability of the firm, emphasising how managerial capabilities allow the firm to maintain sustained competitive advantage through change. Teece (2010, 2017) makes more direct links between management, and in particular Dynamic Capabilities, and innovation within the firm, arguing that management skills are a necessary component in the sustained innovation activity in the firm.

Alternatively, the managerial skills developed in tertiary CE may draw on networks formed during employees' tertiary CE participation to increase the likelihood of successful innovation. A core idea in the NSI literature is that knowledge is the foundation for innovation (Lundvall 2016), and networks between actors in the economy allow for knowledge sharing and can, in turn, lead to higher likelihoods of innovation (e.g., Bell et al. 2019; Bonaccorsi et al. 2014; Cantner and Graf 2006; Dahl and Pedersen 2004; Gonzalez-Brambila et al. 2013). Furthermore, recent US MBA studies on the effects of peer networks on firm policies underscore the importance of collaborations formed during studies for subsequent firm outcomes (Hacamo and Kleiner 2020; Lerner and Malmendier 2013; Shue 2013). A potentially important type of network may be with employees at universities, giving access to collaboration and knowledge sharing with the universities previously linked to innovation (Cohen et al. 2002; Jaffe 1989). As we cannot distinguish between firms' other networks but can investigate collaborations with universities with our available data, we therefore test a second hypothesis: having employees that have participated in tertiary CE leads to higher a likelihood of collaborating with universities for innovation purposes, and also that this is the main channel for tertiary CE's effect on the likelihood of successfully innovating.

11.2.3 Tertiary continuing education in Denmark

The Danish CE system can be divided into short-term labour market education (AMU) and the longer tertiary CE Master's and Diploma programmes (such as MBAs, MPAs, Master's in IT and Diploma in Pedagogy). In this section, we compare the two types of programmes to provide context for the following analysis.[3]

The majority of Diploma and Master's programmes aim at providing participants with management skills. To characterise the content of the tertiary CE programmes, we have collected information on programme content from the Danish Ministry of Education (www.ug.dk) and individual programmes' webpages. Among Diploma tertiary CE programmes, 45% are fully management oriented. Nearly all other programmes, such as the Diploma in Pedagogy, include courses on management specified for the context the course is intended for. Similarly, 42% of Master's programmes are specifically management oriented, including MBAs and MPAs, and most other Master's programmes provide some level of management skills aimed at application to the specific field. One example of the programmes with specific emphasis is the Master's in IT, which allows participants to update their knowledge of recent IT developments while also gaining management-oriented skills relevant for government IT sections and firms. In contrast to the tertiary CE programmes, AMU programmes provide specialised content aimed at building narrow, applied skills including how to use specialised welding equipment (Gregersen and Holek 1996).

The number of CE students in Denmark has increased over time, both in the AMU programmes and tertiary level Master's and Diplomas. Figure 11.1 shows the number of individuals who have started a course, by year and type of programme. From 2000 to 2015 the number of new Master's students rose from five to 5200, and the number of Diploma students rose from 4100 to 24,400 students. This reflects the opening of many new tertiary CE programmes across Danish education institutions. Over the same period, the number of AMU students increased from 173,000 in 2000 to 448,200 in 2009 during the financial crisis, then declining to 198,900 in 2015. The different post-crisis trends reflect different uses of programmes, where AMU programmes are used as unemployment-based training programmes, while tertiary CE is a more substantial time and monetary investment with increased usage over time.

Tertiary CE programmes usually last between one and two years, while the average AMU course lasts four days, and tertiary CE is taken at more intense levels than AMU courses (Gregersen and Holek 1996; Undervisningsministeriet 2010). As a result, AMU courses are taken at less intensive levels than Diploma and Master's programmes. Master's and Diploma students achieve between 0.6 and 1.2 of a full-time equivalent study in a year on their programmes, with intensity declining slightly in recent years. This decline likely reflects a change towards more flexible programmes that allow students to spread coursework over additional years.

11.3 Data and methods

To investigate the hypotheses discussed in Section 11.1, we use the 2007 to 2015 waves of the Danish RDI surveys distributed to between 4000 and 5000 Danish companies yearly.[4] From the survey, we collect information on

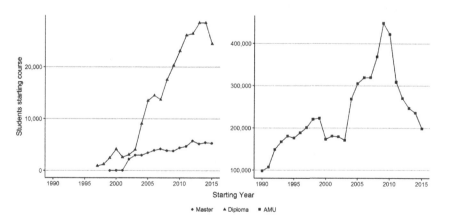

Figure 11.1 Number of students who have started CE by year and type of programme.
Source: Calculations based on Danish administrative data.

innovation activities and collaboration patterns in connection with innovation, which we use as dependent variables.

Our main explanatory variable is a binary indicator for having or not having an employee who participated in tertiary CE in the previous two years.[5] To create this variable we use Danish administrative data containing all individual spells of CE participation at registered education institutions in Denmark. The dataset contains all CE pursued in Denmark at the individual course level from 1974 to 2016.[6] For each period of CE, we can identify the participant, start date, end date, scope in hours, the content of the programme, institution, and whether or not the participant passed the course. We focus on Master's and Diploma level tertiary CE programmes as these are the programmes in which employees are likely to participate, having already been in the labour market for some years.

We obtain several variables at the individual and firm level from administrative data accessed through Statistics Denmark which is available for the full population of individuals in Denmark, as well as all firms from 1980 to 2015. For individuals, these include age, family status, education levels, income levels and their location down to postal code. For firms, they include the number of employees, firm age, industry and location. Finally, we supplement the administrative data with information on the locations of education institutions collected from the Danish Ministry of Education when the institution still exists and found e.g., in historical archives otherwise.

11.3.1 Methods

Our hypothesis concerns the effect of CE on innovation. Firms award employees with tertiary CE which makes the firm more likely to innovate but awarding CE may be endogenous as the innovation process may require employees to participate in tertiary CE. To handle this endogeneity problem and robustly identify the causal effects of awarding CE to employees on the firm's innovation outcome we do two things:

1. We lag the CE variable to ensure that workers are awarded CE before the firm reports on innovation.
2. We instrument CE as even the lagged variable may be endogenous if innovating firms use tertiary CE in anticipation of needs arising from later innovation.

11.3.2 Baseline model

We model firm-level innovation in an augmented innovation production function as is common in the innovation literature (Love et al. 2011; McGuirk et al. 2015). This entails modelling firm-level innovation outcomes as a function of characteristics that are internal to the firm and that can affect the firm's propensity to innovate, augmented with an additional set of regressors capturing contextual factors in the firm's environment that may affect its propensity to innovate. Equation 11.1 describes this framework for firm i at time t, where $firm_{it}$ are firm internal characteristics including our tertiary CE variable, and $regional_{it}$ are firm external factors, which in our data all refer to variables defined at the regional level. We expand on these variables below:

$$Innovation_{it} = f\left(firm_{it}, regional_{it}\right) \tag{11.1}$$

In the findings section, we first show ordinary least squares (OLS) regressions according to Equation 11.1, with an indicator for having innovated within the last year on the left-hand side, and an indicator for having an employee that has participated in tertiary CE in the previous two years as the main right-hand-side variable.

We show two main regressions, first controlling for year fixed effects to capture any fluctuations in overall innovation levels due e.g., to the financial crisis. Secondly, we control for firm and regional level factors that affect firms' propensity for innovation separately from the effects of tertiary CE participation.

The full model with year, firm and regional controls can be seen in Equation 11.2. In the model, λ is the conditional relation between CE participation and firm innovation, and CE is either participation in Master's or Diploma level tertiary CE. $year_t$ is a set of year indicators, $firm_{it}$ a vector of firm-level controls, and $regional_{it}$ the vector of regional controls. We estimate the model using OLS as opposed e.g., to probit or logit modelling and ML estimation to obtain estimates of effect sizes that are readily interpretable from the regression coefficient (Angrist and Pischke 2009, p. 72).

$$Innovation_{it} = \alpha_1 + \lambda CE_{it-2} + \sum_t \theta_t year_t + \gamma_1' \, firm_{it} + \gamma_2' \, regional_{it} + \varepsilon_{it} \tag{11.2}$$

11.3.3 Controls

At the firm internal level, we control for common factors that have been found to correlate with innovation activity. We control for the firm's main branch of economic activity as innovation is naturally more common in some industries compared to others (compare for example the pharmaceutical and construction sectors). We also control for firm size in terms of employment as larger firms have been empirically shown to be more likely to innovate than smaller firms (Cohen 2010), and firm age in years since the firm was established as firms' economic performance has been shown to vary with firm age (Coad et al. 2018). We also control for firm-level inputs to the innovation process by including a variable for the share of researchers in the workforce, as reported by the firm in the RDI surveys.

At the firm external level, we include two controls. The first is a control for the locally available resources for innovation: the share of the regional workforce with tertiary level education. A supply of highly educated labour benefits the firms' innovation activities directly as a resource, and indirectly by allowing the firm increased flexibility when adapting its workforce after the innovation has taken place. We define regions as commuting zones computed from the administrative data. Commuting zones are defined according to Statistics Denmark (2016), as a function of the size of working areas, the distance employees commute, and local economic activity. Around the main cities of Denmark, there are large commuting zones comprised of multiple municipalities, while in the more peripheral areas commuting zones correspond to single municipalities. This means that there are significant differences in the regional innovation systems among our 27 regions. Some are small rural regions with only a few hundred firms, while others are geographically large regions centred around metropolitan university cities with several thousand firms. These differences are likely to correlate with our measure of the locally available resources for innovation, and the share of the local workforce with a tertiary education will thus also reflect differences in regional innovation systems more broadly.

While the first regional variable captures the general conditions for innovation in the regional innovation system, the second regional control variable reflects regional spill-overs that are useful for the specific firm. These are the Marshall-Arrow-Romer (MAR) externalities: a thick labour market, specialised suppliers, and informal interaction (Malmberg and Maskell 2002). To measure the potential for MAR externalities for firm i in region r at time t we use an index for relatedness (Hidalgo et al. 2018; Neffke et al. 2017). That is an index capturing the relatedness between the firm's activities and the other activities in the region-year combination. More related activities entail a thicker labour market, a greater potential for specialised suppliers, and greater scope for informal interaction with peers. The specific index then follows an employment weighted relatedness index as applied in Holm and Østergaard (2018). We compute the index at the level of two-digit NACE[7] industries and for industry-region-year krt. ER_{krt} is interpreted as the share of employment in the region-year, which is in industries that are related to industry k.

11.3.4 Instrumental variable estimation

The OLS regression shows descriptive evidence as to whether there is a relationship between the use of tertiary CE and the firm becoming more likely to innovate. The use of CE may still be endogenous if firms that innovate are simply more likely to have employees participate in CE, for example, because they are expanding their scale of production. To estimate the causal effects of tertiary CE on the innovation process we instrument the CE variable in Equation 11.2.

The instrument for CE is the distance to institutions offering CE. One of the first uses of distances to education institutions as instruments was by Card (1993). Several authors have since extended the approach, including Mountjoy (2019). In our setting, the distance represents a cost, so firms located closer to institutions offering CE are more likely to award their workers with CE. The cost is made up of both the actual cost of transportation, but also as an information cost as firms located near such institutions are more likely to be aware of the possibilities of CE. While the pecuniary cost to the firm of an employee participating in CE is likely to be dominated by the cost of the course itself, there are also personal costs to the participants in terms of time away from home and family if participating in a programme.

The distance between the firm and the institution offering CE is not a perfect instrument for whether firms award CE to their employees. The distance may not be random, as more knowledge-intensive firms tend to locate near educational institutions (Bonaccorsi et al. 2014). There are other ways that the distance can affect innovation outcomes: firms located a shorter distance to educational institutions will have better access to skilled labour, and access to new knowledge produced at the institution – especially if it is a research institution such as a university. However, including the full set of controls as in the methods section will control for both relevant regional and firm characteristics.

The Instrumental Variables (IV) setup is a two-stage least squares (2SLS) approach (Angrist and Pischke 2009). Equation 11.3 is our first stage from which we obtain fitted values for CE participation at the firm level using the instrument and the remaining independent variables from the augmented innovation production function as regressors.

$$CE_{it} = a_1 + \phi Distance_{it} + \sum_t \theta_t year_t + \gamma_1' firm_{it} + \gamma_2' regional_{it} + \varepsilon_{it} \quad (11.3)$$

In the second stage, we use these fitted values in place of CE_{it} in the original model in Equation 11.2 to estimate the causal effects of CE on the likelihood of the firm innovating. For all IV regressions we also include the results from two tests. The first test is an F-test for weak instruments in the first stage, which as a rule of thumb should be above 10 to ensure low levels of weak IV bias in the IV estimate (Angrist and Pischke 2009). We report both the F-statistic and the p-value from the test. The Wu–Hausman test for endogeneity is the second test, which compares IV and OLS estimates to determine if the estimates are statistically different (Wooldridge 2010, pp. 129–134).

11.4 Empirical findings

The OLS regressions presented in Table 11.1 show a strong positive relationship between firm innovation and participation in tertiary CE by the firm's employees. We find a strong positive relationship with both Master's and Diploma CE participation. Firms that have an employee who has received Master's level CE, have a 19 percentage point higher likelihood of having had a product innovation conditional on year fixed effects. When we include firm and regional level controls, the firms are 13.6 percentage point more likely

Table 11.1 OLS regression of innovation outcomes on having former tertiary CE participants among employees.

	Product innovation				Process innovation			
	(1)	(2)	(3)	(4)	(5)	(6)	(7)	(8)
Master's (-2Y)	.190***	.141***			.169***	.125***		
	(.010)	(.010)			(.010)	(.010)		
Diploma (-2Y)			.151***	.124***			.149***	.121***
			(.008)	(.008)			(.008)	(.008)
Employees		.00004***		.00004***		.0001***		.0001***
		(.00001)		(.00001)		(.00001)		(.00001)
Firm age		.0004*		.0004*		-.0001		-.0001
		(.0003)		(.0003)		(.0003)		(.0003)
R&D empl. (%)		.493***		.497***		.257***		.260***
		(.036)		(.037)		(.020)		(.020)
Regional % with tertiary education		.402**		.392***		.213***		.202***
		(.058)		(.058)		(.061)		(.061)
ERirt		.414***		.424***		.159***		.168***
		(.044)		(.044)		(.045)		(.045)
Year FE	Yes	Yes	Yes	Yes	Yes	Yes	Yes	Yes
Industry FE		Yes		Yes		Yes		Yes
N	36,995	36,995	36,995	36,995	36,995	36,995	36,995	36,995

Note: *p < 0.1; **p < 0.05; ***p < 0.01

to have innovated. The relationship is weaker for process innovation at 16.9 percentage points and 12.2 percentage points but remains economically substantial. Firms with employees that have taken Diploma level CE are also more likely to have had product and process innovations. In particular, their likelihood of having had a product innovation is 15.1 percentage points higher than firms without Diploma CE employees without controls and 12 percentage points with controls. The numbers are nearly similar for process innovations.

In summary, the OLS evidence is suggestive of the innovation effects of tertiary CE. Firms with employees who have taken CE are more likely to innovate. The result is robust to including several controls that can impact the firm's innovation process. However, the OLS regressions can only be interpreted descriptively.

Next, we turn to investigate whether the effects we find on innovation can be interpreted causally. Table 11.2 contains IV estimates of the effect of tertiary CE on the likelihood that a firm has had a product or process innovation. The tertiary CE variables remain the same, as do left-hand side variables and firm and regional controls. We instrument lagged Master's and Diploma education with additionally (1–3 years) lagged distances to the nearest education institution providing the relevant type of education.

Firms with Master's level CE participants remain positively and statistically significantly more likely to have product and process innovations when we instrument for CE. It is noteworthy that the point estimate for both product and process innovation remain nearly the same with and without controls. For product innovation, the estimate is 1.722, while it is 0.82 for process innovation without controls, and 0.788 with controls. This suggests that the specification is robust to plausible confounders and that we are capturing causal effects even if the estimates have been sized disproportionately. For Diploma level CE participation and the likelihood of innovating we find mixed evidence. While the likelihood of a product innovation remains higher for tertiary CE participation with and without controls (a point estimate of 1.5), the effect on process innovation becomes negligible and statistically insignificant when controlling for firm and regional variables. Across specifications the first stage F-statistic is above 10, suggesting that the estimates do not suffer from weak instrument bias. Additionally, for product innovation estimations we can reject equality of IV and OLS estimates, and the p-values of the test suggests that there may be fewer issues of endogeneity in the process innovation models.

In total, our evidence suggests that Master's level CE can positively impact a firm's likelihood of having a product and process innovation, while Diploma level tertiary CE has a positive impact on the firm's likelihood of having product innovations.

11.4.1 Collaboration with universities

Collaboration with universities is one potential driver of the effect of tertiary CE on the likelihood of innovation. In the RDI survey, we have access

Table 11.2 IV regression of innovation outcomes on having former tertiary CE participants among employees.

	Product innovation				Process innovation			
	(1)	(2)	(3)	(4)	(5)	(6)	(7)	(8)
Master's (−2Y)	1.722***	1.739***			.820***	.796*		
	(.234)	(.453)			(.238)	(.468)		
Diploma (−2Y)			1.650***	1.476***			.579***	.269
			(.160)	(.251)			(.210)	(.344)
Year FE	Yes		Yes		Yes		Yes	
Industry FE		Yes		Yes		Yes		Yes
Firm controls		Yes		Yes		Yes		Yes
Region controls		Yes		Yes		Yes		Yes
Stage-1 F-stat	42.47	11.20	49.48	18.00	42.47	11.20	49.48	18.00
Stage-1 F p-value	<0.001	<0.001	<0.001	<0.001	<0.001	<0.001	<0.001	<0.001
Wu-Hausman p-value	<0.001	<0.001	<0.001	<0.001	0.005	0.141	0.039	0.667
N	36,468	36,468	36,468	36,468	36,468	36,468	36,468	36,468

Note: *p < 0.1; **p < 0.05; ***p < 0.01

to information on firms' participation in collaborations with universities to increase their likelihood of innovating. In this section, we investigate whether some or all of the effect of tertiary CE on the innovation likelihood can be explained by increased collaboration.

We start by showing that having tertiary CE employees correlates positively with university collaborations. Table 11.3 contains the estimates, where models 1 and 2 show the results for Master's participation, and models 4 and 5 for Diploma participation. Firms which have employees who have participated in CE are 12.6 percentage points more likely to collaborate with universities for innovation compared to firms with no Master's participants when comparing only with year controls, and 10.4 percentage points more likely to collaborate when we include all controls. For Diploma participation, the numbers are 8.9 percentage points and 7.6 percentage points. CE participation is a statistically significant predictor of collaboration, suggesting that this can explain part of the innovation effect we found in the last section.

We also use our instrument to investigate for signs of causal effects. The results can be seen in models 3 and 6 in Table 11.3. The estimates remain positive and statistically significant as we instrument for participation CE, suggesting that we are likely observing causal effects.

If all effects of tertiary CE on the likelihood of innovating can be explained by additional collaboration, then adding collaboration for innovation with a university as a control variable in our primary OLS and IV regressions should remove any independent effect of participation in CE on the likelihood of innovating. Therefore, we next show our main IV regressions but add collaboration with universities for innovation (collaboration with university) as a control to the regressions. The results can be seen in Table 11.4.

We start by investigating the effect of Master's participation on the likelihood of having a product innovation. When controlling for university collaboration, the IV estimate drops only a little, from 1.739 to 1.646, and remains statistically significant. While collaboration does appear to control for some of the effects of Master's participation, there still seem to be other pathways through which CE participation affects the likelihood of having a product innovation.

The effect is somewhat similar when considering the effect on process innovation. The estimate drops slightly from 0.796 to 0.676, but the effect remains statistically significant. Finally, looking at Diploma participation, our results are broadly similar. Controlling for university collaboration makes the product innovation estimate drop from 1.476 to still statistically significant 1.394, whereas controlling for university collaboration in the regression for process innovation leads to a drop from 0.269 to 0.148, both are statistically insignificant.

In summary, while it appears that a higher likelihood of university collaboration is one effect of tertiary CE participation, tertiary CE still has a separate effect on the likelihood of innovating which is largely separate from the collaboration channel.

Table 11.3 OLS and IV regressions of indicators for collaboration with a university on having an employee with tertiary CE degree.

	OLS	OLS	IV	OLS	OLS	IV
	(1)	(2)	(3)	(4)	(5)	(6)
Master's (−2Y)	.126***	.104***				
	(.005)	(.005)				
Diploma (−2Y)				.089***	.076***	
				(.004)	(.004)	
IV Master's (−2Y)			.372**			
			(.157)			
IV Diploma (−2Y)						.325***
						(.100)
Year FE	Yes		Yes	Yes		Yes
Industry FE		Yes	Yes		Yes	Yes
Firm controls		Yes	Yes		Yes	Yes
Region controls		Yes	Yes		Yes	Yes
Stage–1 F-stat			11.20			18.00
Stage–1 F p-value			<0.001			<0.001
Wu–Hausman p-value			0.087			0.009
N	36,995	36,995	36,468	36,995	36,995	36,468

Note: *p < 0.1; **p < 0.05; ***p < 0.01

Table 11.4 IV regressions of innovation outcomes on having former participants in CE among employees and controlling for collaboration with universities for innovation purposes.

	Product innovation				Process innovation			
	(1)	(2)	(3)	(4)	(5)	(6)	(7)	(8)
Master's (−2Y)	1.739***	1.646***			.796*	.676		
	(.453)	(.466)			(.468)	(.485)		
Diploma (−2Y)			1.476***	1.394***			.269	.148
			(.251)	(.258)			(.344)	(.359)
Collab. w. university		.253***		.253***		.306***		.373***
		(.067)		(.046)		(.068)		(.059)
Year FE	Yes	Yes	Yes	Yes	Yes	Yes	Yes	Yes
Industry FE	Yes	Yes	Yes	Yes	Yes	Yes	Yes	Yes
Firm controls	Yes	Yes	Yes	Yes	Yes	Yes	Yes	Yes
Region controls	Yes	Yes	Yes	Yes	Yes	Yes	Yes	Yes
Stage-1 F-stat	11.20	10.25	18.00	16.38	11.20	10.25	18.00	16.38
Stage-1 F p-value	<0.001	<0.001	<0.001	<0.001	<0.001	<0.001	<0.001	<0.001
Wu-Hausman p-value	<0.001	0.112	<0.001	0.008	0.141	0.112	0.667	0.008
N	36,468	36,468	36,468	36,468	36,468	36,468	36,468	36,468

Note: *$p < 0.1$; **$p < 0.05$; ***$p < 0.01$

11.5 Conclusion

In this chapter, we have investigated how firms' use of tertiary CE can impact their likelihood of having either product or process innovations. Participation in tertiary CE, such as Master's and Diploma education has been increasing since the early 2000s. This can be relevant for firms' product and process innovation procedures both by bringing specialised human capital to the firm and by strengthening relations and collaborations with universities that can aid in the innovation process.

We use survey data merged with firm and individual level administrative data to investigate the effects of tertiary CE on firms' likelihood of having a process or product innovation. In descriptive regressions, we find that having at least one employee who has participated in tertiary CE increases the likelihood of having had a product or process innovation. The relationship is robust to controlling for a large set of firm and regional variables that capture both size, age, industry and knowledge appropriation characteristics, as well as year fixed effects.

We then implement IV regressions using distances to the nearest tertiary CE institution as an instrument for having employees who have participated in tertiary CE to estimate whether tertiary CE has causal effects on the likelihood of having product and process innovations. The IV regressions indicate that there is a causal effect of Master's level tertiary CE on the likelihood of firms having both product and process innovations. The estimated effect of Master's level CE is also greater than the estimated effect for Diploma level CE for product innovations. There appears to be no credible evidence for Diploma effects on process innovations.

Finally, to test whether the effects of tertiary CE can be explained through university-related networks and collaborations we first show that both Master's and Diploma CE participation is a strong predictor of firms collaborating with universities to innovate. However, adding university collaboration as a control in our main IV regressions does not substantially change the results. It seems that network and collaboration channels do not explain the effects of tertiary CE on firms' likelihood of innovating, leaving room for further research on how the specialised human capital from tertiary CE impacts innovation.

The increasing use of tertiary level CE in Denmark relative to other forms of CE appears merited as tertiary level CE increases the probability of innovation at the firm level and increases the probability of collaboration between firms and universities. The current study does not give any reason to believe that the effect of AMU-type CE on incremental shop floor innovations has lessened over time and hence cannot suggest that policy should shift focus from the AMU system to tertiary level CE. The study does, however, suggest that policy should attempt to make tertiary level programmes more accessible. This can be achieved by increasing the number of places in Denmark that such programmes are offered at or by lowering the cost of attending the programmes. However, the cost may also represent an important selection mechanism resulting in firms primarily using tertiary level CE when the expected economic benefit is substantial. Another aspect of the costs of participation in tertiary level CE is the degree to which the costs, pecuniary as well as non-pecuniary, are borne by the employee and not the employer. Employees can have a strong incentive to participate in CE to remain adaptive and attractive in the labour market and thus be willing to assume part of the costs. The role of costs is thus complicated, and more research is needed before policy recommendations can be reached.

Finally, our results are only suggestive of the effects of smaller changes to the tertiary CE system, whereas more research is warranted to investigate large scale changes to the tertiary CE system.

Notes

1 Unlike studies investigating short-term training and innovation, a substantial literature investigates effects e.g., on individual employment and wage. LaLonde (2003) and Card et al. (2018) survey the extensive international literature, and Gregersen and Holek (1996) and Danmarks Evalueringsinstitut (2008, 2012, 2019) survey Danish studies focusing also on participants' and firms' experience of the short-term AMU programmes.
2 The upgrade to skills not already available within firms was, in fact, the main purpose for the development of the Danish short-term CE in 1960 (Pedersen et al. 2012; Undervisningsministeriet 2010).
3 Nielsen et al. (2021) provide a more in-depth introduction to the short-term CE programmes.
4 This survey is the Danish version of the Community Innovation Survey run by Statistics Denmark. A full description of the survey is available at https://www.dst.dk/da/Statisti k/dokumentation/statistikdokumentation/forskning-og-udvikling-i-erhvervslivet.
5 The binary indicator for CE participation is a simple threshold indicator. An alternative to the binary indicator is a continuous measure of tertiary CE participation, such as the share of employees who have received tertiary CE, which could capture the intensity of tertiary CE effects on innovation. However, our data on innovation outcomes do not allow us to distinguish between low and high levels of innovation output as we only observe whether a firm has innovated or not. As a result, to avoid unnecessarily complicated functional specifications, we simplify the analysis by focusing on binary indicators on both the left- and right-hand side of regression models we specify in Section 11.5.
6 The data cover all education that is officially recognised by the Danish government as CE. Examples of programme not contained in the register are degrees pursued in foreign countries and online certificates.
7 *Nomenclature statistique des activités économiques dans la Communauté européenne.*

References

Ahern, K. R., Duchin, R. and Shumway, T. 2014. Peer Effects in Risk Aversion and Trust. *Review of Financial Studies* 27(11): 3213–3240.

Altonji, J. and Zhong, L. 2020. *The Labor Market Returns to Advanced Degrees.* NBER Working Paper Series, Working Paper 26959, National Bureau of Economic Research, Cambridge, MA.

Angrist, J. D. and Pischke, J.-S. 2009. *Mostly Harmless Econometrics: An Empiricist's Companion.* Princeton: Princeton University Press.

Audretsch, D. B., Hafenstein, M., Kritikos, A. S. and Schiersch, A. 2018. *Firm Size and Innovation in the Service Sector.* IZA Discussion Paper Series, 12035.

Barney, J. 1991. Firm Resources and Sustained Competitive Advantage. *Journal of Management* 17(1): 99–120.

Bauernschuster, S., Falck, O. and Heblich, S. 2009. Training and Innovation. *Journal of Human Capital* 3(4): 323–353.

Becker, G. S. 1993. *Human Capital – A Theoretical and Empirical Analysis with Special Reference to Education* (3rd ed.). Chicago: Chicago University Press.

Bell, A., Chetty, R., Jaravel, X., Petkova, N. and Van Reenen, J. 2019. Who Becomes an Inventor in America? The Importance of Exposure To Innovation. *The Quarterly Journal of Economics* 134(2): 647–713.

Bertrand, M., Goldin, C. and Katz, L. F. 2010. Dynamics of the Gender Gap for Young Professionals in the Financial and Corporate Sectors. *American Economic Journal: Applied Economics* 2(3): 228–255.

Bhuller, M., Mogstad, M. and Salvanes, K. G. 2017. Life-Cycle Earnings, Education Premiums, and Internal Rates of Return. *Journal of Labor Economics* 35(4): 993–1030.

Bolvig, I., Kristensen, N. and Skipper, L. 2017. *Effektevaluering Af Voksen- Og Efteruddannelsesindsatsen.* KORA - Det Nationale Institut for Kommuners og Regioners Analyse og Forskning.

Bonaccorsi, A., Colombo, M. G., Guerini, M.,and Rossi-Lamastra, C. 2014. The Impact of Local and External University Knowledge on the Creation of Knowledge-Intensive Firms: Evidence from the Italian Case. *Small Business Economics* 43(2): 261–287.

Boneva, T., Golin, M., and Rauh, C. 2019. *Can Perceived Returns Explain Enrollment Gaps in Postgraduate Education?* HCEO Working Paper Series 2019-045.

Børing, P. 2017. The Relationship Between Training and Innovation Activities in Enterprises: The Relationship Between Training and Innovation Activities. *International Journal of Training and Development* 21(2): 113–129.

Cantner, U. and Graf, H. 2006. The Network of Innovators in Jena: An Application of Social Network Analysis. *Research Policy* 35(4): 463–480.

Card, D. 1993. *Using Geographic Variation in College Proximity to Estimate the Return to Schooling.* National Bureau of Economic Research, Working Paper 4483, National Bureau of Economic Research.

Card, D., Kluve, J. and Weber, A. 2018. What Works? A Meta-Analysis of Recent Active Labor Market Program Evaluations. *Journal of the European Economic Association* 16(3): 894–931.

Coad, A., Holm, J. R., Krafft, J. and Quatraro, F. 2018. Firm Age and Performance. *Journal of Evolutionary Economics* 28(1): 1–11.

Cohen, W. M. 2010. Fifty Years of Empirical Studies of Innovative Activity and Performance. In *Handbook of the Economics of Innovation*, Volume 1, ed. Hall, B. H. and Rosenberg, N., 129–213. Amsterdam, NL: North-Holland.

Cohen, W. M., Nelson, R. R. and Walsh, J. P. 2002. Links and Impacts: The Influence of Public Research on Industrial R&D. *Management Science* 48(1): 1–23.

Dahl, M. S. and Pedersen, C. Ø. R. 2004. Knowledge Flows Through Informal Contacts in Industrial Clusters: Myth or Reality? *Research Policy* 33(10): 1673–1686.

Danmarks Evalueringsinstitut. 2008. *Nyt AMU: Med fokus på kompetencer og fleksibilitet.* Copenhagen: Danmarks Evalueringsinstitut.

Danmarks Evalueringsinstitut. 2012. *AMU som springbræt til fortsat uddannelse.* Copenhagen: Danmarks Evalueringsinstitut.

Danmarks Evalueringsinstitut. 2019. *Virksomheders brug og vurderinger af AMU i 2019 - belyst gennem surveys i 2007, 2011, 2015 og 2019.* Copenhagen: Danmarks Evalueringsinstitut.

D'Este, P., Rentocchini, F. and Vega-Jurado, J. 2014. The Role of Human Capital in Lowering the Barriers to Engaging in Innovation: Evidence from the Spanish Innovation Survey. *Industry and Innovation* 21(1): 1–19.

Dostie, B. 2018. The Impact of Training on Innovation. *ILR Review* 71(1): 64–87.

Gonzalez-Brambila, C. N., Veloso, F. M. and Krackhardt, D. 2013. The Impact of Network Embeddedness on Research Output. *Research Policy* 42(9): 1555–1567.

Gregersen, O.and Holek, L. 1996. *Arbejdsmarkedsuddannelserne - En Vidensopsamling*. Copenhagen: Socialforskningsinstituttet.

Hacamo, I. and Kleiner, K. 2020. *Competing for Talent: Firms, Managers and Social Networks*. Kelly School of Business Research Paper No. 17-34, 56.

Hidalgo, C. A., Balland, P.-A. Boschma, R., Delgado, M., Feldman, M., Frenken, K., Glaeser, E. et al. 2018. *The Principle of Relatedness*. International Conference on Complex Systems, 451–457. Springer.

Holm, J. R., Lorenz, E. and Stamhus, J. 2021. Chapter 8: The impact of robots and AI/ML on skills and work organisation. In *Globalisation, New and Emerging Technologies, and Sustainable Development – The Danish Innovation System in Transition*, eds. Christensen, J. L., Gregersen, B., Holm, J. R. and Lorenz, E. Abingdon: Routledge.

Holm, J. R. and Østergaard, C. R. 2018. *Changes in Regional Diversification: The Conditional Role of Knowledge Flows*. Working Paper presented at the Regional Innovation Policies Conference, Bergen, October 11–October 12.

Jaffe, A. 1989. Real Effects of Academic Research. *The American Economic Review* 79(5): 957–970.

LaLonde, R. 2003. Employment and Training Programs. In *Means-Tested Transfer Programs in the United States*, ed. Moffitt, R. A National Bureau of Economic Research Conference Report, 517–585. Chicago: University of Chicago Press.

Lemieux, T. 2006. The "Mincer Equation" Thirty Years after Schooling, Experience, and Earnings. In *Jacob Mincer - A Pioneer of Modern Labor Economics*, ed. Grossbard, S. Boston, MA: Springer.

Lenihan, H., McGuirk, H. and Murphy, K. R. 2019. Driving Innovation: Public Policy and Human Capital. *Research Policy* 48(9): 103791.

Lerner, J. and Malmendier, U. 2013. With a Little Help from my (Random) Friends: Success and Failure in Post-Business School Entrepreneurship. *Review of Financial Studies* 26(10): 2411–2452.

Love, J. H., Roper, S. and Bryson, J. R. 2011. Openness, Knowledge, Innovation, and Growth in UK Business Services. *Research Policy* 40(10): 1438–1452.

Lundvall, B.-Å. 1992. Introduction. In *National Systems of Innovation Toward a Theory of Innovation and Interactive Learning*, ed. Lundvall, B.-Å., 1–19. London: Pinter.

Lundvall, B.-Å. 2016. *The Learning Economy and the Economics of Hope*. London and New York: Anthem Press.

Malmberg, A. and Maskell, P. 2002. The Elusive Concept of Localization Economies: Towards a Knowledge-Based Theory of Spatial Clustering. *Environment and Planning A: Economy and Space* 34(3): 429–449.

McGuirk, H., Lenihan, H. and Hart, M. 2015. Measuring the Impact of Innovative Human Capital on Small Firms' Propensity to Innovate. *Research Policy* 44(4): 965–976.

Mountjoy, J. 2019. *Community Colleges and Upward Mobility*. Working Paper.

Neffke, F. M. H., Otto, A. and Weyh, A. 2017. Inter-Industry Labor Flows. *Journal of Economic Behavior & Organization* 142: 275–292.

Nielsen, P., Lorenz, E. and Holm, J. R. 2021. Chapter 10: Work policy and automation in the fourth industrial revolution. In *Globalisation, New and Emerging Technologies, and Sustainable Development – The Danish Innovation System in Transition*, eds. Christensen, J. L., Gregersen, B., Holm, J. R. and Lorenz, E. London: Routledge.

Østergaard, C. R., Timmermans, B. and Kristinsson, K. 2011. Does a Different View Create Something New? The Effect of Employee Diversity on Innovation. *Research Policy* 40(3): 500–509.

Pedersen, V. H., Andresen, S. and Lassen, M. 2012. *En Fortælling Om AMU: Arbejdsmarkedsuddannelserne i En Verden Af Forandring*. Aalborg: Aalborg University Press.

Peteraf, M. A. 1993. The Cornerstones of Competitive Advantage: A Resource-Based View. *Strategic Management Journal* 14(3): 179–191.

Schubert, T. and Tavassoli, S. 2020. Product Innovation and Educational Diversity in Top and Middle Management Teams. *Academy of Management Journal* 63(1): 272–294.

Shue, K. 2013. Executive Networks and Firm Policies: Evidence from the Random Assignment of MBA Peers. *Review of Financial Studies* 26(6): 1401–1442.

Statistics Denmark. 2016. Pendlingsområder – Metode. *Metode Papir af 22*, November.

Teece, D. J. 2007. Explicating Dynamic Capabilities: The Nature and Microfoundations of (Sustainable) Enterprise Performance. *Strategic Management Journal* 28(13): 1319–1350.

Teece, D. J. 2010. Technological Innovation and The Theory of The Firm: The Role of Enterprise Level Knowledge, Complementarities, and (Dynamic Capabilities). In *Handbook of the Economics of Innovation*, Volume 1, ed. Hall, B. H. and Rosenberg, N., 679–730. Amsterdam: North-Holland.

Teece, D. J. 2017. Towards a Capability Theory of (Innovating) Firms: Implications for Management and Policy. *Cambridge Journal of Economics*, 41(3): 693–720.

Teece, D. J., Pisano, G. and Shuen, A. 1997. Dynamic Capabilities and Strategic Management. *Strategic Management Journal* 18(7): 509–533.

Undervisningsministeriet. 2010. *AMU 50 År Jubilæum*.

Voxsted, S. 1998. Efteruddannelses-systemets Rolle og Muligheder i Det Danske Innovationssystem. *Notat, Erhvervsudviklingsrådet, DISKO-Projektet: Rapport Nr. 3*.

Winter, S. G. 2003. Understanding Dynamic Capabilities. *Strategic Management Journal* 24(10): 991–995.

Wooldridge, J. M. 2010. *Econometric Analysis of Cross Section and Panel Data* (2nd ed.). Cambridge, MA: MIT Press.

Part IV

Green transition and sustainability

12 Firms' contribution to the green transition of the Danish national system of innovation – changes in technological specialisation, skills and innovation

Christian Richter Østergaard, Jacob Rubæk Holm and Eunkyung Park

12.1 Introduction

The Danish system of innovation is facing the challenge of environmental and climate change, which requires a green transition. The green transition entails that both production processes, as well as final goods, evolve towards leaving smaller environmental footprints. This ongoing process has been supported by policies for many years in Denmark, but there is a need for a higher pace in the transition in the coming years. While some green industries like wind turbines and recycling tend to attract the most attention from policymakers, it is important to acknowledge that the green transition is not confined to specific predefined green sectors. It also occurs in many different sectors, including those that are not usually considered to be green (Shapira et al. 2014). In addition, sectors that produce green goods that allow the users to become green might not be green themselves. Therefore, it is necessary to apply a broader perspective of the green transition in analysing the greening of the Danish innovation system.

The public sector, as one of the main actors of the Danish innovation system, plays a significant role in the green transition by controlling the government policy, public investments and public demand. Historically, the Danish environment and energy policy has been critical in promoting certain technologies and industries in the economy (see e.g., Rüdiger 2011). While the role of the public sector is mainly placed on setting the right conditions and environment for making the transition and guiding the direction of the change, the private production system, which constitutes another part of the national innovation system, is the main driving force for realising the transition in the economy. As the Swedish case in the study by Johnson and Jacobsson (2003) has shown, a supportive R&D policy may not be enough for the development of new green industries without active participation of firms in the private sector. Specifically, the production system plays a vital role in the creation and utilisation of knowledge relevant to the green transition. Therefore, this chapter directs focus on Danish firms and how they contribute to the green transition in terms of the development of green technologies, the introduction of environmental innovations, and the demand for skills. While our focus in this chapter lies on the green transition at the national level, we acknowledge that the national innovation system is often influenced by the dynamics at the regional (intra-national) and global level. We will also include relevant regional and global dynamics in relation to the transition of the Danish national innovation system.

Building on the insights gained from the Geography of Nordic Sustainable Transitions (GONST) project which focuses on green transitions in Denmark, Norway, Sweden and Finland, we conduct analyses on technological specialisation, green skills and green innovations of the Danish innovation system. We show that the Danish technological profile in terms of patents has changed considerably during the last 20 years with the increasing share of green patents. This trend can partly be explained by the success of the Danish wind turbine industry, but we see that other patent-intensive industries have also been producing green patents. The analysis of innovations with environmental benefits shows that green innovation happens all over Denmark. It shows which firms undertake green innovation and what requirements this creates for the workforce of such firms, either because these skills are necessary for green innovation, or because they are in demand as a consequence of green innovation. We find that the education and training system in particular, must be adapted if Danish firms are to lead and not just follow in the green transition. Our findings shed light on the challenges and requirements as well as opportunities for the Danish national system of innovation created by the need for making a smooth transition to the greener economy.

The chapter proceeds as follows. In Section 12.2 we discuss previous research on the role of national systems of innovation in shaping the green transition of economies with special focus on the change in technologies, skills and innovations of firms. In Section 12.3, we describe the evolution of patenting towards more green patents in Denmark, showing the technological specialisation of Danish firms in the national system of innovation. In Section 12.4, we present econometric evidence that firms with green innovations often rely on green human capital inputs and create green jobs. Section 12.5 sums up and concludes.

12.2 Green innovations, skills and technologies in the national system of innovation

National systems of innovation can be defined as a narrow concept that focuses on science-based learning and firms' science–technology–innovation (STI) activities, or as a broader concept that also includes doing–using–interacting (DUI) learning in the national economy (Chaminade et al. 2018). The broader definition involves an understanding that knowledge is the most important resource in an economy and that learning is a critical process in creating, diffusing and utilising the knowledge (Chaminade et al. 2018). This definition entails that innovation is an interactive process that involves collaboration between users and producers (Lundvall 2016). Chaminade et al. (2018) argue that the narrow view tends to focus on R&D and radical innovation, while the broader view includes both radical innovation and incremental innovations as well as diffusion of innovations.

We believe that understanding the green transition with a national innovation systems approach entails applying a broader view of the system. The green transition of national innovation systems is not just a question of developing new technologies. Green transition requires a new direction and goal for innovation and learning in the system towards leaving smaller environmental footprints (Lundvall 2016; Schlaile et al. 2017; Fagerberg 2018). Chaminade et al. (2018) argue that national governments play an important role in both enabling and supporting the national innovation systems to generate green innovations and green technologies as well as creating new partnerships and shaping new visions in an emerging phase of a green transition. In later phases, governments become important in providing resources, setting framework conditions and devising policies for the creation of the markets, public procurement and providing incentives for adoption and diffusion of innovations (Chaminade et al. 2018). Similarly, Lundvall (2016) suggests that 'very ambitious combinations of education, life-long learning and labour market policies will be required in order to transform green innovations into wide production and use' (p. 388). However, from the system perspective, the government only constitutes one part of the national innovation system. In order to make the transition happen, the undertakings of the private sector are crucial (Johnson and Jacobsson 2003). Firms in the private sector are often the driving force behind the creation, utilisation and diffusion of knowledge required for making changes towards a greener economy. Therefore, we direct our attention to the commitment of firms in the process of green transition, in terms of the technological transformation, the introduction of green innovations, the demand for green skills and the creation of green jobs.

Seen from the broad innovation system perspective, firms' learning in the process of green transition will involve both DUI and STI modes of learning. In the previous literature, the analyses on the DUI mode of learning have been done through studying innovation processes and skills. In contrast, the analyses on the STI mode of learning focused primarily on R&D and patents activities. Patents represent codified knowledge regarding specific inventions, which may or may not lead to innovation. They contain technological knowledge that could be essential for certain innovations, but analysis on them would only capture limited dynamics of green transition driven by innovation. Our understanding of innovation goes beyond the generation of new technological knowledge. Innovation involves learning in an interactive process from idea to implementation. In addition, innovation does not need to be new to the world. Innovation can also be new to the market, and new to the firm.

Thus, it also includes an element of diffusion of knowledge. Knowing how knowledge diffuses through the learning and skills of various actors in the system, including a firm's suppliers, customers and employees, is critical in understanding the green transition of the national innovation system. While we incorporate both the STI and DUI modes of learning in studying the firms in the Danish national innovation system, we do acknowledge that this chapter focuses on specific efforts of firms by focusing on their technologies, skills and innovations.

Greening an economy requires either utilisation of existing knowledge in a novel way or creation of new knowledge to mitigate negative environmental impacts. Accordingly, firms often need to develop new knowledge and change their technological profile in the process of introducing green innovations.[1] Recent studies point towards the important role of firms' capabilities in generating green innovation (Kesidou and Demirel 2012; Ketata et al. 2015). Developing green technologies and innovations is a more complex task than developing more conventional technologies and innovations, since firms need to include the environmental impact of their technologies and innovations in the development process (Hall and Vredenburg 2003). Therefore, they often need to draw on several different knowledge bases, which increases complexity (Barbieri et al. 2020). As a result, firms introducing green innovations often invest in R&D, have a higher share of highly educated employees and invest in the training of employees compared to other innovative firms (e.g., Horbach 2008; Cainelli et al. 2015). Besides, firms that introduce green innovation are often more open in their innovation process and collaborate more frequently with external partners than other innovative firms (Horbach 2008; de Marchi 2012; Christensen et al. 2019). Thus, for firms, the green transition means a need for new knowledge in the production process both in terms of the skills of the workforce and the codified knowledge of technologies.

Investments in R&D, patents and employment of highly skilled employees are interlinked. Firms that have high R&D spending often patent to protect their intellectual property and employ many highly skilled employees. Furthermore, firms with high internal spending on R&D typically spend most of their money on wages rather than equipment, which is associated with a relatively high share of high skilled workers in these companies. Employees are key contributors in the innovation process of firms since knowledge as the main input to innovation resides in employees, and learning is also done by employees (Grant 1996). Not only do the employees create internal knowledge vital for innovation, but they also determine the firms' absorptive capacity, i.e., the ability to exploit external knowledge (Cohen and Levinthal 1990).

Recently there has been a line of research focusing on green skills and green jobs.[2] For example, Consoli et al. (2016) find that green occupations in the US often have a higher level of human capital and depend on specific cognitive and interpersonal skills compared to non-green jobs. The study also reports that jobs that are becoming greener require a higher level of formal education, increased on-the-job training and more extended work experience (Consoli et al. 2016). The authors consider 111 out of 905 occupations as green and estimate that 9–11% of all US jobs require green skills.

In another study, Østergaard et al. (2019) analyse the extent of green skills based on occupation, education and activity in the economies of the Nordic countries and find a significantly lower level of green skills in these countries compared to the US. The discrepancy in the level of green skills in the two studies may be due to the difficulties in quantifying green skills. Skills depend on several factors such as formal education, work experience and on-the-job training. Nelson and Sidney (1982) define a skill as 'a capability for a smooth sequence of coordinated behaviour that is ordinarily effective relative to its objectives, given the context in which it normally occurs' (Nelson and Winter 1982, p. 73). Thus, skills depend on the match between employees, knowledge and the task content of their work (Autor et al. 2003). Therefore, it might be difficult to identify the extent of green skills, since the match between these factors can change in the process of the green transition. 'Non-green' skills in engineering, for example, might be redirected towards new objectives related to enhancing sustainability. Existing evidence suggests that the green skills might be important for firms engaging in environmental activities (Østergaard et al. 2019), but we need to know more about the changing demand for skills in the process of green transition. That is, if the green transition of the economy leads to a change in firms' demand for particular skills.

12.3 Changes in the technological landscape of Danish firms

The evolution of the technological landscape is illustrated based on patenting activities in Denmark. For this purpose, we utilise patent data from two different sources. The first source is OECD statistics that provide aggregated data on patent applications under the Patent Cooperation Treaty (PCT)[3] filed at the European Patent Office (EPO) by application year and the inventor's country of residence. The OECD identifies patents in selected environment-related technologies (ENV-TECH), which are further divided into sub-categories (OECD 2009b; Haščič and Migotto 2015). We use this data to show the evolution of the technological landscape in Denmark, focusing on green patents. In addition, we use patent data collected in the GONST project from the EPO's PATSTAT (2018b version) based on the EPO y-tags (see Tanner et al. 2019).[4] These data, which are not limited to PCT applications, are utilised to analyse firm-level effort in the green transition. The Danish green patents are identified as green patents (y-tag) that have both inventors and applicants located in Denmark. As mentioned, patents as indicators only capture one side of green transition and therefore the results presented here should be understood in combination with the analyses on other indicators presented later in this chapter.

Figure 12.1 presents the evolution in the share of green patents (ENV-TECH) of total patenting in the Nordic countries, EU28, OECD and the world from 1999 to 2016. The green patents are allocated to the country of the

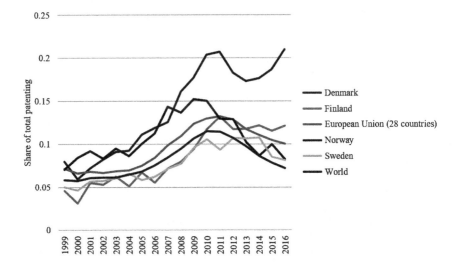

Figure 12.1 Evolution in the share of green patents of total patenting. Source: Patent applications in green patents defined as 'selected environment-related technologies' (ENV-TECH) filed under the PCT inventor country of residence. OECD statistics.

inventor(s). In general, there has been an increase in the share of green patents in the world during this time period. Denmark shows a particularly high share of green patents compared to other countries. The share has increased from 6% to 21% over 18 years. During the period, the number of patent applications by inventors in Denmark increased by almost 70% while the number of green patents more than quadrupled. Figure 12.1 clearly shows the ongoing process of green transition in the Danish innovation system. Denmark is specialised in green patents, i.e., it has a higher share of green patents out of total national patents compared to the average share for the world.

To better understand the technological transformation in Denmark, we visualise the development of green patents in comparison with the development of other technological fields in Danish patents. Figures 12.2 and 12.3 show the same pattern as Figure 12.1: the number and share of green patents by inventors located in Denmark has significantly increased. Other than green patents, the broad medical sector takes up a quite large share of total Danish patenting. The combined share of patents in pharmaceutical, biotechnology and medical technology had accounted for more than 30% of all patents in their highest peak. This is not surprising as the Danish medical sector has for many years shown a particularly strong presence in the Danish innovation system in terms of export, R&D spending and patenting (Møller and Pade 1988; Andersen et al. 2017).[5] However, since 2007, the share of green patents exceeds the share of all other technology fields, including pharmaceuticals, indicating that the

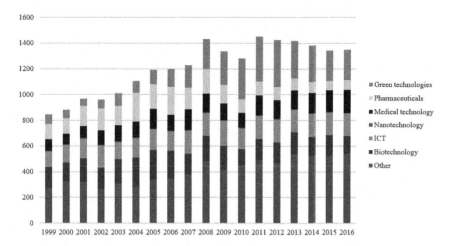

Figure 12.2 Evolution in the number of green patents in Denmark 1999–2016. Source: Patent applications filed under the PCT inventor country of residence. OECD statistics.

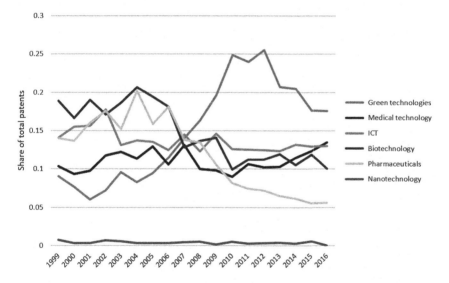

Figure 12.3 Evolution in the share of green patents in Denmark 1999–2016. Source: Patent applications filed under the PCT inventor country of residence. OECD statistics.

technological profile of the Danish economy has become greener in recent years. For most countries the absolute yearly number of green patents applications peak in 2011 and then decline slowly, while the total number of patent application continue to grow. There is no apparent explanation for this decline, but a recent OECD report simply calls for new policies to support development of green technologies (OECD 2019).

Figure 12.4 shows the green patents distributed across eight subgroups. During the last two decades, most green patents have been generated within climate-mitigating technologies related to energy generation, transmission or distribution, while the share of environmental management patents has declined. In this period the number of green patents has increased by more than a factor of nine, while energy related patents have increased by a factor of 46. Looking into the subcategories of the climate mitigating technologies, Tanner et al. (2019) find that Denmark has a strong specialisation within climate-mitigating technologies related to energy, and that there is also a specialisation in technologies related to production or processing of goods. Since the 1970s energy technology has played an important role in the green transition of the Danish economy and the area has been targeted continuously by different innovation-supporting policies (Borup et al. 2009).

At a more detailed level,[6] the main share of the energy patents is within renewable energy generation, i.e., the majority originating from the Danish wind turbine industry. The contribution of the renewable energy sector is also

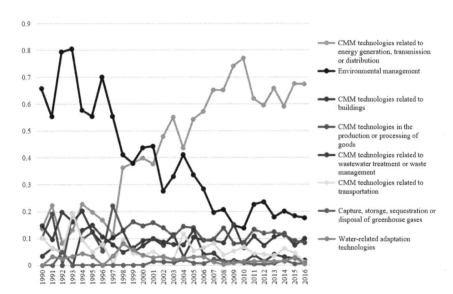

Figure 12.4 Changes in distribution of green patents across subgroups in Denmark 1990–2016. Source: Patent applications based on patent families filed under the PCT inventor country of residence. OECD statistics. Note: climate change mitigation (CMM). The shares sum to more than 100%.

evident in the list of firms producing green technologies (EPO y-tag) as shown in Table 12.1.

A more detailed investigation of the green patents by firms located in Denmark from 2000 to 2017 (see Table 12.1) shows that more than 40% of all green patents in Denmark are owned by firms in the wind energy sector. Vestas, the world-leading wind turbine manufacturer, accounts for almost 30% of the green patents in Denmark. LM Wind Power, which develops and manufactures rotor blades for the wind turbine industry, has 9% of all patents with the second place on the list. Chinese Envision Energy's R&D centre in Denmark accounts for 3% with the fifth largest share. Other than the firms in the wind energy sector, the list reveals many large multinational engineering and biotechnology firms, which suggests a broader engagement in the greening of the Danish economy. More than 500 companies have patented green technologies, but the top 20 accounts for more than 60%. Moreover, the huge contribution of Vestas to the total green patents in Denmark seems to be of a more recent trend since 2007, when the company's share in total green patents exceeded 30% for the first time. The company's share peaked in 2010, when

Table 12.1 The top 20 largest holders of green patents in Denmark 2000–2017.

Name	Total number of green patents	Share of all green patents in Denmark	Share of own green patents with co-inventors located outside Denmark
VESTAS	687	0.297	0.207
LM GLASFIBER	215	0.093	0.149
NOVOZYMES	104	0.045	0.558
HALDOR TOPSOE	89	0.039	0.191
ENVISION ENERGY (DENMARK)	70	0.030	0.000
MAN DIESEL & TURBO	51	0.022	0.118
GRUNDFOS HOLDING	42	0.018	0.143
DANFOSS	37	0.016	0.135
ROCKWOOL INTERNATIONAL	19	0.008	0.368
INBICON	17	0.007	0.059
KAMSTRUP	17	0.007	0.000
DUPONT NUTRITION BIOSCIENCES APS	16	0.007	0.750
UNION ENGINEERING	15	0.006	0.000
FLSMIDTH	14	0.006	0.071
AMMINEX	14	0.006	0.071
PHARMEXA	12	0.005	0.000
NEG MICON	12	0.005	0.167
PP ENERGY	12	0.005	0.083
VKR HOLDING	11	0.005	0.000
MHI VESTAS OFFSHORE	11	0.005	0.182

the company accounted for 47% of total green patents in that year. Although the share of Vestas patents decreased in the following years, it remains in the range 23–41%. This concentration could indicate a potential vulnerability of the Danish innovation system, but patents are only one indicator of performance of the system. The next section takes a broader view on the national innovation system and analyses green innovation and green skills.

Although the patents presented in this table are of Danish origin, generated by at least one inventor located in Denmark and owned by firms in Denmark, the knowledge creation process sometimes involves knowledge that comes from abroad. Table 12.1 also shows the share of patents that involve co-inventors located outside Denmark for each firm. The top three firms that produce the most 'green' patents have relatively high shares of their green patents involving at least one inventor from abroad. Of Vestas' patents 21% have at least one Danish inventor and involve co-inventors located outside Denmark. For the large Danish enzymes firm Novozymes, the share is 56%. The global interaction in patenting can be based on the collaboration between the foreign subsidiaries and the headquarters of Danish firms or the collaboration of Danish firms with other independent partners (firms, universities or research institutes) located abroad. Either way, it suggests that the Danish innovation system is a part of globalised innovation networks and draws on knowledge that resides outside Denmark. More specifically, the green transition of the Danish economy is facilitated by global interaction in the knowledge-creation process.

In terms of technological transformation, Danish firms seem to possess specialisation in green technologies, with an increasing share of green patents in recent years. The technological area in which Denmark seems to have expertise is climate mitigation technologies, particularly renewable energy. We find that large companies within the renewable energy sector possess a huge share of green patents and they often collaborate with actors located abroad in creating new knowledge. Patents represent an STI focus or a narrow view of an innovation system. In order to create new green technologies and make transition towards the greening of the innovation system, companies need employees with knowledge and skills that are relevant for this transition. In the next section, we take a broader view of the Danish innovation system and present analyses on green skills and jobs as well as green innovations in Danish firms.

12.4 Green skills and green innovative firms

In this section, we show some descriptive statistics on green skills in the Danish economy and present results from regression models estimating the relationship between green skills and green innovation in Danish firms. This represents a broader view on the national innovation system and includes DUI types of learning as discussed earlier. While the analyses on patents show the development of technological specialisation in certain green technologies, the analyses on green innovation show patterns of firm innovation related to green transition beyond the boundaries of specific technologies. We note that the analysis of patents is an analysis of inventions during 2000–2017, while the innovation survey data only covers innovations during 2012–2014. Within these time-frames, there are about 570 firms with green patents, while the survey identifies more than 700 green-innovative firms.

12.4.1 Green skills

Table 12.2 is adapted from Østergaard et al. (2019) and shows the share of employees with green skills in each of four Nordic countries in 2014. Three different definitions are used. The first two rely on the job description while the third relies on the description of the employee's education. The first definition of green jobs (broad) is from Vona et al. (2015) who identify green occupations in the US occupation classifications, SOC, and the result is then transferred to the occupation codes used in the Nordic countries, ISCO. The result is rather broad, encompassing, for example, general managers and economists. The second definition contains only occupations with a green description in the ISCO classifications. This results in a narrower definition of green jobs. The final definition relies instead on the description of the employee's education in the International Standard Classification of Education (ISCED) classification system. See Østergaard et al. (2019) for lists of keywords, and of occupation and education codes identified as green. The number of Danish firms with employees with green skills is much higher: 7.8% of the 271,000 firms in Denmark have employees with green skills according to the broad Green Jobs definition, 0.9% according to the narrower definition and 0.4% according to the Green Education definition.

The four countries have a rather similar distribution of green skills across the different definitions, except for Finland which has a higher share of employees with a green education. This might be explained by the fact that the Finnish national system of innovation is relatively focused on engineering. In general, the low share of employees with a green job or green education in this table suggests problems in quantifying green skills. One issue can be that education and occupation do not always reflect the skills applied or task solved. Moreover, firms might only need a few of these employees with green education or occupation in combination with more generic skills and education in order to become greener. An example is Aalborg CSP, which is a Danish SME

Table 12.2 Share of green jobs and green education in 2014.

	Employment 2014	Green jobs, broad	Green jobs, narrow	Green education
Denmark	2,619,627	3.7%	0.9%	0.3%
Norway	2,557,624	5.3%	0.3%	0.3%
Sweden	4,593,586	3.5%	0.8%	0.2%
Finland	2,192,654	4.3%	0.3%	2.4%

Adapted from Østergaard et al. (2019).

that develops and builds solar technological solutions for power plants and district heating. It mainly employs highly skilled engineers with different non-green specialisations and work experience. However, the core of their service, the design of the integrated energy systems and solar solutions, is reliant on a few employees with an engineering degree in energy systems.

Østergaard et al. (2019) show that there is no consistent geographical concentration of the green skills in Denmark except for a higher share in the NUTS region encircling the Copenhagen region. This suggests that the possibilities for firms introducing green innovation are not necessarily limited by the geographical distribution of employees with green skills, but by the general lack of employees with these specialised green skills. It implies that the low number of employees on the labour market with green skills could slow down the green transition of the Danish innovation system, at least to the extent that such skills are a requirement for green innovations. Below we analyse the predictors of green innovation in Danish firms.

12.4.2 Green-innovative firms

In this section we present an econometric analysis of the predictors of green innovation in Danish firms. For this analysis, we use the 2014 edition of the Danish Community Innovation Survey on R&D and Innovation (Danish acronym: FUI) by Statistics Denmark. The 2014 edition was unique as it included a block of questions on innovations with environmental impact. This block of questions was only distributed to firms that had already responded that they had had innovation in the period 2012–2014, and over 90% of firms also responded to the optional module on environmental impact. The share of innovative companies in Denmark is relatively constant at 44% in this period. The share of firms with green innovations is also rather similar to the other Nordic countries in the period (Østergaard et al. 2019).

In the main part of the survey, firms are requested to indicate whether they have introduced 13 different types of innovation (two forms of product/service innovation, three forms of process innovation, three forms of organisational innovation and five forms of marketing innovation). Firms responding negatively to all 13 questions are defined as non-innovative. There are 2217 non-innovative firms in our sample. Firms responding positively to at least one of the 13 questions are then presented to the optional module on environmental impact where they are asked to indicate whether the firm has achieved any of ten environmental impacts on the firm itself or its customers over the period, and, if yes, whether the environmental impact can be attributed to the innovations reported earlier. If the firm's innovations have had any of these ten impacts, then it is classified as green-innovative, and if not, then it is classified as non-green innovative. There are 989 non-green innovative firms and 720 green innovative firms. The total number of observations available for regression analysis is then 3926.

The model predicting innovation activity is a multinomial logistic model[7] (Hilbe 2009). The dependent variable takes three values: 0 for non-innovative firms, 1 for firms that have introduced innovations but not green innovations and 2 for firms with green innovations (green innovators may also have non-green innovations). These three outcomes are indexed by *j*. The multinomial logistic model produces conditional probabilities that firm *i* will belong to category *j* as specified in Equation 12.1.

$$\Pr\left(y_i = j \mid x_i\right) = \frac{\exp\left(x_i' \beta_j\right)}{\sum_{j=0}^{2} \exp\left(x_i' \beta_j\right)} \tag{12.1}$$

y_i is the dependent variable indicating whether firm *i* is non-innovative, innovative but not green or green-innovative. x_i are the independent variables elaborated in this section, including a 1 for the intercept and the β_j are the vectors of parameters to estimate. $j = 0$ will be used as the reference group meaning that the estimates will be relative to non-innovative firms. Therefore $\beta_0 = 0$, and we report the estimates for the two vectors β_1 and β_2. The advantage of a multinomial logistic model is that it allows for a comparison of the three different outcomes. Non-innovators might become either green innovators or non-green innovators if opportunities emerge. Therefore, it is important to analyse the differences in characteristics simultaneously.

The vector x_i contains controls for firm size measured as log total employment in November 2011 and human capital intensity defined as the share of employment in 2011 with at least tertiary education. In order to account for knowledge inputs to the innovation process, we include the share of employees in 2011 with a green education as identified in the GONST project (Østergaard et al. 2019). The 2014 FUI survey also contains information on firms' R&D expenditures in 2014 which we use in log form as a control for generic inputs to the innovation process, despite this being an imperfect control as it is measured in 2014. x_i also contains controls for the region of the main address of the firm defined at the NUTS2 level and for sectors defined following Eurostat's taxonomies for high-low tech sectors and Knowledge Intensive Business Services with 'other services' and 'primary sector, construction and utilities' added for completeness. We use the 'calibrated weights' supplied by Statistics Denmark and report robust standard errors.

Table 12.3 shows the result of the multinomial logistic regression predicting innovation outcomes 2012–2014. The results show that as firm size increases, the probability that a firm has green innovation compared to no innovation goes up too. R&D is, not surprisingly, positive for both types of innovation, while the share of employees with tertiary education is only positive for non-green innovation, and the share of employees with green education is only positive for green innovation.

Effect coding is used for the categorical variables so that the estimates are relative to the national average and not relative to a reference category. The results show that non-green innovation is predominantly observed in high-tech manufacturing and not in low-tech manufacturing, while green innovation

Table 12.3 Model on characteristics of green innovative firms compared to non-green innovative firms.

	Non-green innovation	S.E.	Green innovation	S.E.
Intercept	−1.072★★★	0.155	−3.216★★★	0.254
Size	0.011	0.040	0.254★★★	0.063
Log(R&D)	0.241★★★	0.022	0.375★★★	0.027
Share tertiary education	0.0069★★★	0.0021	−0.0012	0.0043
Share green edu.	−0.053	0.071	0.130★★★	0.037
Prim. Constr. Util.	−0.052	0.183	0.782★★★	0.243
High-tech manufacturing	0.494★	0.266	0.497	0.340
Medium-high-tech manufacturing	0.214	0.195	0.789★★★	0.215
Medium-low-tech manufacturing	−0.046	0.180	0.115	0.247
Low-tech manufacturing	−0.524★★★	0.197	0.129	0.243
High-tech KIS	0.122	0.136	−0.244	0.266
Financial KIS	−0.103	0.239	−1.597★★★	0.417
Market KIS	−0.086	0.130	0.098	0.230
Other KIS	−0.162	0.287	−0.659	0.678
Other services	0.143	0.102	0.090	0.170
North Jutland	0.010	0.147	−0.310	0.212
Central Denmark	−0.008	0.099	0.135	0.142
South Denmark	−0.055	0.104	0.136	0.142
Capital	0.049	0.086	−0.049	0.145
Zealand	0.005	0.139	0.088	0.186
−2LogL Model	22,977.575			
−2LogL Null	25,157.398			
N	3926			

Multinomial logistic regression with weights. Reference: 'no innovation'. Estimate for linear predictor and S.E. of estimate. ★: $p < 0.1$; ★★: $p < 0.05$; ★★★: $p < 0.01$. Effect coding used for region and sector. KIS: knowledge intensive services.

is mostly on primary/construction/utilities and in medium–high-tech manufacturing. It is not surprising that firms in medium–high-tech manufacturing sectors are more likely to be green innovators, since the Danish wind turbine industry, mechanical industry and chemical industry are in this sector. These are also among the most active in green patenting, see Table 12.1. The sector 'primary/construction/utilities' contains agriculture, where organic farming is increasingly important, implementation of building solutions to conserve energy and water and the supply and production of electricity. It is thus not surprising that firms in this sector are relatively more likely to have green innovation rather than no innovation. Firms in the financial knowledge-intensive services are significantly less likely to have green innovation, which could be expected given the type of innovation. However, it could also indicate a lack of focus on green innovations and an untapped potential for improvements.

No regional variations in innovation outcomes are found, which also corroborates the even geographical distribution of green patents described earlier.

The results show that employees with green education make a firm relatively more likely to have green innovation, whereas the same is not true for tertiary education in general. R&D, on the other hand, is an important input to both types of innovation processes. This suggests that the 'green skills' among employees and not the 'generic absorptive capacity' are important for green innovation and for the green transition in Denmark.

12.4.3 Job creation by green-innovative firms

In the previous section, we showed that green skills matter for creating green innovation. Here, we show the type of jobs created by firms with green innovation. Table 12.4 shows the results of five separate ordinary least square regressions estimating the relationship between innovation outcomes and job creation at the firm level.

We measure job growth in five different employee groups, which are four groups by skill: green-skill jobs, low-skill jobs, mid-skill jobs and high-skill jobs, and finally total employment. The definitions of high-, mid- and low-skill jobs follow the literature on job polarisation (Goos et al. 2014). This means that high-skill jobs are managers, professionals, associate professionals and technicians. Mid-skill jobs are clerical jobs, craft and related trades, assemblers and plant and machine operators. Low-skill jobs are service and sales and elementary jobs. For green-skill jobs, we merge the two definitions of green jobs described above in connection with Table 12.2. This allows a broad definition of green jobs which includes both jobs with a narrow green content as well as the more broadly defined jobs that are affected too. g_{ki} is job growth at firm i of job group k measured as change in employment in the group from 2014 to 2016 relative to the average employment in 2014 and 2016, cf. Equation 12.2.

$$g_{ki} = \frac{\left(l_{ki,2016} - l_{ki,2014}\right)}{\left(l_{ki,2016} + l_{ki,2014}\right)/2} \tag{12.2}$$

The five separate regressions then follow the general shape illustrated by Equation 12.3, where z_i is a vector of explanatory variables elaborated below including a 1 for the intercept, α_k are the parameters to estimate and the ϵ_{ki} are classic errors.

$$g_{ki} = z_i'\alpha_k + \epsilon_{ki} \tag{12.3}$$

The vector z_i contains the same variables as x_i in the multinomial regression models presented earlier with two exceptions. The first is that inputs to the

Table 12.4 Job creation by innovative firms 2014–2016.

	Green	High	Mid	Low	Total
Non-green innovation	0.026	−0.019	−0.054	−0.014	0.002
S.E.	0.040	0.042	0.044	0.047	0.025
Green innovation	0.089*	0.069	0.052	0.026	0.069**
S.E.	0.047	0.055	0.061	0.068	0.029
Size	−0.045***	0.017	−0.035**	0.007	0.008
S.E.	0.014	0.017	0.016	0.018	0.009
Share tertiary edu.	0.0004	−0.0001	0.0003	0.0032***	0.0004
S.E.	0.0007	0.0009	0.0010	0.0010	0.0005
Productivity	0.0004	0.0030	0.0139***	−0.0007	0.0017
S.E.	0.0013	0.0031	0.0029	0.0017	0.0018
R2	0.012	0.006	0.009	0.010	0.009
N	3638	3638	3638	3638	3638

Separate OLS regressions with weights. Dependent variables are the growth in green jobs, high-/mid-/low-skill jobs and total jobs. Estimate followed by robust SE. *: $p < 0.1$, **: $p < 0.05$, ***: $p < 0.01$. Models also include an intercept and controls for sector and region.

innovation process, i.e., the share of employees with a green education and log (R&D), are replaced by a three-level categorical variable for outputs from the innovation process. The categorical variable takes the value 0 if the firm had no innovation 2012–2014, 1 if the firm had innovation but not green innovation and 2 if the firm had green innovation. The second exception is that we include productivity defined as value-added per full-time equivalent employee in 2014 as a control for firm performance. We again use the 'calibrated weights' supplied by Statistics Denmark and report robust standard errors.

As can be seen in the final column, firms with green innovation 2012–2014 had 6.9% higher growth in total employment 2014–2016 compared to firms with no innovation. Firms with non-green innovation were not significantly different from non-innovative firms. The estimated effect is 0.2% and it is not statistically significant. The first four columns show that the job growth at firms with green innovation was among jobs that require green skills and related jobs in particular. Firms with green innovation are estimated to have had 8.9% higher job growth in such green jobs compared to firms without innovation. No difference is observed with respect to the generic skill level in job creation.

All five regression models presented in Table 12.4 have low R-squared indicating that they only explain a minor share of firm level job growth. The main take-away from the regressions is thus that there is a statistically significant partial correlation between green innovation and green job growth, and between green innovation and total job growth, while there are no statistically significant correlations between non-green innovation and job growth. Combining the evidence of this section shows that, on average, green innovation processes require green knowledge inputs in terms of the education of the workforce, and green innovations create green jobs broadly defined. Thus, in order to facilitate the green transition, the national system of innovation needs to supply green education, and to facilitate that relatively generic employees in occupations such as management, economics and engineering can adapt and occupy jobs with a more green-task content.

12.5 Conclusion

The purpose of this chapter was to analyse the green transition of the Danish economy with a special focus on green patents, green skills and green innovations of firms. The evolution in the Danish technological specialisation through patent analyses shows a rather drastic change towards green technologies. Green patents have had a high growth since the 2000s, and the data from 2016 shows that green patents account for almost 18% of all Danish patents. This is partly driven by the success of the Danish wind turbine industry, which contributes to more than 40% of green patenting in Denmark. Technologically, the greening of Danish innovation system seems to be concentrated in certain sectors and firms. This suggests that there are some sectoral and technological innovation systems related to green technologies within the Danish national innovation system. Borup et al. (2009) identify five different technological innovation systems within energy technology in the Danish innovation system. These have different properties and challenges, but they have also interdependencies as a part of the Danish national innovation system. Malerba (2002) also argues that it is necessary to complement the analysis of national innovation systems with the analysis of sectoral innovation systems since growth and changes at the national level are often determined by leading sectors located in particular regions in the country. This is also relevant to the greening of the Danish innovation system, as the wind turbine industry concentrated in the central Jutland region is driving the transformation.

When it comes to the geographical aspect of the green transition, it is also essential to consider the global interaction of firms in the national innovation system. As is shown by the extent of global connectivity in the patenting of the large green firms in Table 12.1, the success of these firms also depends on their ability to collaborate with inventors outside Denmark. Thus, the green transition in terms of patenting also relies on the absorptive capacity of the Danish firms. As noted by Lundvall (2016), the traditional national innovation systems literature has somehow neglected these globalised knowledge flows, and the analysis of national innovation systems needs to include the learning from knowledge flowing through global value chains and distributed innovation.

We also showed that green patenting, green innovations and green employment are interconnected in the effort of firms making the green transition. In order to conduct green R&D and make green inventions, firms need to hire highly educated employees with green skills. Our regression analysis shows that firms with employees with green skills are more likely to introduce green innovations. While the analysis of patents revealed a concentration in particular sectors and firms, the analysis of firms' likelihood to do green innovation shows a broader trend of the green transition. The medium-high-tech manufacturing sector, high R&D spenders and large firms were more likely to do green innovations compared to other types of innovation. But the traditionally low-innovative industries like construction, utilities and primary industry were also more likely to develop green innovations. There were also no signs of a geographical concentration of green innovators within Denmark. However, the broader scope of transition in terms of green innovation compared to green technologies could be from how these concepts are identified and measured in our analysis. Innovations with environmental impact per definition can be generated across a wide range of technologies and sectors.

Furthermore, we find that green innovators have higher employment growth than other innovative firms and also a higher growth of green jobs. This suggests that the green transition of the Danish economy can be self-reinforcing, as increased green innovation creates more green jobs thus increasing the scope for further green innovation in terms of incremental shop floor innovations, increased absorptive capacity for green innovations and thus increased demand and increased potential for diffusing green innovations in export markets. The positive effect of green jobs and education for the likelihood for green innovation opens the possibilities for supportive innovation policy in terms of increasing and diversifying the supply of green education and training. It could be worrying that the green patenting in Denmark is highly reliant on a few firms within the wind turbine industry and that R&D spending is concentrated in few large firms, which makes the green transition of the Danish economy somewhat vulnerable. Furthermore, the apparent low level of green innovations in the service industry, which accounts for the majority of employment in the Danish economy, calls for further research.

As pointed out earlier, firms are an important part of the national innovation system as well as different regional, technological and sectoral innovation systems. They are highly dependent on institutional frameworks in these systems, including the role of demand, financial system, government, public sector, political system, broader knowledge infrastructure and other actors (Fagerberg 2018). Considering the pattern of the green transition of firms in Denmark shown in these analyses, developing policy instruments that encompass different levels of innovation systems to deal with balanced development of technologies, skills and sectors would be necessary.

Notes

1 Our definition of green innovation follows how the Community Innovation Survey (2014) defines 'environmental innovation'. We see green innovation as innovation with environmental benefits within the firm or for users or both. While green patents are defined as patents in environmental-related technologies (OECD 2009b), green innovations are not necessarily associated with specific technologies and industries. This

definition does not require that the environmental benefits were the main objective of innovation.

2 The International Labour Organization (ILO) defines green jobs as: 'they reduce the consumption of energy and raw materials, limit greenhouse gas emissions, minimise waste and pollution, protect and restore ecosystems and enable enterprises and communities to adapt to climate change' (International Labour Office 2018, p. 53), while skills are 'defined as the ability to carry out the tasks and duties of a given job' (International Labour Office 2012, p. 11).

3 The PCT procedure allows applicants the possibility to seek rights in multiple countries with one international application at a single (receiving) patent office. In 2006, the share of PCT application was 62% at the EPO, and since the early 2000s this share keeps increasing (OECD 2009a).

4 Both ENV-TECH and EPO y-tags have in common that both systems identify sets of technologies that are environment-related. However, these are two independent classification systems and there may be deviation in the patents identified by the two systems. See Tanner et al. (2019) for a detailed explanation on the different coverage of the two systems.

5 According to the recent EU Industrial R&D Investment Scoreboard 2019, Denmark has 45 companies on the top 1000 list of R&D spenders, of which 12 are within the pharmaceutical and biotechnology sector. Their total R&D spending accounts for 56% of the total. The large Danish wind turbine company Vestas is fifth on the list, and its joint venture with Mitsubishi is 22nd.

6 The detailed level is not shown in Figure 12.3 but is available from the authors upon request or at OECD stats.

7 The advantage of a multinominal model is that it allows for a comparison of the three different outcomes. Non-innovators might later become either green innovators or non-green innovators. Therefore, it is important to analyse the differences in characteristics simultaneously. A Heckman selection model could also be used to control for unobserved differences between non-innovators and innovators in a sense that some non-innovators might not innovate because they do not want to innovate. However, this represents a rather linear innovation thinking. Demand from customers or regulation or technologies from suppliers might present a company with unexpected opportunities for innovation – regardless of the initial innovation strategy.

References

Andersen, T. M., Bentzen, J., Jensen, S. E. H., Smith, V. and Westergård-Nielsen, N. C. 2017. *The Danish Economy in a Global Context*. Copenhagen: Djøf Publishing.

Autor, D. H., Levy, F. and Murnane, R. J. 2003. The skill content of recent technological change: An empirical exploration. *Quarterly Journal of Economics* 118(4): 1279–1333.

Barbieri, N., Marzucchi, A. and Rizzo, U. 2020. Knowledge sources and impacts on subsequent inventions: Do green technologies differ from non-green ones?. *Research Policy* 49(2), 103901.

Borup, M., Andersen, P. D., Gregersen, B. and Tanner, A. N. 2009. *Ny Energi og Innovation i Danmark*. Copenhagen: Jurist-og Økonomforbundets Forlag.

Cainelli, G., De Marchi, V. and Grandinetti, R. 2015. Does the development of environmental innovation require different resources? Evidence from Spanish manufacturing firms. *Journal of Cleaner Production* 94: 211–220.

Chaminade, C., Lundvall, B.-Å. and Haneef, S. 2018. *Advanced Introduction to National Innovation Systems*. Cheltenham: Edward Elgar Publishing.

Christensen, J. L., Hain, D. S. and Nogueira, L. A. 2019. Joining forces: Collaboration patterns and performance of renewable energy innovators. *Small Business Economics* 52(4): 793–814.

Cohen, W. M. and Levinthal, D. A. 1990. Absorptive capacity: A new perspective of learning and innovation. *Administrative Science Quarterly* 35(1): 128–152.

Consoli, D., Marin, G., Marzucchi, A. and Vona, F. 2016. Do green jobs differ from non-green jobs in terms of skills and human capital? *Research Policy* 45(5): 1046–1060.

De Marchi, V. 2012. Environmental innovation and R&D cooperation: Empirical evidence from Spanish manufacturing firms. *Research Policy* 41(3): 614–623.

Fagerberg, J. 2018. Mobilizing innovation for sustainability transitions: A comment on transformative innovation policy. *Research Policy* 47(9): 1568–1576.

Goos, M., Manning, A. and Salomons, A. 2014. Explaining job polarization: Routine-biased technological change and offshoring. *American Economic Review* 104(8), 2509–2526.

Grant, R. M. 1996. Toward a knowledge-based theory of the firm. *Strategic Management Journal, 17*(S2): 109–122.

Hall, J. and Vredenburg, H. 2003. The challenge of innovating for sustainable development. *MIT Sloan Management Review* 45(1): 61.

Haščič, I. and Migotto, M. 2015. *Measuring Environmental Innovation Using Patent Data*. OECD Environment Working Papers. No. 89. Paris: OECD Publishing.

Hilbe, J. M. 2009. *Logistic Regression Models*. Boca Raton, FL: CRC press.

Horbach, J. 2008. Determinants of environmental innovation—New evidence from German panel data sources. *Research Policy* 37(1): 163–173.

International Labour Office. 2012. *International Standard Classification of Occupations 2008 (ISCO-08): Structure, Group Definitions and Correspondence Tables*. Geneva: International Labour Office.

International Labour Office . 2018. *World Employment and Social Outlook 2018. Greening with jobs*. Geneva: International Labour Office.

Johnson, A. and Jacobsson, S. 2003. The emergence of a growth industry: A comparative analysis of the German, Dutch and Swedish wind turbine industries. In *Change, Transformation and Development* (pp. 197–227). Heidelberg: Physica.

Kesidou, E. and Demirel, P. 2012. On the drivers of eco-innovations: Empirical evidence from the UK. *Research Policy* 41(5): 862–870.

Ketata, I., Sofka, W. and Grimpe, C. 2015. The role of internal capabilities and firms' environment for sustainable innovation: Evidence for Germany. *R&D Management* 45(1): 60–75.

Lundvall, B.-Å. 2016. *The Learning Economy and the Economics of Hope* (p. 377). London and New York: Anthem Press.

Malerba, F. 2002. Sectoral systems of innovation and production. *Research Policy* 31(2): 247–264.

Møller, K. and Pade, H. 1988. *Industriel Succes*. Copenhagen: Samfundslitteratur.

Nelson, R. R. and Winter, S. G. (1982). *An Evolutionary Theory of Economic Change.*

OECD. 2009a. *OECD Patent Statistics Manual*. Paris: OECD Publishing.

OECD. 2009b. Patents in environment-related technologies. In *OECD Science, Technology and Industry Scoreboard*. Paris: OECD Publishing.

OECD 2019. *Innovation and Business/Market Opportunities Associated with Energy Transitions and a Cleaner Global Environment*. Issue Paper. Paris: OECD Publishing.

Østergaard, C. R., Holm, J. R., Iversen, E., Schubert, T., Skålholt, A., Sotarauta, M., Saarivirta,T. et al. 2019. *The Geographic Distribution of Skills and Environmentally Innovative Firms in Denmark, Norway, Sweden, and Finland*. Aalborg: AAU, Department of Business and Management.

Rüdiger, M. 2011. *Energi i Forandring*. Copenhagen: DONG Energy.

Schlaile, M. P., Urmetzer, S., Blok, V., Andersen, A. D., Timmermans, J., Mueller, M., Fagerberg, J. et al. 2017. Innovation systems for transformations towards sustainability? Taking the normative dimension seriously. *Sustainability* 9(12): 2253.

Shapira, P., Gök, A., Klochikhin, E. and Sensier, M. 2014. Probing "green" industry enterprises in the UK: A new identification approach. *Technological Forecasting and Social Change* 85: 93–104.

Tanner, A. N., Faria, L., Moro, M. A., Iversen, E., Østergaard, C. R. and Park, E. K. 2019. *Regional Distribution of Green Growth Patents in Four Nordic Countries*. Copenhagen: DTU.

Vona, F., Marin, G., Consoli, D. and Popp, D. 2015. Green Skills. *National Bureau of Economic Research Working Paper Series*, Working paper No. w21116.

13 The measurement and performance of the Danish innovation system in relation to sustainable development

Birgitte Gregersen and Björn Johnson

13.1 Introduction

It is increasingly acknowledged that limiting climate change, biodiversity loss, pollution and other major environmental problems requires fundamental changes in the structure and development of production and consumption of goods and services (Stern 2006, 2015; Rockström 2015). The conviction that 'sustainable transformation' of contemporary societies is necessary for the long-term survival of human civilization has probably never been as firm and widespread as at present. It is obvious that new knowledge and innovation are needed to realise developments towards sustainability (Fagerberg et al. 2015; United Nations 2019a). It is, however, important to stress that not only technological innovations are necessary. Without social innovations, institutional innovations and policy innovations it will not be possible to make such a sustainable transition. This means that innovation systems need to be well functioning in order to support the necessary transformation towards more sustainable societies (Markard et al. 2012; Fagerberg 2018). In other words, the performance of national innovation systems should, thus, reflect how well the innovation system contributes to sustainable development.

Nevertheless, performance is not a simple concept. It can be delineated and measured in many different ways. First, performance may be delineated both narrowly and broadly. A narrow definition of a national innovation system may focus on the research and development system, and the meaning of performance is then rather straightforward. It can be thought of as research and development-based technical product and process innovations. Performance indicators are, for example, scientific publications, patents and new products and processes as measured by innovation surveys. If this approach is applied to sustainable development it could be specific scientific publications, patents and new products and processes related to any of the 17 Sustainable Development Goals (SDGs), for instance the so-called 'green patents' analysed in Chapter 12 (this volume) by Østergaard et al. (2021).

Second, it is important to distinguish between how good the system is at producing goods, services and other things we value in a sustainable way and how good it is at generating the capabilities in forms of competences, skills and experiences, needed to produce such values (Teece et al. 1997). There is, thus, a difference between a utility-based and a capability-based approach. In a long-term sustainable development perspective, the capability to learn and innovate is, obviously, crucial and a discussion of innovation system performance has to reflect this.

Against this background the overall question raised in this chapter is how well does the contemporary Danish innovation system perform in relation to sustainable development? To answer this, we start in Section 13.2 by taking a closer look at the United Nations 17 SDGs and related targets as overall performance measures for sustainable development. The SDG performance measures play a central role as policy-informing tools, as they reflect the 2030 commitments at the national level. Although the prevailing monitoring of how far or how close the Danish innovation system develops to reach the 17 SDGs at the national level may serve as important signposts and wake-up calls for policy action, we argue in Section 13.3 that these measures should be supplemented by a *learning* and *capability building* approach to performance measurement. Capability building is understood here as building capability and capacity to enhance knowledge, competences, skills, experiences and institutions to be capable of propelling a transition to a sustainable development path. In Section 13.4 we widen the perspective on sustainable development and raise the question if the meaning of sustainable development needs to be rethought in the Anthropocene era with significant human impact on the Earth's eco-system. Section 13.5 discusses some overall policy implications and concludes the chapter.

13.2 UN Sustainable Development Goals as performance measures

13.2.1 *OECD and UN performance assessments of Denmark in relation to the SDGs*

In the literature, sustainable development is conceptualised in different ways. Very generally, it may be thought of as the ability of the economy to function within the capacity provided by the Earth's ecosystems (Dietz and O'Neill 2013). Referring more specifically to human needs the Brundtland report defined sustainable development as development that 'meets the needs of the present generations without compromising the ability of future generations to meet their own needs' (UN 1987 Brundtland report). It can also be defined and operationalised, specifically and broadly at the same time, as the United Nations 17 SDGs. This section takes its point of departure in the latter.

The 17 SDGs[1] adopted in 2015 in the '2030 Agenda for Sustainable Development' are accompanied by 169 sub-goals or targets describing more specific goals and actions in order to stimulate a transition towards a global sustainable development. To be able to measure status and assess development, a global indicator framework was developed by the Inter-Agency and Expert

Group on SDG Indicators (IAEG-SDGs) in 2017. Annual refinements of indicators have taken place, and in the 2020 report the indicator framework consists of 247 indicators of which 231 are unique indicators as a few indicators are repeated under two or three different targets.[2]

The final selection of sub-goals and indicators is of course a pragmatic solution based on the one hand on what makes sense from an overall perception of 'sustainable development' including what type of indicators are relevant and what data is available on a systematic and worldwide scale, and on the other hand, what is negotiated and accepted politically by the 193 UN member states. Although the 17 main goals and the related 169 sub-goals or targets are global targets meant for all countries, it is clear that some (or most) are easier to achieve for high-income countries (mainly situated in the North) than emerging economies or low-income countries (the latter mainly situated in the South). For these reasons it is also stressed that countries should supplement the UN-monitoring activities with more specific sub-goals and indicators relevant as signposts for country specific actions. We return to a Danish example of supplementary indicators later in this section.

Different international, governmental and non-governmental initiatives have been launched for monitoring and assessing SDG performance on different levels and for different topics. The UN provides annual progress reports (see for instance United Nations 2019b) on selected SDGs and cross-cutting themes on the global level including larger (WHO) sub-regions.[3] Eurostat is measuring progress on SDGs focusing on existing EU policies. The OECD has developed an approach to 'measuring distance to the SDGs targets' on a country level, and the Bertelsmann Foundation in co-operation with the UN Sustainability Development Solution Network (SDSN) publish the 'SDG Index and Dashboard Report' and rank the 193 countries according to their overall performance. In parallel, several initiatives exist for monitoring specific aspects of the overall sustainable development agenda with UN Intergovernmental Panel on Climate Change (IPCC) among the most well-known, essential and directly related to SDG 13 (climate action).

It is not possible here to list, compare and discuss the many different approaches to measure various aspects of 'sustainable development'. All have their strengths and weaknesses. Neither is it possible to dive deeper into each of the 17 SDGs and the 169 related targets. Instead, we take the point of departure in the OECD 'distance to SDG targets' and the 'SDG Index' by the SDSN as reference points, since these are the ones that most governments and organisations relate to when national SDG progress reports are published. It is also the case for the Danish government.

The OECD 'distance to SDG targets' analysis from 2019 (OECD 2019) covers 101 of the 169 SDG targets and is based on 127 available indicators. According to the report, in 2019 Denmark achieved 20 out of the 169 2030 targets, and for several of the remaining targets, the 'distance' is relatively small, while for others the achievement seems to be far away from meeting the targets. If we take a closer look, it is a mixed picture depending on the selected indicators for each goal and how these indicators are weighted and what data is available. One example is SDG 3 on good health and wellbeing. Overall, Denmark has a high performance in most of the health-related indicators but seems to be far away from meeting for instance the specific target related to rates of tobacco consumption (measuring target 3.a). While there are many indicators for SDG 3 on health and SDG 4 on education, there are only two indicators related to each of the goals 10, 11, 12 and 14. As pointed out by the OECD, inclusion of more indicators on these goals might shift the overall picture. This conclusion becomes clear if we instead take a look at the second well-established approach developed by the SDSN, where more indicators are included, see Figure 13.1:

Since the SDSN published its first SDG index in 2015, Sweden, Denmark and Finland have topped the SDG global ranking positions. According to the Sustainable Development Report 2020 (Sachs et al. 2020), Denmark is ranked second (Sweden first) with an overall SDG index score of 84.6 (out of 100).[4] Despite the relatively high overall SDG performance score, a closer look at the average performance by SDG reveals that since 2015 for some of the 17 goals Danish society seems to have moved in the wrong direction. According to the 2017 report (Sachs et al. 2017), Denmark had achieved the 2030 target for six out of the 17 goals (1, 3, 4, 9, 10 and 17) by 2017. In 2018 only two goals met the 2030 targets (1 and 10) (Sachs et al. 2018). In 2019 (Sachs et al. 2019) three goals (1, 10 and 16) and in 2020 the 2030 target was achieved for 'only' SDG 1 (no poverty) and SDG 10 (reduced inequalities) (Sachs et al. 2020). This means that different degrees of challenge still persist for the remaining 15 goals. For SDG 12 (responsible consumption and production), SDG 13 (climate action) and SDG 14 (life below water) the challenges are classified as major, for SDG 2 (zero hunger)[5] and SDG 11 (sustainable cities and communities) challenges are classified as significant, and for the remaining 10 SDGs challenges continue to exist although with moderately improving trends for most of the SDGs compared to the 2019 report.

These performance rankings can be interpreted differently depending on the perspective. On the one hand, as the reporting indicates, in general and in relative terms (global and regional score) Denmark is performing well in relation to the SDGs, and the 2030 targets seem within reach. On the other hand, the reporting clearly indicates that important challenges remain and may even increase over time if no action is taken. From a sustainable transition perspective, it is worrying that Danish society faces significant challenges in meeting the 2030 targets relating to sustainable cities and communities (SDG 11), responsible consumption and production (SDG 12), climate action (SDG 13) and life below water (SDG 14). Reaching the 2030 targets for these SDGs will require major changes in existing consumption and production patterns, infrastructure and transport systems, energy production and the way farming and fishery are executed.

From the two examples on reporting, it is clear that it is a rather complex issue to provide an accurate picture of the SDG status for Danish society (or

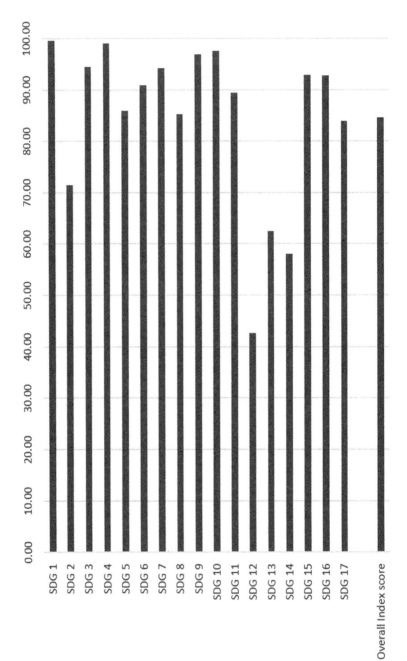

Figure 13.1 Overall and average performance by SDG, Denmark 2020.
Source: Sachs et al. 2020; data from online database for Sustainable Development Report 2020.

any other country). Different approaches have selected different indicators. The indicators used as background for the performance measures used by the UN SDSN (Figure 13.1) do not fully comply with the indicators suggested by the IAEG-SDGs. Data might not be available for all countries and when they are available, they may be outdated or not reliable. As an illustration, the 2020 SDG performance index for Denmark includes data from 2010 as the most recent up to 2020 depending on the specific indicator. As is generally the case when constructing a composite index, you often end up 'adding apples and pears' and the result depends on the relative weighting of the selected indicators. In the SDG performance index (Figure 13.1) all indicators are given the same weight when constructing the average performance per SDG. As many of the 17 goals are mutually interdependent, this approach is problematic, and it might lead to wrong policy initiatives if a goal is singled out and removed from context. Another important issue is how activities in one country affect SDG targets internationally. One example on this is when Denmark is used as a showcase on 'genuine green growth' defined as a decoupling of greenhouse gas (GHG) emissions from economic growth (measured by GDP) (Stoknes and Rockström 2018). Increasing energy efficiency is part of the explanation, but a main explanatory factor is that coal is substituted by imported biofuel originating mainly from Baltic forests; similarly, when emissions from international shipping and air traffic are not included in the CO_2 emission calculations but at the same time the income generated from international shipping and air traffic are included as part of the GDP (Danish Council on Climate Change 2019).[6]

13.2.2 Specific supplementary Danish indicators and targets

As mentioned earlier, countries are encouraged to supplement the UN monitoring activities with more specific sub-goals and indicators relevant as signposts for country-specific actions. Denmark took part in the first (2017) voluntary national review initiated by the High-Level Political Forum (HLPF) on sustainable development, and in accordance with the 2030 Agenda, the Danish government formulated an Action Plan (2017) as part of the review in order to adapt the SDG targets to the Danish circumstances. The Action Plan took its point of departure in the OECD approach mentioned earlier and it was formulated around the 5 Ps (People, Planet, Prosperity, Peace and Partnerships). The liberal government formulated 37 related but more specific targets, each with one to two national indicators that are measurable and quantifiable (Danish Ministry of Finance 2017). At the election of the Danish parliament in 2019 climate came very high on the agenda, and the newly elected social democratic government has formulated a very ambitious climate act that received support from most parties in the parliament. The climate act aims at Denmark being 'climate neutral' in 2050, for emissions from GHGs to be reduced by 70% by 2030 compared to 1990, for an 'indicative target' to be set for 2025, and for the government to present a yearly progress report in order to document that the country is on track according to the targets.[7] The 2019 climate act became a key argument for Denmark being able to jump from 15 to 5 on the Climate Change Performance Index (CCPI) (Burck et al. 2019). Since no country qualifies for positions 1–3, position 5 is relatively good compared to, for instance, the SDG Index Score on SDG 13 mentioned earlier. The CCPI has existed since 2005 as an independent monitoring tool for tracking countries' climate protection performance. It is published yearly by Germanwatch, the New Climate Institute and the Climate Action Network. The CCPI tool is an example on how sensitive the benchmarking is on the methodological approach and data sources. The CCPI assesses countries' performance in four categories with different weight: GHG emissions (40% of overall score), renewable energy (20% of overall score), energy use (20% of overall score) and climate policy (20% of overall score).

Following the need to develop relevant indicators, in 2019 the Danish 2030-Panel[8] together with Statistics Denmark initiated an open SDG development project with the overall aim to establish supplementary Danish indicators on the status of the SDGs in Denmark. An important purpose of the indicator project (named 'Our Goals') was to raise the awareness and engagement of Danish citizens, institutions, organisations and companies for the 17 SDGs by calling for input and participation in public debates on how a status for the SDGs should be measured so it would become as relevant as possible in a Danish context. During autumn 2019 and spring 2020 the project organised public debates and workshops on each of the 17 SDGs in different parts of the country – and online after the COVID-19 outbreak – in order to involve as broad a group of people and interests as possible. Experts from universities, Statistics Denmark, NGOs and consultancies were 'called in' in order to prioritise among the many suggestions. After a round of public hearings on preliminary reports, the final baseline report was published in September 2020 (2030-Panelet 2020) suggesting adding 197 supplementary indicators. Three types of examples may illustrate the importance of supplementing the overall UN monitoring with country-specific indicators in order to mobilise for action.

The first example concerns SDG 1 (no poverty). According to UN monitoring, Denmark has achieved the 2030 target. However, this does not mean that *relative* poverty does not exist in Denmark and that no policy action is needed. By adding more nuanced supplementary indicators such as, for example, the number of homeless persons, number of persons on long term public support, share of families that suffer material deprivation (in relative terms) and distribution of wealth it becomes clear that SDG 1 is also relevant in a Danish context. The second example is SDG 12 (responsible consumption and production) where the Danish SDG performance indicates a long distance to the 2030 target. A key issue here is waste handling including waste reduction, and the result of the 'Our Goals' project is 13 supplementary indicators that in a more detailed form can monitor, for instance, recycling of material, waste of food, share of ecological food consumption as signposts for increasing awareness, policy interventions and actions from both private and public consumers and producers. The third and final example is related to SDG 9 (industry, innovation and infrastructure) where the supplementary indicator project ended up with 13 supplementary indicators. In the UN global monitoring, the SDG 9 indicators mainly focus on the general level of industrialisation, access to the internet and more narrow research and innovation indicators such as R&D expenditure (% of GDP), number of patents (per million population), scientific and technical journal articles (per 1000 population). In the Danish supplementary indicator project the focus for SDG 9 has been on selecting indicators that can monitor development of a green transition of not only industry (understood as manufacturing) but also of services and transport of goods and people. New knowledge and new technological solutions are necessary for realising a green transition and the supplementary indicators thus emphasise to what extent R&D activities, patents, etc. are targeting green innovation and sustainable transition. If the 197 supplementary performance indicators identified in the 'Our Goals' project are institutionalised as part of Danish society's monitoring of the 17 SDGs, they will evidently improve the knowledge base for policy formulation and action towards sustainable development because these indicators are embedded and contextualised in local/national formal and informal institutions.

Despite the many problems related to these performance measures and benchmarking activities they may function as a wake-up call for policy makers and play an important role as a basis for policy action and assessment. It is definitely important to be able to find ways to measure to what extent progress is made on both a global and a local (national) scale even if these approaches do not give much information and help to actually formulate a policy strategy. In other words, a pragmatic approach is to see these performance measures as being a great deal better than nothing. It is also clear, that both the selection of relevant indicators and the availability of systematic and reliable data are in progress.

However, even with these improvements, a yearly status report on the performance measures only reflects a comparative static approach and does not in itself provide insights into how different learning and innovation capabilities driving the process of innovation depend and feed upon each other. In other words, it calls for what can be labelled a capability-based performance measure for sustainable development where learning and capability building are at the centre.

13.3 Towards a capability-based performance measure

In Section 13.2 the focus was on the national level and the SDG targets Denmark as a country has to accomplish by 2030. In that sense the SDG targets at the country level are to be seen as the overall targets for the Danish national innovation system. What then are the implications of applying an innovation system approach for policy-informing performance measures? In the current context we argue that the most prominent 'feature' is stressing the importance of linkages, interactions and learning processes. In a long-term sustainable development perspective, the capability to learn and innovate is, obviously, crucial and a discussion of innovation system performance has to reflect this. The learning and innovation capabilities of a national innovation system depend on many factors like R&D, education, vocational training, life-long learning opportunities, ICT facilities, availability of different types of capital, established modes of innovation, triple helix relations, the distribution of income, wealth and power, social cohesion and inclusion, and so on.

We are thus looking for a performance measure that can help indicate to what extent a national innovation system is enhancing its learning and innovation capability to transform towards a more sustainable society. Inspired by the 'learning organisation' and 'learning culture' approaches, we may define a learning society towards sustainable development as a society (Johnson and Lundvall 1994; Gregersen and Johnson 2005; Lundvall 2016):

- where learning, creativity and innovation fostering sustainable development are valued
- where investment in education and possibility for life-long learning towards a more sustainable production and consumption pattern are given high priority
- where time and other resources for learning and innovation targeting a transition towards a more sustainable society are available
- where interaction, co-operation and knowledge synergies between people, organisations and disciplines are stimulated
- where participation in the transition process is encouraged by giving learners voice and legitimacy in decision-making
- where learning opportunities are created and shared equitably among all citizens so 'no one is left behind'
- where processes exist for a socio-economically sustainable distribution of the values created, including institutions and policies to compensate victims and handle conflicts related to sustainable structural changes and 'creative destruction of knowledge'.

Performance indicators that reflect learning and innovation capability are necessary starting points for formulating and implementing policies for transition to sustainable development. Agreeing on the targets and monitoring the distance to the targets are crucial as mobilising for action but building the learning and innovation capabilities to implement the transition is a prerequisite.

Education and competence building in the broad sense is of course a basic ingredient. However, it is not only the general level of education or the extent of vocational training opportunities that are important, but also that creativity and innovation are stimulated through the education and training system and continue to be so in the way work is organised. Availability of supportive resources for learning and innovation influences not only the creation and diffusion of new knowledge in the innovation system but also which ideas are realised and implemented in product and process innovations. Interaction, collaboration and knowledge synergies between people, organisations and disciplines reflect key characteristics of the national innovation system and the importance of such linkages for the creation, diffusion and utilisation of new knowledge is well documented in the innovation literature. Finally, we state that fair and equal distribution of learning opportunities and costs and benefits of technological changes among its citizens is part of a sustainable development. Not only because social cohesion, innovativeness and wealth seem to be interrelated when seen in a long-term perspective, but also because equal learning opportunities and a social fair distribution of the costs and benefits of structural changes and 'creative destruction of knowledge' is relevant in its own right (Gregersen and Johnson 2005).

Recalling the introductory definition, performance measure should measure to what extent the innovation system delivers what is selected and defined as wanted and valued. This, of course, does not need to be the same for each national innovation system. In other words, targets should, in principle, be tailor-made as signposts for a sustainable transition process for the specific national innovation system or group of national innovation systems in question. For this we need an active approach trying to broaden the perspective in order to create a future demand for relevant indicators and data collection that emphasises performance as a dynamic capability-building process rather than as static single-point exercise. In that way, such performance measures can better support policy formulation and policy evaluation. This is a critical task for the innovation system community to take up as a constructive supplementary contribution to formulating policies towards sustainable transition.

We have argued that a national innovation system approach to analyse performance in relation to the 17 UN SDGs implies a rethinking of (or at least supplements) the prevailing SDG performance measures and indicators. It calls for a dynamic capability-based performance framework where learning and capability building is at the centre. It follows from that, that a broad definition of a national innovation system in combination with a broad definition of performance is needed where the interdependency between technical, organisational and institutional change is emphasised as a point of departure for formulating policies that stimulate a transition towards a more sustainable society. That well performing national innovation systems are crucial for adequate sustainability transitions becomes even more evident if we take into account new challenges related to changes in the total Earth system. In next section we briefly develop this argument.

13.4 A wider perspective on sustainable development

The very idea of sustainable development is increasingly challenged by a growing scientific and political awareness of a number of global challenges related to the onset of the Anthropocene era (Crutzen 2002; Gaffney and Steffen 2017).[9]

The biophysical system is becoming more complex, contingent and volatile and cannot be used as a fixed background for economic and social development in the same way as before. Humans are, so to speak, not any longer the sole actors on the scene. The Earth system with its many subsystems is changing and interfering with the development of human societies (Descola 2013; Steffen et al. 2015; Steffen et al. 2018).

> Human and biophysical systems are coupled: human actions affect biophysical systems; biophysical forces affect human well-being, and humans respond in turn to these forces. (p. 149) … Because the two sides of coupled systems are highly interactive, we cannot explain—much less predict—the behavior of these systems without treating both sides as endogenous.
> (Kotchen and Young 2007, p. 150).

Or as Kotchen and Young (2007) express:

The onset of the Anthropocene implies that we need to implement transformative, structure-changing policies based on long-term thinking, often (a bit indefinably) referred to as 'sustainability transition'. There is a need for transformative capacity, i.e., an ability to mobilise major innovation and investment activities to restructure society to meet the Anthropocene challenges. In such a transformative approach many kinds of innovation will be needed, from minor improvements of technologies already in use to transformative innovation restructuring production and consumption to keep society within planetary boundaries. It seems clear that meeting the challenges of the transition from the Holocene to the Anthropocene requires a new development path including strengthened learning and innovation capabilities as pointed out in Section 13.3. At the same time, because of the urgent time perspective, we need to cope with necessary immediate action in relation to climate change, loss of biodiversity, soil destruction, ocean acidification, etc. In sum, the Anthropocene challenge for a transition to sustainable development is to reconcile three different and partly conflicting imperatives: take immediate action, increase resilience, mitigation and adaptability, and implement transformative structural change in a world which appears more unstable and uncertain than ever before.

The SDGs do not explicitly take the Anthropocene challenge on board, but we may – as argued in this chapter – use the SDGs as pragmatic temporary approximations of the needs for transformative change in the transition from the Holocene to the Anthropocene. However, to some extent they do indirectly reflect an Anthropocene perspective: issues related to environmental sustainability play important roles in 12 out of the 17 goals. They are global and refer to 'mankind' and not only nations or classes. They refer to the need to transform our world and they integrate social, economic and environmental aspects. They imply major changes in existing structures and tendencies and they often refer to technical and institutional innovation as both necessary and effective instruments. At the same time, it is important to note that the 17 goals do not add up to an adequate definition of sustainable development in the Anthropocene. Interdependencies between the different goals, tipping elements in different environmental processes and some critical planetary boundaries are not receiving the attention they deserve from an Earth system perspective.

13.5 Conclusion

As demonstrated in this chapter, the Danish innovation system is performing relatively well in relation to the UN SDG performance indicators but still with major challenges before the 2030 targets are achieved – especially in relation to sustainable cities, consumption, production, climate action and life below water. Despite the general weak spots of the prevailing SDG performance indicators, they play an important role in stressing that no country has yet managed to achieve all 17 SDG targets and that implementation will require considerable changes in ways of living, production and consumption in order to meet the 2030 targets on both a global and a national level. Such a transition calls for action from all parts of the innovation system including consumers, firms, knowledge institutions and policy makers.

Forming directions for sustainable development with such specific targets as the 17 SDGs, mobilising finance and other resources, coordinating policies across policy areas (e.g., energy, research and innovation, social, education, labour market, health) are necessary ingredients of a sustainable transition process. When the economy is viewed as a process of change rather than as an equilibrium system, innovation and learning become crucial and basic concepts. Furthermore, when the economy is looked upon as changing from within, constantly in the process of becoming something else, innovation and learning come forward as a means of change, as the process through which transformation is implemented. Technical innovation, organisational innovation, policy innovation and institutional innovation are the very processes, which create or detect novelty and introduce it into the economy and distribute it. This is why the prevailing UN SDG performance indicators need to be supplemented by a learning and capability perspective that emphasises closing the gap of competences, skills and experiences to implement a transition to more sustainable societies.

Successful implementation of the goals in the context of an increasingly insecure Earth system depends crucially on a number of institutional factors. SDG 17 considers implementation issues: it is stated that a massive redirection of public as well as private investment is needed to deliver significantly on the sustainable development goals. This is not only a responsibility for governments and international organisations like the UN. It requires partnerships between governments, the private sector and civil society on global, regional, national and local levels building on a shared vision, and shared goals that place people and the planet at the centre. The European Green Deal is one such important step. With the Green Deal the EU has agreed to take a series of initiatives to protect the environment and boost the green economy in order to reach the target to be climate neutral by 2050. Another example is the UN Science, Technology and Innovation Forum and the many UN partnership organisations targeting the SDGs. If a general and global popular movement could be built around the SDGs rather than around nationalistic agendas different real existing capitalist systems might converge and serve as a platform for moving towards a more sustainable future.

Still, national agendas of technical and institutional change for greener solutions in different specific areas will be necessary parts of a global move towards navigating the Anthropocene in a way that respects the health of the biosphere and other planetary boundaries. Learning and innovation capabilities become vital. The need for strong national systems of innovation will increase as a result of the Anthropocene challenge to sustainable development.

Notes

1 SDG-1: no poverty; SDG-2: zero hunger; SDG-3: good health and wellbeing; SDG-4: quality education; SDG-5: gender equality; SDG-6: clean water and sanitation; SDG-7: affordable and clean energy; SDG-8: decent work and economic growth; SDG-9: industry, innovation and infrastructure; SDG-10: reduced inequality; SDG-11: sustainable cities and communities; SDG-12; responsible consumption and production; SDG-13: climate action; SDG-14: life below water; SDG-15: life on land; SDG-16: peace, justice and strong institutions; SDG-17: partnerships for the goals.
2 For detailed information on updates of the official UN SDG indicators, see https://unstats.un.org/sdgs/indicators/indicators-list/
3 The Sustainable Development Outlook 2020 edition (United Nations, Department of Economics and Social Affairs 2020) looks at how the COVID-19 pandemic may influence the SDG target progress in different ways. While the planet may have gained, targets related to people and prosperity are facing setbacks on a global scale.
4 In the 2019 report, Denmark 'outperformed' Sweden and scored 85.2 (out of 100), or in other words, average performance by some SDGs seems to have moved in the wrong direction from 2019 to 2020.
5 The full title of SDG 2 is 'end hunger, achieve food security and improved nutrition and promote sustainable agriculture'. The prevalence of obesity defined as BMI $\geq$ 30 is 19.7% among the Danish adult population.
6 An alternative approach is the so-called consumption-based emission accounting framework that aims at looking at the whole value chain (see for instance Lund et al. 2019).
7 However, formulation of concrete action plans is being delayed due to the COVID-19 crisis and it is yet to be seen if the COVID-19 pandemic will stimulate the necessary transition to more sustainable production and consumption patterns or the result is a setback not only in the short term.
8 The 2030-Panel is an advisory body established by the Danish parliament's All Party Coalition for the Sustainable Development Goals in 2017. The panel has 23 members, including members from Danish industry organisations, labour organisations, regions, educational institutions, university experts.
9 The impacts of the human actions on biophysical systems are so comprehensive and deep that many observers now speak of human-dominated ecosystems and argue that we have entered a new planetary era best described as the Anthropocene (Kotchen and Young 2007).

References

2030-Panelet. 2020. *Gør Verdensmål til Vores Mål – 197 danske målepunkter for en mere bæredygtig verden* [in Danish], Vores Mål projektet. ('Our Goals' project).

Burck, J., Hagen, U., Höhne, N., Nasciento, L. and Bals, C. 2019. *Climate Change Performance Index. Results 2020*. (CCPI). Germanwatch, New Climate Institute & Climate Action Network. http://www.climate-change-performance-index.org

Crutzen, P.J. 2002. The anthropocene. *Journal de Physique IV*. France. 12 10 1–5. doi:10.1051/jp4:20020447

Danish Council on Climate Change [Klimarådet]. 2019. *Status for Danmarks klimamålsætninger og forpligtelser 2019*, Copenhagen: Klimarådet.

Danish Ministry of Finance. 2017. *Report for the Voluntary National Review. Denmark's Implementation of the 2030 Agenda for Sustainable Development*, Copenhagen: Danish Ministry of Finance.

Descola, P. 2013. *Beyond Nature and Culture*. Chicago: University of Chicago Press.

Dietz, R. and O'Neill, D., 2013. *Enough Is Enough: Building a Sustainable Economy in a World of Finite Resources*. San Francisco: Berret-Koehler Publishers

Fagerberg J. 2018. Mobilizing innovation for sustainability transitions: A comment on transformative innovation policy. *Research Policy*, 47(9), 1568–1576. https://doi.org/10.1016/j.respol.2018.08.012

Fagerberg, J., Laestadius, S. and Martin, B. eds. 2015. *The Triple Challenge for Europe – Economic Development, Climate Change and Governance*. Oxford: Oxford University Press.

Gaffney, O. and Steffen, W. (2017). The Anthropocene equation. *The Anthropocene Review*, 4(1), 53–61.

Gregersen, B. and Johnson, B. 2005. *Performance of Innovation Systems: Towards a Capability Based Concept and Measurements*. Paper presented at The Third Globelics Conference, Innovation Systems as framework for the promotion of economic growth, social cohesion and political development, Pretoria, South Africa, October 31–November 4.

Johnson, B. H. and Lundvall, B.-Å. 1994. The learning economy. *Journal of Industry Studies*, 1(2), 23–42.

Kotchen, M. J. and Young, O. R. 2007. Meeting the challenges of the anthropocene: Towards a science of coupled human-biophysical systems. *Global Environmental Change*, 17, 149–151.

Lund, J. F., Bjørn, A., Simonsen, M. B., Jacobsen, S. G., Blok, A. and Jensen, C. L. 2019. Outsourcing og omstilling: De danske drivhusgasudledninger genfortolket. *Samfundsøkonomen*, 4, 15–24.

Lundvall, B.-Å. 2016. *The Learning Economy and the Economics of Hope*. London: Anthem Press.

Markard J., Raven R., Truffer B. 2012. Sustainability transitions: An emerging field of research and its prospects. *Research Policy*, 41, 955–967.

OECD. 2019. *Measuring Distance to the SDG Targets 2019: An Assessment of Where OECD Countries Stand*. Paris: OECD Publishing. https://doi.org/10.1787/a8caf3fa-en.

Østergaard, C.R., Holm, J. R. and Park, E. 2021. Firms' contribution to the green transition of the Danish national system of innovation – changes in technological specialisation, skills and innovation. In Christensen, J. L., Gregersen, B., Holm, J. R. and Lorenz, E. eds. *Globalisation, New and Emerging Technologies and Sustainable Development – the Danish Innovation System in Transition*. Abingdon: Routledge.

Rockström, J. 2015. *Bounding the Planetary Future: Why We Need a Great Transition*. Great Transition Initiative (April 2015), http://www.greattransition.org/publication/bounding-the-planetary-future-why-we-need-a-great-transition.

Sachs, J., Schmidt-Traub, G., Kroll, C., Durand-Delacre, D. and Teksoz, K. 2017. *SDG Index and Dashboards Report 2017*. New York: Bertelsmann Stiftung and Sustainable Development Solutions Network (SDSN).

Sachs, J., Schmidt-Traub, G., Kroll, C., Lafortune, G. and Fuller, G. 2018. *SDG Index and Dashboards Report 2018*. New York: Bertelsmann Stiftung and Sustainable Development Solutions Network (SDSN).

Sachs, J., Schmidt-Traub, G., Kroll, C., Lafortune, G. and Fuller, G. 2019. *Sustainable Development Report 2019*. New York: Bertelsmann Stiftung and Sustainable Development Solutions Network (SDSN).

Sachs, J., Schmidt-Traub, G., Kroll, C., Lafortune, G., Fuller, G., Woelm, F. 2020. *The Sustainable Development Goals and COVID-19*. Sustainable Development Report 2020. Cambridge: Cambridge University Press.

Steffen, W., Richardson, K., Rockström, J., Cornell, S. E., Fetzer, I., Bennett, E. M., Biggs, R., Carpenter, S. R., de Vries, W., de Witt, C. A., Folke, C., Gerten, D., Heinke, J., Mace, G. M., Persson, L. M., Ramanathan, V., Reyers, B. and Sörlin, S. 2015. Planetary boundaries: Guiding human development on a changing planet. *Science*, 347(6223), 736. doi:10.1126/science.

Steffen, W., Rockström, R., Richardson, K., Lenton, T. M., Folke, C., Liverman, D., Summerhayes, C. P., Barnosky, A. D., Cornell, S. E., Crucifix, M., Donges, J. F., Fetzer, I., Lade, S. J., Scheffer, M., Winkelmann, R. and Schellnhuber, H. J. 2018. Trajectories of the earth system in the anthropocene. *Proceedings of the National Academy of Sciences of the United States of America (PNAS)*, 115(33), 8252–8259, doi:10.1073/pnas.1810141115,

Stern, N., 2006. *The Economics of Climate Change: The Stern Review*. Report to UK Government 2006, available online https://webarchive.nationalarchives.gov.uk/20 100407172811/http://www.http://hm-treasury.gov.uk/stern_review:report.htm

Stern N. 2015. Economic development, climate and values: Making policy. *Proceedings of the Royal Society London B*, 282, 20150820. http://dx.doi.org/10.1098/rspb.2015.0820

Stoknes, P. E. and Rockström, J. 2018. Redefining green growth within planetary boundaries. *Energy Research & Social Science*, 44, 41–49.

Teece, D. J., Pisano, G. and Shuen, A. 1997. Dynamic capabilities and strategic management. *Strategic Management Journal*, 18(7), 509–533.

United Nations. 1987. *Our Common Future* (Brundtland report), Report of the World Commission on Environment and Development.

United Nations. 2019a. *The Future is Now – Science for Achieving Sustainable Development*. Global Sustainable Development Report 2019.

United Nations. 2019b. *The Sustainable Development Goals Report 2019*. New York: United Nations.

United Nations, Department of Economic and Social Affairs. 2020. *Sustainable Development Outlook 2020 – Achieving SDGs in the Wake of COVID-19: Scenarios for Policymakers*, New York: United Nations, Department of Economic and Social Affairs.

Index

Note: page references in italics indicate figures; bold indicates tables.

Acs, Z. J. 53
Alasoini, T. 186
angel investment 39, 61
Arntz, M. 191, 192
artificial intelligence (AI) *see* robots and AI/ML
Arundel, A. 137
automation 46, 54, 102, 189–192, 199–203; *see also* robots and AI/ML

Bauernschuster, S. 210
Baumol, W. J. 54
Bessen, J. 191
Bhidé, A 63
Birch, D. L. 53
Bolvig, I. 211
Børing, P. 210
Borins, S. 132
Borup, M. 247
bottom-up perspective 132–133, 138, 141, 203
Bowles, J. 190
Brynjolfsson, E. 149, 165
Bryson, J. M. 138
bureaucracy 56, 74, 177
Burns, T. E. 171
Busenitz, L. W. 54
business promotion 42, 72–83, *74*, *76*; *see also* private sector

Canales, R. 65
capabilities 4, 39, 46, 93, 116, 120, 124, 125, 139, 211, 234, 252–253, 259–264
capital 22, 39, 55, 58, 61–64, 72, 79, 114, 260; human capital 79, 198, 208–211, 224, 232, 234, 243; relational capital 116, 119, *119*, 122, 125; social capital 3, 78, 79, 113; *see also* funding; grants
Card, D. 216

Chaminade, C. 233
Chesbrough, H. W. 130
China 239
Christensen, J. L. 83n
Coad, A. 56
collaboration on innovation 3; and green transition 233, 234, 240, 247; and performance of the innovation system 33–34, 38–42, 43–46; and policy on innovation 16–17, 21, 23–25, 27; and ports 111–126, *119*; public sector 130–143, **134**, **135**, **138**, **140**, **141**; and regional innovation policy 73, 78; and robots and AI/ML technology 150, 193; and supplier firms 95, **97**, 97–98, 102, 105–107; and sustainable development 261; tertiary education and private sector 209, 212, 214, 221–224, **222**, **223**; and work policy 193, 200–201, 203
competition and competitiveness 1, 4, 14, 20, 45, 53, 63, 91, 93–95, 107, 112–117, 124, 132, 133, 150, 166, 186, 209, 211
Consoli, D. 234
Cornett, A. P. 70
COVID-19 3–4, 45, 48, 55, 62, 66
Crosby, B. C. 138
crowdfunding 61

Dahl, M. S. 56, 62
Dauth, W. 191
Davidsson, P. 63
digital technology 4, 39–40, 43, 44, 46, 60, 61, 75, 91, 107, 151, 190, 199, 203
discretionary learning 153, 155, 166, 177, 179, 182–185, *184*
Doloreux, D. 113
Dostie, B. 210
Drejer, I. 83n

education and training: and
entrepreneurship 54, 56, 60, 61, 62,
64; and green transition 232, 234–235,
248; and performance of the innovation
system 37, 39, 40, 44–46; and policy
on innovation 17, 19, 23–24, 26; and
regional innovation policy 77, 79; and
robots and AI/ML technology 150–151,
154, *157*, 157–158, 162–164, 166; and
supplier firms 98, 102, 105–106; and
sustainable development 255, 260, 263;
tertiary continuing, and private sector
innovation 208–225, *213*, **218, 220,
222, 223**; vocational 166, 198, 200, 201,
203, 260; and work organisation 173;
and work policy 190, 195, 198–203;
see also learning; skills; universities
employees: and entrepreneurship 54,
56, 57; and green transition 234–235,
240–247; public sector 131–132, 138,
139–143, **140, 141**; and robots and AI/
ML technology 150–159, 162, 165,
166; and supplier firms 97, 98, 101,
102, 105, 106; and work organisation
169–177, 182–186, **183**, *184*; and work
policy 191, 193, 194, 199–203; *see also*
education and training; learning; skills
employment *see* automation; employees;
human resources; job creation; labour
market; skills; unemployment; work
organisation; work policy
energy 21, 37, 49; wind 21, 37, 117, 231,
232, 238–239, 244, 247, 248
entrepreneurship 53–66; and performance
of the innovation system 39, 45–46,
54–55, 59–63; and regional innovation
policy 60, 61, 73; and tertiary continuing
education 211
environment *see* green transition;
sustainable development
European Union (EU) 25, 35, 37–38, 40,
42, 47, 48, 60, 70–71, 78, 80
experimentation 48, 54, 63–66, 78

Finland 174, 179, 186, 232, 241
flexicurity 189, 193–194, 206, 207
framework conditions 20, 22, 23, 38,
43, 55, 60, 62, 71, 75, 81, 91, 199,
233, 254
Freeman, C. 16, 17, 169, 190
Frey, C. B. 190–191
funding 14, 16, 22, 35, 37, 38–40, 44, 45,
47, 49, 60–62, 66, 73, *74*, 75, 79–81,
131, 186; *see also* capital; grants; subsidies

generation shifts 114–121, 124, 125
Germany 101, 105, 210
Gjerløv-Juel, P. 56
globalisation 1–3, 6, 62, 94, 169, 189
grand challenges 49
grants 23, 39, 40, 45, 58, *74*; *see also*
capital; funding; subsidies
green transition 45–47, 231–248, *236*,
237, *238*, *239*, **241**, **244**, **246**; *see also*
sustainable development
growth: and entrepreneurship 53, 54, 56–
62; and green transition 245–248; and
performance of the innovation system
39, 40, 42; and policy on innovation
14, 16, 17, 19, 20; and ports 111, 114,
116–118, 120; and regional innovation
policy 71–81; and supplier firms 105;
and sustainable development 257; and
work policy 192, 206, 207
Guzman, J. 56–57

Hall, P. V. 121
higher education *see* education and
training; universities
high-performance work systems (HPWS)
169–173, 177, 179, 185
holistic policy on innovation 19, 26, 27,
34, 42, 48, 49
Hollanders, H. 137
Holm, J. R. 97, 152, 176, 177, 191, 192,
200, 216
human capital 79, 198, 208–211, 224, 232,
234, 243
human resources 45–46, 49, 73, 169;
see also employees; labour market

incubators 39–40, 42, 54, 60–62
industry: and entrepreneurship 54,
57–58, 62, 63, 66; and green transition
231–232, 238–239, 244, 247; and
performance of the innovation system
41, 45–46, 48; and policy on innovation
14, *15*, 21–22, 24; and regional
innovation policy 71, 77, 78; and robots
and AI/ML technology 149–151,
154–159, 162, 166; and supplier firms
91–93, *92*, 95, 97, 101; and sustainable
development 259; and work organisation
169, 183; and work policy 190–193,
199; *see also* ports; private sector
infrastructure 3, 4, 40, 44, 62, 245, 248;
physical *see* ports
innovation studies 17, 19, 26, 35, 59, 77,
169–170, 210

innovation systems thinking 2–3, 13, 17–19, *18*, 23, 26, 33, 46, 59, 72, 81, 259, 261
intrapreneurship 54, 56

Jacobs, W. 121
Jacobsson, S. 231
Japan 14, 169, 177, 179
job creation 53, 71, 245–247, **246**
Johnson, A. 231

Kerr, W. R. 63, 64
knowledge 3; and entrepreneurship 58, 65; and green transition 232–235, 240, 243, 244, 246–248; and performance of innovation policy 33, 35, 40–42, 44, 48–49; and policy on innovation 16–17, 20, 21, 23–27; and ports 113–115, 121–122; and the public sector 131–133, 136, 139; and regional innovation policy 70, 71, 72, 73, 77, 79; and supplier firms 106, 107; and sustainable development 252, 259, 260–262, 263; and tertiary continuing education 208, 212, 217; and work policy 199–200, 203; *see also* learning
Kotchen, M. J. 262
Kringelum, L. B. 94

labour market 3; and entrepreneurship 55; and green transition 233, 242; and regional innovation policy 73; and robots and AI/ML technology 150, 165; and tertiary continuing education 208, 212, 214, 216, 225; and work organisation 186; *see also* human resources; work policy
labour unions 150, 166
large companies 33, 41, 53, 54, 64, 65, 240, 248
lean work organisation 153, 156, 159, 164, 166
learning 3; discretionary 153, 155, 166, 177, 179, 182–185, *184*; and green transition 232–234, 240, 247; and performance of innovation systems 34, 45, 46, 48; and policy on innovation 27, 34, 48; and ports 112, 118, 121, 125; and the public sector 138, 143; and robots and AI/ML technology 152–159, *157*, 162, 166; and supplier firms 93, 107; and sustainable development 253, 259–262, 263, 264; and work organisation 170–171, 173–175, 177,

179–182, **180–181**, **182**, *184*, 184–186; *see also* education and training; knowledge; skills
Levin, R. C. 16, 28n
Lindgreen, A. 97
Lindholm-Dahlstrand, Å. 65, 66
linear model 16, 19, 35
links *see* collaboration on innovation
Liu, J. S. 35
Lorenz, E. 97, 152, 176, 177, 200
Lundvall, B.-Å. 4, 169–170, 182, 233, 247
Lykkebo, O. B. 133, 137

machine learning (ML) *see* robots and AI/ML
macroeconomics 22, 53
Malerba, F. 247
managerial skills 209, 210, 211–212
market failure 55–56, 70, 72, 76–79, 81, 82
Mazzucato, M. 66
Mintzberg, H. 171, 177
Morgan, K. 78
Mountjoy, J. 216

Nelson, R. R. 17, 235
neoclassical economics 72, 79–81
Netherlands, The 37, 60, 179
networks 40, 64, 208–209, 212, 224, 240
new businesses 53, 54, 56, 57, 59–60, 65, 73, 79, 81, 114
Nielsen, K. 64
Nielsen, P. 158
Nightingale, P. 56
Nordic countries 91, 97, 137–139, 143, 179, 186, 232, 235, 241, 242; *see also specific countries*
norms 3, 78, 79, 177, 179
Norway 60, 101, 105, 175, 210, 232

organic work organisation 171
Organisation for Economic Co-operation and Development (OECD) 2, 17, 23, 25, *36*, 36–37, 71, 73, 76, 253–257
Osborne, M. 190–191
Østergaard, C. R. 216, 235, 241–242
outsourcing 4, 6, 54
Özcan, S. 56

patents: and entrepreneurship 57; and green transition 232, 233, 234, 235–241, *236*, *237*, *238*, **239**, 244–245, 247–248; and performance and the innovation system 35, 37, 40; and policy on innovation 16; and sustainable development 252, 259

Pavitt, K. 93
Perez, C. 17, 190
performance of the innovation system
33–49, *36*; and entrepreneurship
39, 45–46, 54–55, 59–63; and green
transition 240, 246; learning approach to
measurement 253, 259–262, 263, 264;
and policy on innovation 17, 34–35,
39–49; and regional innovation policy
41–42, 49; and sustainable development
46–47, 252–253, 259–264; and work
organisation 169–171, 173, 175, 182
place 70, 78, 80–81, 83
policy on innovation 13–28, *15*, *18*; and
entrepreneurship 53–66; and green
transition 231, 233, 238, 248; and
performance of the innovation system
17, 34–35, 39–49; and ports 112–114;
and the public sector 22, 27; and robots
and AI/ML technology 150, 151, 166;
and supplier firms 91; and sustainable
development 252–254, 257–263; and
tertiary continuing education 209–212,
224, 225; and work organisation
186; work policy 189–204, **194**, *194*,
195, **196**, *196*, *197*; *see also* regional
innovation policy
Porter, M. 80
ports 111–126, *119*; port of Aalborg
115–118, **118**, 125
private sector 3; and entrepreneurship
58–61; and green transition 232,
242–245, **244**, 247; and performance
of innovation systems 37, 39–44;
and policy on innovation 22, 25,
27; and ports 116, 118, 120; and
public sector innovation 130–132,
136–137, 139, 141–142; and regional
innovation policy 77–79; and robots
and AI/ML technology 149, 153;
and sustainable development 263; and
tertiary continuing education 208–225,
213, **218**, **220**, **222**, **223**; and work
organisation 170, 171, 175; *see also* large
companies; new businesses; small- and
medium-sized companies
proximity 119, *119*, 120–122, 125
public good 16, 79
public sector 1, 130–143, **134**, **135**, **138**,
140, **141**; and entrepreneurship 56,
58, 61; and green transition 231, 233,
248; and performance of the innovation
system 35, 37–45, 48; and policy on
innovation 22, 27; and ports 118, 120;

and regional innovation policy 73, 75,
77–79, 81, 130, 131, 133–34, 136, 139;
and sustainable development 263; and
work policy 198, 199

R&D *see* research and development
Reagan, R. 14, 54
regional innovation policy 20, 25, 70–83,
74, *76*; and entrepreneurship 60, 61, 73;
and green transition 232, 245, 248; and
performance of the innovation system
41–42, 49; public sector 73, 75, 77–79, 81,
130, 131, 133–134, 136, 139; and robots
and AI/ML technology 151, 159, 162; and
sustainable development 263; *see also* ports
Reichstein, T. 56
relational capital 116, 119, *119*, 122, 125
research and development (R&D): and
entrepreneurship 58, 66; and green
transition 231, 233, 234, 239, 242,
243, 245–248; and performance of the
innovation system 33–42, *36*, 44–45,
49; and policy on innovation 14, 16, 17,
19, 21, 23, 25; and regional innovation
policy 72–73, *74*, 81
risk 54, 55, 56, 57, 62, 64, 79, 82, 121, 122
robots and AI/ML technology 149–167,
152, *154*, *156*, *157*, **160–162**, **163–164**;
and performance of the innovation
system 46; and ports 111; and work
policy 190, 192, 193, 195
Rothwell, R. 14, 17

Sarasvathy, S. D. 55, 64, 65
Schumpeter, J. A. 17, 53, 56
science policy 13, 14–16, *15*, 40, 77
Shane, S. 56
silos 38, 40, 42, 46
skills: and entrepreneurship 57, 58, 62,
64; and green transition 232–235,
240–242, **241**, 247–248; managerial
209, 210, 211–212; and performance
of the innovation system 45–46; and
policy on innovation 25, 26; and the
public sector 26, 140; and robots and
AI/ML technology 150–151, 153–158,
156, 162–166, **163–164**; and supplier
firms 102; and sustainable development
252, 253, 263; and tertiary continuing
education 208–212, 217; and work
organisation 172–173, 182, 186; and
work policy 190–193, 195, **196**,
197, 199–203; *see also* competencies;
education and training; learning

small- and medium-sized companies 24, 33, 38–43, 54, 55, 62
smart specialisation 49, 66, 78
Smith, P. 138
social capital 3, 78, 79, 113
Sørensen, E. 140
spill-overs 76, 79, 192, 202–203, 216
spin-offs 40, 61, 62, 65–66
Stalker, G. M. 171
start-ups 39, 55–57, 61–63, 65
Stern, S. 56–57
subsidies 21–23, 79; *see also* grants
supplier firms 16, 22, 25, 82, 91–109, *92*, **96**, **97**, **99**, 132, 216, 234; detached *100*, 101–105, **102**, **103**, **104**; integrated *100*, **102**, **103**, **104**, 106, 107; technology-focused *100*, **102**, **103**, **104**, 105
sustainable development 2, 252–264, *256*; and entrepreneurship 54; and performance of the innovation system 46–47, 252–253, 259–264; and ports 111, 115–116, 118–121; *see also* green transition
Sweden 21, 60, 101, 105, 111, 137, 174, 179, 186, 231, 232, 255
system failures 72, 77, 81

Tanner, A. N. 238
taxation 1, 14, 21, 22, 39, 58, 61, 116, 131
Taylor, M. P. 56
technology 2; digital 4, 39–40, 43, 44, 46, 60, 61, 75, 91, 107, 151, 190, 199, 203; and entrepreneurship 54, 58, 60–61, 63, 65; and green transition 232–240, *236*, *237*, *238*, *239*, 247; and performance of the innovation system 35, 37, 39–41, 43, 44, 46–49; and policy on innovation 14–17, *15*, 21–22, 23, 25; and ports 112, 114–115, 125; and the public sector 131, 136, 140; and regional innovation policy 73, 76, 78–80; and supplier firms 94, *100*, 100–101, **102**, **103**, **104**, 105–106; and sustainable development 252, 259, 261, 262, 264; *see also* robots and AI/ML technology
Teece, D. J. 211
Thatcher, M. 14, 54
top-down perspective 131, 132–133, 143, 172, 202
Torfing, J. 132, 140, 143

training *see* education and training
Truffer, B. 49n
trust 3, 77, 94, 113, 121, 122, 124, 125

UK Regional Development Agencies (RDAs) 71
UN Conference on Trade and Transport (UNCTAD) 114–115
unemployment 1, 7, 21, 55, 57, 62, 193, 195–198, *196*, 201–203, 206–207, 213; *see also* welfare
United Kingdom (UK) 14, 16, 17, 21, 71
United States of America (US) 54, 56, 63
universities 16–17, 25–26, 37, 39–40, 44, 54, 57, 58, 60–62, 65, 75, 78, 111, 121, 141; *see also* education and training; knowledge; public sector; research and development (R&D)
UN Science, Technology and Innovation Forum 264
UN Sustainable Development Goals *see* sustainable development

Valeyre, A. 176
value chains 4, 6, 91, 94, 107, 112, 114
value creation 39, 44, 93–94, 98, 100, *100*, 106, 111–125
Van den Berg, R. 119
Verheul, I. 58
voluntarism 166, 190, 192–193, 200
Vona, F. 241
Von Hippel, E. 130
Voxsted, S. 208, 210

waste 56, 258
welfare 1, 49, 131, 193, 195–198, 202, 207
Wihlman, T. 138
wind energy 21, 37, 117, 231, 232, 238–239, 244, 247, 248
Winter, S. 17, 235
work organisation 169–186, **172**, **174**, **176**, **178**, **180–181**, **182**, **183**, *184*; lean 153, 156, 159, 164, 166; and robots and AI/ML technology 151–159, **152**, 162, 164–166; and supplier firms 97
work policy 189–204, **194**, *194*, **195**, **196**, *196*, *197*
World Bank 1, 43, 60

Young, O. R. 262

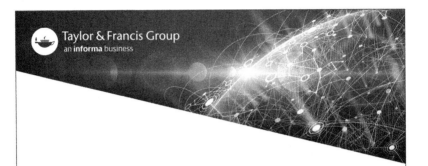

Taylor & Francis Group
an **informa** business

Taylor & Francis eBooks

www.taylorfrancis.com

A single destination for eBooks from Taylor & Francis
with increased functionality and an improved user
experience to meet the needs of our customers.

90,000+ eBooks of award-winning academic content in
Humanities, Social Science, Science, Technology, Engineering,
and Medical written by a global network of editors and authors.

TAYLOR & FRANCIS EBOOKS OFFERS:

A streamlined
experience for
our library
customers

A single point
of discovery
for all of our
eBook content

Improved
search and
discovery of
content at both
book and
chapter level

REQUEST A FREE TRIAL
support@taylorfrancis.com

 Routledge
Taylor & Francis Group

 CRC Press
Taylor & Francis Group

Printed in the United States
By Bookmasters